Behind the Seen

HOW **WALTER MURCH** EDITED *COLD MOUNTAIN*

USING APPLE'S FINAL CUT PRO AND WHAT THIS MEANS FOR CINEMA

New Riders

CHARLES KOPPELMAN

BEHIND the SEEN: HOW WALTER MURCH EDITED COLD MOUNTAIN USING APPLE'S FINAL CUT PRO
AND WHAT THIS MEANS FOR CINEMA

Charles Koppelman

New Riders
1249 Eighth Street
Berkeley, CA 94710
510/524-2178
800/283-9444
510/524-2221 (fax)
Find us on the World Wide Web at: www.peachpit.com
To report errors, please send a note to errata@peachpit.com

New Riders is an imprint of Peachpit, a division of Pearson Education
Copyright © 2005 by Charles Koppelman

Executive editor: Marjorie Baer
Editor: Douglas Cruickshank
Production editor: Hilal Sala
Copyeditor: William Rodarmor
Proofreader: Evan Pricco
Technical editors: Sean Cullen, Ramy Katrib, Zed Saeed
Photo editing and research: Kristin Piljay
Indexer: Emily Glossbrenner, FireCrystal Communications
Cover design: Aren Howell
Cover photo: Steve Double/RETNA
Interior design and composition: Kim Scott

ISBN 0-7357-1426-6
9 8 7 6 5 4 3 2 1
Printed and bound in the United States of America

For my mother.

CONTENTS

FOREWORD

By Anthony Minghella

Years ago, as an eager young playwright, I spent two weeks at an English Stately Home, working with an encouraging group of actors and a director. It was my first contact with professionals and I had a thrilling time, writing, rehearsing, learning. My group was one of seven at this sponsored fortnight for promising young writers and directors, and we were scheduled to present some aspect of the work we had been doing at the end of the workshop. Our days were frantic and intense and we paid little attention to our surroundings, except to note—with some amusement, with some disdain—that our formidable residence was still at least partly occupied by an eccentric aristocracy, complete with butlers and maids. We would glimpse activity, at the end of a hall, at the edge of the ha-ha: an elderly gentleman in a bathchair, brandishing an ear trumpet; the sudden squeal of a nurse. I was more class-conscious, perhaps, in those days and was dismissive of these goings-on as I tried to write about the slow death of the fishing community in the North of England, where I then lived.

It came to our last day and the presentations. My group did well to make something out of the very little I had managed to make for them. Others had been enormously productive. We watched, discussed, enjoyed. It came to the final group, Group Seven. Their leader apologized. They had nothing whatsoever to show for their two weeks. We were taken aback. But then one of the actors appeared with an ear trumpet. Another pushed on a bathchair. Another appeared in a nurse's uniform. And all of us—utterly duped, and delighted to have been—began to applaud.

Charles Koppelman's excellent, original, and tremendously informative book pulled me back to this experience. I thought I knew most of what happened over the course of making *Cold Mountain*, but reading *Behind the Seen* led me to realize that there was the equivalent of a Group Seven in play throughout pre-production, filming, and post-production, led by the incomparable Walter Murch, to whom this book is a deserved love letter. Frequently, Koppelman's account reads like a thriller as he foregrounds the massive experiment that was going on just inside my peripheral vision. Walter and his Group Seven gang, here known as the DigitalFilm Tree gang (Ramy, Zed, Edvin, Walt, Tim, Dan, Mark, and their colleagues), with the extraordinary Sean Cullen as a serene co-conspirator and problem solver, pulled off an audacious coup. They persuaded me, my producers, and the film studio to endorse editing an ambitious and expensive movie using software which was unproven at this level, and whose own manufacturer was of two minds about lending whole-hearted support. It was a very good job I hadn't read some of these chapters before I began shooting!

Almost unremarked, there has been an astonishing revolution in cinema and *Behind the Seen* invites us to pay attention to it. I entered a dozen drafts of my handwritten screenplay into my G4 laptop using an excellent program called Final Draft. I ended work on *Cold Mountain* using Final Cut Pro. From Final Draft, then, to Final Cut and in between, using the same computer, I compiled location photographs, made storyboard animatics, reviewed casting sessions and budgets, wrote my notes and emails, contemplated dailies, watched various cuts, considered effects shots, title sequences, prepared ADR scripts, and tested music cues. This happened on planes, in bed, on locations, in restaurants, on trains in many different countries, at the most eccentric times of the day and night. It's only a handful of years ago that not one of these activities would have been possible without my visiting a studio facility of some description, without my needing a whole host of accomplices, without the benefit of different and bulky machines. Film has practically disappeared from filmmaking. I barely saw any celluloid during *Cold Mountain* and one of the most exciting chapters in the process was working on the digital grading of the movie. Finally, the same degree of precision and care can be applied to the way each frame *looks* as has long been taken for granted in the way each moment *sounds*. It can only be a matter of time before digital projection becomes the norm and, beyond that, albeit on an approaching horizon, is a method of digital capture which truly competes with the pointillist mysteries created by film chemistry. Parallel with these changes—and equally profound—is the implicit democratization of the movie-making process produced by the size, cost, and portability of capturing devices. All this, coupled with the facility to make visual effects, sound effects, picture edits, and music on the same lightweight and mobile machine—and the opportunity to stream that information on the Internet—will surely alter what all of us understand by filmmaking. At the very least it will present enormous challenges. Even if Apple doesn't emerge in this book as quite the ally I had supposed on *Cold Mountain*, Steve Jobs and his team have been and will be as important to the story of cinema as Fellini or Spielberg or Disney.

For the moment, though, making a movie remains a gargantuan and sometimes grotesque marathon. So many people are involved, so many dollars spent, so many days and months consumed, so much tilting at windmills endured, so much effort poured into an odyssey which sometimes produces a couple of hours of entertainment and only very occasionally something more, and lasting. *Behind the Seen* celebrates this glorious folly. The view from the boiler room, where Koppelman's book is situated, is not always the same as the view from the bridge, and the diaries and notes Walter has shared with Charles are, like all such accounts, subjective. But that, of course, is the point. *Behind the Seen* achieves something remarkable: a chronicle about technology and data, machines and methodologies that also manages to record a story of friendships and dreams—not least the dreams I have been lucky enough to share with my friend and editor over three films and for almost a decade. If you read this book you will be left in no doubt that Walter Murch is a marvel. And he is.

Anthony Minghella
Old Chapel Studios, London
Summer 2004

INTRODUCTION

I first met Walter Murch at the Saul Zaentz Film Center in Berkeley, California in the mid-1990s when he was editing *The English Patient,* directed by Anthony Minghella, and I was developing, *Dumbarton Bridge,* my first feature film as a writer-director. We had a couple of lunches together, he agreed to look at my treatment, and then my screenplay. The idea that someone of Murch's stature was reading this first-time director's script was, well, a thrill and a confidence-booster. Nearly a year went by as I struggled to raise independent financing and assemble a filmmaking team. By that time *The English Patient* was released to great acclaim. I had not been in contact with Walter for quite a while. One very early Saturday morning, just after dawn, while I was strolling my sleepless infant daughter, Gaby, through the neighborhood, I chanced upon a young man sitting on his front steps reading. I glanced at the cover—it was Murch's book on film editing, *In the Blink of an Eye,* which I had read before I first had lunch with Walter.

"You're reading *Blink of an Eye!*" I said to the stranger.

"Yes, it's amazing," he said.

I said I knew Murch. The young man's eyes lit up.

I felt this coincidence might be a portent—and I needed to act.

Later that morning, after waiting until a more reasonable hour, I nervously phoned Walter at home. I explained the situation to him about my film and how I needed help. He asked what he might do. Understand—an independent filmmaker pulling a project together through sheer will and chutzpah learns to lose all sense of propriety and protocol. I steeled my will and requested he consider editing.

There was a silence that seemed to go on forever.

"I'm starting the re-edit of Orson Welles' *Touch of Evil,*" he said, "so I'm pretty committed. But I will be working on it at the Zaentz Film Center, so I could be around for some advice if you want."

Right then he agreed to be the consulting editor. Later he connected me with the wonderfully talented editor I hired for *Dumbarton Bridge* (Robert Grahamjones, his former assistant editor). Two weeks before my first day of principal photography Walter walked me through his script notes. (Yes, I did a rewrite after that.) During post production he came into our edit room whenever I needed advice, and he attended screenings of each new assembly.

This was my introduction to Walter Murch—the best possible way for beginning to get to know him—through active engagement on a film project. Credit goes to Frank Simeone for acquainting us.

Several years later, in the summer of 2003, I'd heard Walter was editing *Cold Mountain,* the film directed by Anthony Minghella, using Apple's Final Cut Pro system. There was already a lot of buzz about this in the film community, especially in the San Francisco Bay Area, because this had never been done before. Like everyone else, I was curious to know why he chose this $995 software to edit an $80 million studio film, and the creative and technological consequences.

Around that same time, Lisa Brenneis, a friend and author of books on Final Cut Pro, put me in contact with Peachpit Press Executive Editor Marjorie Baer. Peachpit had published several successful books on digital film editing. I asked Marjorie if she'd be interested in a book about Walter Murch using Final Cut Pro to edit *Cold Mountain*. Marjorie, being the well-informed editor she is, knew of Murch and his groundbreaking venture. And having confident intuition, she said yes, then and there. And in your hands is the consequence of her decision.

• • •

This book takes a particular and unusual point of view about feature filmmaking. In most other accounts, the editor is either completely invisible or a shadowy, unfocussed presence. By putting the editor in the spotlight, and concentrating on the events surrounding the completion of the film, the inevitable consequence is that other, more familiar perspectives become foreshortened. I apologize in advance for not being just as thorough about every department's crucial contributions to *Cold Mountain*, but it would have been impossible to achieve without expanding *Behind the Seen* far beyond its original mission.

Taking this kind of journey with Walter Murch would never have begun had Anthony Minghella not said yes to my proposal. He did that quickly, enthusiastically, and with no small amount of personal and professional risk. I could only write this book by being on the scene, with complete access to the creative process as it unfolded. Anthony allowed me free rein during the editing in London for ten days in September 2003, and for a week during the final sound mixing, also in London, during November 2003. I also had the privilege of attending two preview test screenings in the New York area.

This kind of inside view of a major motion picture still in-progress is usually denied to an author because it is such a sensitive time with so much at stake. Anthony, I will always be in your debt.

Cold Mountain producers Sydney Pollack, Bill Horberg, Albert Berger, and Ron Yerxa welcomed me and the idea of this book, which I appreciate.

In addition to seeing *Cold Mountain* unfold in real time, I was blessed to have an ocean of background materials from Walter Murch. On my first research trip to New York, he offered to make his emails and personal journal available to me so I could chart the course he took on *Cold Mountain*. He's been a serious journal-keeper for 30 years, and I knew immediately this and his electronic correspondence were going to prove bountiful for my research. When I began to read this material, and subsequent installments, I realized I had more on my hands than simply helpful background information—here were heartfelt and dramatic reports from the front lines that belonged in this story. So within these pages are generous excerpts from Walter's 18-month journal on this project, and his 2,111 pages of email.

Sean Cullen, Walter Murch's assistant editor, was an incomparable resource for me. He never failed to provide thorough, well-explained answers to my oft-repeated, frequently naïve questions—be they another explanation of reverse-telecine, or which Underground line to use.

Ramy Katrib and Zed Saeed at DigitalFilm Tree have been devoted in their support and enthusiasm for this book, while also giving me priceless information and details.

Tim Bricknell, Cassius Matthias, Karen Cattini, and everyone at Mirage Enterprises in London always made me feel at home, and for that I'm very grateful. Walter Slater Murch, Dei Reynolds, and Susannah Reid made room for me in their cramped edit space at the Old Chapel and they were great companions.

Likewise, being able to write amidst friends and colleagues here at Fantasy Inc. and the Saul Zaentz Film Center is a pleasure: thanks especially to Steve Shurtz, Scott Roberts, Paul Zaentz, Bill Belmont, Terri Hinte, and Nancy Eichler.

Appreciation to L. Wayne Alexander who helped put this enterprise together, to Dayna Holz who got me organized, to Debra Kalmon for her fine, enthusiastic transcribing, to Melanie Laird for helping set the stage, and to Bunny Alsup for being a Looking Glass guide.

Jenni McCormick of American Cinema Editors (ACE), Michael Horton at the L.A. Final Cut Pro Users Group, and Philip Hodgetts at IntelligentAssistance.com all provided key background research assistance. Edie Ichioka generously filled in many blanks.

There are an abundance of wonderful images herein: Greg Williams of London took the terrific shots at Minghella's Old Chapel Studio. Thanks to Kristin Piljay for her expert photo editing and research, and to Steve Maruta for his photography and tireless work preparing images. Katrin Eismann and Sandee Cohen pitched in with location photos on the east coast. Shelley Wanger was generous in her advice.

Kim Aubry, Anahid Nazarian, James Mockoski, and Rachel Eckerling at American Zoetrope, along with Kathleen Talbert—thanks for all your assistance.

Miramax Films generously provided movie images from *Cold Mountain* and for that, thanks go to Harvey and Bob Weinstein, Steve Hutensky, and Brad Buchanan.

Steve Jobs, Will Stein, Bill Hudson, and Brian Meaney at Apple have been forthcoming, generous, and supportive—I am appreciative.

Thank you to Marjorie for saying yes, and for always being there with everything I needed. My gratitude to Nancy Ruenzel, the publisher of Peachpit, for saying yes to Marjorie and marshalling the resources. Everyone at Peachpit took this book into their collective heart, including Paula Baker, Harriet Goldberg, Rebecca Ross, Scott Cowlin, Kim Lombardi, Susan Nixon, Mimi Vitetta, and Evan Pricco. Special thanks to Damon Hampson and Sara Jane Todd for their creative marketing and publicity. And very special thanks to Hilal Sala for her patient and thorough project management.

I was blessed to have a team of thoughtful, careful editors: Marjorie Baer, Kaitlin Quistgaard, William Rodarmor, and especially Doug Cruickshank. Not only did Doug's sharp eye, good sense, and informed opinion keep this book focused—he became a friend in the process.

This volume looks so good because of Kim Scott's attentive layout and design work on the interior, Aren Howell's on the cover.

I would not have had the proper approach nor the observational tools to undertake this book had it not been for my experience making documentaries, writing scripts, and directing a feature film. Many, many people made that possible and I thank them all—not the least of whom is my late father, Howard, a filmmaker, writer, and film editor who never forsook his upright Moviola.

Walter Murch's family—Aggie, Walter Slater, Beatrice, Connie, and Carrie—thank you for allowing me to include you in this account. It's richer for it.

My family gave me time and space to become as fully immersed in the work as I needed to be. Walker, Gabriella, and Jonah—your spirits of curiosity and strength can be found in here, too—and yes, Daddy's done with the book now. My wife, Deb Sibony, gave her all (and more) for over a year, along with wise counsel and steadfast support.

Finally, I wish to thank Walter. But words here will never be enough. May the book that follows suffice.

Charles Koppelman
September, 2004
Berkeley, California

CHAPTER 1

The Last
Preview

If people consider film editing at all, they
think of the editor as being the person who takes material
selected by the director, cuts out the bad bits, and then puts
everything together into a coherent whole. Sometimes that's
exactly what happens, of course. But in a motion picture
industry dominated by specialists and highly trained craftspeople, the editor needs to be as much a generalist as a spe-
cialist, as much an artist as a technician, as much a diplomat
as a good soldier. He must take the initiative as often as he
follows a producer's or director's lead. He needs to be as
comfortable with complex databases as a corporate systems
manager, and also have the communications skills of an
international ambassador when telling the director a scene
may not be working as he shot it. In between these extremes
are utilitarian duties some directors may not even know are
happening for the benefit of their film—like spending two

hours tweaking the speakers and Dolby sound system inside a working theater to make sure the sound presentation is not just adequate, but superior. This is something Walter Murch will do in Edgewater, New Jersey, when he arrives there tomorrow for the final test preview screening of *Cold Mountain*.

Murch has kept a detailed journal for 30 years. He makes entries faithfully every day, grabbing moments here and there. More than simply a detailed record of his activities as a film editor, the journal is like a transcript of conversations Murch has with himself. On departing London September 30, 2003, he writes: "Today screen film and travel to New York. God willing, all will be well. Thank you for guidance yesterday." The journal will pick up hours later: "Here we are now landing @ JFK 8.15 pm. May this next leg of our journey be fortuitous. Got through customs immigration ok."

OCTOBER 1, 2003—NEW YORK CITY

At 8:00 a.m. Murch, a tallish man with a graying beard, spectacles, and a Lincolnesque face stands waiting on Thompson Street in lower Manhattan. He carries a plain black computer briefcase over his shoulder and wears a blue blazer, open dress shirt, dark slacks, and running shoes. A black Town Car is already parked in front of the hotel, waiting to take him and his son, also named Walter, from SoHo to the theater in New Jersey. Young Walter, 35, is the second assistant editor on *Cold Mountain*, and came along from London. He wheels a hand cart bearing the film in its seven Goldberg cans to

Goldberg cans with the work-in-progress of *Cold Mountain*. They had their own ticket from London to New York under the passenger name "Film Murch," so they could be hand-carried onto the plane without a hassle for the trip to the last preview.

the car, and asks the driver to pop the trunk. The film traveled on the same flight as the two Walters. Like many tools and gadgets in the film business, the cans' cognomen comes from the name of their first manufacturer—in this case, the Goldberg Brothers of Denver. With three ten-pound reels of 35mm film or magnetic sound in each carrying case, the Lincoln's rear end takes a noticeable dip.

On the drive from lower Manhattan to the Lincoln Tunnel, the car passes a large apartment building on 23rd Street in Chelsea where Murch's parents first lived when they moved to New York from Toronto in the late 1920s. Murch gazes up from the back seat and muses about his home town's "Cartesian grid of streets and irregular stalagmitic buildings—it's the opposite of Paris, with its spider web of streets and uniform buildings dressed in suits." His father, also named Walter, was an artist who made an impact on the New York art scene, going against the grain of abstract expressionism during the 1940s, 1950s, and 1960s. His paintings such as *Transformer*, *Electrons*, and *Measurement and the Cosmos*, placed industrial objects within still-life compositions.

Like some kind of New Jersey put-down joke, the driver immediately gets lost coming out of the tunnel, despite having a printed set of driving directions. A wrong turn puts the Town Car inside a parking garage. Directions from the attendant get the driver oriented properly and heading along the top of the Palisades north toward Edgewater. Given that Murch has flown in the night

"Radio," 1947, oil on canvas. Painting by Murch's father.

before from London and needs to prepare a screening for a major motion picture, one might expect him to show some anxiety or stress. Instead, after a few moments of silence, he asks if anyone knows the origin of the word "Kodak." Sensing that no one does, Murch continues. "Back in the 1880s, George Eastman hired a linguist to come up with a name that he wanted to be pronounceable by people all over the world. *And* it had to sound like the click of a camera." Walter pauses and says it, savoring the syllables: "koh – dak."

The car arrives at the Edgewater Multiplex Cinemas—14 stadium-style theaters with the same floor plan and color scheme of any mall cinema in the suburbs of St. Louis, Seattle, or Cincinnati—and stops at the south entrance. The elder Murch peers through the glass doors while his son pulls the Goldberg cans out of the trunk, stacks them on the hand cart, and joins his father at the door. The concession stand is up and running even at 9:30 a.m., but no one is in sight. Young Walter taps on the glass door bearing the small decal, "National Amusements"—meaning that Sumner Redstone's mega-company (parent of Viacom), owns this theatre complex. No response. Then he pounds on the door. Still no one. A word from Murch, and his son is on the cell phone calling a Miramax post-production person in Manhattan who in turn calls Tim Carroll, the Dolby consultant, who is already somewhere inside the theater, setting up the hard-drive sound system. Another five minutes, and Tim comes downstairs with the manager to let them in.

"Electrons," oil on paper, 16 x 20 1/2. Painting by Walter Murch's father.

The Edgewater Multiplex theatre in New Jersey where several preview test screenings for *Cold Mountain* were held. The skyline of Manhattan's upper West Side, where Murch grew up, is in the background.

All told, what with getting lost and waiting to be let in, Murch is running nearly an hour behind schedule. Since he allots 11 hours for his tasks today—from leaving the hotel to starting the actual screening—this isn't a problem.

The manager, a bouncy woman in blue uniform pants and matching vest, leads the group across the enormous lobby, which is hung with eight-sheet posters for *Pirates of the Caribbean*, *Freddy vs. Jason*, and other summer releases. Crazy sound effects and a thudding bass from the theater's video game room fill the empty space. She opens a door marked "Private." Down a barren hall is the freight elevator for the ride up one floor. The two Walters, Tom from Dolby, the manager, and the hand truck with the Goldberg cases all squeeze in. The door creaks closed.

"I hate this elevator," the theater manager says with a grimace. Up it goes, very slowly, to the projection rooms. Murch stares at the closed doors. Past, present, and future converge today. He's been working on *Cold Mountain* for well over a year and the movie will be released in just three months, on Christmas Day. All that effort comes together tonight, in Theater 4 in front of 310 hand-selected, demographically correct suburbanites. Will the film run properly and the temporary mix sound satisfactory? And then what's in store? Will the audience respond well? Will the producers demand major unforeseen changes, pressing Murch and director Anthony Minghella up hard against the delivery deadline? Metal clanks against metal, the elevator shudders, then jerks to a stop.

"Thank you, God," the manager says. The door hesitates, then opens. "Right this way."

Anthony Minghella, the director of *Cold Mountain*.

This preview, like all screenings for a film before it's released, is cobbled together to simulate as nearly as possible a true film experience for the audience. A preview does no one any good if viewers are distracted because technical glitches constantly remind them they're watching a work-in-progress, whether those flaws are visible splices or poor sound, for example, or scenes with colors that don't match from one shot to another. At this point picture and sound aren't even physically joined. The images are shown on a 35mm film "workprint," before the final visual special effects have been completed and incorporated (such as adding stars to a night sky), and before final dissolves and fades have been included. Since scenes are not finalized, either in length or placement, shots are physically spliced together so they can be pulled apart and re-cut or re-ordered later, if necessary. Murch edits *Cold Mountain* digitally, on an Apple Macintosh, and a "conformed" workprint must be continuously kept up to date to match his digital version so the film print can be screened at previews like these, for producers, and at early press screenings. With a few exceptions, no crucial viewing is held using a video monitor; only a theatrical screen will do.

Murch inhabits two very different worlds: analog and digital.

The 35mm film workprint that young Walter wheels down the hallway is the only film version that now exists of *Cold Mountain*. It partly consists of "dailies"—film that was printed overnight by Kodak Cinelabs on location in Bucharest so it could be screened during production by the director, cast, and crew the next day (hence, "dailies")—along with temporary visual-effects shots. The workprint, true to its name, has a few scratches and dirt from previous showings and trips through the rewinds at the assistant's editing bench.

The soundtrack for these preview screenings is in a digital file, not so different from downloaded music files, though of course the soundtrack contains much more data—three gigabytes, to be precise—stored on a Kingston hard drive, hand-carried from London. Walter is as amazed by this technology as anyone, even though he pioneered the use of hard drives in preview screenings. Prior to this the sound would have been built up from 12 standard reels into one giant reel of 35mm magnetic film, six feet in diameter.

This preview embodies both old film methods and emerging digital technologies. Like most feature film editors working today, Murch simultaneously inhabits two very different worlds: analog and digital. The images begin on film, migrate to digital video, and come out on the other end on film for theaters. Movie sound begins as digital information and stays that way, for the most part. Today in New Jersey, with the soundtrack in a digital file and the picture on celluloid, the two must somehow run in sync—that is, sound and picture must be synchronized exactly so when an actor speaks, his words match the movement of his lips. Normally this is accomplished in the film lab or in the edit room when sound and picture are first brought together. Right now advances in audio are ahead of film—so the high-quality, professionally edited soundtrack can be stored on a single portable hard drive, 5 by 8 inches square. Sound and image, though physically separated, must somehow "speak" to each other to be in sync. This is accomplished by a special attachment to the projector that generates a bi-phase signal that is sent to the hard drive along an electrical cable.

Will the sound and picture stay in synch? Will the hard drive seize up, or otherwise fail to generate proper sound? Murch has used separate digital sound like this in test screenings for several years. Still, it feels a bit like Chuck Yeager taking the Bell X-1 rocket plane out to break the sound barrier in 1947 before knowing for certain that old-fashioned welded rivets could withstand the punishment they'd take from a new-fangled supersonic jet engine. Murch also has basic film worries: Will the splices hold, or might the film itself go flying apart? All one can do is plan for disintegration, think through each worst-case possibility, have a backup plan, and work smart. For example, Walter brings a second hard drive with a clone of the soundtrack, in case one drive goes down for some reason. For the workprint it means using the N-VIS-O splicing system—Murch invented it in the 1980s—which maximizes adhesion and keeps visible splice marks from showing on the screen when each edit passes through the projector gate. Being attentive to detail means spending the entire morning prepping the theater, checking sound levels, and doing a complete three-hour run-through of film and sound ahead of time. There is too much riding on a preview screening to be any less vigilant.

Other than projectionists, theater workers, and film editors showing preview screenings, very few people see the "back office" of a movie theater. When glamour gets projected onto movie screens and seeps out into the culture at large, it doesn't start here. The fluorescent-lit halls are lined with supplies: huge shrink-wrapped packages of toilet paper, palettes of soft drink cases, boxes of paper towels—the cineplex infrastructure. Around the corner and through a propped-open door is a 300-foot-long, dimly lit room. Fourteen Christy halogen projectors, seven on each side, lean forward, pressing up against glass panes overlooking the theaters. With switch boxes on the walls, carts here and there, and the constant hum of equipment being cooled and powered, this could be a corridor in a hospital surgery wing.

"Hey, Walter, how are you?" It's Eddie the engineer, a short muscular guy with an earring. Howie, the projectionist, big and heavy, is dressed all in black with a short, cropped beard. He comes over to shake Murch's hand. "I brought the split reels this time," Howie says in his heavy Jersey accent, "and the gang synchronizer." He laughs loudly. "If I hear about a gang synchronizer again, I'll go over there and hang myself." At the previous preview, in Charleston, South Carolina, Walter needed the tabletop-geared mechanism to fix a splice, and none was available.

Howie and Eddie are expert projectionists who travel the country, running preview screenings exclusively for Miramax Films, the studio behind *Cold Mountain*. Tests like this are too important to leave to the local theater hires—often teenagers who, for minimum wage, handle film prints worth thousands of dollars on projectors that cost six figures. This is the fourth preview screening that Eddie, Howie, and Tim have been through on *Cold Mountain*. Murch attends every one, so the team is accustomed to one another, and to Walter's precise, demanding way of working.

Young Walter takes two small metal cases the size of a shoebox out of his backpack. These are the Kingston drives (a main and a backup); each holds two tracks of sound within a matrix that plays back four tracks inside the theater when decoded properly.

"SR encoded," he tells Tim, meaning it uses Dolby's patented cinema noise-reduction system.

WHAT'S A
RELEASE PRINT?
———

Images and soundtrack are married together for films shown in theaters. Alongside each frame of picture are continuous strips of digital data that contain all the sound—music, dialogue, sound effects—mixed with each other for proper volume and equalization. Older prints use an optical track—sound waves played by the projector's optical sound reader. The worst thing that can happen to a release print is that it breaks. Otherwise it delivers a finished film to the screen every time.

There's a sense of mission and dedication in the projection room. "It's like the Secret Service has arrived," Murch whispers. "They're in control now, as opposed to local projectionists who don't handle these test screenings."

Murch announces that the running time of *Cold Mountain* is now 16 minutes shorter than the last version.

"Oh, this is like a holiday for me," Howie says. "Short show!"

"It's been on the Atkins diet," Murch says.

Kidding aside, there's work to be done, a problem to solve. At a run-through in London the day before, Murch noticed the film went out of rack. A replacement shot that included a new digital effect was inserted into the workprint, and it was two sprocket holes off. That one-half frame of extra film threw the rest of the reel out of registration from that point forward, and actors' heads wound up at the bottom of the screen. There was no time to correct this in London before catching the New York flight, so Murch would take care of it here, at projection, in the multiplex.

The offending reel, number nine, is up on the rewinds. Murch has his hands on the film and examines it over a light box on the editing table. He tilts his head sideways and looks at the frame, like a doctor examining a patient's X-ray. "This is it!" he says.

"Do you want me to do the honors?" his son asks.

"Sure."

Several hours later, Murch walks out of the multiplex. He has finished a complete run-through of *Cold Mountain*, all alone in the theater, after carefully adjusting the audio levels and equalization of the theater speakers. A few hundred yards away, the Hudson River separates the two worlds of New Jersey and Manhattan. Murch observes his surroundings. He points across the river to the city's West Side, which seems very close. "There," he says, finding Riverside

The N-VIS-O splice, invented by Walter Murch, and made here on a guillotine splicer (left) with a special industrial-grade adhesive tape. The tape is very narrow (center), covering only the frame-lines between an edit, and is invisible when projected. The result is a seamless work-in-progress screening. A standard splice (right) uses clear acetate tape and covers part of each adjoining film frame. Murch first used the N-VIS-O system on *Julia* (1977).

Church with its soaring bell tower. "That's where Aggie and I got married in 1965 and that's the block of 119th Street where I grew up." It's a whimsical statement, as if he were saying, "Look how far I've come in 60 years: I've crossed the Hudson."

It takes Murch a few moments to walk from the new New Jersey of the Edgewater Multiplex Cinemas and the Promenade Mall to the old New Jersey on the other side of River Road. There, the River Gorge Cafe is tucked under the Palisades. With its old stone walls inside and out, it feels like a grotto, which is appropriate as it is two blocks from the Hudson. The flagstones shine with a patina of cigarette smoke, fried cooking, and river moisture that has been accumulating since the 1920s.

The restaurant manager gets up from the table where she's sitting, having a smoke break, and greets Murch.

"Still open for lunch?" he asks in his commanding but amiable voice.

"Of course," she replies. "Back again?"

Murch had been at this eatery only six weeks before, on August 20, for a prior test screening of *Cold Mountain*.

Murch's son, also named Walter, is the second assistant editor on *Cold Mountain*. He trims off a half-frame of workprint from reel nine to get the film back into proper framing before the last preview screening in Edgewater, New Jersey. He reassembles the cut with an N-VIS-O splice.

Film editor Walter Murch at the River Gorge Cafe in Edgewater, New Jersey, before the final preview screening of *Cold Mountain*.

"You're the producer, right?"

"No, the editor. The film editor." The River Gorge is a quiet harbor amid the fast-running tides of a major motion picture preview, and this seems to be a good time to inquire about broader questions before director Minghella's work-in-progress faces "a meat-eating audience," as Murch describes what lies ahead that evening.

How is he capable of stepping back, after spending 15 months working on this film, looking at 600,000 feet of footage, much of it hundreds, even thousands of times, and still retain any objectivity about what's been done, and what must still be accomplished?

"In a good sense, that's exactly what a preview is for because it grabs you by the hair and yanks you out of your own mind-set," Murch says. "For a new audience watching it cold, all things are possible. It's always good to be reminded of this in various ways."

Robert Grahamjones, who assisted Murch on *The English Patient* and *The Unbearable Lightness of Being*, says that the hardest thing about editing a film is to sit down and look at it the second time, and then the third, and the fourth, and to keep doing that with fresh eyes every day, for as long as 18 months.

Murch is silent for a moment. Then he responds to that idea. "In a way you can also use the opposite technique—to try *not* to be objective, because in my case it's kind of hopeless. Instead I tend to plunge even deeper into subjectivity in the hope that if I push one opposite as far as I can, it sort of meets the other thing coming around the corner."

"When I'm working on a film, the image I have is of myself swimming in a fast-moving river. The film is always changing and I'm kind of in the middle of it. Objectivity would mean trying to swim to the shore, clambering up, and looking at the river go by. The dangerous thing about doing that is that's when most people drown—when you're trying to get out of the water. On the other hand, if you relax and let yourself be carried along, and even swim in the direction of the current—somehow, given the editor's particular dilemma, that's a better thing to do than to try to go back and forth from objectivity to subjectivity. Heightened subjectivity means learning to listen to very tiny voices that you hear in the corner of your head that say, 'What if? What about this? What about that?'"

"For example, 'I wonder what it would be like if the sky were green.' With film you have an opportunity to make that happen. You can make the sky green in a film—literally, because of what we can do with visual effects now. But I also mean figuratively in terms of structure: What would happen if we did something counterintuitive, flipped those two scenes around? So your unconscious, which is your deeply subjective self, is always whispering things to you. But in the middle of the clatter of all the urgent practicalities of making a film, and schedules, and getting on flights for London and New York, those voices can sometimes get drowned out. So, it's learning to find ways to amplify them, or create zones in which things are a little quieter so they can be heard. Luckily for me, on this film I can walk to work, so that gives me a good half hour of 'tiny voice' time."

The manager takes Murch's order—early dinner or late lunch, it's not clear which, nor does it matter. For Murch it's 10:00 p.m. London time, and this will be his only meal of the day since he won't get back to his hotel in SoHo until after midnight. He picks up his thoughts about seeing and subjectivity using a different comparison—one drawn from lighting technique. "An interior might have four different sources of light in it: the light from the window, the light from the table lamp, the light from the flashlight that the character is holding, and some other remotely sourced lights. The danger is that, without hardly trying, you can create a luminous clutter out of all that. There's a shadow over there, so you put another light on that shadow to make it disappear. Well, that new light casts a shadow in the *other* direction. Suddenly there are fifteen lights and you only want four."

"As a cameraman what you paradoxically do is have the gaffer turn off the main light, because it is confusing your ability to really see what you've got. Once you do that, then you selectively turn off some of the lights and see what's left. And you discover that, 'OK, those other three lights I really don't need at all—kill 'em.' But it can also happen that you turn off the main light and suddenly, 'Hey, this looks great! I don't need that main light after all, just these secondary lights. What was I thinking?'"

"Editorially we do that by removing or transposing scenes. You can take out a scene that seems absolutely essential to the film—a scene that's like the main light—and sometimes you realize, 'Hey, we don't need that scene at all,' because it was telling us something too overtly, perhaps in words spoken by the main character, that in fact was present in all these other scenes in much more interesting and subtle ways. Even if you wind up putting the main scene back, looking at the film without it allowed you to see things that you couldn't otherwise."

Young Walter suddenly appears outside through the window, walking past the restaurant. He had stayed behind in the theater solving a Final Cut Pro problem on his iBook. Tonight he will use his laptop to run a Final Cut Pro version of *Cold Mountain* in real time alongside the projected film. It's a tool for re-syncing picture and sound should the film break during projection. Just as Murch stands up to get his attention, his son turns and sees him in the restaurant. He comes inside to the table looking happy.

"I tend to plunge even deeper into subjectivity in the hope that if I push one opposite as far as I can, it sort of meets the other thing coming around the corner."

Eddie, the projection engineer, watches as the preview of _Cold Mountain_ plays simultaneously in Final Cut Pro on young Walter's iBook "clamshell" and in 35mm film on the motion picture platter system.

"It was the RGB"—the red-green-blue color setting—"versus the something-else setting; very straightforward."

"Fantastic," Walter says, relieved. "Those are the problems we love."

"It's very funny being up there hearing those guys talk," Walter's son says after ordering his meal. He is referring to Howie, Eddie, and Tim. "When you were testing sound, they were saying, 'Yeah, you know, I'll listen to him. That guy's no bullshit. He doesn't bullshit you around. He knows what he's talking about.'"

Murch smiles while his son continues, imitating Howie. "Some guys, you get in there and they're spouting off. They don't know what the difference is: 80 db this, 90 db that; listening to the surround speakers. The real test, you go to a totally new theater and he's in there and he's saying 'Up here,' and 'Down there.' The levels—perfect."

Theater 4 is waiting silently on the other side of River Road, ready to go. Its 343 seats are empty, its doors closed, and two hours and 37 minutes of film lies on a stainless steel platter in one giant flat reel. Why is the final test pre-view screening of *Cold Mountain* so important? What is the purpose of these previews? What will Minghella, Murch, the producers, and the studio get out of it?

There is an old adage in Hollywood, attributed to the screenwriter William Goldman, about the unpredictability of the film business: "No one knows any-thing." Regardless, producers are like gamblers at the track with their *Racing Forms*, tout sheets, and lucky charms; if there's any way to get an advantage, improve the odds, they'll use it. Testing films in front of selected, representa-tive audiences is one of those ways: studios and producers want to know if films they finance are on the right track while there's still something they can do about it if they aren't. Many a film has had its ending changed because a test audience didn't like the hero dying. If you consider film an art, this is like letting a jury pass judgment on a painting by Picasso. If you believe motion pictures are commercial ventures, meant to attract the largest possible audi-ence, then testing the "product" on potential consumers makes perfect sense.

Not that films should be made in a vacuum. Only the most personal experi-mental film might be made and previewed by a single person. In fact, most filmmakers—whether they make documentaries or fiction films—no matter what the budget, screen their works-in-progress for friends, peers, and poten-tial audience members. It's the only way to get reactions and responses to the material before it's set in stone. If a sequence is unintelligible or confusing, a filmmaker wants to know about it.

"Fantastic. Those are the problems we love."

"Anthony Minghella describes his physical sensation at previews as being 'skinless'— all of his nerve endings are exposed."

But testing major studio films aspires to the level of a science, much in the way new merchandise and its advertising campaigns are put through all manner of market research, product testing, and consumer scrutiny. It's not simply a matter of making a motion picture better. Backers and distributors want to know a film's projected payoff, in part so they can decide how many millions of dollars to spend on advertising. Preview testing is not new. Even in the 1930s, studios insisted on getting audience reactions before a film was completed.

For directors and editors who need to complete a film on schedule, with artistic integrity, and an eye toward success (who wants failure?), preview screenings are taken like cod-liver oil. No one involved in the day-to-day making looks forward to them, but they're "good for you," and hopefully good for the film.

Murch has been at hundreds of work-in-progress screenings for pictures he's still editing, presumably while he's also still vulnerable to criticism. Does he get nervous?

"Anthony describes his physical sensation at previews as being 'skinless'—all of his nerve endings are exposed. The slightest touch is electric. The experience is intense for me, but I've never felt skinless at a preview where I was the editor. I think it's just the difference between being a writer-director and an editor. I certainly *did* feel like that when we were previewing *Return To Oz* [a feature film Murch directed in 1985], so I know exactly what he's talking about. But I think that intensity helps focus your attention. It puts you in a different emotional state, which makes you see different things in the material. When you go to work every day in the same room and you're looking at the film all the time in the same environment, there's a certain routine metabolism that is comforting, but it can lull you into a false security. All of that disappears here, when you're looking at the film with strangers in a different environment. With consequences."

And since Murch handles not only story issues, but also technical problems, the added question "Will it run?" can be unsettling. During the previous preview, in Charleston, the hard drive seized up and the film was stopped for ten minutes while things were reset, put in sync, and started again. Film on a platter system can't be rewound, so the audience not only had its viewing interrupted, it missed part of one scene.

"The technology has the ability to kick back at you like what happened to us in Charleston. Whereas if something like that happens in the edit room, you just stop and restart it, and off you go. So there's a performance level here that's more intense—it's an unstoppable juggernaut—but that's good because it adds to the intensity. If the film is like an architectural model you've been working on, looking at it for months from the same perspective, now circumstances yank you up and plop you down so you're looking at it 90 degrees to

Walter Murch and Fairuza Balk on the set of "Return to Oz" (1985). The film, which Murch directed, also starred Nicol Williamson, Jean Marsh, and Piper Laurie.

the side. Suddenly you're seeing around the back and making connections you hadn't before: 'Oh, if the stairway goes down *there*, we don't need this little portico *here*.' Whereas before, you intellectually *knew* there was a stairway back there, but you didn't *see* it. So previewing the film—with all these different people looking at it—helps to reveal the film as a dimensional thing, which in turn kicks off different ideas. It's a psychic component that you pick up from the people sitting there taking it in for the first time."

There are also reactions of the director and the producers, who will each provide notes to Murch after every screening.

"It's hard to pick all of that apart at the time. You're feeling the whole gestalt at once. After Charleston, Anthony felt that the audience had a more muted response. Whether they were really muted or whether it was his heightened skinlessness from showing the film to a Southern audience, I don't know. In fact the numbers from the Charleston preview were among the highest we've had. But it became a benchmark for him and informed his attitude toward the next round of changes."

It's nearly dark outside. The meal is over and dessert is ordered. Murch has a further thought about audiences. "Think of the comparison between a vacuum tube—an old-style radio tube—and a theatre. They're both devices to amplify something. If you stick two electric wires up into a glass bulb, with no air in it, the current would normally jump from the end of one wire to the other. But then something revolutionary was discovered around the turn of the last century. When the current is leaping through the vacuum from one wire to the other, it is in a highly suggestible state. It is very easy to influence it when it is in the middle of its trapeze act. If you take a little grid of metal— a wire screen—and put it in the gap, and attach the screen to another, weaker electrical signal, the strong current will pick up the vibrations of the weak signal as it jumps through the screen. So at this point you have two things coming into the vacuum tube. One of them is very powerful but simple current coming from the wall. But then you also have a very intelligent, but very weak current—Beethoven's Ninth Symphony coming from an antenna that shows up as electrical oscillations within the screen. The simple but powerful current leaps through the screen and on the way picks up the shape of Beethoven's Ninth. The current that lands on the second wire is powerful *and* it's Beethoven's Ninth. That's amplification, pure and simple. Ultimately the current is going to be powerful enough to push the coil of a speaker back and forth in the same pattern as the music, and you hear Beethoven's Ninth in your living room."

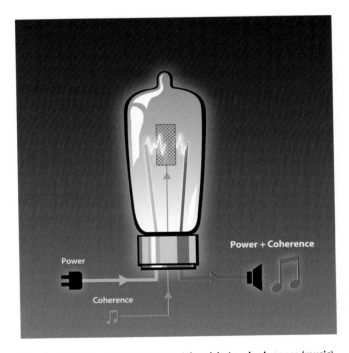

A radio tube brings together power (electricity) and coherence (music).

"That's essentially the setup you've got when you're in a theater. The power—the energy—isn't coming from the film. It's coming from the collective lives and emotional world of the audience. Say it's a big theater—there are a thousand people there, and the average age of that audience is 25. You have 25,000 years, three times recorded history, sitting in the audience. That's a tremendously powerful but unorganized force that is looking for coherence. That's why they pay their eight bucks. They reach some point in their own life when they say, 'I need coherence,'" Murch says, laughing. "They didn't articulate it that way, of course. It came out as, 'Let's go to a show.' But what really is getting them to leave home is a temporary dissatisfaction with where they are, craving something that will cohere them, at least temporarily, within the self and with a bunch of like-minded people."

"So there they are, waiting for the film to begin, but they've all got their own histories: tragedies, love affairs, heartbreaks, triumphs, you name it. It's all collected there, waiting. That's the equivalent of the current coming out of the wall. And then the screen lights up in the darkness. It's not really that powerful a light. If you measure it with a light meter, it's probably about as bright as this tablecloth. But it's very coherent because 250 people for two years collectively worked on it, made that movie. So there are 500 'man-years' of work in that particular play of images and sounds. It's as if somebody started out on their own to make this film in 1503, and now, here in the year 2003, brought it to Edgewater and said, 'I'm done.' Well, that's a piece of work. That's the number of years of endeavor that something like this film represents."

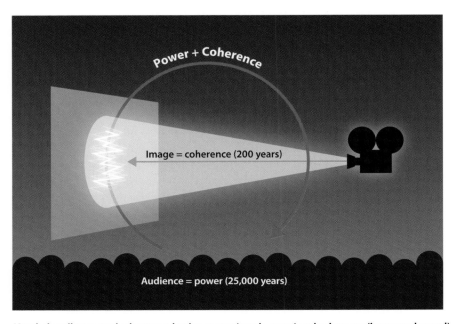

Murch describes a movie theatre as having power (movie goers) and coherence (image and sound).

"Radio Telescope," 1955, Oil on canvas, 18" x 18." Painting by Walter Murch's father.

The manager comes over. "Would anybody like fresh coffee?"

"Just a little bit for me, thanks," Murch says.

"So, you get this beam being projected on a screen; not in an air vacuum, but in the vacuum of darkness. And people are sitting there in the dark, which is kind of strange when you think about it; that 343—or a thousand, or six—people would choose to pay money to go spend two hours with strangers in the dark. But they do it, and they do it willingly. Then this flickering image and some fluttering speaker cones play their relatively modest energies. But the power that film has over the audience is not its physical strength, but its coherence and the fact that 25,000 years of human history is coiled there in the dark, ready and anxious to make a leap. It's a powerful combination when it works. It's like that spark in the tube. It's *ready* to leap into the void; the audience is ready to let go and abandon itself to the vacuum of darkness. In the moment of that leap, when you've let go of who you are and all of your specific concerns, you are highly suggestible to the coherence of the film. What comes out the other side—the audience after they have seen a good film—is, simultaneously power *and* coherence. The theater's vacuum of darkness is where those two things come together."

It's nearly 6:00 p.m. when the two Walters leave the River Gorge Restaurant, jaywalk across River Road, now clogged with evening commuters, and make their way to the multiplex. They approach the lobby entrance, which, nine hours ago, was uninhabited. Now it's full of activity—regular filmgoers coming in, buying tickets, and stopping at the massive concession area for popcorn and super-sized drinks. It's easy to overlook the fact that a sensitive and secret preview screening is about to take place, unless you notice the proper-looking woman holding a clipboard, guiding a wide range of New Jerseyites, mostly working class, 20 to 50 year-olds, around the ticket lines and toward Theater 4. There are many couples and lots of Latinos, not unlike the rest of the patrons. The *Cold Mountain* audience is here by invitation, intercepted over the last week by recruiters, either at the multiplex or the nearby mall. It's not a sneak preview, in the old sense of going to a film without knowing anything about it. They were given a brief description of the film: "a major motion picture, set during the Civil War, starring Nicole Kidman, Renée Zellweger, and Jude Law." The preview audience knows the film will be followed by a written survey questionnaire, and for 24 of them, a follow-up focus group to be held right then and there.

Aside from the clipboard lady, several movie industry executives, looking very non-New Jersey, congregate in small knots just beyond the popcorn and Coke, exuding a combination of intensity, nervousness, and power. These are some of the *Cold Mountain* producers: Ron Yerxa and Albert Berger of Bona Fide Productions, and Bill Horberg representing Mirage Enterprises. Bona Fide and Mirage initiated *Cold Mountain* as a film when they optioned the novel in 1997 with backing from the United Artists studio. Yerxa, with spiky gray hair and starched white shirt, and Berger, quiet and cerebral-looking, both produced the films *King of the Hill*, *Election*, and *Pumpkin*, among others. Horberg's credits include *The Quiet American*, *Heaven*, *The Talented Mr. Ripley*, and *Sliding Doors*. He stayed on to help produce *Cold Mountain* after leaving Minghella's production company for Dreamworks SKG. Nearby stands executive music producer T-Bone Burnett, famously of *O Brother Where Art Thou?* and its hugely successful soundtrack album. Burnett, a tall drink of water all in black, just flew in from Nashville, where he's been recording new songs for *Cold Mountain*. Sydney Pollack enters the lobby. He is Minghella's partner in Mirage, which co-ventured with Bona Fide to develop *Cold Mountain*. Pollack began his career in film as an actor (he still acts occasionally: *Eyes Wide Shut*, *The Player*), before moving into directing (*The Way We Were*, *Three Days of the Condor*, *Absence of Malice*, *Tootsie*), and producing. He's been nominated for a directing Oscar three times, and won once, for *Out of Africa*. Pollack greets the others in his friendly-assertive way.

At last, Anthony Minghella arrives wearing rumpled black slacks and t-shirt, a wool cap pulled over his shaved head, eyes twinkling as usual. He exhibits an openness and warmth unusual in film directors. He greets his producers in a barely audible voice, nodding more than talking. He looks rough, having just worked 18-hour days in Nashville, recording music with T-Bone Burnett, while also doing final aerial photography from a helicopter over North Carolina.

The screening will start at 7:00 p.m., so there's still time for Murch to have a few words with the producers and to update Minghella on what he's been doing in London.

Everyone seems friendly and considerate. This group has worked together for over a year since production began in Romania in mid-July 2002. For some, including Minghella and Pollack, it's been six years since the original *Cold Mountain* deal was put together. Behind the small talk and catching up one can picture invisible *Cold Mountain* scars from battles won and lost, egos bruised and burnished. In spite of having all the reasons in the world to be jaded and cynical, this bunch is still excitable. There's a film to see. And just like civilians going into the other 13 theaters to see *Pirates of the Caribbean* or *Freddy vs. Jason*, these movie professionals get the same rush of anticipation for what Murch called "the great coherence"—when that weak beam of light reaches the screen and is energized tonight by 10,290 years of collective life.

"There they are, waiting for the film to begin. But they've all got their own tragedies, love affairs, heartbreaks, triumphs."

Cold Mountain producers Ron Yerxa, Albert Berger (top left), William Horberg (top right), Sydney Pollack (bottom left), and executive music producer, T-Bone Burnett (bottom right).

All during this time, a handful of staff people from Miramax have been keeping to themselves. They stay behind in the lobby, waiting for someone or something, as Murch and the others make their way down the hall toward Theater 4. As he passes beneath each marquee with its red LCD readout, Murch imagines this multiplex as if he owned it, quietly announcing tonight's showings: "*8 1/2, Citizen Kane, Last Year at Marienbad.*"

In obvious ways this isn't a typical movie night. Two security guards at the doorway inspect handbags and carry-on items, as if it were an airport. The studio wants to prevent anyone from sneaking a digital video camera inside that will put *Cold Mountain* on the Internet tomorrow, playing across the world in its half-finished state. To make extra sure, every 10 or 15 minutes a guard will stand at the front of the theater during the screening, scanning the crowd with a pair of night-vision goggles to pick up any infrared beams being emitted from a video camera.

Harvey Weinstein, Miramax co-chairman and *Cold Mountain* Executive Producer.

It's a few minutes past 7:00. Inside, the seats are almost all taken. Walter is in the seat taped off for him, smack dab in the middle of the theater, two-thirds of the way up. He has three tools in his lap for the preview: a little orange box with a black knob to control the sound level, should he decide that the temporary sound mix he finished two days ago in London needs mid-course adjusting; a walkie-talkie to communicate with young Walter, should there be problems in projection that can be solved quickly, such as the film being thrown out of focus by any of the N-VIS-O splices; and a G4 PowerBook with its screen darkened to note any ideas he may have during the screening.

Finally, at 7:15, a burly man dressed in black pants and a white shirt with black suspenders leisurely enters the theater, carrying a black suit coat and accompanied by a young assistant. He sits down in a reserved row near the left aisle. It's Harvey Weinstein, co-founder and co-chairman of Miramax Films. Only now do the lights go down. The final test screening of *Cold Mountain* begins, 465 days after Walter Murch drove from his home in West Marin to San Francisco International Airport for his flights to London and later to Bucharest, where *Cold Mountain* was set to begin filming.

The lagoon near Blackberry Farm.

CHAPTER 2

Running on the Fault Line

To this day, if you go to the San Francisco Bay Area and want to find the town where Murch lives, don't look for a sign. It disappears whenever the Department of Transportation puts one up. Over the last 34 years, 22 signs have been pulled down; the people who live here would rather no one else found it. The community, located north of San Francisco on the coast, is a magical village of Victorian farmhouses and clapboard homes, surrounded by green pastures and redwood forests overlooking the Pacific Ocean. The adjacent lagoon that empties into the ocean forms a moat to the south and east; there is ocean to the west and wild forest to the north. From the beach you can see pale apartment

Walter and Aggie moved from their houseboat to Blackberry Farm in 1973. George Lucas waits on the shore to help.

Lena Olin as Sabina, at Blackberry Farm, as seen in the motion picture, *The Unbearable Lightness of Being*.

buildings on the hills of San Francisco, only seven miles away as the crow flies. Driving to The City, however, is no easy task—the first half of the trip is over convoluted mountain roads and then, as a bracing contrast to the bucolic drive, you run the gauntlet of a commuter-jammed Golden Gate Bridge. It's over an hour, one way, on a good day.

The town's basic mix of farmers, fishermen, and working professionals is peppered with artists, musicians, writers, second-homers, and drop-outs. A few are poor and homeless, and some quite wealthy. With residents bicycling into town to run errands and catch up at the community bulletin board, even a big-city attorney can't help but want to work at home amid the eucalyptus and clean, salty air. It's just too idyllic not to.

In 1987, when Director Philip Kaufman needed a closing American locale for *The Unbearable Lightness of Being*, he chose Blackberry Farm, one of the 19th century farm houses just outside the town. It wasn't merely a good-luck find by an astute location manager; it happened to be the home of the film's editor, Walter Murch. He and his wife, Aggie, and their two children, Walter (then 4) and newborn Beatrice, moved here in 1973 from the Sausalito houseboat where they had been living since 1969. With two children, life on the water in relatively cramped conditions no longer seemed like such a good idea. Sisters Connie and Carrie Angland (then aged 10 and 11) came to live permanently with the Murches in 1975.

It just wasn't in the cards for Walter to move back to Los Angeles where he had gone to graduate film school at the University of Southern California. Other budding sound editors and mixers might find steady work there, at the center of the American film industry, but Murch and his college friends all had something else in mind besides getting good jobs in Hollywood. The group included Francis Ford Coppola (for whom Murch had already done sound work on *The Rain People*), Carroll Ballard (director of *The Black Stallion, Never Cry Wolf*, and *Fly Away Home*), Matthew Robbins and Hal Barwood (Robbins directed and Barwood produced the film *Dragonslayer*; they were uncredited writers of *Close Encounters of the Third Kind*); Robert Dalva (film editor on *The Black Stallion, Jumanji, Jurassic Park III*, and director of *The Black Stallion Returns*), and George Lucas.

Coppola, Lucas, and Murch and their families moved to the San Francisco Bay Area in the spring of 1969 to complete *The Rain People*, launch Zoetrope Studios, begin work on *THX-1138*, and establish an approach to filmmaking independent of Hollywood that was more in keeping with the low-cost, collaborative way they had made films at USC and UCLA. This was well before Lucas's success with *American Graffiti* and *Star Wars*, and with what became Lucasfilm, Skywalker Sound, Industrial Light & Magic, and Pixar. It was prior to Coppola directing *The Godfather*. And it was six years before Saul Zaentz, the Berkeley-based producer, would win Best Picture and four other

Director Philip Kaufman, left, and Daniel Day-Lewis, center, on the set of *The Unbearable Lightness of Being.*

Aggie Murch.

Beatrice Murch.

Connie and Carrie Angland.

Walter Slater Murch.

JOHN KORTY CARROLL BALLARD TIM HUNTLEY JOHN MILIUS GEORGE LUCAS ROBERT DALVA STEVE WAX WALTER MURCH JIM McBRIDE
BARRY BECKERMAN AL LOCATELLI FRANCIS COPPOLA
LAWRENCE STURHAHN DENNIS JAKOB

The gang from American Zoetrope in 1969. Walter Murch is second from right. Coppola (fourth from right) holds a zoetrope, invented in 1834. When sequenced photographs are viewed through slits in this device they produce the equivalent of a motion picture. The word "zoetrope" is a combination of Greek words meaning roughly "wheel of Life."

major Oscars for *One Flew Over the Cuckoo's Nest* (1975). By the late 1970s, Coppola's vision of a Bay Area network of artists and craftspeople had become reality: a critical mass of filmmaking talent and financing that could flourish outside of Southern California.

JUNE 1, 2002—BLACKBERRY FARM

It's a windy and sunny Saturday. Murch has lived here now for nearly 30 years. To a casual observer, it is another day for pleasant diversions in this Northern California Shangri-la. Surfers in wetsuits find the curl that breaks off the point. Daytrippers drop into the local café for cappuccino. Honeymooners in rental cars drive up Highway 1, not realizing (since there is no sign) they've just passed the real deal—a more authentic Mendocino than the town up the coast they'll sleep in that night.

Only 27 days ago Murch was in Berkeley at the Zaentz Film Center on the last day of editing and mixing *K-19: The Widowmaker*, directed by Kathryn Bigelow, starring Harrison Ford and Liam Neeson. As usual, he spent over a year on this single project, and worked consecutive 16- to 18-hour days for the last several weeks to make the release date. So now, with his work done,

From *The Rain People*, directed by Francis Ford Coppola, on which Murch did the sound montage and was the rerecording mixer.

Walter is prone to what he calls "parade syndrome;" not simply a letdown, it's a physical sensation. Imagine sitting in the bleachers on Manhattan's Central Park West, as Walter used to do when he was five, and watch the Macy's Thanksgiving Day parade go by. "After the last float, I'd look down at the asphalt," he says. "It seemed to be oozing in the other direction, left to right. I knew it couldn't be so, and yet there it was, the result of a reflex motion of my eyeballs. The effect wears off in about five minutes, but while it lasts it is totally fascinating and disorienting to a child. The same kind of thing happens at the end of a film. For a year, I'm used to seeing the film grow, change, evolve, organize, and get more coherent. And then suddenly—very suddenly—it's done and the film stops changing. But instead of just stopping, there is some mental reflex and the film seems to be disintegrating each time I look at it, leaving me slightly seasick. The film is done, how can it be coming apart? It will take at least six weeks to get my land legs back."

Despite any queasiness, there is too much to do today to lie low. Walter reviews galley proofs of *The Conversations: Walter Murch and the Art of Editing Film*, the book novelist Michael Ondaatje has written based on discussions about film and film editing he and Murch had over the last year and a half. Murch is also on a deadline to finish an article for *Mix* magazine on the history of sound in film over the last 25 years.

In three weeks Murch will depart for London and Bucharest to start work on *Cold Mountain*. For logistical, technical, and artistic reasons, he gets involved right from the start of shooting. Technically, film needs to be processed and printed; oversight and troubleshooting at the lab are the responsibility of the editing team. If things go wrong at this stage—improper processing of exposed film, sound incorrectly synched up with picture, or footage printed and organized incorrectly, for example—it could mean expensive reshooting or losing precious time in the editing schedule for delivering the finished film. Most studio pictures begin shooting with an established release date—for *Cold Mountain* it's Christmas 2003—and the studio organizes its marketing and exhibition plans based on that date.

While on location, the editor supervises the preparation of film dailies so the director, director of photography, and other crew members can view the results of their work. Each department head will be given the opportunity to check his or her own work as it appears on film. Sometimes cast members are invited to see "rushes," as dailies are also called (from being "rushed" through the lab for urgent viewing). The purpose of seeing footage immediately is partly technical: to make sure everything "is there," in case material needs to be reshot while actors are available and sets are still in place. Also, the director needs to evaluate his own staging and the subtleties of the actors' performances after the momentary thrill of the take is passed. The cinematographer wants to review his work artistically and confirm that choices of lenses, camera moves, and film stock are appropriate.

"25 Years of Film Sound: Making Movies in the Digital Era"

By Walter Murch, excerpted from *Mix* magazine, July 2002

Large-format film sound in 1977–79 had finally reached a level of technical fidelity that had been the longed-for dream of the earlier Eras. *Star Wars, Close Encounters of the Third Kind*, and *Apocalypse Now*, with their 6-track, Dolby-encoded 70mm magnetic sound, had finally eliminated surface noise, expanded reproducible frequency range to its practical limit, and expanded the dynamic range to the threshold of pain.

So, here we are in 2002, 25 years on. A whole era has passed, and what has changed? Well, technically, many things—most notably the complete digitization of what used to be a completely analogue process—but remarkably not a significant increase in audio quality when you compare… frequency response, dynamic range, noise threshold, and channel array.

Does the transformation of the technical landscape go along with an improvement in the aesthetic quality of the soundtracks produced today? Well, there is always a developmental synergy between the creative urge and the technical means—a kind of yin-yang interdependence. If you listen to the pre-Dolby films of the early '70s, you can often hear the sound straining against the technical limitations of the time. Back then, we wanted to achieve more than the equipment would allow, so we "souped up" the old sound engine to its maximum and relied for effect on unusual juxtapositions of image and sound… the urge was already there; it was not elicited by the new technology.

Listen to the complex, provocative integration of image and sound in Fritz Lang's *M* (1931) or Orson Welles's *Citizen Kane* (1941) and *Touch of Evil* (1958). They are technically primitive by today's standards, but it is sobering to realize that on the creative, conceptually daring level, we probably haven't made as much progress.

The editor begins reviewing footage as soon as it becomes available, logging notes that get incorporated into a massive database in preparation for editing. As soon as enough film has been accumulated—usually after a week or so of shooting—the editor starts to cut the material into scenes and sequences, beginning the lengthy process of assembling film. "The first compilation helps flush out subtle continuity problems that may have snuck under everyone's radar," Murch says, "and begins to give the director a sense of how the finished film will look and feel." Also there is simply a logistical issue of using available time efficiently: if the editor were to begin assembling the material only after shooting was completed—with a backlog of 40 or more hours of film, in the case of a major studio film—it could add months to the editing schedule.

Like all members of a film crew, Murch must be willing to go where the work is. In 1976, this meant editing *Julia* in London for director Fred Zinneman. Directing *Return to Oz* involved another two-year stint in London in the mid-1980s. *K-19* was shot in Toronto and finished in Los Angeles.

The Cinecittà Studios outside Rome, Italy, where Murch edited *The Talented Mr. Ripley.*

Murch situates his editing rooms within easy striking distance of the set—but not too close. For example, on *The Talented Mr. Ripley*, his base was the Cinecittà film studios near Rome, while filming took place at various locations around Rome and Italy. Murch may meet actors on the set, or socially, but he intentionally keeps a certain distance. He will be living with the performers and their characters in his edit room for over a year, and will wind up knowing their onscreen tics and habits perhaps better than they do. Being outside the typhoon of film production not only safeguards Murch from its gale-force winds of emotion, physical exertion, and stress, but it gives him a degree of much-valued objectivity. However, getting ready for a project still means preparing physically, as well as creatively and logistically. Going 8,000 miles from home to work in a former Soviet-controlled state will make it more of a challenge for Murch to do things the way he likes, and put him far from the support systems of familiar film labs and edit facilities. It also means being away from family and friends. The journey to Romania will be an expedition to an unfamiliar world where unknown tests and adventures await.

Walter Murch with the director of *Julia*, Fred Zinneman.

Even in the edit, far from the set, there will be long nights, missed meals, and tensions, so Walter uses the time leading up to a film's start date to get in good physical condition. This being the week of the summer solstice, there is ample daylight to schedule four- or eight-mile runs every day. Sometimes he'll go out along the open ridge tops bordering the seashore, where on days like this, you can see the Farallon Islands 30 miles out into the Pacific; other runs are through shadowy coastal glens where bay trees give the redwood forests a tangy scent.

Arroyo Hondo trail.

June 7, 2002, Murch's Journal

Run Arroyo Hondo, which is exactly 2.5 miles. On the trail, I suddenly come across a woman taking a piss by the side of the road. "Hello" I say. She says nothing. Later on, I meet two guys coming back toward me—they were probably all camping together, and the guys had taken a hike so she could do her business. Maybe.

Thirty years earlier, in the fall of 1973, when Cold Mountain was a just another peak in North Carolina, Murch took a noteworthy eight-mile run that began, as they all do, down the dirt driveway through his front field. Murch had *The Conversation* on his mind—his first film as a film editor. He made a right at the street and headed west. Four miles down the road, the aging asphalt gives way to dusty dirt. It's an ideal run, since few cars travel here. Walter had been working for almost a year on *The Conversation*, written and directed by Francis Ford Coppola, starring Gene Hackman as Harry Caul, the idiosyncratic eavesdropper, and expert in sound bugging whose anti-hero point of view lies at the heart of the story. At the moment, thought Murch, things weren't going well.

Up until *The Conversation*, Walter had created sound effects and edited them to fit the picture. He'd also been a re-recording mixer—the artist/engineer sitting at a mixing board who, at the very end of the filmmaking process, brings dialogue, music, and sound effects together at proper volume levels and equalization. By 1973 Murch's feature film credits included Coppola's *The Rain People*, (sound montage and re-recording mixer), George Lucas's *THX-1138* (co-writer, sound montage, and mixer), *The Godfather* (supervising sound editor), and Lucas's *American Graffiti* (sound montage and mixer). He'd also edited picture on some documentaries, commercials, and educational films.

It is unusual for sound editors to cross over into picture editing. The film business is traditional and hierarchical; craft boundaries are strict and were even stricter in 1973. In part this is because each skill—be it lighting, cinematography, wardrobe, or editing—requires years of apprenticing and experience before you achieve proficiency. Then too, it can take longer to solidify your reputation in the business, becoming well enough known among producers and directors who make hiring decisions.

So it was a creative risk for both men when Coppola brought Murch on to edit picture as well as design sound and do the mix for *The Conversation*. Coppola wrote the screenplay in the mid-1960s, then put it away for several years. When he formed Zoetrope Studios in 1969, *The Conversation* was part of Zoetrope's proposal of future projects to Warner Brothers. The package included *Apocalypse Now*, and *American Graffiti*, among others. As Walter dryly puts it years later, the executives at Warner Brothers felt these "weren't interesting films," and turned the package down. This devastating rejection led indirectly to Coppola's signing with Paramount to direct *The Godfather*— a script that Elia Kazan, Fred Zinnemann, and Sergio Leone had already turned down.

But when *The Godfather* was released and became an instant critical and commercial success—at that time the highest grossing film ever—Hollywood became very interested in Coppola. Paramount wanted him to get started immediately on a sequel, *The Godfather: Part II*, but Coppola would only agree if the studio would first let him make *The Conversation*.

The problem was how to squeeze in *The Conversation* between the end of *The Godfather* and the start of production on *The Godfather: Part II*. The solution was for Coppola to be less involved with editing *The Conversation* on a daily basis, and that was a precondition when he asked Murch to edit the film. Coppola would plunge into development on *The Godfather: Part II* as soon as he was finished shooting *The Conversation*—casting, choosing locations, rewriting the script, and all the thousands of overwhelming tasks that occupy a writer/director/producer. The plan on *The Conversation* was that Coppola would show up every month or so, once Murch and associate editor Richard Chew (it was his first feature, too) had the film assembled. The three of them would screen it, spend a couple of days together going over ideas and making lists of things to try out. Then Coppola would disappear for another month into the maelstrom of *The Godfather: Part II* preproduction.

"The first assembly of *The Conversation* was long," Murch continues, "just under five hours, so one overriding issue was how to get the film down to a releasable length. Needless to say, this wasn't the usual kind of editor-director relationship. But it was my first feature editing job, and since I had nothing to compare it to, it seemed normal. Richard and I were working on Zoetrope's new KEM 8-plate editing machines and relished the technical challenges and the freedom. Francis told us that if we thought of anything that wasn't on the list we had, we should just go ahead and try it out without bothering him; he would see it when he next came back to town. The first assembly was completed at the beginning of May 1973—about six weeks after the end of shooting—and we went along like this for the rest of the summer: screening every month, then revising and shortening the film."

Gene Hackman as Harry Caul in *The Conversation*, directed by Frances Ford Coppola. The first film edited by Walter Murch.

Gene Hackman in *The Conversation*.

From *The Godfather*, directed by Francis Ford Coppola. Its success made it possible for him to then direct *The Conversation*.

Adding to the uncertainty of making a comprehensible motion picture was the fact that ten days of shooting never took place. Because the picture had gone over budget and was behind schedule, 15 pages of the original screenplay—10 percent of the needed material—was never shot.

"There were three areas of struggle," Murch said later. "Trying to reduce the overall length while keeping things coherent; finding some way to re-knit the story line to compensate for the missing days of shooting; and a more fundamental issue of balancing the story's two thematic elements—character study and thriller—since Francis had conceived the film as an unlikely fusion of Herman Hesse and Alfred Hitchcock."

Murch and Chew made progress in finding solutions to the first two problems, but the third—balancing the two themes—proved to be more difficult. Coppola's monthly screenings in the projection room at his home in San Francisco would always include several "civilians" who knew nothing about the film or indeed nothing about the film industry. These audiences admired the work-in-progress but were unclear about what had really happened at the end of the movie. More crucially, they also found it hard to identify with the introspective, socially uncomfortable central character of Harry Caul, and felt the thriller parts of the story did not integrate with the character study, or vice-versa. The editors tried different solutions, but audience reactions remained the same. By September, five months after finishing the first assembly, Coppola was getting worried. He was about to start shooting *The Godfather: Part II*, and *The Conversation* remained unfinished and problematical.

Murch and Chew flew to Lake Tahoe with the latest version of the film. Coppola was shooting the spectacular, party scene for *The Godfather: Part II*. They screened *The Conversation* in the evening and developed a new series of notes, but everyone could see that Coppola was consumed by the logistical and creative demands of *The Godfather: Part II*. At the beginning of October, Coppola called Murch with a bombshell: he had decided to suspend work on *The Conversation* until after *The Godfather: Part II* was finished.

On the outbound leg of that run in 1973, Murch passed a Coast Guard facility. There, overlooking the ocean, what look to be conceptual sculptures support webs of antenna wires. This array uses great power and coherence for ship-to-shore communications, and it would fascinate someone caught up by all things audio, like Harry Caul—or Walter Murch. But on that day Walter was focused on what to do about *The Conversation*. Should he go along with Coppola—his mentor, the first director to give him a shot at picture editing—and halt the edit?

Richard Chew, who co-edited *The Conversation* with Walter Murch, went on to win an Oscar for editing *Star Wars*, along with Paul Hirsch and Marcia Lucas.

The dirt road soon comes to a dead end and the coast trail begins. Four miles to the east lies the San Andreas Fault. This is where the Pacific plate, moving northwest, meets the North American tectonic plate traveling southeast. Their grinding together caused the 1906 San Francisco earthquake. Ground zero was not far away. In a single violent moment, the earth now under Walter's running shoes had leapt 20 feet to the north. Many violent temblors like the one in 1906 have been bringing most of Northern California and Southern California closer together for millions of years. This geologic activity, an excruciatingly slow conveyor belt, keeps nudging Hollywood (on the Pacific plate) inexorably closer to the Northern California film community (on the North American plate) at an average rate of 35 millimeters (the width of motion picture film!) every year. In a little over 16 million years, Sunset Strip will lie just offshore of San Francisco.

By now, Murch was running back the way he'd come. And he had made his decision. He describes the moment 30 years later, still fresh as highland water: "I decided to kick against the idea of postponement, convince Francis that I could fix what was wrong with the film—somehow find the right balance between the thriller and the character study—and come up with a plan to finish it on time."

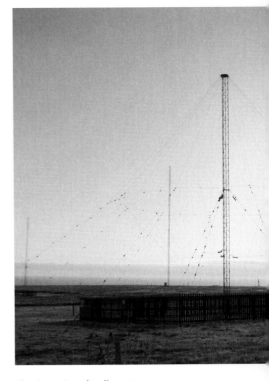

The Coast Guard radio antenna array along the route of Walter's run.

Coppola agreed to let Murch have one final crack at the film, and when they screened it a couple of weeks later the new version seemed to have done the trick. *The Conversation* was released in the spring of 1974 at the height of the controversy over Nixon's Watergate tapes; it went on to win the Palme d'Or at the Cannes Film Festival. *The Godfather: Part II* was released in December of the same year, and both films received Academy nominations for Best Picture of 1974. *The Conversation* was also nominated for Best Original Screenplay and Best Sound. *The Godfather: Part II* was nominated for eleven

Oscars and won six, including Best Picture, Best Director, and Best Adapted Screenplay, boosting Coppola's career to an even higher level than it had reached with *The Godfather*. Murch later won two British Academy Awards for his editing and sound work on *The Conversation*.

"If we had postponed," Walter says now, "*The Conversation* would have probably come out in late 1975, but with a cloud over it which would have been blamed on me—a re-recording mixer who had never edited a feature before. And the crucial topicality of Watergate would have been lost. Both Francis and I had a lot invested in the film coming out on time." Murch couldn't know it then, but the challenges he faced in *The Conversation* as a rookie editor—solving major structural, storytelling problems, often working autonomously of the writer/director—would soon become as familiar to him as his favorite running trails.

The Conversation begins with a young couple, Ann and Mark (played by Cindy Williams and Frederic Forrest) walking through San Francisco's Union Square at lunchtime, having a conversation they don't want overheard. Harry Caul, the "private ear," has been hired by the young woman's husband (the "Director," played by Robert Duvall) to record the couple with several hidden long-range microphones. Back in his workshop, Harry Caul uses his sophisticated technology to uncover a key line from the partially garbled conversation, as spoken by Mark: "He'd kill us if he had the chance." Harry becomes more and more convinced that the Director might be planning to have the young couple killed because they are having an illicit affair. This weighs on Caul's guilty conscience: it won't be the first time his snooping resulted in someone's murder.

Work-in-progress audiences were having problems understanding the intricacies of the plot because Harry himself doesn't fully understand what he has gotten involved in, and the story is told strictly from his point of view. Given the structure of the screenplay, there was no easy way to swing outside events and show them in wide shot, so to speak.

During production, while Frederic Forrest and Cindy Williams were still easily available, Murch took them to Alta Vista Park, a quiet square in a residential neighborhood of San Francisco, to record a complete take of their conversation, audio only, in case he needed "clean" dialogue to augment the original production sound which was being spoiled by microwave interference. In that "wild sound" recording with Murch, Forrest did one reading of the "kill us" line with an unintentionally different emphasis. Instead of saying, "He'd *kill* us if he had the chance," implying that the couple is in danger, Forrest accidentally read it as, "He'd kill *us* if he had the chance." Says Murch: "That makes you imagine three dots at the end of the line, and in parentheses at the end of the line, the implied conclusion: 'So we have to kill *him*.'"

CON - 5021-22

Frederic Forrest as Mark and Cindy Williams as Ann in *The Conversation*. Notice Gene Hackman (Harry Caul) on the park bench.

Murch re-recorded dialogue for this scene, and by chance got a line reading he later used in editing to clarify the story.

"I noted that reading at the time," Murch continues, "and filed it away as being inappropriate. But a year later during the mixing of the film I suddenly thought, let's see what happens if we substitute that 'inappropriate' reading with its different inflection into the final reel. It might help tip audiences into understanding what had happened: that the 'victims' were really the 'plotters.' So I mixed it into the soundtrack in place of the original reading and took the finished film to New York where Francis was halfway through shooting *The Godfather: Part II*. I prepared him for the change and wondered what his reaction would be when he heard it. It was a risky idea because it challenged one of the fundamental premises of the film, which is that the conversation itself remains the same, but your interpretation of it changes. I was prepared to go back to the original version. But he liked it, and that's the way it remains in the finished film."

"Harry Caul is sophisticated technically but stunted emotionally," Murch says, "and he used all of his sophisticated technical filters to uncover that one critical line of dialogue. But the significant distortion he didn't remove was the one in his mind. He was falling in love with Ann (the Williams character) at a distance, and he so needed to believe she was a victim that he subconsciously placed the emphasis on *kill* rather than *us*. At the end, after the Duvall character is discovered to have been murdered in the hotel room, the mental distortion falls away and Harry hears the line the way it really must have been all along."

Another example of Murch's active participation in constructing *The Conversation* was seizing an opportunity to add intrigue, and coincidentally help fill the hole created by unshot footage. Just past the halfway point in the film, after attending a surveillance trade show, Harry Caul invites his colleagues and acquaintances to come back to his loft office for an informal party. There's drinking and continued confrontation between Harry and Bernie Moran, his rival, played by Allen Garfield. Moran's assistant Meredith (Elizabeth MacRae) seems to be intent on seducing Harry. The tape of Ann and Mark's Union Square conversation is still up on Harry's tape recorder.

"One of the things that emerged in the editing of the film was the idea of making Meredith steal the tapes," Murch says. "In the film as it was shot, she stayed with Harry, slept with him in his office, and was gone when he woke up, having stolen some electronic diagrams that Moran had coveted. But I found if we could insinuate that she had stolen the tapes, then several lines of the story would come together—implying that her boss Moran was in cahoots with the Director's assistant Martin Stett (Harrison Ford) to get the tapes which Harry was holding on to. But all of that was constructed in the editing. In the end we found we had to shoot just one extra shot—Harry's hand on an empty reel—to tie it all together."

How the Toilet Scene in *The Conversation* was Conceived

From Walter Murch's commentary on *The Conversation* DVD:

"Francis got the story to the point where Harry was in a room in which a murder has ostensibly taken place. The room was perfectly clean, and Francis wanted the evidence of the murder to be present, yet hidden at the same time. When he gave me the script to read, he said, 'If you can think of anything let me know.' Well, I did."

"Well, I thought of this image of me as a preteen. I had gotten hold of some pornographic magazines and was reading them when I heard my parents coming home. I panicked and cut the magazines up and tried to flush them down the toilet. Well, of course the opposite happened, and the toilet blocked up and these pornographic magazines, fragments of them, kept gurgling out of the toilet when my father came to fix it. He was horrified but secretly amused, as parents are under those circumstances."

Murch suggested a version of this scene to Coppola, in which Harry Caul sees the toilet backing up with bloody evidence the murderers thought they had flushed away.

"Francis shot the scene in a brilliant way, and I was able to cut from the first hint of blood to an unexpectedly low angle, at dead level with the toilet, where you don't see anything yet. But the focus of attention is, 'What was that in that toilet?' Slowly, slowly the toilet begins to brim, then overflow with this horrible red liquid. As happened to me with my porn magazines, the thing the murderers most wanted to get rid of got stuck in the toilet and came back up to accuse them."

From *The Conversation*.

Something of Murch is in the Harry Caul character. They're both fascinated by sound, recording equipment, and how audio can be manipulated and its meaning redefined. They don't mind—maybe they prefer—working alone. Harry plays the saxophone, which seems to be his only form of relaxation. Walter considers editing a musical form—visual music. This superimposition of character and film editor became evident during the edit of *The Conversation*. One late night, on the edge of exhaustion and deep inside movie space, Murch was working on a scene in which Harry Caul stops his tape recorder. Murch couldn't understand why his KEM editing machine didn't also come to a stop on Harry's command. Who was controlling whom? It's an obvious question: did Coppola model Harry Caul on his freshman editor when he wrote the screenplay for *The Conversation*?

The experience of working so independently on *The Conversation* gave Murch the methods, approach, sensibilities, and confidence that would define his editing work for the next three decades. In Murch, directors like Coppola, Zinnemann, Minghella, and others know they'll be working with a skilled film editor, no question. But more than that, they will be bringing a creative partner aboard: a co-pilot capable of flying the plane when the director needs to focus attention elsewhere; a flight engineer who can respond to mechanical problems with elegant solutions to keep the machine airborne; and a navigator finding added meaning and poetry that were never fully spelled out in the flight plan.

The party scene in *The Conversation*. Murch reconstructed the end of the scene to imply that Meredith, played by Elizabeth MacRae, steals Harry Caul's tapes.

AGGRESSIVE COLLABORATION

From Walter Murch's commentary on *The Conversation* DVD:

"It was a wonderful challenge. I'd come up with new ideas in the course of that month, and then give Francis a call, and if he was available he'd come back and screen the film again, and there'd be many surprises because I'd simply gone ahead and done many things we didn't talk about, like the transition of this scene into two different scenes at two different times; but Francis enjoyed that, he likes that kind of initiative and sort of aggressive kind of collaboration. I certainly enjoyed it, even though it was the first film I edited. I certainly felt it was a challenge on many, many different levels."

Artwork for *The Conversation* poster.

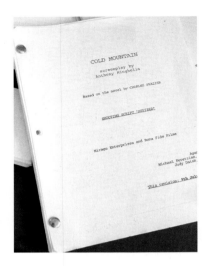

The screenplay of *Cold Mountain*.

From:	Walter Murch
Date:	6/8/02
To:	Anthony Minghella

Dear Ant:

Have received and am reading the new CM - wonderful work! - and will finish it today, have a timing for you hopefully Monday - Tuesday. I like the longer opening in CM before we go to war. Have an idea about that transition, but will wait to think more about it until I finish.

Have a great time location scouting!

And congratulations again on the new version!!

Love,
Walter

Now, 30 years and 27 films later, Murch is preparing for another plunge into the bracing waters of a high-budget, high-profile, studio-backed motion picture: *Cold Mountain*. For this he needs to reread the screenplay, write up his notes for director Anthony Minghella, and perform a ritual "script timing." This involves reading the screenplay to himself in "film time," measuring each scene's duration with a stopwatch as it plays in his head. He'll do this exercise three separate times to see if the film "runs" consistently. If it does, fine; he's found the bedrock of the film's tempo and length. If the timings do not agree, that may indicate a fault line running under the film's surface—a fissure that could cause rumblings later in the editing. This is certainly not the last window of opportunity to raise concerns with a director about structure, tone, and comprehensibility. Walter and Anthony will sit with these issues every day, like family at the dinner table, throughout the filmmaking process. But this is the only chance for Murch to share his thoughts and worries about story and character before the tornado of production moves in and sucks up most of the oxygen. And since they still exist only on paper, for the moment these issues remain theoretical problems, snugly confined to the upstairs office in Murch's barn.

Cold Mountain has a story structure that is the antithesis of the one in *The Conversation*. Instead of being locked into a single protagonist's point of view, the award-winning, best-selling novel by Charles Frazier uses a parallel, multiple point-of-view construction. Inman (played by Jude Law), is a Confederate soldier injured in the Battle of Petersburg who deserts from the army and travels as an outlaw for many months over hundreds of miles to return to the woman he loves, Ada Monroe (Nicole Kidman). Ada is an aristocratic minister's spinster daughter who waits for Inman in Cold Mountain, North Carolina. There she struggles against Home Guard vigilantes, hard winters, and her own inadequacies to hold onto her farm, Black Cove, after her father has died. Inman and Ada have had a brief taste of romance before secession leads to war and forces them apart, but the film tells of their respective travails separately. Only at the end are they reunited.

June 9, 2002, Murch's Journal

Eight Miles. Last three up the hill and then another mile on ridge trail south, and back. Lovely weather, the triptych smell of pine, eucalyptus, and bay laurel in hot sun, three braids intertwined. Town lovely and mysterious 1000 feet below. Why mysterious?

I went for a swim in the channel—cold—but not crampingly so. I told myself that this is the ritual baptism, allowing me to be reborn from K-19 onto Cold Mountain. I went in three times, each time a little longer, and by the end of the third, floating out to sea, I could not feel the cold. In fact, it felt in some metaphysical way warm. Lovely day, blue sky, warm inland wind, the town putting on its finest for me, who is about to leave it.

Among Murch's many working methods is "The Memo": a set of notes, usually six to eight pages long, that he gives a director before principal photography begins. Sometimes, as Murch describes it, The Memo is the first and last thing he does on a film. A few directors have changed their minds about having Murch edit their film, once they read the extent of his critique and grasped how intimately involved he would be in the project. Either way, these first notes serve Murch well.

From:	Walter Murch
Date:	6/10/02 2:06 AM
To:	Anthony Minghella

Dear Ant:

Congratulations on the new draft—a couple of tear-stinging moments for me, even though this is the third read.

I am going to be timing it tomorrow and Tuesday, if I can keep the rest of my life at bay and find that lovely stopwatch.

Structurally, of course, lots (50+) transitions back and forth in space and time. Presents its own challenge, as we know from EP [The English Patient], which had 40 transitions. But it will be wonderful.

However, how to articulate the moment when back and forth in time becomes back and forth in space? It is a little confusing to track it now, if I put on my audience hat.

When Inman nods to Mrs. Morgan (page 26), a clock starts ticking faster, faster, and the sooner he gets out on the road the better.

Once Veasey and Ruby enter the film, it rockets along.

I have put so many check marks (good!) on almost every page from 35-100 it is stunning. Lines and moments that any film would be happy to have a half dozen of, here there are scores and scores.

I wonder, that the interlude with Sara, and the fact (debatable, but still…) that Inman and Sara sleep together, undercuts his meeting with and sleeping with Ada. The two scenes are in such close proximity. And then the fight with the Northerners, and Inman's actions to save Sara and her baby, are similar in tone to his actions against Teague and Co. to save Ada and Ruby. There is a kind of musical reiteration, thinking of it symphonically, that may undercut the most important moments, which are those with Ada and the shootout with Teague & co. Perhaps I am missing something…

Is there a way to hint at the ambiguity of Inman's death, the way the book did? If we know he is dead, then the coda feels more… coda-like, and a little too sweet, somehow.

Relationship between Ada and Inman:

More tension, and more class distinction. Make it more IMPOSSIBLE, UNTHINKABLE for these two to get together, so that when it does, it is the more rewarding. What she goes through on Black Cove Farm causes her to grow in stature, and understand and love Inman. The early scenes are all pretty easy now, except for Inman's taciturn nature. Everyone (Sally, Monroe) is kind of nudging them together. And Ada is very willing. Make her less so, more complex, and paradoxically less self-aware: a dose more Scarlett O'Hara, not as completely accepting of Cold Mountain's charms and people.

All of this is present, latent, in the structure now, but I am suggesting finding a way to draw the bow a bit further back at the beginning so the arrow has more force.

=========

Excuses, as always, for the lack of "perhaps" and "maybe" and "it seems to me" which are hovering invisibly around every phrase of these comments.

It is and will be a fantastic film.

Love,
Walter

Minghella, who is having production meetings and scouting filming locations in North Carolina, answers Murch two hours later:

From:	Anthony Minghella
Date:	Mon, 10 Jun 2002 07:16:24 EDT
To:	Walter Murch

brilliant brilliant notes, and I'm intrigued by each of them. I don't know how to address them all, but I am already contemplating new moments and improvements. I'm particularly keen to make the return of Inman to Ada sing more. And I understand what you mean about Ada and Sara. It's one of the things which prompted me to cast Natalie, who is so young, and finally not a real threat to Ada, but but but. I also know what you mean about Ada and the absence of thistle between her and Inman. I know I can make it better. I know that the budget battles, continuing today with a big meeting on our one

Nicole Kidman as Ada Monroe in *Cold Mountain.*

Jude Law as W.P. Inman in *Cold Mountain.*

> rest day of the technical survey (on which I'm also scouting) means that my brain is more occupied by numbers, by cuts, by the indifference to content, than it is with issues of content.
>
> I am so happy to get your mind patrolling this material. Keep scratching away. I'm thrilled that you see what we have here; I'm thrilled that you'll push me to make it better. Did you look at the storyboards? They're already simplifying and simplifying, and I'm very conscious of the sequence in terms of length, but I'd love your scouring of their implications and their narrative transparencies.
>
> off to battle myself
> ant

According to time-honored Hollywood tradition, film school graduates who want to become movie executives break into the system by taking a job in a studio mail room. In fact, many entertainment industry agents-to-be still begin their climb to the top by wheeling mail carts through the decorous halls of such big talent agencies as Creative Artists Agency (CAA), William Morris, and International Creative Management (ICM). Similarly, Walter Murch's first paying film job was nowhere near an editing room or film set, though it did involve legendary Hollywood director George Cukor (*Dinner at Eight, The Philadelphia Story, My Fair Lady*).

When they were all students at USC, Murch's friends George Lucas and Matthew Robbins saw a bulletin board posting for a temporary job over winter break. It turned out that George Cukor needed people to help wrap and deliver his annual bounty of Christmas gifts. Lucas quit after one day, so Robbins recruited Walter as his replacement. In Cukor's attic they found a pyramid of gifts—at least 250 of them—for the director's closest friends, actors, actresses, and film business cronies. Robbins and Murch soon became expert in wrapping techniques, as well as navigating their way around Beverly Hills, Brentwood, and Bel-Air. They tootled around in Robbins's VW van, ringing doorbells, with Walter going up to imposing front doors and announcing to the butler or maid, "A gift from Mr. Cukor." Occasionally Cukor would appear at the door of his attic to monitor progress. Murch still remembers Cukor's advice (borrowed from Benjamin Disraeli): "Never complain. Never explain." It became a saying the film student would retain and rely on: work hard, get the job done, and don't bother explaining why something didn't get finished. No one cares about excuses.

(Walter later figured out that Cukor was using the holiday seasons to recruit Christmas helpers for his own extra-curricular entertainment: "the elves in the attic," as Walter calls them. "That year he struck out. But he was very good-natured about it.")

After leaving USC in 1967, Murch first went to work in the film business—for real this time—at Encyclopedia Britannica Educational Films (replacing Robbins, who was moving on to something else), and he soon got his chance to edit picture. Later he went to Dove Films, a commercial production company run by two cinematographers, Haskell Wexler and Cal Bernstein. At both places, Murch was working with the Moviola editing machine.

Forty years earlier, before the invention of the Moviola, the edit room was a quiet place outfitted simply with a set of rewinds, scissors, and editor's intuition. Stitching together a film was analogous to sewing, and many editors in those days were women. After seeing new footage projected once, editors went over the film with a magnifying glass, choosing where to make cuts based on their recollection from that one screening. Their only rule of thumb: a length of film held from the tip of the nose to the end of an outstretched hand would run for about three seconds. Strips of film were put together with paper clips and sent off to another room to be hot-spliced together with acetone film cement. After this new assembly was screened for the director and producer, the editing process continued, with adjustments made as necessary until the final version was approved.

Editing department, Triangle Pictures Corporation, 1917.

So things remained until Iwan Serrurier, who was neither an editor nor a film worker, invented the Moviola, the world's first editing machine. A Dutchman, he came to the U.S. at the turn of the 20th century, made a fortune in real estate, and became intrigued by the technical advances taking place here. Serrurier's initial idea was to invent a film-viewing machine for the home, (comparable to the Victrola for playing records)—the first home entertainment system. He built a model with beautiful cabinet work, and got it patented; one of his five children named it in a family contest. Priced at $600 in 1920 (about $5,600 in today's dollars) his machines were beyond the reach of a normal household. So who could afford them? Serrurier thought studio executives might use the Moviola to view dailies in the comfort of their own offices.

Serrurier went to the movie studios but succeeded in selling just three machines. Only after going to the Douglas Fairbanks Studios (the same facility where Walter worked on *K-19* some 75 years later) did Serrurier finally see how movies were being put together. He watched an editor trying to move the film back and forth by hand to get the equivalent of a moving picture. The man told Serrurier he might be interested in the machine if it were modified for use on an editing bench. Over a weekend, Serrurier retooled the Moviola for professional use, stripping it of its varnished wood cabinet, and on Monday brought the revamped prototype back to the editor. The Moviola was a hit, and in 1924 Serrurier sold his first editing machine to Fairbanks Studios for $125 (about $1,370 today—not much more than the cost of Apple's Final Cut Pro edit system).

Demand for Moviolas took off during the 1930s, then boomed during World War II, when hundreds of military and propaganda films were being produced each year. All the newsreels shown in theaters to keep Americans abreast of the latest war developments were cut on Moviolas. Serrurier's company added a small editing bench and splicer and shipped these self-contained postproduction units overseas. The first "broadcast journalists" shot, processed, and edited short films on location, then sent the newsreels home. They were the precursors of today's field reporters, who use satellite-linked cameras to send TV and Web-delivered news clips of events as they occur.

An upright Moviola editing machine, the type Murch first used when he began working in the film industry.

By the time Walter Murch first encountered the Moviola, it had been in use with few changes for over four decades. It still had its beefed-up sewing machine motor, forward and reverse foot pedals, exposed flywheel, and a hand-brake. The editor, working standing up or perched on a stool, watched a smallish image flicker on a viewfinder no bigger than a postcard. With the help of an assistant who stood behind hanging up "trims" (small clips of film), the editor slowly built up a reel of good takes. Each reel had a maximum capacity of 1,000 feet, or just over 11 minutes. For sound, the Moviola could handle one separate reel of audio that had been transferred from ¼-inch tape to 35mm magnetic film—essentially audiotape in 35mm gauge.

The frustrations of editing on a Moviola are legendary. The machine loves to eat film, scratching or chewing up workprint inside its uncompromising steel mechanism. The intermittent motion of the film clatters noisily. The viewing image is small. And by only being able to run one audio track at a time, it gives the editor little control over sound, aside from dialogue.

The first flatbed film editing system, an alternative to the Moviola, was introduced in Germany by Wilhelm Steenbeck in 1931. The Steenbeck, like the later model made by KEM, provided a larger image viewing area, virtually silent operation, a rotating-prism lens, three tracks of sound, and a generally more comfortable working environment. The editor could now work sitting down as if at an office desk, instead of standing up at the Moviola like a lathe operator. When Coppola began planning his edit for *The Rain People* on a trip to Europe in 1967 and brought back a Steenbeck editing machine, it was the first flatbed to be used, by editor Barry Malkin, on a motion picture in the U.S.

So in 1972, another challenge for Murch on *The Conversation*, in addition to editing his first feature and dealing with seemingly intractable story problems, was the new editing machine he was using—this one a huge, gray, ultramodern KEM Universal "8-plate" flatbed, similar to the one that Thelma Schoonmaker had used to edit *Woodstock* in 1970. Until *The Conversation*, all of Murch's picture editing experience had been on the traditional upright American Moviola. The sleek German KEM had two rotating-prism screens,

A KEM Universal flatbed editing machine.

was push-button operated and capable of playing three tracks of sound at the same time. But it required film workprint to be strung together in large 1000-foot (11-minute) rolls of consecutive shots, rather than spooled into cupcake-sized individual takes a minute or two long, as used on a Moviola. The two machines require working in different modes, which Murch likens to a sculptor using different materials: instead of building up the "sculpture" of the film from small bits of "clay," as would have been the case with a Moviola, editing with a KEM involves chiseling away chunks of "marble" from large blocks of film, ultimately revealing the movie hidden inside.

Although it is a mechanical device, the Moviola is in fact a non-linear system with more organizational similarities to random-access computerized editing than to the linear KEM system. Consequently Murch's change to the linear KEM from the non-linear Moviola actually required more of a wrenching conceptual shift than the shift he would eventually make from film-based editing to digital editing. After *The Conversation*, Murch would switch back and forth between KEM and Moviola over the following 20 years, depending on the director he was working for and the editorial style of the film.

From *Apocalypse Now*, directed by Francis Ford Coppola. Murch used an Avid to edit *Apocalypse Now Redux*, the director's cut, released in 2001.

Thus began, on his first feature film, Murch's participation in the search for the filmmaker's Holy Grail: a technique for assembling motion pictures that would be fast, cheap, and transparent; immediately responsive to creative ideas without the process itself getting in the way; and a method of reproducing film image and sound as near as possible to what audiences experience.

As early as 1968, Coppola, Lucas, and Murch had been investigating a precocious attempt at computer-controlled editing. The CMX film-editing computer, like mainframes of the day, was expensive and bulky, filling an entire room with hardware, but it gave Murch a glimpse of the future. A few years later, Coppola and Murch proposed using a more developed CMX system to edit parts of *The Godfather*, but the studio turned them down, citing unreliable data storage and exorbitant costs.

By the late 1970s and early '80s, as the personal computer came of age and began to revolutionize home and work, many different computer-based film editing systems came along: E-Pix, EMC, D-Vision, Lucasfilm's EditDroid, and others. As Murch points out in his 1995 book, *In the Blink of an Eye*, "A tremendous amount of research and development was invested in these systems, particularly when you consider that, although professional film is an expensive medium, there is not a lot of professional film equipment in

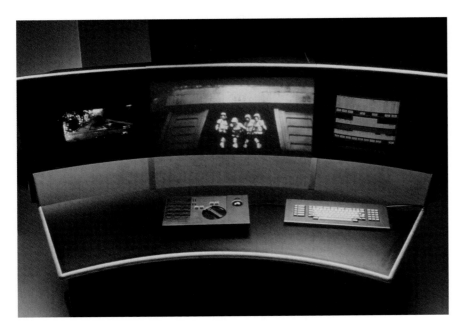

Lucasfilm's EditDroid, the first computer based, non-linear editing systems.

the world (compared, for instance, to medical equipment)." Of course, television offered more business opportunities, and digital post-production took off worldwide in the broadcast industry. In all of these early systems, the computer was used simply to control the movement of analogue media (VHS tapes, laserdiscs, etc.) stored on transport devices that were umbilically linked to the computer.

By the late 1980s, speedier processors and better data storage capabilities made it possible to digitize film images directly to a computer's hard drive. After getting its inauguration on commercials and high-end documentaries, the Avid editing system for film began to appear in feature-film editing rooms. Murch's initial experience with Avid was on a music video for Linda Ronstadt in 1994, and for a short, layered sequence in the 1994 film, *I Love Trouble*. The first feature film he edited entirely on the Avid was *The English Patient*. The Avid was his system of choice on the next several films: *The Talented Mr. Ripley*, the recut of Orson Welles's *Touch of Evil*, *Apocalypse Now Redux*, and *K-19*.

But the Avid had certain limitations and difficulties. For one thing it is relatively expensive. The Avid Film Composer, which simulates film editing and contains the necessary film-to-video conversion protocols, cost $80,000 to $100,000 when Murch first used it in the 1990s, so feature-film budgets would normally allow for only two machines, at most. (Some films limped along with only one.) Even with two machines, one of them is usually dedicated to doing all the "housekeeping," such as file management and making tapes for other crew members—sound editors, music composers, producers. The Avid is a "closed" system, meaning its architecture is designed to run only proprietary software, and its way of digitizing and replaying the image is unique. Expensive new versions and upgrades have to be purchased, and only from Avid. Finally, for a long time the company was infamous for providing spotty technical support and resisting innovation and input from filmmakers.

As he worked on Avid systems, Murch kept his eye on other developments in the digital editing world. Premiere, by Adobe Systems, came out in 1991. The software was suitable for commercials, documentaries, and other projects originating on video, but it couldn't translate 24-frame-per-second film into 30-frame-per-second video.

Meanwhile, the San Francisco-based media software developer Macromedia was having great success with programs for multimedia and Web development, such as Director, Dreamweaver, and Flash. It had been working on a digital editing system called Key Grip, that could operate on Apple's Macintosh, but the company was concentrating on Web tools and didn't see much future for its new editing application, and so sold it to Apple in 1998

Murch first used the Avid Film Composer on *The English Patient* when he had it set up in his office at home. Assistant editor Edie Ichioka, seen above, describes it as, "a surreal setting for editing, with a wood-burning stove, and chicken clucks in the morning that aren't coming out of your edit machine, but are actually coming out of chickens in the barn below."

before ever releasing a finished product. In 1999 Apple released a revamped version of Macromedia's application as Final Cut Pro, a digital editing system designed to compete with Premiere for consumers, students, and low-end professionals. This caught Murch's eye, as it caught the attention of other film editors on the lookout for technological advances. He had been using a Macintosh since 1986 and has always been a fan of Apple. He liked the company's belief in supporting professionals in the creative arts with tools that were innovative and responsive to users' needs.

In June 2002, Walter was preparing to leave for Romania to start work on *Cold Mountain*. The project meant being out of the country for a year and a half. He'd barely had time to catch his breath, having finished sound mixing on *K-19* only four weeks earlier. This would be his third picture with director Anthony Minghella, so Walter knew how Minghella liked to work: shooting an abundance of material for later review and editing; constantly re-examining assumptions about story, structure, and character; and revising picture and sound right up to delivery of the final mix and cut negative. As with their two previous films, Murch would be both picture editor and re-recording mixer.

Now, as if he didn't already have enough challenges ahead of him, Walter was thinking about making another dramatic jump-shift in editing methodology: editing *Cold Mountain* with Final Cut Pro—Apple's $995 off-the-shelf software. Had his desire to find the Holy Grail of film editing become an obsession? Was Murch getting too far ahead of the pack, becoming an errant knight? He may intrepid, but Murch isn't reckless. His longtime assistant editor, Sean Cullen, helped Murch weigh the risks and locate the most qualified sherpas available to guide their journey—but they were not in Cupertino. People at Apple reacted variously to the news about Murch's intention to use Final Cut Pro, ranging from euphoria and excitement to caution and deep misgivings. So for help, Murch and Cullen instead went to a 1920s Tudor-style building on Sunset Boulevard in West Hollywood, halfway between the Whisky a Go Go and the Roxy nightclubs.

Ralph Fiennes and Kristin Scott Thomas in *The English Patient,* the first motion picture Murch edited on an Avid Film Composer digital editing system.

Walter Murch edited the motion picture *K-19: The Widowmaker* on an Avid editing system in 2002 at The Lot.

CHAPTER 3

Kicking the Tires

EARLY JANUARY 2002—WEST HOLLYWOOD, CA

Walter Murch is at the former Warner Hollywood Studio, now called The Lot, editing *K-19*, starring Harrison Ford and Liam Neeson, and directed by Kathryn Bigelow. His first assistant, Sean Cullen, comes into the room. Murch is editing on his Avid system. He works standing up, the way some writers do. "Walter," Sean asks during a pause, "what do you think about this Final Cut Pro thing?"

Apple Computer's Final Cut is considered to be a "prosumer" application, midway between professional and consumer, though it is widely used to edit documentaries, TV commercials, and low-budget independent films. Hobbyists, students, and filmmaker wannabes love it because it's cheap and easy to learn. For a film editor of Murch's stature to consider using FCP on a big movie could presage the long-predicted convergence of consumer-level digital video tools and the Hollywood film industry.

"Hmm," Walter murmurs. "Let's keep an eye on it." An understated response, but to people who know him as well as Sean does, it means, "I'm interested!"

Over the course of nearly eight years, Cullen had worked at Murch's side on *The English Patient*, *The Talented Mr. Ripley*, the restored Orson Welles classic, *Touch of Evil*, and *Apocalypse Now Redux*. They make a great partnership. Cullen is fearless when facing technological challenges. At the Yale School of Drama he received an MFA in Technical Design and Production in 1994. Cullen's master's thesis on motion control in theater included designs for a new Apple Macintosh interface. Cullen knows that Murch's commitment to advancing film and sound technology goes back to when Murch got started in feature films in 1969, on *The Rain People* for Francis Ford Coppola—the first American movie to be edited (by Barry Malkin) on a flatbed Steenbeck editing table and re-recorded (by Murch) on a KEM flatbed mixing system. Ten years later, on *Apocalypse Now*, Murch and Coppola invented what later became known as the "5.1" sound format for movies when Murch mixed the film's soundtrack (on cinema's first automated mixing board) so helicopters could be heard flying in 360 degrees around the theater. Only problem was, no audio system could accommodate the effect then, so Coppola had speakers added

Sean Cullen has worked as an assistant editor with Walter Murch since 1994. Prior to his film work, Cullen did technical design at the San Francisco Opera and was technical director at the Berkeley Repertory Theatre.

or rewired in movie houses across the country, paying out of his own pocket. In the 1990s, this pioneering audio technology filtered down to consumers, who could begin listening to "surround sound" in their living rooms. So now, having spent his career seeking out and often inventing breakthroughs in post-production technologies, it was perfectly in character for Murch to explore the possibility of changing editing platforms for *Cold Mountain*.

When Apple Macintosh computers arrived in the mid-1980s, Walter became a fan, and not just for personal use. He always had a Mac in the edit suite for note-taking and logging information. If there is a filmmaker who personified Apple's "Think Different" campaign, it is Walter Murch.

He had migrated from film-based editing to the Avid digital system in 1995 on *The English Patient*, though his initial motivation had nothing to do with technology *per se*. Murch needed to work out of his home in the Bay Area while filming continued on location in Italy and Tunisia. His son, Walter, had to undergo emergency surgery for a brain tumor, and it was only by going digital that Murch could stay near his son in California and keep up with the schedule. His Academy Award for Best Editing on *The English Patient* made it the first such Oscar for a film edited on a non-linear digital system.

By the late 1990s Avid had a strong foothold in the film industry, as well as in television news and advertising, where it first made its mark. But Murch and Cullen were looking for an alternative.

Avid, headquartered in Tewksbury, Massachusetts, has a reputation among film editors and assistants for holding onto useful but expensive improvements for years at a time. Cullen and other assistant editors find the company's backup support sketchy. Cullen says, and other assistant editors concur, that Avid systems are not easily accessible for troubleshooting problems. So a system crash can be a real crisis, often requiring an Avid-certified technician to help them recover, which can cost an editor days of work. Avid technicians have been known to ascribe problems to configurations that use non-Avid peripherals, such as an NEC monitor. Cullen describes using an Avid to be, "like dancing with a gorilla, and the gorilla always leads." Murch and Cullen were looking for a digital editing system that could give them more flexibility, would cost less (affording them more workstations), and if it did crash, one they could more easily fix on their own.

With their gift for problem solving, appreciation for Apple's creative tools, and zest for challenges beyond mere editing, Murch and Cullen were ready to consider Apple's Final Cut Pro, even if it hadn't been fully road-tested.

Just for fun, when the two were editing *Apocalypse Now Redux* at American Zoetrope in San Francisco in 1999 and 2000, Sean tried the newly released Final Cut Pro 1.0. The immediate problems with the application had more to do with housekeeping than anything else. With its corresponding FilmLogic

Sound mixing *The Godfather: Part II*, 1974. Left to right, Mark Berger, Francis Ford Coppola, Walter Murch.

Murch first worked with Francis Ford Coppola on the motion picture, *The Rain People* (1969). Both enjoy seeking out the latest technical filmmaking advances, and in some cases, inventing them.

Murch holds his two Oscar awards for editing and sound mixing *The English Patient* (1996), directed by Anthony Minghella.

software, FCP could track only key numbers—the coding system for tracking every frame of film negative—then used by Kodak. But *Apocalypse Now* had been shot in the 1970s, so the alpha/numeric stamps on its negative were long out of date. "I could probably get around that," says Sean, "but it was too 'ka-chunk'—too labor-intensive."

By 2002, two years later, Final Cut Pro had reached version 3.0. For Murch and Cullen, the prospect of doing an $80 million studio film on software costing $995 is too seductive to disregard, as is the prospect of living in Apple's friendly interface and object-oriented, cut-and-paste world. With Walter's encouragement, Sean uses his spare time to do technical research, pore over Apple's Web site, and play with the software on his laptop. He starts coming across an outfit in West Hollywood called DigitalFilm Tree. "When I did a Google search, DigitalFilm Tree kept coming up—either a reference to them, or to Ramy Katrib, who had spoken at some conference." Sean talks to Walter again: "There's these guys in town, DigitalFilm Tree, and I'd like to give them a call. How would you feel about me saying we might do the next show on Final Cut?"

"Sure," Walter says. "Let's see what develops."

The historic Sentinel Building in San Francisco, offices of American Zoetrope, Francis Ford Coppola's production company. Here, while working on *Apocalypse Now Redux* (2001) with Murch, Sean Cullen first experimented with Apple's Final Cut Pro 1.0 to see how it handled film.

Office of DigitalFilm Tree, located on the Sunset Strip in Los Angeles. Sean Cullen contacted the company to find out more about using Final Cut Pro.

Ramy Katrib had formed DigitalFilm Tree in 1999 expressly to help film editors, as opposed to video editors, learn and properly configure Final Cut Pro. FCP wasn't originally released with the idea of editing film, so there was a dearth of reliable information and technical support. Katrib quickly found a niche within the post-production community of editors looking for advice and TV and motion picture productions seeking consultation. The information went full circle, since Apple itself came to DFT for FCP development ideas and feedback from users in the field.

At the beginning of 2002, serious planning for post-production on *Cold Mountain* hasn't even started. All Sean and Walter know for sure is that Anthony Minghella is directing; they don't know where the film is going to be shot or edited. Tom Cruise is actively negotiating to take the role of Inman, which Jude Law will eventually play. Cullen and Murch understand this much: *Cold Mountain* is going to be a big-budget, high-profile, studio-backed film with a star-driven cast. Characteristic of the motion picture business, there are no deals, contracts, or handshakes. Anthony simply sent Murch an early draft of the script in the summer of 2001, and Walter enthusiastically agreed to edit the film. Still, it was incumbent on Cullen to be careful when contacting people that word about the project didn't get out.

When Cullen calls DigitalFilm Tree, Scott Witman picks up the phone. "I'm thinking about doing this film and using Final Cut Pro," Cullen says. "I want to talk to you guys about what's possible and what you've done before, and just whether or not you think this could even have a chance of working."

Witman's answer might have ended the whole venture right then and there. "Well, we're pretty busy right now," he says. "A lot of people are asking for advice. We can't give out free help any more."

Sean assures Witman he has a professional relationship in mind: "No, no, not free. We'd pay you to consult—to find out what's going on."

"In the first conversation," Sean recalls, "I sort of held back a little bit. I said it's a large film, that we'd probably shoot half a million feet, and shoot for a number of months—maybe six months. They were starting to get interested. Witman said, 'We'll give you a call back.' I just left my first name and the phone number."

With his dark bedroom eyes and customary three-day growth of beard, the founder of DigitalFilm Tree is known among women in the digital film community as "beautiful Ramy." He first began exploring the unmapped terrain between film and desktop digital video in 1998 while working the night shift at Magic Film & Video Works in Burbank. It was then considered the largest negative-cutting house in the world, where film negative was conformed for shows like *E.R.*, *NYPD Blue*, and *Spin City*, along with most of New Line's feature films. Ramy was the telecine operator, doing film-to-video transfers.

Ramy Katrib, founder and president of DigitalFilm Tree.

"When you walked in, the smell of chemicals and cement just overwhelmed you," says Ramy. "They had ten splicing stations, old German machines with foot pedals, all going click-click, click-click. At the time that I worked there they had 70 employees, all negative cutting." (As a measure of digital editing's invasion of the film world, only 15 workers remain.)

"Negative cutting is the scariest post work I've ever seen," says Ramy. "If you make an error you lose your job. I hated it." But in retrospect, the experience was fortuitous both for Ramy Katrib and for Walter Murch. "I stopped being scared of film," says Ramy. "I touched it. I rolled it."

Ramy Katrib's life began far from Hollywood. He was born in Beirut in 1970 of Lebanese-Christian parents. His father was an evangelist, his mother an English teacher. They settled in Loma Linda, east of Los Angeles, in 1975. From there Ramy went to U.C. Riverside and to Columbia College in L.A., where he learned hands-on film crafts. "School was all about learning how to edit, how to shoot; I liked that," he says. "But everyone in my family was freaking out. They perceived L.A. as Sin City, even though it was only 50 miles away."

On off-hours from his job at Magic Film & Video Works, Ramy produced his own documentaries. "Of course I wanted to be a filmmaker, just like every Joe out here," he says. One project—still unfinished—was about the writer Mardik Martin, who wrote *Mean Streets* and *Raging Bull*. The other documentary was about proton treatment—the convergence of nuclear particle physics and medical treatment. For that project, Ramy bought one of the first Canon XL-1 digital video cameras when they came on the market. He was spending his own money, so finding ways to work cheaply and quickly was always a priority. Avid, which sold its low-end machines at $100,000 or more, was out of the question. Having both film and digital video footage to edit, Ramy's challenge was to find a way to get film footage into a cheap desktop digital video system, such as Adobe's Premiere, and then get it out accurately. At the time, this was uncharted territory.

Edvin Mehrabyan, known as "The Finisher" for his top-notch negative cutting.

Ramy was on the verge of buying a Fast-601 edit system that had Avid-like capabilities but cost $13,000 when he heard about Final Cut Pro. The Mac computer and FCP software together cost less than $4,000.

Even though Katrib did telecines at Magic Film & Video on a machine using a sophisticated Silicon Graphics computer and operated a DaVinci color-correction workstation costing six figures, he didn't own a personal computer or even use email at that time—hard to believe, given his desire for taking FCP beyond its domain. But Cullen doesn't know any of that when he reaches out for help with FCP. All he knows is that Ramy and DigitalFilm Tree are at the nexus where film editing meets Final Cut Pro.

Ramy calls Sean back and asks what kind of help he needs.

"Right now, we're trying to stay low profile," Sean replies. "We don't want anyone to say, 'What are you talking about?' and short circuit things. We want to keep it quiet. Is that something you can do?"

"Oh, absolutely," Ramy replies.

Sean continues. "It's *Cold Mountain* with Anthony Minghella. Walter Murch is the editor."

Ramy pauses to catch his breath. "Whoa!"

By early 2002, Ramy had built DigitalFilm Tree into a considerable force with help from two colleagues at his old telecine job, Henry Santos and Edvin Mehrabyan. During long nights on the graveyard shift, the three discovered a shared interest in pushing computer-based, non-linear editing software past its original purposes. Mehrabyan, a Russian-Armenian, was supervising all the negative cutting at Magic. He was nicknamed "The Finisher," says Ramy. "Everyone knew him. People who had botched negative cutting jobs would come to him in a crisis from all around Los Angeles. He could fix negative tears by artificially slicing on the frame line and splicing it himself."

Santos started working at Magic a year or so after Ramy. He was 18 then, a kid out of high school, but he already had excellent skills as a colorist—the person who corrects hues and tones in film and video transfers. "He was a sharp kid," says Ramy, "so I brought him in as an apprentice to work in telecine." Ramy already was demonstrating the kind of entrepreneurial, team-building instincts that would later serve him well in making DigitalFilm Tree a reality.

The next principal to join DFT was Tim Serda, a Macromedia certification engineer who worked on Final Cut Pro, which then had the code name Key Grip. Serda had moved to Apple when it acquired the application from Macromedia.

Once he had his own Final Cut Pro software, Ramy brought his burgeoning brain trust together to see if they could force FCP to accurately cut film. An essential element—the missing link—was FilmLogic, an application for transplanting video's 30 frame-per-second databases and edit lists into the realm of 24 frame film. Ramy located Loran Kary, the father of FilmLogic, and invited him to Los Angeles to join in the experiment. Without telling anyone, they all gathered at Magic Film & Video Works one weekend.

Ramy had finagled Sony into lending him a $15,000 DVCAM DSR 2000 digital video deck for a week. "We did something really simple—we transferred film dailies to a DV format, which was unprecedented," he said. "For us, that was like—whoa! No one was doing this. I took that tape home and put it my Final Cut system. I put it in my little DVCAM deck, lined it up, captured it. And it behaved the same way that video behaved on an Avid. I knew we were onto something. It was too dramatic. And the fact that I was even approaching a place where I'm doing something with film that wasn't on an Avid Film Composer—I was just smart enough to know that this was big."

Loran Kary developed FilmLogic, a database for taking 30 frame-per-second video information and converting it into 24 frame film. Apple later acquired the program and renamed it CinemaTools.

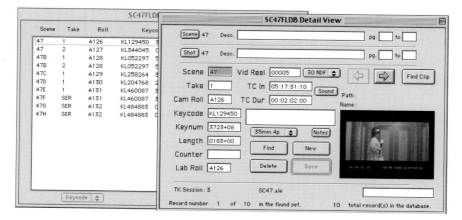

The interface for FilmLogic, the application used in conjunction with Final Cut Pro to convert information for 30 frame-per-second digital video to 24 frame-per-second film.

Katrib, Edvin Mehrabyan, and Loran Kary prepare to begin the test in Katrib's apartment.

Video monitors show a sample scene being cut in Final Cut Pro.

Loran Kary uses a loupe to inspect cut camera negative—the end product of the successful Final Cut Pro test. Mehrabyan is on the left.

The group's accomplishment was considerable for two reasons: first, Final Cut Pro software had been tricked into doing something Apple never had in mind when it designed and released the product solely for video; and second, an affordable, open-format, user-friendly competitor to Avid was being hatched in front of their eyes. Within a year Apple caught on to the implications, bought FilmLogic, renamed it Cinema Tools, and hired its creator, Loran Kary.

"The day we documented that test was when we launched DigitalFilm Tree," says Ramy. "I don't know why I decided to document it, because really, if you go back to that day, no one thought anything about anything; it was just kind of hanging out. I even remember a little grumbling from some of the people because it was a 16-hour day. It was no money, no nothing. But we cut a sequence in my apartment, where my system was. We generated a cut list out of FilmLogic. We went back to Magic, and Edvin cut it. And it lined up. It was just like an Avid cut. It was perfect; and everyone was there to verify it."

"Once we did that test, I became an evangelist, like my dad," says Ramy. "I was preaching it to everybody. And that's when I started talking to Edvin and Henry—telling them this was going to change the whole landscape for film. We went through the process of hiring a lawyer, formed an LLC, and started DigitalFilm Tree."

It's nearly two years later when Sean Cullen drives out onto Santa Monica Boulevard from The Lot. He heads west toward Sunset Boulevard and finds DigitalFilm Tree's home: a two-story English Tudor-style house, cater-corner from Larry Flynt's Hustler Store. From the outside, the place looks like the location for Steve Martin's failing production company in the film *Bowfinger*— a long-neglected, stereotypically noir Hollywood building. But once he goes inside, Sean sees the future of feature film editing.

Sean recalls that first encounter: "I outlined not only what I thought we might be doing, but some of the politics of *Cold Mountain* and a description of Walter's personality. I told them he will say, 'Oh, this is wrong. It's off a few frames.' I said, 'You really want to be careful, because he's always right. And you might say, 'No, that's in sync.' And he'll go, 'No, it's out of sync one frame early. Fix it, and then give me a call.' And sure enough, it's out of sync one frame early. I said, 'Watch out, because Walter has a really sharp eye.'"

"The more we talked," Sean says, "the more we realized we were perfect for each other. They were doing what nobody else was doing. They were ground-breaking because they were doing the first features. It was clear this was where the smart people were." What had begun with DigitalFilm Tree saying, "We can't give out free help," quickly becomes "We'll figure out the money later."

Cullen describes the sort of relationship he and Murch want to have with DFT. Changing editing platforms means they would need all kinds of troubleshooting and problem solving, especially since Final Cut Pro has never been used to edit a major feature film with so much footage. They will need to be in constant communication, night and day; the inevitable fire alarms will demand an instantaneous response. Sean needs to know if Ramy and DFT can provide that kind of backup and go the distance for well over a year. Barely containing his enthusiasm, Ramy says they can and will.

Cullen then talks about possible deal breakers. "There are a number of things that, unless they are provided to Walter, he isn't going to do the film on Final Cut." Sean tells DFT, "If we can't make these things work—either because I don't understand how they work, or they can't work—then the deal is off, and we'll do the show on Avid.'"

One requirement is being able to watch the same material on the computer screen and on the TV screen. By this, Cullen means that in addition to the normal computer monitor, Murch has to be able to use a large-screen TV in his edit room for viewing completed edits. Cullen also insists that both the computer and TV monitors be capable of displaying the same images, simultaneously, cleanly, and crisply by running digitized material at true 30 frames per second. Being a surrogate for the audience, the film editor needs to be immersed in the movie, free from technical distractions, even if he watches a single scene less than a minute long.

"I knew that Final Cut, when you took it out of the box, couldn't support a reverse telecine process," Cullen says later. "You couldn't watch 30 frames per second on the TV. Avid does this, so I knew that we were going to have to do it. Walter needed to be able to have the record monitor and the TV both play back in real time, simultaneously, not switching one from the other."

Ramy takes all these requirements in stride, telling Cullen they can be realized. To prove it, Ramy turns to their Final Cut Pro setup and runs some sample footage. Cullen isn't impressed.

"Guys, the stuff on the right-hand monitor looks like crap," he says.

"What do you mean?"

"Walter won't go for that. That looks bad. It's jumpy and tearing from the interlace." For Cullen, the image is compromised and contains artifacts—lines that are jagged instead of straight—due to the low data rate by which media is being sent to the computer.

But Ramy sees the glass as half full. "Well, it's not that bad," he says.

"Okay, wait, stop," says Sean. "We need to understand each other. If I say Walter isn't going to go for it, he's not going to go for it. And that isn't good enough for us."

"Guys, the stuff on the right-hand monitor looks like crap."

```
The cut list in construction order:

Shot   Time    Duration  Keycode      In Frame  Out Frame  Roll
Scene  Take

     01:00:00:00 to 01:00:00:14 Fade-in of 12 frames (00:15)
     In-coming KI 73 0819 from 6328&11 to 6329&02

001  01:00:00:00  00:16:04  KI 73 0819  6328&11   6347&17   A33
1     4

002  01:00:16:04  00:01:12  KI 73 0819  6569&02   6570&15   A33
1A    2

003  01:00:17:17  00:04:16  KI 73 0819  6429&04   6434&12   A33
1     5

004  01:00:22:03  00:05:02  KI 73 0819  6810&08   6816&09   A34
1A    3

     Note -- 1 frame was added to the end of this cut.
005  01:00:27:05  00:01:19  KI 73 0819  6451&11   6453&09   A33
1     5

006  01:00:28:24  00:04:19  KI 73 0819  6818&09   6823&19   A34
1A    3
```

An edit decision list (EDL), a database listing every cut in a movie that is generated by a digital editing system, such as Avid Film Composer or Final Cut Pro.

"Well, we know we can get it better," says Ramy, "just not on this machine." Like many functions in the Final Cut Pro system, the data rate can be customized—in this case upward.

Sean is still dubious. "Okay, but I guarantee when Walter comes in, he's going to need to see it looking really good on both the computer and the TV."

Ramy later says, "It didn't take very long to realize that Sean was a force of nature, a heavyweight. Sometimes when you talk to people, you can feel that some of it is registering and some of it isn't. With Sean, everything was registering and he was coming back for more."

One hugely threatening issue remains, and Sean, Ramy, and the others at DFT talk it through: the fact that Final Cut can create an Edit Decision List (EDL) for conforming the film workprint but cannot track subsequent changes to that list—an essential procedure in any big-budget feature.

A cut list, or EDL, is the blueprint for how scenes of a film finally get put together. It lists the shots to be used, in order, with each beginning and end point, measured in feet and frames. All effects such as dissolves or fades are also noted. At the end of the editing, when the picture is "locked," or declared finished, this cut list goes to the negative cutter. Up to that point the film that was originally exposed on the set has remained untouched, except to make the workprint. It's been sealed in cans, safely locked away in the film lab vault. There is only one original camera negative, and it can never be replaced. Only when all the decision making on the picture editing is done, does the final negative cutting process begin.

Negative cutting is done in a dust-free environment. The cutter wears white cotton gloves and makes splices using cement. There can be no mistakes. Each cement splice destroys one frame of negative, since the adjacent frame must be scraped to make a "hot splice." Negative cutters work alone, for the most part. In the film business, they are the only crew members for whom a compulsive, sometimes neurotic personality is considered a job requirement, if not an asset. They work much like gem cutters, where a mistaken move can ruin the goods—except that a feature film negative is worth far more than most diamonds.

During post-production, the film editor is essentially creating the "pattern," or template, that the negative cutter will later use to cut the whole cloth into a finished garment. That cut list must be exactly correct in referring to the original film negative. The basis for indexing all that film footage (114 miles of it in the case of *Cold Mountain*) is the *key codes*. Each frame of film has a unique address or marker. These alphanumeric inscriptions reside on the edge of the film negative, in the area outside the viewable frame. They occur once every foot (16 frames), pre-burned into the film stock when it is manufactured. A second set of tracking information is applied to the film workprint, or dailies.

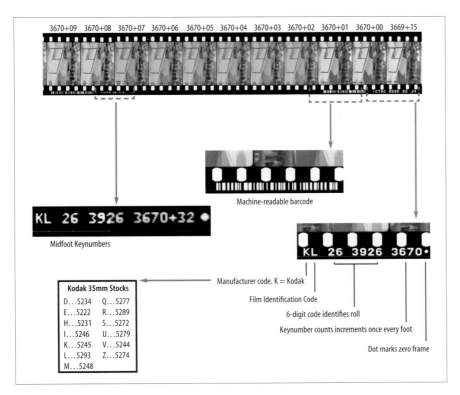

3670+09 3670+08 3670+07 3670+06 3670+05 3670+04 3670+03 3670+02 3670+01 3670+00 3669+15

Machine-readable barcode

KL 26 3926 3670+32 ●

Midfoot Keynumbers

KL 26 3926 3670•

Manufacturer code. K = Kodak

Film Identification Code

6-digit code identifies roll

Keynumber counts increments once every foot

Dot marks zero frame

Kodak 35mm Stocks	
D...5234	Q...5277
E...5222	R...5289
H...5231	S...5272
I...5246	U...5279
K...5245	V...5244
L...5293	Z...5274
M...5248	

A sample of 35mm film showing negative key codes imprinted by Kodak at the time of manufacture. This system gives every frame of film its own unique address so editors can keep track of their whereabouts throughout the long process of film editing.

These are called *edge numbers* or *print codes*. They are stamped onto the edge of the film by an assistant using an Acmade numbering machine. The format is usually a seven-digit code, like a telephone number. The first three digits refer to the camera roll number, the last four to the footage. Different inking colors can be used to create sub-levels and categories. For example, you might code all footage using visual effects in red.

Keeping track of all the footage in a feature film is a major systems challenge. Typically, a two-hour feature film might have a shooting ratio of 20:1. That is, for every minute of film in the final release print, 20 minutes were shot. Even that shooting ratio is misleading, because a fair amount of film stock is wasted in normal operations: starts and stops, film run through the camera to thread it up, and hunks of leftovers that are not long enough to record a complete take ("short ends"). However, in some films, such as Coppola's *Apocalypse Now*, the shooting ratio is much higher—100:1 or more.

The accounting method in day-to-day assembling of a film relies on the edge codes printed onto the workprint. These are what the editing team will use to conform the 35mm workprint to the arrangement of shots edited in the computer. Key codes on the negative don't come into use until the end of the process, when the negative must be cut. However, both sets of numbers are encoded from the beginning, before editing irretrievably mixes up all the footage. With non-linear digital editing like Final Cut Pro or Avid, a lot of data—starting and ending key codes and print codes for each take—must be added manually by an assistant when the footage is digitized or brought into the computer.

Whether a film is edited on an upright Moviola, on a flatbed, or in a digital system such as Final Cut Pro, the same thing will eventually be delivered to the negative cutter: an EDL listing all the correct edit points. When a film is cut only using workprint, the edit list is manually written. The negative cutter also has the edited film workprint and its printed-through key codes as a guide for double-checking, but the list is paramount. When digitally editing, the alphanumeric key codes entered at the beginning remain embedded in the media files, hidden but available. They emerge in the cut list when it is generated on the computer.

Creating an EDL automatically is one of the most valuable timesaving benefits of non-linear editing. With a couple of keystrokes, you can produce a complex database that, in the analog world might take an assistant a week to make—with inadvertent errors a likelihood. EDLs from a non-linear system also have a built-in feature to check for any duplicate frames. Since every cut to the negative eliminates one neighboring frame (remember, it's called "destructive editing"), the negative cutter needs to know ahead of time if any of those abutting film frames must be used somewhere else in the film. If so, an assistant will ask the lab to make a duplicate copy of the take in question, a *dupe negative*. Cut lists must be absolutely frame-accurate. Should a decision list go to the negative cutter with inaccuracies, disaster results. Needed frames may be mangled or—even worse—an incorrect version of the film may get printed at the lab.

Long before an EDL is required for the negative cutting, film assistants need a similar cut-by-cut database called a *change list* to do their work. The change list catalogs all the variations between two different edited versions of a film. The assistants use this to re-cut the workprint on their editing benches, conforming the projectable film to its digital counterpart. Sound editors also use the change lists to conform their soundtracks to match new versions; otherwise their audio work will be out of date or out of sync. Another beauty of digital editing is the ease with which this information can be communicated from the picture department to the sound editors.

Getting a reliable edit decision list out of Final Cut Pro was not a problem. But Cullen had to know if and when FCP would be able to generate dependable change lists. Did Apple at least have it in the works? Ramy replied that it was being developed, but he wasn't sure it would be ready in time. Troubling news, but for an assistant film editor, there is no such thing as a perfect world. It helps, however, when variables such as this are known ahead of time.

All digital editing systems crash, lose media, or otherwise throw uncertainties into the path of a feature film barreling down the road to completion on a tight schedule. As Sean says, "I noticed working with the Avid on *English Patient,* things like media crashes and corruption all had the same amount of difficulty to solve. But when Avid told us, 'That's not a problem, just get over it,' those were the things that really stuck in our minds. When they were open and up front about it, even though we were putting in the same amount of work, we thought, 'Oh, that's just part of the cost of using Avid.'"

"I didn't want to get into a situation where I had suggested that we go the Final Cut route, knowing there were things that were going to be a problem," Sean says. "Either not telling Walter, or minimizing problems, then having them come up. That's always a pain." Cullen wants to go through all the things with DigitalFilm Tree—both good and bad—that might materialize, to get a sense of how much of a problem they are going to be and how much energy it will take to do workarounds. Says Sean: "If it was something that wasn't going to be fixed but I could solve, I could say to Walter, 'It's a problem, but I'll take care of it.' On an Avid, you're taking care of things all the time. I knew there was going to be a certain amount of that going on."

One of Final Cut Pro's big advantages is price. Murch can have four fully loaded Final Cut Pro editing systems for less than the cost of one Avid system. Having four machines means backup and redundancy, thus avoiding project-wide crashes or breakdowns and making serious downtime much less likely. Apple's Final Cut Pro system is relatively immune to serious crashes because it is a software-only system (except for a third-party card for digitizing) that is designed to run on Apple hardware. And because it can also run on a laptop, FCP gives an editing team great flexibility and mobility.

"I was immediately reminded of the fact that most kitchen stoves have four burners," Walter says later. "When you're cooking a big meal for the family you use all those burners. And in retrospect, looking back at all those shows I've done with two stations, it was very similar to trying to cook a banquet on two burners. There's a lot of, 'Well, I'll take off the cauliflower and put that to one side. Meanwhile cook up the onions... Oops, the cauliflower has to go back on again!' There's just so much juggling because of all the different tasks you have to do at the same time."

Shawn Paper, film editor on *Month of August* (released in 2002), the first feature film to use Final Cut Pro.

A "four-burner" configuration for *Cold Mountain* will provide one station for Walter to work on and a second for Sean to do syncing up of dailies, file management, and some editing. Of the two other stations, one will digitize "in" and the other will digitize "out." That is, station three will be connected to a Beta SP videotape deck for the purpose of transposing videotapes of film dailies into the QuickTime digital files that FCP uses. Station four will take dailies, scenes, and assemblies from FCP and put them onto other media—sometimes VHS tapes but most often DVD—so that producers, the studio, and other post-production crew can view versions of the film as a work-in-progress.

"I enjoy collaborative work," says Murch. "One of the profound implications of FCP is that it is so inexpensive that anyone with a PowerBook—and one of the machines we had was an old clamshell iBook—can download media and edit with it. So I was giving scenes to the assistants and apprentices for them to cut their teeth on. It's a great teaching tool. Plus, it gave us a great deal of reliability and flexibility, in addition to being a system that I found completely transparent and enjoyable in the day-to-day cutting of the film."

When Final Cut Pro first surfaced, the post-production community in Los Angeles didn't take it seriously. It was not ready for an alternative to Avid. "People ridiculed it," says Ramy. One day a film editor, Shawn Paper, who had always used the Avid system, came to Ramy and said, "I've got Final Cut Pro at home. Can I do this?" And Ramy said yes. And with help from DigitalFilm Tree, Paper cut the first feature film, *Month of August*, on Final Cut Pro.

That led to DFT working on several other motion pictures using FCP, such as *Full Frontal* in 2001, which was directed by Steven Soderbergh and edited by Sarah Flack, and featured David Duchovny, Catherine Keener, and Julia Roberts. DFT also supplied Final Cut Pro systems for *The Rules of Attraction* (2002), directed by Roger Avary and edited by Sharon Rutter, starring James Van Der Beek and Shannyn Sossamon. Then, in the spring of 2002, Sean Cullen and *Cold Mountain* walked in the door.

What Do You Drive?

"Some [editors] were concerned that working with cheaper equipment might mean that editors would command less respect."—from a May/June 2001 *Motion Picture Editors Guild Magazine* article reporting on a Final Cut Pro/FilmLogic seminar presented in part by DigitalFilm Tree.

Since the first meeting went well, Sean wants to bring Walter to DigitalFilm Tree to "kick the tires," as he put it. He requests a system that looks good on both monitors—record and playback—and he wants some footage available that Walter can cut. He reminds DFT that they still have made no financial arrangement. They tell Sean not to worry.

In the meantime, Ramy runs out to buy the second edition of Murch's 1995 classic book on film editing, *In the Blink of an Eye*. He is shocked to find a long passage about Final Cut Pro and FilmLogic in the afterword. (That section, new to the 2001 edition, is called "Digital Film Editing: Past, Present and Imagined Future," and fills fully half of the book's 146 pages.) "How does Walter know about this stuff?" Ramy remembers thinking. "It was so new. When I told some of the people we work with that the next Final Cut Pro project could be for Walter Murch, they freaked out. People who come from the editing community were stunned. I wondered, 'Why is Walter Murch even talking to us? We're nobody.'"

Sean phones DFT a few days before he brings Walter to the company. "How's it going? Are you guys ready?"

"Yeah, we're all ready."

"How good does the video look?"

"It looks great."

"I need to know: does it look great, or does it look so-so? Because if it looks so-so, I'll get Walter ready now."

"No, it looks great."

Sean doesn't prompt Walter before they go together to see DigitalFilm Tree. Nevertheless, on the way over, he zeroes in on the potential problem.

"How's the video?" Walter wants to know.

"It should be good," Sean tells him.

Walter and Sean arrive at DFT and are introduced to Edvin Mehrabyan, Tim Serda, Walter Shires, John Taylor, and Dan Fort. The group then goes into the edit suite, which doubles as a training room for Final Cut Pro users and students. Ramy and his team are smiling, feeling both sanguine and nervous. They have a brief discussion about what Murch and Cullen want to accomplish while they are there, and then… it's showtime!

As Sean later remembers it, "The video image was good. Walter said it could get better, but it was definitely passable, that he could do a show on it." Though he tries not to show it, Ramy is ecstatic.

Later, Ramy recalls the impact of having Walter Murch come to DigitalFilm Tree: "It wasn't simply his award-winning credits. It wasn't that he was the first Academy Award-winning editor we worked with. He was the third or fourth. It was the fact that he was wearing tennis shoes when he came here. The fact that he was down to earth, that he later sat right down to check his email. That's when we started to appreciate that he was different. He would ask things and we would just look at each other. He wasn't a pushover; his questions were brutal." A silent stare from Murch can be intimidating, even for someone who is technically savvy. Ramy, freely admitting he was the least knowledgeable about technical things and editing, describes how during that first session with Murch at DFT, he intentionally put himself out there with incomplete information to force the other DFT people to chime in with more complete answers to Murch's questions.

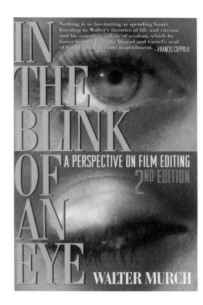

Walter Murch's book on film editing theory and practice, *In the Blink of an Eye.*

"We mostly told him what was bad about Final Cut," Ramy says. "It will do things that are heart-stopping, and we knew this going in. We never sat down and tried to sell him. After you have spent months cutting a show, FCP can dish up an error message saying, 'Sequence won't open,' or 'File not found,'" Ramy says. One editor describes FCP as "jackass-put-together, dumb-shit code, a bullshit program." Even Ramy, who is an evangelist, admits FCP is an application often constructed out of "sheer voodoo." He says: "Things happen that make no logical sense. You can lose your project, or you're doing a color-correction job, and all of a sudden it's gone, like vapor, and you can't find it." Given that FCP is an application first developed by Macromedia, then rushed into its first release version by Apple, Ramy calls it "a hack on top of a hack."

Still at DFT, Walter goes through what Sean calls "the artistic stuff": how the interface feels, what other editors had problems with, how fast it is and how quickly sequences load—things that he knew he would be doing day in and day out. In his mind, he was weighing FCP against the Avid. "A lot of his questions, as mine had been, were referenced off the Avid," Sean said. "We were on an Avid, we had used Avid. We knew the Avid problems, knew the Avid strengths. So a lot of it was comparing. Very much to DigitalFilm Tree's credit, they never said, 'Final Cut's better.' They were very honest: 'Well, Avid is better at that, but Final Cut is still passable.' Or, 'Final Cut really doesn't have that,' or 'Final Cut is much better at that than the Avid.'"

Three major concerns emerge by the end of the meeting at DFT: 1) how to generate accurate change lists to keep a 35mm film workprint version conformed to match the Final Cut Pro version; 2) how to transfer soundtracks on Walter's machine—"sequence information"— to the sound editors' ProTools workstations; and 3) whether FCP could swallow, digest, and play back so much media—a first assembly that might exceed five hours of running time. Sean admits he is less concerned about list-making functions because he won't need them for nearly a year. DFT isn't too worried about transferability of sequence information since they had access to programmers and engineers who are experienced with OMF (Open Media Format, the file format for transferring audio material between applications). DFT also knows that Apple is working on developments that might give Final Cut Pro a mechanism for exporting edited audio tracks to digital audio workstations (DAW).

Walter isn't so easily satisfied, however. "He really wanted to know about the sequence transfer to the sound department," Sean recalls, "because he's very much a sound person, and he has a lot of experience working with sound departments. Walter knows that the more friction you have [between picture and sound departments], the harder the whole process is."

"What if Apple doesn't do it?" Walter asks. "What are we going to do?" The question hangs in the air.

In a way, the money discussion is easier. It comes down to Ramy saying: "Just as long as you take us on board when you do the film, this will all be pro bono work. And if you don't take us, we'll get a lot of good experience researching this."

Sean and Walter come away from their meeting feeling that DigitalFilm Tree will be their "men in Havana," but they haven't quite decided to adopt FCP. They need to know more. Sean, Walter, and DFT agree to divide the next round of research. Walter will talk to editors who have done work on Final Cut Pro. Sean will investigate whether FileMaker, the program they use for organizing their code books, logs, and databases, will work well with Final Cut. DFT will look into the remaining technical hurdles and design issues.

After the meeting, Ramy calls his contacts at Apple to give them the head-line: Walter Murch is interested in using Final Cut Pro on his next feature film. "I'm chatting with Apple people who are enthusiastic—I'm talking to higher tier managers, foot soldiers, not with the people who run the company. And I'm telling them that Walter's here, and they're downright giddy." Ramy informs Walter and Sean that Apple is excited, that the company loves the idea of him using FCP.

At this point, Ramy reaches across the country for more help, getting in contact with Zed Saeed, a FCP fellow traveler on the East Coast. Saeed had put Oxygen Media on Final Cut Pro, the first television network of any substance to use the application. When he began working at Oxygen they had two Final Cut Pro systems; when he finished they had 200. Zed in New York, much like Ramy in Los Angeles, saw the future possibilities of Final Cut Pro in film editing. And since he was one of the few people on the East Coast to understand both technical and user needs, Zed had most of the new opportunities to himself. He also became a post-production consultant to Showtime Networks, designing and managing their film-based editing systems using Final Cut Pro.

Zed Zaeed, senior post production coordinator at DigitalFilm Tree.

Born and raised in Pakistan, Zed Saeed came to the U.S. in 1983 to attend Hampshire College in western Massachusetts. By 1984, he had won his first Student Emmy Award for his short film *Back to School*. Of all the Final Cut Pro specialists none might be more excited about Murch using the system than Saeed. "There was nothing I ever wanted to do more than just make films," he says. "My friends and I, we lived films: we ate film, we made films, we slept films. When I was in college we were obsessed with *The Conversation*, because as film students we were taught it was the height of sound design. We actually recorded the soundtrack of *The Conversation* from the videotape to ¼-inch audiotape—just like Harry Caul! We would be in our dorm rooms playing the reel-to-reel, listening to the soundtrack of *The Conversation* over and over and over again. I mean, that's how obsessed we were with Walter Murch's work. And it wasn't like we thought it was a Coppola thing; we knew

Harry Caul's reel-to-reel tape recorder from the film, *The Conversation.* Zed Saeed: "We would be in our dorm rooms playing the reel-to-reel, listening to the soundtrack of *The Conversation.*"

it was a Murch thing. We had researched it and found out he had put it together and it was his ideas. I'm not making this up after the fact. You can call my friends up and they'll tell you, 'Yeah, yeah, we used to do the reel-to-reel thing all the time.'"

Ramy Katrib and Zed Saeed first met in Las Vegas at NAB, the National Association of Broadcasters annual electronic media trade show. "We had a hysterical time in the hotel room where the DFT guys were all staying," says Saeed. "Right then and there we both agreed that somehow, some day, I'd have to come out to L.A."

After Murch and Cullen return to The Lot to complete *K-19*, Ramy continues talking to Apple about *Cold Mountain* and the kind of assistance DFT needs so that it can help Murch and Cullen. "The response was fabulous, giddy, salivating," says Ramy. "I can point to like four or five different individuals who were giving very positive feedback. It was all positive."

Murch informs director Anthony Minghella about the possibility of using Final Cut Pro on *Cold Mountain*. Minghella, who is an Apple user and also savvy about digital editing, begins his own research into Final Cut Pro. In an April 28 email to Murch, he reports on his findings. "I see Soderbergh just made *Full Frontal* using Final Cut and may do the same for *Solaris*... there was mention that the system can now make change lists. True?" Minghella is open to Murch using Final Cut Pro, but he also knows enough about editing and digital technology to maintain a healthy skepticism.

MAY 7, 2002—BERKELEY, CALIFORNIA

While Walter completes the sound mix on *K-19* at the Saul Zaentz Film Center, Sean wraps up his work in Los Angeles and sees to it that the film negative cutting is underway and going smoothly. In the months since *K-19* entered its final finishing stages, vast changes have taken place in the *Cold Mountain* universe: Tom Cruise, originally cast as Inman, has been replaced by Jude Law, and Nicole Kidman, Cruise's ex-wife, has been signed to play Inman's lover, Ada Monroe. Equally far-reaching, the production has shifted from the United States to Romania, where more than 70 percent of the film will be shot. The plan is for Murch to leave for the United Kingdom after a few weeks' break, then set up the *Cold Mountain* edit in London while film production gets underway in Bucharest. Then, on May 11, Walter receives word from Anthony Minghella that editing for *Cold Mountain* will not begin in London as originally planned. Instead, Anthony wants Walter to set up shop closer to the set, in Bucharest.

To:	Walter Murch
From:	Anthony Minghella
Date:	May 11, 2002

Dear friend, a wave to you. I am pretending to examine the script but am, in fact, hostage to issues of schedule, budget, score, etc. The more I learn about Romania, the more I feel that there would be some real wisdom in your being based in Bucharest rather than London. I can't imagine how I could profit from your work during shooting otherwise, and it looks like John [Seale, director of photography] will be using the lab there. I'm particularly thinking about the Crater sequence at the beginning of the movie and how it will need your help in ensuring we've collected the material we'll need in the cutting room. Where are you? How is your inner being? Your outer one? Love and blessings. Ant.

Walter responds to Anthony with a series of questions: What's the support system like there? The lab? The telecine? Anthony does not immediately know the answers. "We were already stretching the envelope, but if we were doing the stretching in London, at least we'd be in the orbit of people who knew about these things. But Romania?" asks Walter.

A few weeks later, on May 30, out of the blue, Ramy is asked to join a conference call with some Apple executives. "They said they had weighed the pros and the cons, and they would not engage *Cold Mountain*, Walter, or any part of our effort," Ramy says later.

Now Ramy has to call Murch with the bad news: "Walter, I don't know how to say this, but Apple said we shouldn't do this, and that they will not be involved at all."

"Why? Why are they doing this?" Walter wants to know.

"My best explanation is I think the liability is too high for them," Ramy says. "They think that this project is too big for Final Cut Pro, that Final Cut Pro isn't ready for something like this. I think some of the people I was talking to don't appreciate who you are and what you represent to the community. Some of them weren't the same people who had been enthusiastic, who did appreciate it."

"Well, what if I still want to do it," Walter asks firmly, "in spite of Apple? What if I still want to do this?"

There was such forcefulness in his voice that Ramy responds without hesitation. "We're there! We'll go with or without Apple."

"There was no fear in the fact that Apple wasn't going to go," Ramy says late one night two years later, sitting at his desk across from Zed Saeed. "It was the strength of his voice, the way he said it. To me, it was just certain. There was nothing that I had to talk about to my partners. We were going to go. That's when it started to settle in that we were going to be on a long ride—that this was going to change our lives."

Zed jumps in, as is his wont, finishing Ramy's thought with exuberance and passion. "This is Walter Murch, man, who's seen action on *Apocalypse Now!* He's asking us to jump into the fire with him. Hell, yes! What are we going to say, 'Sorry, Walter...'?"

Adds Ramy, "We couldn't say, 'Well, if Apple's not going, I think we'll pass.'"

"We're there," he says softly, reliving the moment.

The day after the conversation in which Ramy and Walter tentatively decide to proceed with plans to edit *Cold Mountain* on Final Cut Pro, Walter sends him this email: "Dear Ramy: Good talking to you yesterday, and I am hopeful it will all work out. Any chance of getting a phone number for Steve Jobs? Thanks, Walter M."

Walter Murch's office, upstairs in a converted barn.

CHAPTER 4

Give me a Reason
Not To

From: Walter Murch
Subject: Final Cut Pro
Date: 6/2/02 10:44 PM
To: Steve Jobs

Dear Steve Jobs:

Greetings, and thanks for all you have done for the world through Apple and Pixar, and most likely many other things I don't know about, but from which we all have reaped an indirect benefit.

My name is Walter Murch, and I am a film editor and sound mixer, working mostly in the Bay Area for the last thirty-three years. I started out with Francis Coppola and George Lucas in the early days of American Zoetrope, back in 1969 when we all moved up to SF from LA.

I am going to be editing "Cold Mountain" for Anthony Minghella, for whom I edited "The English Patient" and "The Talented Mr. Ripley." The studio is Miramax. The film is based on the best-selling book by Charles Frazier about the closing days of the American Civil War. We start shooting in the middle of July. The film stars Jude Law, Nicole Kidman, Renée Zelwegger, Philip Seymour Hoffman, Donald Sutherland, and will be an expensive, high profile project.

We intend to use Final Cut as our editing program, and we have had conversations with a company in LA, DigitalFilm Tree, about advising us. They have personal links to people at Apple who were instrumental in the development and promotion of Final Cut, and when initial approaches were made in March of this year, the attitude at Apple was very receptive to the idea of our collaboration, to say the least.

But last week there was a follow-up phone conference between Ramy Katrib at DFT and Apple. This time around, Apple declined to give us the logistical support that they were enthusiastic about offering a couple of months ago.

I am still optimistic that this will work out. I have been using Macintoshes in the cutting room since 1986, and "English Patient" was the first digitally-edited film to win an Oscar for editing. My assistant Sean Cullen is very much for it, and extremely knowledgeable about how to make sometimes difficult situations flow easily. Ramy Katrib at DFT is also still enthusiastic. Is there anything that you can do to help us?

Anthony Minghella is a good friend of Steve Soderbergh's, and in private conversations (notwithstanding the Soderbergh/Final Cut ads that Apple is currently running) not only was Soderbergh's advice to Anthony not encouraging, it turns out that he (Soderbergh) will not be using Final Cut on his next film. If we now find that Apple itself won't offer us support, even in token, it makes it more difficult for me, politically and technically, to move forward with Final Cut Pro on "Cold Mountain."

I hope that you will see the advantage to everyone in somehow making this work.

My sincere good wishes, and thanks for taking the time to read this email,
Walter Murch

The following morning, less than eight hours later, Steve Jobs sends a brief email reply to Murch. He writes that someone from the Final Cut Pro team will contact Murch. Jobs then asks Murch why director Steven Soderbergh no longer feels favorable to Final Cut Pro.

Murch tries to find his own answer to that question. He contacts Sarah Flack and Susan Littenberg, editor and assistant editor, respectively, of Soderbergh's *Full Frontal*.

June 3, 2002, Murch's Journal

Talked to Susan Littenberg who assisted Sarah, even though she is an editor herself, and is working on Solaris. *They have reservations about FCP, don't think it is ready for working on features.*

Later that same day, as Steve Jobs promised, an email exchange ensues between Murch and Apple's top Final Cut Pro product managers, Bill Hudson and Brian Meaney.

Date: Mon, 03 Jun 2002 17:12
Subject: Final Cut Pro
From: Bill Hudson
To: Walter Murch
CC: Brian Meaney

Dear Mr. Murch,

Our friends at Digital Film Tree tell us you are exploring the use of Final Cut Pro for your next movie, "Cold Mountain." We are flattered that you would consider using our product for this important film and we'd like the opportunity to speak with you so we can fully discuss Final Cut Pro's capabilities and limitations.

Let us know how best to reach you.

Regards,
Bill

Bill Hudson
Strategic Accounts Manager
Professional Applications
Apple

From: Walter Murch
Subject: FCPro
Date: 6/4/02 3:40 PM
To: Bill Hudson

Dear Bill:

Good talking to you today. I have passed your email and phone number on to my assistant, Sean Cullen, and he will be contacting you in the next day or so to discuss in more depth the issues that you raised.

I am excited about the prospect of using Final Cut Pro on Cold Mountain, and particularly excited by the prospect of helping the program evolve to a point where it becomes the standard in the film industry.

All best wishes,
Walter Murch

A meeting is set up for June 18 in Berkeley among Murch, Cullen, Hudson, and Meaney to discuss Final Cut Pro and how a working relationship between *Cold Mountain* and Apple might be structured. A few hours later Murch gets a discouraging follow-up email from *Full Frontal* assistant editor, Susan Littenberg:

Date:	Tue, 04 Jun 2002 18:33
Subject:	Re: Thanks
From:	Susan Littenberg
To:	Walter Murch

Walter,

It was an honor to converse with you. A few more points have come to mind that I'd like to share, and possibly coerce you to seriously consider trying FCP on a small project before putting it to the test on a big feature...

Littenberg warns Murch about "real time" rendering of effects in Final Cut Pro, such as dissolves between shots. FCP can easily preview such an effect on a computer screen, but to see it on a TV monitor, or on tape, requires "rendering," or being saved permanently, which is time-consuming. Since *Full Frontal* originated on digital video, not film, Littenberg expresses doubt whether FCP can even work in 24 frame-per-second film mode.

The following day Murch makes a foray to the shop Steve Jobs built. No, not Apple, but his other company—Pixar Animation Studios in Emeryville, California. Jobs bought Pixar from George Lucas in 1986 when it was the computer graphics division of Lucasfilm, Ltd. The success of *Toy Story* in 1995 put Pixar on the map. Over the following eight years Pixar released *A Bug's Life*, *Toy Story 2*, *Monsters, Inc.* and *Finding Nemo*—five blockbusters with an accumulated worldwide box office gross of more than $2.5 billion. And that figure doesn't include revenue from home video, DVD, or merchandise sales. Pixar combines original storytelling, its highly advanced RenderMan software, smart filmmaking, and voices of the stars to mine an ever-deepening, gold-

The entrance to Pixar Animation Studios, where Murch went to learn more about Final Cut Pro.

veined niche in animation. The company is a child of two first cousins: the adventurous, tradition-breaking Bay Area spirit that brought Lucas, Coppola, Murch, and others from Los Angeles to San Francisco in the 1960s, and the entrepreneurial high-tech inventiveness of Silicon Valley, only an hour or so to the south, personified by Apple CEO Steve Jobs.

Like a perfectly constructed haiku, it's as inevitable as the seasons that Murch should go to Emeryville so he can run his idea of using Final Cut Pro past two Pixar editors he has known for many years: Torbin Bullock and Robert Grahamjones. After a few email exchanges they invite Murch for lunch and show-and-tell.

Emeryville had always been a small but puissant blip on the Bay Area map. Even before Pixar arrived, Emeryville was a host for entertainment services, just of a different sort: gambling, card clubs, the Chinese lottery, and the first dog races in the U.S. Its mayors and district attorneys traded places with each other, often with a jail stint in between for extortion, rackets, and other underworld activities.

Emeryville cleaned up in the 1970s and went straight, using its well-developed political muscle for broader economic benefits. First it courted high-tech companies needing to stretch out beyond the Santa Clara/San Jose area. Then the town sought out biotechnology and software companies such as Chiron and Sybase to locate here. When Pixar outgrew its home in nearby Point Richmond, a similar post-industrial bayside town, Emeryville made Jobs a tax-incentive, development offer he couldn't refuse. In 1998 Pixar broke ground on a 225,000-square-foot facility, built from scratch on the site of an old Del Monte cannery right across the street from Emeryville's 1903 Deco-style, copper-domed City Hall.

Pixar's two-story building is surrounded by well-kept lawns, and its masonry commingles 515,000 specially made ruby, mojave, coral, brown, and black bricks. The pattern of shapes and colors seems to be random, selected by some imaginative, free-associating bricklayer. One row is set ends out; the next five rows are placed the long-way. But there is a visual code embedded in those walls. Horizontally set bricks are the rectangular shape of digital video pixels, the ones laid square the shape of computer graphics pixels. Squint and you can discern Pixar's story—computer-generated imagery trans-figured into video for all the world to behold.

The patterns of the exterior walls at Pixar represent pixel shapes.

Pixar's lobby rivals the atrium of any Hyatt Hotel. It's a vast open area, its south wall made almost entirely of glass. A commissary, the Luxo Café, is tucked into one side and the tables spill out onto the main floor. The Pixar receptionist calls Torbin Bullock. "He'll be right out," she tells Murch.

Torbin Bullock, an editor at Pixar.

Murch and his wife, Aggie, first met Bullock as an embryo. While they were living on their houseboat in Sausalito, Aggie was one of the first Lamaze natural birth teachers in the area. Torbin's mother was in her class. Coincidentally, Torbin's father, Tom Bullock, was a film editor. Over the years the Bullocks and the Murches, along with their kids, crossed paths at social functions and film events. Torbin and Walter's daughter, Beatrice, are good friends.

Murch and Bullock collect their pasta from the Luxo Café and go sit at an outside table. Torbin, in his early 30s, is husky and Nordic-looking, with short, cropped blond hair.

"You want to cut *Cold Mountain* in Final Cut Pro?" asks Torbin, incredulously. "In Romania?" He pauses, dramatically. "Are you out of your mind?"

Before this get-together Murch reached out to Bullock by phone. "Walter told me, 'We're thinking about using Final Cut Pro on Anthony's next picture. What can you tell me about it—good things, bad things.' I thought he was crazy—or should I say, a braver man than I am. Especially since Final Cut Pro 3 had only just come out and hadn't really been put through the wringer."

After having worked on a number of studio and independent films in the Bay Area, Bullock started working at Pixar in 1995 as second assistant editor on *Toy Story*. By 2003 he was promoted to associate editor on *Cars*. In high school Torbin worked in his father's studio, synching up dailies and conforming sound tracks. He tried to imagine another path, spent a few years in college at San Francisco City College and at SUNY Purchase, but just couldn't shake his genealogically stamped future. He was a "film kid," as he puts it, like an Army offspring who refers to himself as an Army brat. And like other Bay Area film kids, Torbin attended "the Droid Olympics," annual film parties at Murch's Blackberry Farm. There Murch, Lucas, Tom Bullock, and dozens of other editors, directors, and film crew got together for a day of fun, frolic, and competitive post-production contests, such as the 1,000 foot picture and sound rewind event.

Over lunch, Torbin tells Walter what he'd be concerned about if he, Torbin, were Murch's assistant. "Make sure you buy the most hot-shit computer you can, make sure you have two of them, load them up with as much RAM as you can, and bring backups of your secondary monitor boards and stuff like that." He speaks to the issue of networking the computers so they can share media files: "Put together a RAID (redundant array of independent disks) system so if you lose any of your data, or if one of your drives goes bad, and you're in the middle of fucking nowhere, at least you can yank that drive out, hot-swap it, and shove in a new one that rebuilds the system on the fly. That's the way you want to be in feature-land." A feature film in post production should never grind to a halt because the equipment goes down.

The Droid Olympics were held for many years at Murch's house.

The "Stacking Film Boxes In Order" event.

Murch celebrates on winning film box stacking.

Art Repola competes in the "1000 Foot Rewind Race."

Bullock has never actually
worked for Murch, though he
came close on *The Talented
Mister Ripley,* the previous
Murch-Minghella collaboration.
"Walter called and asked me to
run the film conforming. I was
very tempted—any assistant
would be—but I'd been asked
to be first assistant on *Monsters,
Inc.* The choice between doing
conforming and running my
own ship as a first assistant, well,
it was more challenging to stay
at Pixar. If Murch had asked me
to be a first assistant on *Cold
Mountain,* to go to Romania and
London, I'd have said, 'Sorry, got
to go!' That would have been the
opportunity of a lifetime. To be
honest, I'm still a little envious.

"I not only envy them their
physical adventure, going off to
another country. But I envy their
adventure in doing this in FCP. I
had been an assistant editor for
12 years, so it makes you a glut-
ton for punishment. I couldn't
tell him not to use it—only the
things to look out for."

Not having actually worked for Murch but knowing him outside the film
world his whole life, Bullock is in a good position to make observations.
"Walter does his research, but once he makes up his mind, he goes for it. I
think he made up his mind when he first spoke to me. He just wanted to see
if I could talk him out of it. Walter wanted someone to come up with a reason
not to use Final Cut Pro. And really the only reason not to was a question of
courage and a question of making sure everyone knew it was going to be a
work-in-progress."

Murch and Bullock talk mostly about Final Cut's problems from an assistant's
point of view. There are four big concerns, as Torbin describes them to
Murch:

1. Rendering time for effects—the length of time it will take the machine to
   permanently digest an effect, like a dissolve or fade, and save it into a cut.

2. Media management for large amounts of digitized material: how to organize it and have it be easily and quickly accessible. His understated, pre-
   scient observation: "To get into these issues with third-party cards can be
   messy."

3. Having multiple users on multiple computers. Bullock says that up to now
   "sneaker net" has been the only reliable networking solution for FCP—that
   is, walking external hard drives around from one station to another.

4. In general things are "a little flaky in Final Cut Pro 3," as Torbin puts it.
   "Sometimes footage just disappears"—which Ramy Katrib had also told
   Murch.

But the biggest concern for Torbin is Final Cut Pro's change list functions.
"The rest of it," he says, "like the hardware issues, we can get around. Give it
enough money and you can set up your infrastructure so risk is at a manage-
able level—down to 10 percent, which is just as good as anything else, including Avid. But the change list is a serious issue."

Murch is fully aware from his discussions with DigitalFilm Tree that the edit
decision list (or "cut list") function in Final Cut Pro 3 is untested for a film
with the volume of footage he expects in *Cold Mountain*. And there is no
change list function at all. "I warned him about the cut list factor," Bullock
says later. "No one had really run that much footage through. There was no
way to know when it would fall apart. In theory it could handle any number of
files, but even Avid has its upper limit. But Walter continually invites trouble.
It isn't that after 20 years he'll just decide to try something different. It's like
his move to use flatbed editing tables from the old upright Moviola. He's
tried all the new editing systems that came along, because they were better or
worse, not because they were simply different. He's interested in new ways of

technology. He gets bored. I'm convinced he gets bored. That's why he willingly puts himself into positions of challenge."

As their lunch at Pixar wound down, Robert Grahamjones comes outside to join Murch and Bullock. Murch warmly greets his former assistant on *The English Patient* and *The Unbearable Lightness of Being.* Like many others in this field, Robert, a sturdy, bantam-sized man with a ready laugh, gravitated to film from photography. One of his first film jobs was working as a driver on the locally produced animated feature, *The Plague Dogs.* In addition to shuttling animation cells from studio to lab and back, Robert took director Martin Rosen to and from the sound mix at the Zaentz Film Center in Berkeley.

It wasn't long before Grahamjones made contacts that led to apprentice editing on two of director Rob Nilsson's locally made independent films, *On The Edge* and *Signal 7.* Soon Bay Area film editors were keeping Grahamjones busy working as an assistant. His first contact with Murch occurred in 1985 on George Lucas's $20 million Michael Jackson video, *Captain Eo*, directed by Francis Coppola, that was installed at Disneyland. Grahamjones was already on the project when Murch came in to help Lucas finish the project, which stretched out well beyond its original budget and schedule. From there Murch hired Robert to be a film assistant on his next feature, *The Unbearable Lightness of Being*, directed by another Bay Area director, Philip Kaufman.

After lunch Robert leads Walter down the dimly lit halls at Pixar to his windowless edit room. The former assistant, now host to his mentor, will give Murch his first demonstration of Final Cut Pro. It's as if the master bricklayer on that Pixar building turned to his hod carrier for a better method of laying bricks.

"I was surprised when we started going through things," Robert says later. "He hadn't touched Final Cut before—he really didn't know how to move this thing to there, how to make a cut. He hadn't messed with the machine. He was about to embark on *Cold Mountain* and he hadn't really used it!"

Murch heard about Final Cut Pro systems issues from Torbin Bullock. Now he was interested in learning interface and editing gestalt from Grahamjones, who straddles the film/video/digital worlds and knows Walter's way of working. They share a special relationship, not unlike firemen in an engine company. The intense experience of working together on a major film is deep and mutually dependent. Robert could talk Walter's language, using the kind of shorthand an assistant and an editor come to rely on.

Each editor uses an identical system differently, just as novelists will use word processing software in their own ways. A good tool is adaptable. The Final Cut Pro system is flexible, allowing the same task to be performed in a multitude of ways. This is one of its attractions to Murch, who is all about customizing his tools and work environment to fit his style.

Robert Grahamjones, an editor at Pixar and Murch's former assistant on *Unbearable Lightness of Being* and *The English Patient.*

USING FINAL CUT PRO 6,000 MILES FROM CUSTOMER SUPPORT

Torbin Bullock: "Say a piece of gear goes out. Let's think about this: the closest shipping source is say, from London. That's if they even *have* the part that works with American gear. So maybe you get it counter-to-counter in a day, or more likely it's two or three, with customs and paperwork. So you have to tell your producer the video card went out, and you're spending $400 and it will cost $200 for counter-to-counter. And what if the CPU blew? Or, God forbid, it's something more serious?"

"He's had an Apple computer forever," Grahamjones says later, "and he loves doing things on it. The prospect of being able to cut a film on his own desktop computer just really kind of tipped it. He was willing to go into unknown territory just for that fact alone. As far back as 1986, on *Unbearable*, we did lots of database things on FileMaker using Mac SEs. If Final Cut had been, say, a program only available on the PC platform, it wouldn't have got his attention."

Going to work for Murch on *The Unbearable Lightness of Being* meant Grahamjones was pulled into all sorts of experiments with editing equipment and work flow. *Unbearable* was the first time Murch used his custom-made picture boards, for example; an alternate way of seeing the film in progress through still photos pasted onto large black foamcore boards. It's a system he's used on every film since, including *Cold Mountain*. Murch selects from one to eight representative frames from every set-up—"defining moments," he calls them—that best represent the "story" of that particular shot, emotionally or visually. On *Unbearable* Grahamjones used a copy stand mounted with a 35mm single lens reflex camera to photograph each frame of film that Walter marked. Mounted side by side, in story order (or, as the story was written in the screenplay) these postcards from the movie create an imagistic, dream-like pattern. Walter uses the picture boards because it lets his eyes dance through the film and discover hidden patterns and rhythms, new ways of relating to the material. For *Unbearable* there were 4,000 stills and 40 boards to hold them. With computer-based digital editing Walter's picture board images are captured with a keystroke—a screen shot.

Grahamjones recalls that day at Pixar. "A lot of what he was coming to me for wasn't the specifics of how to press button A, B, C, or D—mainly what he was looking for was to make sure it was flexible enough for him because he doesn't want to get into a situation where there's only one way to do certain things."

Grahamjones shows Murch how Final Cut allows editors to cut sound in "sub-frames," or fractions of film frames. A 35mm film frame equals 1/24 of a second running at normal projection speed. On an Avid system at that time, soundtracks could only be cut right on the frame line. So, an editor gets stuck working in 1/24 second chunks. (When sound editors work in their native software programs, such as ProTools, they have much more latitude.) This may seem adequate, but a frame is a large block of time in the film continuum. For a breath, a beat of music, or a sound effect to be heard exactly where the Avid editor feels it belongs, he must build in tiny fades or dissolves to create the equivalent of sub-frame edits—again, a time-consuming process. "That was one of the exciting things to him," Grahamjones reports later. "He said, 'Oh, sub-frames! I like that!'"

After three hours, Murch finishes his session with Grahamjones. "It was fairly inconclusive," as Grahamjones describes it. But Murch didn't come to Pixar

From *The Unbearable Lightness of Being* with Juliette Binoche and Daniel Day-Lewis.

to decide whether to sign on for Final Cut Pro. He was looking for reasons *not* to go forward. Murch saw the system's ergonomics, the way it cuts footage, and that seems to work well for him. "The big unknown," according to Grahamjones, "was how it was going to mesh into a system overall because the way I'm using it, I told him, I can't help with that. That's going to be the make or break thing. But he left feeling very Walter-like, I think. Mission accomplished."

Indeed there was still much to be figured out—issues Grahamjones didn't have to manage in his own work, since he was cutting projects that were shorter than full-length features, without a huge volume of film dailies. Also, the end product for most of what Grahamjones worked on was videotape, not 35mm film. Final Cut was designed to work properly in video and had already been used extensively on commercials, documentaries, and major television shows. Could the application be nudged into the spotlight of big-time feature films before Apple's design team believed it to be ready? Murch first considered using Final Cut Pro instead of Avid on *Cold Mountain* because the Apple system offered him economies of scale—more workstations at less cost. Some consequences of that choice appear to promise more elegant ways of working, like editing sound in sub-frames. But choosing Final Cut for such a big project may also cause difficulties and lead to troubling work-arounds to handle so much media, get reliable cut lists, and transfer sound editing information.

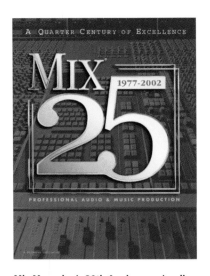

Mix Magazine's 20th Anniversary's edition with an excerpt of the article written by Walter Murch.

Nearly six hours after finishing their lunch together, Murch walks into Torbin Bullock's edit room. "What are you still doing here, Walter?"

"Is there any way we can look up something on the Internet and also check my email?" Walter asks.

"Sure," Bullock says, "but I've got to go then, Walter. You kinda came in on my ticket, and I can't just leave you here by yourself if I'm not here!"

Murch quickly checks his email and researches an item for the *Mix* magazine article. Then he and Bullock walk out to the Pixar parking lot and say their good-byes.

June 6, 2002, Murch's Journal

Finish the article for Mix at 2am, send it off to Tom. It is a couple hundred words too long.

After visiting Bullock and Grahamjones at Pixar, Walter spends time the following week reading the *Cold Mountain* script and making his notes for Minghella.

June 8, 2002, Murch's Journal

Finishing Cold Mountain. Whole middle section very moving. Harder at the beginning, like the book but in a different way. Tear sting a couple of times, around the murder of Esco, Maddy, etc. I wonder how it will end. A swallow: trapped (how?) in the east part of the office, flying around, chirping. I raise the blind, open the window, and it circles seven times and then, lowering its spiral, flies out to freedom. My heart leaps. Thank you.

This won't be the only time Murch deals with a trapped bird in the course of *Cold Mountain*. It's one of those synchronicities that seem to insinuate themselves in and around Walter—one month hence Anthony Minghella will deliver a final version of the *Cold Mountain* screenplay, this one dated July 9, 2002, and marked, Shooting Script *Revised.* It contains a new scene, number 18, which is entirely without dialogue:

```
INT. CHAPEL, COLD MOUNTAIN TOWN. DAY. SPRING 1861

A BIRD IS CAUGHT INSIDE THE NEWLY COMPLETED CHAPEL.
It flies in short, terrified bursts, hitting windows.
Ada is there, then Inman enters. Gradually she and
Inman close in one the bird; Inman removing his coat
to use as a net.
```

There is still a lot Murch must do in terms of making the decision to use Final Cut Pro as his editing system. And he hasn't even tried the system yet with his own hands. Although Steve Jobs indicated support for Murch in that earlier email, Murch's working relationship with Apple and its Final Cut Pro development and support teams is still up in the air. At this time the *Cold Mountain* producers and studio people handling budgeting and logistics are not even aware Murch is thinking of alternatives to the Avid system they assume he will use. Murch does not want to broach the subject until he is sure he himself wants to make that change. And then he will do so only when he has answers about cost savings, creative benefits, and workflow effects on the other film departments. Meanwhile, Ramy and DigitalFilm Tree are feeding Murch results of their ongoing research and investigation of FCP. They're also preparing a list of help items Murch and Cullen will ask from Apple at the upcoming meeting in Berkeley.

What did Minghella think about Murch using Final Cut Pro as his new editing system? Many months later Minghella summarizes his attitude: "I have such trust in Walter that if he'd said he was going to cut the film on an adapted bicycle, I would say, well, okay. Because I would just rely on him to understand the implications."

June 10, 2002, Murch's Journal

Talked to Ramy K: Things are boiling. Some at Apple are with us, some are not—they are working on FCP 4, and this would take effort away. Ramy working on a short list of fundamental issues, drawbacks, which are keeping FCP from being all it could be. Foot draggers at Apple are people facing immediate reality, but this (CM) is bigger than all of them, says Ramy. OMF is a moving target right now, Brooks one of the designers, could fix everything in a week if the API [application programming interface] is there. If it isn't, it could take three months. He was very happy to hear about Brad and Iron Giant pushing Steve J. from the Pixar angle. "That's it then, it's a done deal," said Ramy. I had the idea of bringing TC and LS to the meeting on the 18th if they are available, God willing.

Ramy and Sean continue talking nearly every day about systems and technical concerns even while Sean is on vacation with his family in Germany and Italy. The drive toward making the technical decision about using FCP continues at full speed but Walter needs to spend more time with mouse in hand to be comfortable with it creatively. For that he goes to the "home office"—the Saul Zaentz Film Center in West Berkeley, where Murch spent much of the previous 15 years film editing and sound mixing. This is where he just finished mixing sound for *K-19: The Widowmaker*, where he edited and mixed *The Talented Mr. Ripley*, *The English Patient*, and *The Unbearable Lightness of Being*, and prepared the re-cut of Orson Welles' *Touch of Evil*.

When Saul Zaentz took over Fantasy Records in 1967, it was a small, quirky San Francisco jazz label with artists such as Dave Brubeck, Cal Tjader, Mongo Santamaria, and satirist Lenny Bruce. The company's catalogue grew to be one of the world's largest for jazz, rhythm and blues, gospel, and soul after Zaentz and his partners acquired record companies such as Riverside, Contemporary, Prestige, Stax, and Specialty.

The company had a rock-and-roll label, Scorpio, that recorded local bands, including The Golliwogs, four guys with a distinctly down-home sound. Before Fantasy released their first album, the group and its lead singer, John Fogerty, came up with a new name for the band, Creedence Clearwater Revival. They blew the roof off the place. Zaentz soon got involved with motion pictures, helping to produce *Payday* (as executive producer without screen credit). Released in 1972, starring Rip Torn, it didn't go too far. But a few years later, with Michael Douglas, Zaentz produced *One Flew Over the Cuckoo's Nest*, and he had a hit the second time out.

Being committed now to producing more films, and also being a good businessman, Zaentz expanded his post-production editing and sound-mixing facility. The two-story offices grew into a seven-story building, still the tallest in that part of Berkeley. Its preformed concrete walls embedded with river rocks house the Zaentz Film Center, the record company, and state-of-the-art recording studios. When the Film Center isn't being used for Zaentz's own films, like *The Unbearable Lightness of Being*, *The Mosquito Coast*, or *The*

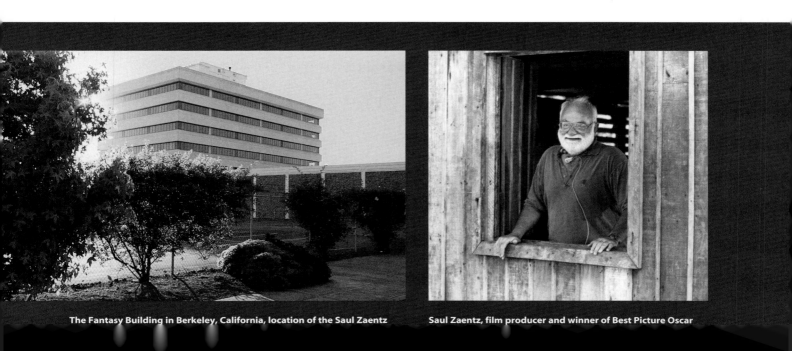

The Fantasy Building in Berkeley, California, location of the Saul Zaentz

Saul Zaentz, film producer and winner of Best Picture Oscar

English Patient, clients from Hollywood make the trip north to work in the center and use its talented band of sound editors, engineers, and mixers.

It is appropriate for Murch to come back to the Film Center for his first test drive on Final Cut. Not only had he edited and mixed some great pictures here, he likes the people and the place. And the feelings are mutual. The staff, house editors, mixers, and engineers appreciate Murch and his approach to filmmaking. Michael Kelly, director of special projects at the Film Center, says having Murch working on a project in the Film Center means doing things "way different" from when other film personnel come in to use the place.

"If he decides he wants to figure out problems or a process, you're in for it, because he's going to ultimately figure it out at philosophical and subatomic levels. With Walter, if you can't answer his questions, you'll end up questioning your own assumptions—discover the limits of your own understanding. He doesn't do this to get at you but to find the boundaries of logic around systems. It's Socratic. In small or large ways the Film Center changes the way we do our work because Walter finds better ways to do things. New functions are discovered. They get adapted permanently—or at least temporarily, to appease him."

Actor Rip Torn in *Payday,* the first motion picture Saul Zaentz produced.

Jack Nicholsen in *One Flew Over the Cuckoo's Nest,* produced by Saul Zaentz and Michael Douglas.

Tom Christopher, a film editor and early user of Final Cut Pro.

The third floor at the Saul Zaentz Film Center, where Walter Murch frequently works.

One week after visiting Grahamjones and Bullock at Pixar, Murch goes to Berkeley to see Tom Christopher, a sandy-haired film editor in his late 40s with the agile bearing of a shortstop. Christopher began in post production as an MRO—machine room operator—at Coppola's Zoetrope facility in San Francisco. He first worked there in 1980, on *Dragonslayer*, the film co-written and directed by Murch's college friend, Matthew Robbins. Murch also mixed *Dragonslayer*. Being comfortable with computers and high technology, Christopher found himself in more demand as editing and mixing began to move toward digitally based systems. "Walter and I have been talking about non-linear editing—forever." Indeed, Christopher gave Murch his first introduction to EditDroid, the laser disc-based non-linear editing system that George Lucas developed in 1984.

"Walter was here in the Film Center in the spring of 2002," recounts Christopher. "It was in the kitchen on the third floor, during a mix break on *K-19*. I mentioned I was looking into this new Final Cut Pro software. I had already used Adobe Premiere on a few projects. I told him I was very impressed with Final Cut Pro, and he went, 'Ahhh.' That registered with him." Murch asked Christopher for his contact information. Not long afterward an acquaintance of Murch's was looking for someone to edit a PBS special on local restaurant owner and celebrity chef Alice Waters. Murch referred Tom Christopher, he got the job, and the program became the first *American Masters* show edited on Apple's Final Cut Pro.

Murch later called Christopher about the FCP lab of sorts he had going at the Film Center. "We were very hot on it at that point," Christopher says later, "and we were hearing from other editors, 'Yeah, yeah it's an interesting toy.' But we were seeing it differently; it wasn't a toy. I had a think tank up here, had the Apple people up here, along with other editors, and had roundtable discussions and talked with the Apple Development Team about what our needs were and how we wanted to use this new technology."

"I received a call in June 2002 from Walter saying he was very interested in using FCP as his next platform. He had worked out a plan and he had contacted Apple and he wanted to have a meeting up here with me and go over what I was doing. I set up the room so we could have a little platform for him to get warmed up on. What was evident that day Walter came in by himself was he hadn't really mastered the software at all. But the fact it was new to him didn't matter."

"You sit down in front of one of these machines and you're clueless for the first few minutes, an hour, even days, because you've just come off something else, a different editing system. You have to get in the zone. I had Final Cut set up the way I liked to work: the video monitor in the center, and two computer monitors flanking left and right. Walter took charge, as he is wont to do, starting to sculpt the digital environment so it was the way he wanted it to be. Walter got into the zone pretty quick. He started to adjust things. For example, he reset the parameters of the trim window—changing the default parameters."

"It was a couple of hours and then he wanted to just work on his own. I left him alone, backed off, checked in with him every once in a while. He was fine. He got as far as he wanted and then he took off."

June 13, 2002, Murch's Journal

Good session with TC on FCP. Made me nervous about changing "instruments" but… flushed out some questions but some answers too.

Got windshield fixed on Subaru.

Walter later described the anxiety he felt that day in Room 305 at the Film Center, his old editing room during *The English Patient*, trying Tom Christopher's Final Cut Pro edit system. "I had the tiniest whiff of 'uh-oh.' I was confronted with the fact that I was going to do it—here it is. I was metabolizing that information. If I were a pianist, it'd be as if I were changing instruments and found the pedals were in a different position on this piano. In the middle of the third movement would I have a wrong reflex—go for the pedal here but find it was now over there?"

So far so good. None of the editors he met with—Bullock, Grahamjones, and Christopher—are giving him a make-or-break reason not to use Final Cut Pro on *Cold Mountain*. While Sean and DFT are finding handholds for systems and workflow issues such as change lists and EDLs, networking workstations, integrating audio files with ProTools, and managing the high volume of film material, Walter is getting more accustomed to the interface, keyboard, and functionality of Final Cut Pro. In ten days Murch will leave for Europe.

Dan Fort helped create the Cinema Tools application used with Final Cut Pro for film editing.

John Taylor, film editor and one of the DigitalFilm Tree's stable of experts.

Timing the script: It took me three hours to get to 1/5th—so it will take fifteen hours total. At any rate, I timed the first fifth, and the mpp [minutes per page] is 1.66, which makes for a total over three hours: 3.06 fast, 3.20 slow. I wonder what it will work out to be in the end?

[WM's later insert here: It was 2.52 fast, 3.10 slow.]

Didn't finish timing today—takes about 12 hours to do it (timing each scene twice)—will finish tomorrow

The meeting in Berkeley with Hudson and Meaney of Apple is three days away. Sean Cullen returns from vacation, giving him and Murch just enough time to make a one-day trip to Los Angeles on Monday, June 17, for their final visit to DigitalFilm Tree. Cullen prepares a background document for the session at DFT—a two-page description of the workflow he plans to use on *Cold Mountain* to prepare dailies every morning during production. Based on how he works using the Avid editing system, it's a step-by-step process that begins with receiving just-printed film rolls from the lab and ends with digitized media on Walter's desktop ready to edit. In his introduction to the document Sean writes, "There are a number of workarounds that I have to use to trick the Avid into behaving..." which are so extensive he leaves them out, for brevity's sake.

When Sean and Walter sit down in DFT's training room the following day, they learn more perhaps than they ever wanted to know about the kinds of workarounds Final Cut Pro would soon be demanding from them. They each sit at one of the ten Final Cut Pro stations outfitted with Cinema Display monitors normally occupied by pupils of DFT's Final Cut Pro training classes. Beside Ramy Katrib, the others are chief technology officer, Tim Serda, who will be responsible for integrating and testing the *Cold Mountain* editing systems; managers Henry Santos and Edvin Mehrabyan; trainer and then DFT president, Walt Shires, FCP and Cinema Tools editor/consultant Dan Fort; and DFT editor John Taylor, who is especially versed in the differences and similarities between the Avid and FCP systems. Serda and Shires are from the original Final Cut team when it was being developed at Macromedia, before the program was sold to Apple. So for Murch and Cullen, sitting in this room with some of the editing system's original planners and designers is an opportunity to range freely through Final Cut's nervous system. Similarly, Dan Fort was influential in the development of Cinema Tools—the additional application that allowed FCP to be used for film editing.

The initial discussion is about logging footage in Final Cut Pro: film measurement (feet and frames) versus video measurement (timecode). Timecode is the electronic indexing system used in video that encodes unique time stamps on every frame using a system of hours, minutes, seconds, and frames (30 per second). It is video's equivalent of key code numbers used on film. *Cold Mountain* will live in both video and film worlds, so they want to have an easy way to convert between the two logging systems. And while Cinema Tools is the basis for translating the film numbering database to video timecode, and back again, there are process issues about when to convert timecode material into feet and frames, and how to track both. This is Sean's primary area of responsibility, so Walter stays quiet for the most part, injecting questions occasionally. The conversation is brisk, focused, and serious.

Apropos the topic at hand, Ramy mentions that *Star Trek*, the television show, had just sent its entire post-production team, including all the editors, to DFT to learn Final Cut Pro. "Walt was training all nine of them," Ramy says, "until this 'bug' came up about 24 frame film versus 30 frame video." *Star Trek* uses many short bits of visual effects that originate in film, so conversion from feet/frames into timecode requires a labor-intensive, cumbersome, manual data-entry process for the assistant editors. "Because of this 'bug,' *Star Trek* didn't go with FCP," Ramy says, "and we reported to Apple because they wanted to know why it didn't happen."

Walter breaks in to ask if Apple's Final Cut Pro managers are up to date on the problem—a window into the computer company's sensitivities to entertainment industry needs.

"To the extent they understand anything about 24 frame," Ramy says sardonically. "They've never worked on a film project. See, 99 percent of FCP users aren't affected by something like this. It's such an infinitesimal thing. But it could be addressed in an afternoon if they [Apple] have the will to do it."

Murch is all too familiar with the film business being a tiny drop of economic demand as far as major manufacturers and suppliers are concerned. "We have needs for very fine tolerances in equipment and gear, but the capital base is tiny compared to medical products or ski equipment," he says.

Walt Shires believes Murch's involvement will trigger changes to Final Cut Pro, based simply on his status in the movie business. Murch tells the group about his emails to and from Steve Jobs—that his friend Brad Bird, a film director at Pixar, is also contacting Jobs. "I think there is some heat on solving some of these problems," Walter tells the group.

The discussion continues. Sean is informed that when he first opens a newly digitized clip from film dailies, he should expect to find the timecode numbers to always be wrong.

"Always?" Murch asks. "Good. A reliable bug—that's much better."

"This is a rock-solid bug!" Ramy says, to much laughter.

The discussion continues about another sticking point: there is no counter built into Final Cut Pro for keeping track of elapsed time in feet and frames. In Avid it's a simple toggle to reset the counter from feet and frames, to timecode. "But Final Cut will only count timecode," John Taylor says. "Sean will have to maintain two separate databases in his log book: one for negative key codes and the other for workprint ink numbers."

Dan Fort volunteers he could write a filter, or mini-program that would do that conversion for Sean.

"It would be easy for Apple to write something and decode feet and frames," Walt says, "but it is a matter of this being a very niche-y toolset for someone like Apple."

Fort also points out such a workaround would have to operate on OS 9.

"Then you're going to run into the fact that Steve [Jobs] officially pronounced OS 9 dead," Shires says. "No work or budgets will be spent on OS 9."

Later, after lunch, the group reconvenes in one of DFT's small edit rooms where Sean starts putting Final Cut Pro through its paces. He asks if the font size on the interface can be enlarged since Murch edits standing up, is farther from the screen, and needs larger type.

"No!" someone says, mockingly, a dig at intransigent software designers. But of course it can.

"I suppose you want to remap the keys, too?" John asks rhetorically, referring to editors who like to customize their keyboards for frequent shortcuts. This joke isn't so funny.

"Yeah, I know," Sean says dejectedly, without prompting. He's already aware keyboard remapping, a function native to Avid, is unavailable in FCP 3.

Finally Walter sits down at the keyboard. With everyone quietly observing, like an expectant audience awaiting the first chord at a piano recital, Murch tries out some basic functions and edits on Final Cut Pro. This is not a trivial moment. The group, which is quickly becoming the FCP/*Cold Mountain* support team, feels the gravity.

At the end of their day together, Ramy sets up a conference call for Sean and Walter with Brooks Harris to talk about the thorny problem of getting sound files from Final Cut into ProTools. At the heart of this is FCP's inability to provide OMF compositions (edited audio information) that can be emailed to the sound department and then re-linked to their raw audio files. FCP can only provide OMF export with audio embedded—that is, carrying the sound media with it. Normally that may seem convenient, but sound editors need to work with raw audio files of the highest quality. For *Cold Mountain* Murch wants the sound to be delivered at 24 bits. The higher the number, the more precisely the original audio signal will be reproduced. (Standard CDs use a bit rate of 16.) However, Final Cut Pro can only handle sound files with 16-bit sound information. Using embedded sound exported from FCP will compromise the quality of sound that was originally recorded at 24 bits.

The other problem with embedded sound information is that Murch wants to be able to send the sound editors his blueprints for the building (edits points where his cuts occur, levels, equalization, etc.), not the bricks, mortar, lumber, and drywall—all the building materials—which is clumsy, inefficient, and unnecessary. So, if Brooks Harris, one of the original developers of OMF who helped develop OMF Tool Kit, an application used by the post-production community, can circumvent these hurdles, all the better for Murch, Cullen, and the sound editors on *Cold Mountain*. Everyone stands around the speakerphone in Ramy's smallish office. On the wall is a full-size Bebe fashion poster featuring a model in her underwear. Two years later, it will be replaced by a one-sheet of *Cold Mountain*.

"Walter and Sean are meeting with Apple tomorrow," Ramy tells Harris, "so everything's coming to a head. This sound problem—not being able to transfer composition-only sound from FCP—is one of the top three issues that's on the table right now."

"If they just gave me access to the API," Harris responds, "I could do it through OMF." There is more discussion about details and options. But in the end, a solution seems possible, and from a top programmer that DigitalFilm Tree knows and trusts.

"That was encouraging," Ramy says after the call is finished.

"Yeah," Sean says cheerfully, "and Brooks seems to be a pretty pessimistic individual."

JUNE 18, 2002—BERKELEY
Walter and Sean arrive at the Fantasy building in West Berkeley for their meeting with Apple Final Cut Pro managers, Brian Meaney and Bill Hudson. They convene in Murch's old editing room, No. 305, with Tom Christopher—who is hosting the get-together—and his assistant editor, Tim Fox. Sound editor and sound supervisor Larry Schalit, with whom Murch had worked on *The Talented Mr. Ripley* and *K-19* is also there. Schalit will contribute to the issue of sound file transferability between Final Cut Pro and the ProTools application. Christopher has spent considerable time with both Meaney and Hudson on previous occasions as a beta tester for FCP.

"Coming into the Apple meeting," as Sean later described it, "all of the momentum was towards Final Cut Pro. I had essentially decided that Final Cut Pro was the way to go. The only question was the best way to approach it. My sense at the time was that Walter hadn't decided—that he was still kind of like, 'Hmm.' But I certainly had decided, and DigitalFilm Tree had decided, that they really wanted this to happen."

As Tom Christopher points out, the meeting is a natural outgrowth of Apple's aggressive marketing campaign of Final Cut Pro to the film industry: "A two-page, full-color spread on FCP in film trade magazines? That little flip of a page sent out a message. And this meeting between Walter and the Final Cut development team is the culmination. When you advertise in *Variety* you're not attracting the high school drama market, you're not going for industrial clients, you're going after movie people. And here you have a movie person, and he wants to do it now."

Two years later, also looking back on that Berkeley meeting, Bill Hudson, Apple's senior manager of Market Development and Strategic Accounts for Professional Applications, says, "We wanted to make sure someone of Murch's experience understood what the workflow was going to be—making sure there were no blind spots. If you go into something with your eyes wide open and you know what to expect, you can address things as they come up."

In the corner room on the third floor of the Zaentz Film Center, Sean Cullen presents his *Cold Mountain* game plan to Hudson and Meaney, what systems he plans to use, and how he will put together the edit room. Cullen presents several unresolved issues based on his research during the last several weeks. He proposes that Apple help solve them.

"They were basically giving a brain dump of post-production needs for this project," Christopher recalls. "The wants, the wish list. It was the most elaborate Final Cut Pro scheme probably ever devised." Hudson and Meaney listen quietly. Cullen does not get much of a response.

In essence, Murch and Cullen are asking Apple for Final Cut Pro functions and attributes that are not likely to be available until the next version release. Christopher, having been in many development sessions like this with Apple, knows this is a line that cannot be crossed. Christopher tells Cullen that Apple is being non-responsive because neither Cullen nor Murch have a non-disclosure agreement with Apple.

"Hudson turned to me," Christopher recalls, "and said, 'Thank you.' Because these are the rules they run by. You have to talk about what things are important for your workflow. You're not allowed to come around and say, 'When can I have it? Will it be part of the next release?' You can't buttonhole these guys, because they're not allowed to talk like that. But they do take the information you give them; they take that home."

First off, Hudson and Meaney feel Sean will have problems getting the FileMaker database program to work with FCP. Cullen says, "Everything I've seen shows me that it's just the same as using it to work on an Avid, so that's not a problem. I'm expecting to have to do that kind of work."

Sean is warned that FCP might crash.

"I'm expecting to have crashes. Crashes happen all the time. That's not a problem."

"Media might get corrupted."

"Media gets corrupted all the time. I've got videotapes."

Brian Meaney, part of Apple's Final Cut Pro team.

Apple does not seem to understand the amount of strategic thinking Sean, Walter, and DigitalFilm Tree have already done on their own. Sean also senses they hold Avid in too much regard. "I think they had an impression that the Avid was much more turnkey than it was. Their impression of Avid was the sort of big brother—that it can't do anything wrong, that Avid's perfect."

"Up until that point," Brian Meaney explains later, "many of the people we had met in the higher end of the film community, with studio productions, didn't understand Final Cut Pro and its nuances—didn't understand its differences from the Avid or other systems that they may be used to working on—at a tech level as well as the editing itself, to some degree."

Then the issue of systems versions that Walt Shires alluded to at DFT the day before in Los Angeles comes up. Bill Hudson says the Final Cut Pro team has been instructed from the highest levels at Apple that all advancements, all software development must be in OS X. According to Tom Christopher, "He was basically saying, 'None of this can happen for you, Walter, Sean. You're in 9.2.2. You can't have any of this. We can't do this for you. We are doing things that you will like, but those things will only be usable in OS X.' That was a sobering moment. I wouldn't call it chilling, because it didn't chill these guys. But it basically set the stage for this being a space walk with no leash. If you're on the Shuttle and you go out to fix something, you have a leash. The astronauts have a leash. Bill basically said you're going to be a space walk with no leash, no net, walking out with no net."

While understanding the partnering relationship Sean and Walter would like to have with Apple, Meaney implies that FCP is still fundamentally a consumer application, not intended—not yet, anyway—to withstand the demands of a full-length feature film of *Cold Mountain*'s magnitude. He intimates there are reasons, technical things, that Walter and Sean don't know about that could hurt them.

"Brian Meaney is a really good technical Apple product manager kind of guy," Tom Christopher says later. "I've been at trade shows with him. He has this rocket delivery of stuff. Very confident. Here, the nervousness level was quite high. He was getting more intense at this meeting. I could just see he was nervous."

"We knew for a fact that OS X wouldn't work," Sean recalls, "because DigitalFilm Tree identified a number of problems with it." *Cold Mountain* would be using a SAN (shared area network) because Sean and Walter will network together four or more computer stations that share audio and video from one central storage data bank via a fiber channel. No SAN solutions run on OS X, either from Apple or any third-party company. Another problem with OS X is that Aurora, a third-party hardware developer for Apple, has not completed a capture card driver to use with OS X. Aurora's Igniter card, which DFT will include in Murch's system, is the most reliable and proven method to capture 29.97 frame per second (fps) video dailies to 24 fps video in FCP and provide 29.97 output and viewing, all in real time. Finally, at this time OS X is an unknown quantity in general.

For Cullen, System 9 versus OS X was a red herring: "We said to Apple, 'We're going to do it on Final Cut Pro, and that's what matters. We don't care about System 9 or X. We can switch over to OS X later in post production.'" The push for OS X, which Meaney and Hudson admit comes from "top management," has to do with Apple's mission to eliminate OS 9 from the scene. When a major computer maker like Apple introduces a new system version, it wants it to become the gold standard as quickly as possible. But software upgrades are not like launching the Euro and simultaneously taking all the old European currencies out of circulation. To this day in fact, OS 9 is still used to run most advanced Final Cut Pro systems because of the lack of third-party software and hardware development for OS X.

"We hadn't come across anyone yet," Brian Meaney says later, "who has spent the time to understand these things. What we don't want, and what we worked very hard to do, was to not have false expectations out there in the industry. Many times that means not going in to make lots and lots of sales, and we're fine with that and always have been. We had reservations that this might not be a good idea."

"They were very much between a rock and a hard place," Sean recalls, speaking of Hudson and Meaney. "I can certainly understand their concern and their trepidation. Myself and DigitalFilm Tree, we had already decided we would be able to make it work. It was a question now of how much would Apple help. How much easier will they make it? Before the Apple meeting I said to DigitalFilm Tree, 'It's important that we have a solution that gets us all the way through post production to the delivery of the film that will be successful if Apple goes out of business tomorrow, because we can't tie the fate of this film to the fate of a software company. Apple came a little too late to block the flood."

"They really were saying, 'We don't want you to do it, because we're not ready,'" Cullen recalls later. "I could hear a little corporate doublespeak. There was a little bit of, 'We know what's going on, but we can't tell you. We don't want to share information with you directly. We'll only share information with you in an indirect manner.'"

The session in Room 305 ends in a stalemate of sorts. Sean and Walter shared their plans to use Final Cut Pro on *Cold Mountain* and their requests for how Apple might smooth the road. Apple had a punch list of needs and wants to take back to Cupertino from a top feature film editing team that would soon be pushing the limits of its editing software. The atmosphere was cool but not unfriendly. They adjourned for lunch to the Westside Bakery, a light and airy café across the street from the Fantasy building.

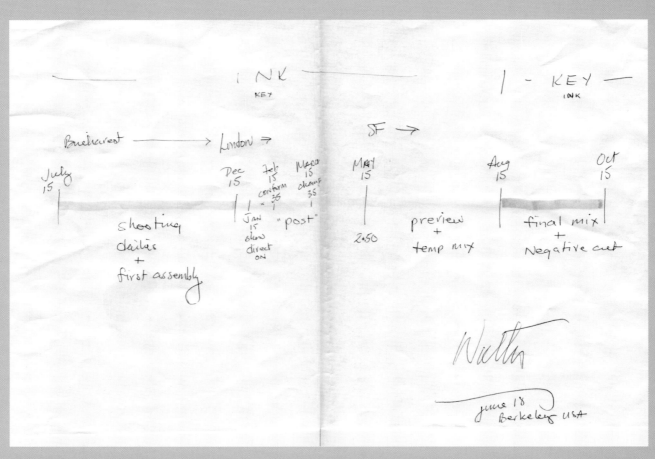

Murch's sketch of the workflow he planned for *Cold Mountain*, as drawn during his meeting with Apple in Berkeley.

At lunch the conversation continues about film editing and Final Cut, though less intensely than earlier. Murch excuses himself for the rest room. Tom Christopher turns to Hudson and Meaney, who sit across the table from him. "Walter is very determined and he will figure it out. His crew will make it work. They're tired of doing it the way everyone else is doing it. You're not dealing with some guy in a garage on Cahuenga Boulevard in North Hollywood. And you're not going to dissuade him by saying 'It's a scary tunnel you're going into, Walter.'"

Larry Schalit was also at the lunch and later recalled: "I sensed Walter was very disappointed by the end of the lunch at the Westside. He was disappointed Apple wasn't going to help him out. Apple could have been enthused, like DFT. They were nice guys, but it seemed they never really got what an opportunity this was and who Walter really is. And they didn't really give him the respect. Here they were, sitting across from the one guy who could take FCP to the big leagues, to big features. I don't think they realized that."

Bill Hudson remembers it differently. "When we were driving back to Cupertino," he says later, "Brian and I were going like, 'Okay, wow, he is totally getting it, and he's seeing the benefit in working a different way.' Not a lot of people are willing to set aside the tools that they've honed their craft on and have the confidence in their craft, and he does. Walter is a great exception. And that was really exciting and invigorating for us."

But Hudson and Meaney also realized that with OS X eclipsing OS 9, they could not do all they might want to assist *Cold Mountain*. "We could make improvements," Meaney continued later, "but any improvements were going to be on System X. And he [Murch] wasn't going to benefit from those. We don't do special builds, special fixes, to try and help out individual clients. We do a lot of software for a lot of people. We needed to make that clear. In addition to that, if he hit any particular problem, we weren't going to be able to help."

Hudson sighs. "Yeah," he says, ruefully agreeing with Meaney.

June 18, 2002, Murch's Journal

Meeting with Apple Bill Hudson and Brian… Larry Schalit, Tom Christopher, Sean, Me, and Tim Fox. All seems good or tending that way. They were greatly relieved to meet us (i.e. Sean) and feel our competency and enthusiasm. We told them about our reservations and they listened to us attentively. **Tired… Nice evening with Bea and Kragen and Hana sitting on the sofa.**

Soon thereafter Walter asks Ramy to send him a budget comparison between Avid and Final Cut Pro. He will use that information to prepare his final pitch for using Final Cut Pro. Interestingly, Murch puts a positive spin on the meeting with Apple in his email to Minghella and producers Bill Horberg and Iain Smith.

DEAR COLD MOUNTAINEERS: JUNE 20, 2002

We had a very good meeting with Apple (Bill Hudson, Strategic Accounts Manager and Brian Meaney, Product Designer) on Tuesday, regarding Final Cut Pro, and they are as enthusiastic about the project as they are about giving us technical support. So it looks like this is the system we will be using. Cold Mountain would be the first "high profile" 35mm feature film project to use FCP, which makes a powerful statement to the industry, and Apple will get much free publicity out of this. How we can parlay that to our further advantage, I leave to your large brains.

I am very happy for a number of reasons, but mostly I am impressed with the programming architecture of Final Cut, which uses the Macintosh's native abilities and is thus inherently elegant and effective. I can put sequences on my G4 laptop, with all the associated media, and show things to Anthony "live." (Avid, by contrast, is a clunky hardware & software "add on" which is becoming more and more of a dinosaur.)

And then there is the question of cost: Final Cut systems are many times less expensive than Avids. Our plan is to install four FCP editing stations for less than the cost of one Avid station. This will allow us to multi-task—editing, assisting, digitizing, and making tapes at the same time, plus having a station available for the second unit and VFX, etc. It also assures us a certain amount of redundancy: if a problem develops with one of the machines we can keep rolling on three wheels rather than, as on *"Ripley"* with the Avids, grinding to a halt until someone could come down from London to fix the problem.

I will include at the end of this letter a list of all the equipment, down to the most trivial, but let me just say by way of explanation that there are four interlocking pieces of the puzzle: 1) the FCP G4 computers which are the core of each station—this is where the editing, digitizing, etc. is actually done; 2) the hard-disk storage, where the media (the images and sounds) are kept. Each station accesses this media through a Fibrechannel network; 3) the outrigger equipment such as tape decks, mixers, CD players, etc.; and 4) the more conventional 35mm editing room equipment: a Steenbeck, benches, rewinds, splicers, etc.

Our savings come with the first puzzle-piece—whether we use Avids or FCP, the other three pieces would remain the same.

I would like to have this equipment in place in Romania by the week prior to shooting, so that we have time to shake it down.

I am leaving for London on Sunday the 23rd, and will be there with Aggie for a week, arriving in Bucharest Sunday night June 30. I will be on email and phone. Sean Cullen can also handle any specific questions about any of this.

All very best wishes from

Walter Murch

Avid system vs. FCP: Avid would cost $62,000 to purchase (edit point). We would need two of them for $124,000. We get four [FCP] stations for $54,000 = $13,500 each. Not much more than what I paid for the Pro Tools stations back in 1998. Wrote FCP letter and list to Ant and Bill and Iain. Godspeed!

Then, on Sunday morning, June 23, after a few days spent wrapping up his affairs, including getting a bad tooth pulled, Walter departs for the San Francisco airport to catch his plane to London where Aggie arrived a few weeks earlier, to care for her ailing mother.

June 24, 2002, Murch's Journal
Arrive at London, no one from the film to meet me as planned. I took the train in, too much luggage to handle myself, but I did it. Didn't have any pound coins for the trolley, but the ticket lady gave me change. Then the first trolley I got at Paddington had a wonky front wheel, so I switched to another one which worked fine, then got a cab to Kingstown Street, and there was Aggie!

Bucharest, Romania.

CHAPTER 5

Keys to the Kingdom

JUNE 24, 2002—LONDON, ENGLAND

The filming of *Cold Mountain* in Romania starts in exactly three weeks, yet final approval of the editing platform Walter Murch will use to edit the movie is still up in the air. As of yet nothing is authorized. In the entertainment business, decisions like these typically get made "just in time." No one seems panicked. As Walter says later, "If I even know where I'm going to *be* three weeks in advance, that's a long lead time."

On arrival in London, Murch emails Minghella an updated set of script notes he wrote on the plane from California:

From: Walter Murch
Subject: Script Notes
Date: 6/24/02 10:36 AM
To: Anthony Minghella

Dear Ant:

Here are some notes on the first forty pages, as a .pdf file. Don't be afraid that there are thirteen pages! I am writing about everything and anything that comes into my head, also writing down applause. As always, there is "I think" and "It seems to me" and "maybe" hovering around everything, all written in the hopes that maybe 5% makes sense or might trigger something in your approach to the material. I made it to London, and am just about to jog around Regent's Park to get some oxygen in me from the flight over. Weather is lovely. Lots of love and good wishes. W.

Meanwhile, since Murch wants to have his edit rooms in Bucharest set up and operating before filming begins on July 15, he must keep an eye on the progress of ordering and shipping his equipment. He sends an email to on-location producer Iain Smith that mostly concerns arrangements for visual effects design, and concludes: "Also, any progress on getting the FCP Apple editing equipment? We should have it on the ground and ready to install at the end of the first week of July. All best wishes, Walter."

Murch spends the following week with Aggie at their house in Primrose Hill, attending to family matters. During that time DigitalFilm Tree finalizes an equipment list for four Final Cut Pro editorial stations using Mac G4s networked together with 1.2 terabytes of storage using a Rorke Data shared area network (SAN) with all the required monitors, video cards, cables, and accessories. On June 25, Ramy sends an email to producer Bill Horberg with this itemized breakdown. The total comes to $133,904. Of this, $56,000 is for four Final Cut Pro stations—hardware, software, the Aurora capture system for proper digitizing, five monitors, extra memory, and cables. The remaining $78,000 is for the data storage systems, hard drives, other accessories, and supplies. The next day Ramy forwards a copy of that message to Zed, who is still in New York. Ramy gets a response early the next morning: "Awesome stuff, dude! I'll be praying. Zed."

A conference call among Ramy, producer Bill Horberg, and Linda Borgeson, the post-production supervisor for Miramax, is set up by Horberg's assistant for late afternoon that same day to review the equipment list. By email Ramy alerts Walter in London, and Sean, who is still in San Francisco preparing to leave for Romania.

A few hours later—and before the conference call—Ramy gets Walter's return email message: "I talked to Linda Borgeson a couple of weeks ago and she is very keen on FCP. Bill is keen on saving money. Emphasize how much $$ saving in comparison to Avid, and Apple's interest and support of this project. Protect the idea of four stations as being crucial to the way we are multi-tasking: editing, assisting, file management, making tapes, and digitizing, all at the same time. On 'Ripley' in Rome, with two Avid stations, we would grind to a stop until someone from London could fly down to fix the problem… Good luck! Walter M."

The conference call goes well. Horberg agrees in principle to go with Final Cut Pro. Questions remain to be answered, however. Who will provide support for Walter on the ground in Bucharest? Should the systems be leased or purchased? What items might be obtained in London, where post production will continue once filming concludes in Romania?

In a matter of days, these questions are getting answered. A London-based rental house, Edit Hire, will rent Beta SP decks, VHS decks, CD players, timecode and film code burners, and other hardware. The film production office will purchase stock and expendables—blank videotapes for telecine transfers from film, blank DVDs for burning copies of digitized film dailies to be sent to Miramax and to the other producers, paper, labels, and other supplies. With information now being exchanged about shipping logistics, it looks like it becomes a done deal at the moment Walter is in the air, flying to Bucharest.

One major question remains: Who will go to Romania to put the systems together? DigitalFilm Tree always planned to assemble and rigorously test everything in Los Angeles before shipping, but once it all arrives in Bucharest someone needs to be there who can help get the systems configured.

From:	Bill Horberg
To:	Ramy Katrib
Subject:	Update/DFT systems
Date:	July 1, 2002

…it seems the critical path will be a support person on the ground here next week with the equipment for set up and commencement of smooth running operation… we are anxious to know who that individual might be… we really need to know today or tomorrow a.m. where we stand.

Regards,
Bill

The pressure is on DFT to come up with an on-site technical person, otherwise Horberg might quash using FCP. Ramy immediately puts out email to the DFT network of FCP experts with the subject line: "Update/DFT Murch Support—Important!!" to see who among Walt Shires, Zed Saeed, Mike Stroven, Shawn Paper, and Tim Serda is available and wants to go to Bucharest. "We have to pick a candidate for Romania soon… Everyone, please advise. As you all know, there is a little history here in the making. — Best, Ramy."

Zed recalls Ramy phoning him to follow up on this email: "I remember sitting with a friend and the phone rang and Ramy said, 'Zed, this is Ramy. I need you to go to Romania.' I didn't ask anything. I said, 'Yeah, sure!' It didn't work out because of my passport situation. This is the post-9/11 world, remember, and I've got a Pakistani passport. Not exactly the credentials you want for flying to Romania at that time."

As it turns out, Jim Foreman will go to Romania. He is from Aurora, the company in Michigan that is supplying the Ignitor capture card for digitizing, outputting, and viewing video in Final Cut Pro. He will first come to Los Angeles to join DFT in assembling and testing the systems.

July 1, 2002, Murch's Journal

Arrive Bucharest. Feeling is Italy 1963 and Havana 1989, with Marriott Las Vegas 2002, Paris 1889, and Moscow 1955.

On arriving and checking into the Marriott, Walter takes a two-mile run around deposed Romanian dictator Ceaucescu's former palace, now the Palatul Parlamentului—the biggest building in Europe. Later, just after midnight Bucharest time (afternoon in Los Angeles), Ramy receives final word from Miramax by email approving purchase of the Final Cut Pro setup. "This email confirms that Cold Mountain Ltd. will purchase and/or lease computers, editorial software, media storage, and peripherals based on the breakdown in the 6/25/02 quote #5085 provided by DigitalFilm Tree.... I understand that you will immediately begin ordering and assembling the systems with the intent to ship from LA to Romania by Friday July 5... Best, Linda Borgeson; VP Post-production; Miramax Films." A momentous idea becomes reality.

Former Romanian dictator Ceaucescu's Palace.

Even a film company as large and well known as Miramax must set up an account and get credit approval from Apple. There are credit applications, purchase orders, and wire transfers to process. Apple's managers are caught up in end-of-quarter financial matters and their attention isn't focused on DigitalFilm Tree's need to complete purchase and lease arrangements. The schedule for getting the equipment off to Bucharest in time for Walter to begin working with initial footage is now falling behind. Ramy and the DFT staff still have to receive the software and hardware in Los Angeles, plug it all together, test it, dismantle it, and ship it halfway around the world to a former Soviet-bloc nation with uncertain customs procedures. Ramy has no choice but to make the plunge, even if it might put DFT out of business.

JULY 3, 2002—LOS ANGELES, CALIFORNIA

At 1:00 a.m. Ramy makes a decision and sends email to Miramax and to DFT's purchasing contact at Apple: "Hello everyone. On Tuesday DigitalFilm Tree began ordering system components. A director of financial services at Apple will check on the credit approval process now taking place at Apple/London. We trust all will go well as we are ordering on our credit to facilitate faster delivery, — Best Regards, Ramy."

Sean Cullen later recalls the situation, "We had done a lot of, 'We're ready! We're ready!' but the money hadn't come through, and DigitalFilm Tree ended up basically saying, 'We're going to buy these things for you now and ship them off to you, and we are going to assume that we are going to get paid.' They took a big risk—a major risk. We said, 'That would save us. Are you sure?' And Ramy said, 'Yeah, because we care about it. We've worked on it, we've done it, we're going to do it.'" That kind of impassioned faith is unusual in any business. But in the film business, where checks are rarely used anymore—money only moves by wire transfer—this sort of trust is unheard of.

Now, less than three hours after Ramy received the email from Linda Borgeson at Miramax approving DFT's quote, he gets the first electronic notice from the Apple purchasing system confirming acquisition of four Mac G4s and four Cinema Tools 1.0/Final Cut Pro 3.0 bundles, totaling nearly $16,000: "Dear Apple Reseller, Thank you for placing your order with Apple Computer, Inc. Your order has been successfully received and is currently being processed... Thank you again for choosing Apple Computer!"

For Walter, the first order of film business in Bucharest is to select a location for what will become the home of the *Cold Mountain* edit. That means going to visit Kodak Cinelabs Romania, and Castel, a Romanian production company.

Great day at Kodak the lab of our dreams. Good rooms, great people, etc. etc. As soon as our equipment arrives, we should be moving in. They were plastering the walls as we looked at them.

Walter can locate his editing rooms on the second floor of the lab's facility, which means timely access to film dailies and to telecine transfers—the videotape copies the lab makes from those film dailies. Kodak Cinelabs is one of a handful of far-flung "pocket" film labs Kodak is locating around the world to better service local and regional filmmakers. They can do this by utilizing the same kinds of miniaturized technologies used by one-hour photo processing shops. The lab is nearly three hours drive from the *Cold Mountain* sets in the Carpathian Mountains which, after extensive location scouting in the U.S., Canada, and Europe, director Anthony Minghella decided best resemble mid-19th century North Carolina. Setting up here, in Bucharest, and being self-contained and efficiently organized, is more of a priority for Murch than having access to actual filming many miles away. Arrangements will be made to get film dailies up to the set for Anthony and the producers to review.

Like most professional director-editor relationships, Walter Murch and Anthony Minghella's is a close creative partnership. Their association has a specific style with its own particular procedures, customs, and unspoken

Kodak Cinelabs in Bucharest, Romania. Murch's edit room will be located here, on the second floor.

understandings. They each keep creative boundaries that best serve the interests of the film. For example, Walter is invited to read and make notes about the screenplay very early in Anthony's writing process—in the case of *Cold Mountain*, a full year before commencing production in Romania. For Anthony, Walter isn't simply an editor vetting the script for discontinuities, story flaws, or other hard-edged editorial concerns, such as, "If we saw Inman in town, we'd better see him leave town before he shows up in battle." What Anthony draws on from Walter, first off, is his "story sense"—observations, analyses, and emotional responses.

On the other extreme—keeping viewpoints separated—Walter holds to a mutually agreed-on "Don't tell me, let me discover it myself" ritual. He doesn't want to see Anthony's on-set notes before he forms his own first impressions of the material. That information exists, of course—the script supervisor keeps a detailed log of the director's reactions to each numbered take, such as "NG" (no good), or specific comments about particularly good line readings, or questions of camera focus. When Murch first watches dailies (alone in the lab's projection room, not with Minghella, cast, or crew) he does so as a clean slate, without anyone else's opinions to influence him. It's a way of staying separate from the thrill (or agony) of production. The adrenaline rush that comes naturally during filming can make a so-so take seem wonderful, just as low blood sugar can make a great shot seem terrible. These sorts

Director Anthony Minghella in Bucharest watching dailies at the start of production.

of distortions can easily find their way into the on-set script notes. That's why an editor's obligation, as Murch sees it, is to experience the footage without filters. The only value to him is what's on the screen. Murch will not look at Minghella's notes until his second viewing of the footage weeks later, just before he begins the actual cutting. For much the same reasons—keeping himself immune from inappropriate influences—Murch doesn't make any effort to visit the set, or even get to know actors face to face. Indeed, during the four months of shooting *Cold Mountain,* Murch will go to the set only four or five times.

"I am the kind of editor who doesn't like to go on the set," Murch says. "I joke about it: If I *have* to go I look at the floor"—as he says this he shields his brow with his hands and looks down—"until I find the director's shoes and I look up (Murch glances up), talk to him, and look back down again." (Murch shields his brow again with his hands and looks down.) "I don't want to know what it's really like. I want to see only what's on the screen because that is all the audience will ever see. And the editor has the responsibility to be *the* person on the film who isn't influenced by the reality of the location or the mood of the set at the time. Or how difficult that shot was to get. Or how cold it was. The editor's innocence about these things is a counterweight: 'Looks good to me!' or, 'Doesn't look so great, no matter how much it costs.' Everyone else who works on the film at this stage—director, producer, camera, sound, design, costume—can 'see around the edge of the frame,' so to speak."

The construction of Black Cove Farm, where Ada Monroe (Nicole Kidman) lives in *Cold Mountain*.

Set builders working on Cold Mountain town near Brasov, Romania.

Trip up to Carpathian Locations. Walter, Sean and me. Driven by Mike the Mathematician. See Battlefield: Black Cove Farm, Cold Mountain Town, Swangers. Very impressive work—needs to be shagged up a little when it is done. Signs though are too weathered. Meet Nicole Kidman at the Villa Hotel. Anthony there too, good to see him, good for Sean and Walter to see him. Meet the Tintype Man: Stephen. They are taking pictures of the locations using the old glass plate technology. Also pictures of Ada and Inman. Stephen was the guy that Barry Malkin suggested and I passed on to Tim—glad it worked out. He took a picture of me, a closeup.

July 5, 2002, Murch's Journal

See rehearsal at Killing Fields and suggest that Brendan say his lines about Ruby based on a look from Teague, rather than the command to go to the tree. The command follows Brendan's lines about Ruby, and then Brendan is defiant when talking about Pangle's hat. [In the end this suggestion wasn't followed.] Finished Notes for Ant—four pages of distilled notes, at 4am.

A tintype of Walter Murch.

L to R: Stephen Berkman, Sean Cullen, Mihai Bogdan, Walter Slater Murch on the set of *Cold Mountain* with Berkman's equipment for making tintype photographs.

From *Cold Mountain*: Characters Stobrod and Pangle in the campfire scene.

Breakfast meeting with Ant, discussed script, Kodak, things in general in a brief meeting. Talked about the "tang" effect.

MINGHELLA AND TANG

Minghella's "falling in love" with a book is his prerequisite for making a movie based on it. *The English Patient*, *The Talented Mr. Ripley*, and *Cold Mountain* are all examples of this. The challenge in making any film adapted from fiction is deciding what to keep, what to lose, and how to take abstract, often interior moods created in words and present them in pictures on the screen. On *Cold Mountain,* as on the other two films, Minghella is both screenwriter and director, so he adapts the story twice—first from book to script, then when turning his screenplay into images and sounds. He approaches a novel with respect and admiration, and does not begin adapting it into a screenplay until he feels immersed in its historical facts, geography, language, culture, and so on. Minghella spent one entire year just doing research before starting to write the script for *Cold Mountain*. He is fully prepared for the surgical process of getting the book into script. It's a painful one, he says, because by definition it means losing the form and details that drew him to the story initially. To make it less traumatic, he doesn't even have the book nearby when he adapts it. Describing the process of adapting Michael Ondaatje's *The English Patient*, Minghella says he went into seclusion and brought piles of research materials and books but left the novel itself behind, for fear he might simply transcribe it word for word into screenplay format—that's how much he loved it.

On assuming the director's mantle (he never really stops being the writer), Minghella takes his screenplay and transmutes it into film. This director's adaptation, while wholly different from the writer's, is no less drastic. A new set of accommodations and adjustments get made based on practicalities such as locations, schedules, budget, and creative surprises—both good and bad.

The admixture of love and death is a thematic combination to which Minghella has consistently been drawn, starting with his first film, *Truly, Madly, Deeply*. The story of *Cold Mountain* is certainly predicated on this motif. In love, but separated and surrounded by death, the protagonists Inman and Ada spend most of the film apart. Inman goes off to war with the Confederate Army, receives a near-fatal wound after the Battle of Petersburg, and recuperates in a hospital by the sea before beginning a dangerous journey on foot back to Ada and Cold Mountain. Ada, alone in Cold Mountain, struggles to manage Black Cove Farm after her father dies, while she fends off Captain Teague—the leader of the vigilante-like Home Guard—and learns how to survive on the farm from Ruby, a local mountain girl. Both lead characters experience many separate violent episodes. Other than at the very beginning and very end of the film, there are no romantic scenes between Inman and Ada to leaven the brutality.

A week after arriving in Romania, Murch gives Minghella a new set of script notes. One of the issues Murch raises with Anthony is the challenge of integrating the story's piquancy (or "tang," as a line from that draft of the screenplay expressed it) with its romance—found, postponed, and regained. The sharply detailed hand-to-hand combat of the initial Civil War battle scene, as well as individual killings and shootings along Inman's journey back to Cold Mountain, have to be stitched into a fabric of longing and desire between Inman and Ada. Not an easy accommodation in the film world, where stories tend to lean toward one genre or the other.

Surprisingly, especially for such a congenial, sensitive, soft-spoken person, Minghella chose to occasionally write even more "tang" into the screenplay than was written into the novel—not simply in the visual details he wants to show, but in the plot itself. One good example is a scene late in both the novel and the motion picture when Inman, nearing the end of his long trek back to Cold Mountain, is given shelter from a storm by Sara, a struggling young farm widow with a sickly baby.

This episode appears in the chapter "Bride Bed Full of Blood," about two-thirds into the novel. Inman, the injured, starving Confederate soldier who left the war and "wandered the mountains for days, lost and befogged through a stretch of wretched weather," is finally nearing Cold Mountain, where he hopes his love, Ada, still waits for him. A little man named Potts tells Inman about "a good gal down the road three or four mile that will feed you and ask no questions." Sara is only 18 years old, and "a pretty thing, little and slim and tight-skinned." All she has of value is some chickens and a hog she's been fattening up. She lets Inman into her cabin, fixes him dinner, and gives him a place to sleep in the corn crib—until later in the night, when she invites him into her bed for platonic company and to "bear witness to her tale." The next morning Inman wakes to a raid by three Union soldiers. He escapes out a window and watches as the men harass Sara, put her infant girl out into the cold, and finally steal her chickens and hog. Inman follows the Federals through the woods, ambushes and kills them, and returns to Sara's with the chickens (two are now cooked) and the hog. He spends another night with Sara after they butcher the hog together. Since Sara's baby girl, "had a croupy cough, Inman figured there was little reason to expect it to come out the other side of winter alive." Being restless, Sara sings to the baby, her "tones spoke of despair, resentment, an undertone of panic. Her singing against such resistance seemed to Inman about the bravest thing he had ever witnessed." The baby sleeps and Sara then sings "a murder ballad called 'Fair Margaret and Sweet William,'" which includes the lyrics of the chapter's title:

I dreamed that my bower was full of red swine,

And my bride bed full of blood.

FROM WALTER MURCH'S SCRIPT NOTES TO ANTHONY MINGHELLA

Cold Mountain—Notes, July 7, 2002

Balance of "tanginess" and romance: how to find the right tone which will embrace both the blunt rawness of some of the situations, and the romance. The two do not naturally alloy to each other, and there will be some members of the audience for whom *the vile stew of blood and innards* [a descriptive line from the screenplay]—along with the various rooster, goat and sheep decapitations and skinnings (people being generally more squeamish about animal than human violence)—will make it impossible for them to feel warmly romantic when the time comes. As we discussed yesterday morning, perhaps it is the richness of the nature that surrounds our characters that might provide the key.

Then, with "a reduction of sadness" as written in the novel, Inman and Sara sit in the cabin together, and "though they talked but little the rest of the evening, they sat side by side in front of the fire, tired from the business of living, content and resting and happy; and later they again lay in bed together. The next morning Inman continues his journey back to Ada."

In the screenplay for *Cold Mountain* this scene also appears at the two-thirds point. And it begins much the same way, except there is no Potts guiding Inman to Sara. On Inman's arrival outside Sara's cabin he first hears the cries of the sick baby—now a baby boy—even before he hears or sees Sara. She is a more guarded, frightened creature than the character of the book, shouting out to Inman, "I've got a gun." Inside, Sara nurses baby Ethan. She tells Inman about the hog and Inman offers to help her kill and butcher it, since she doesn't know how. The screenplay proceeds as in the book, with Inman in the corncrib, then in Sara's bed. The morning follows likewise, when the raiding party of three Union soldiers arrives and Inman hides out back. But now, in Minghella's screenplay, while the baby is outside in the cold, the lead soldier forces Sara back inside her cabin to rape her. Outside, the youngest soldier begins to take pity on baby Ethan. The third soldier goes into the cabin to take his turn with Sara. But Inman is inside hiding. He slits the first Union soldier's throat, and when the other soldier comes in, he gets axed in the back by Inman. Sara runs out to rescue her baby. Inman responds to the young soldier's sympathies for the baby and lets him escape after forcing him to take off his trousers and boots. But Sara, standing behind Inman, shoots the young soldier in the back as he runs away. Then the screenplay returns to the thread of the book. With Sara's hog hanging upside down, slaughtered in the front yard, Inman does the butchering and Sara renders the fat into lard. Now, while she washes the hog's intestines—not as in the novel, when she sang this to her baby—we hear Sara:

I dreamed that my bower was full of red swine,

And my bride bed full of blood.

Then the screenplay extends the Sara scene into new territory. When she checks on the baby, he won't nurse. "THE BABY IS DEAD," reads the screenplay. She returns outside to take Inman some food, then goes back inside with his knapsack. As Inman eats the food Sara cooked he hears "the sudden shooting report of a revolver." By Inman's reactions we know Sara has shot herself. At dusk we see Inman dig two graves. Inside the house are two bundled bodies, one very small.

Murch circled a couple of dozen items in the first version of Minghella's *Cold Mountain* script he read (dated August 21, 2001). He drew one of those circles around the screen direction, "THE BABY IS DEAD." Something about this distressing moment caught Murch's attention in that early reading. In part it's the "tang" of the scene, but he also took notice of timing and structure issues,

Natalie Portman as Sara.

specifically the idea of introducing such a potent, self-contained scene with a new principal character (Sara) so late in the story. The "Sara scene" and its evolution from novel to screenplay, then to first film assembly and finished motion picture, will be a good case study to follow for understanding the powerful ways in which editing influences story and character.

Wrangling the Gear

Murch's first assistant, Sean Cullen, and Murch's son, Walter, the second assistant, have now arrived in Bucharest. They begin to nail down the workflow that they will soon be responsible for: from film to telecine to preparing dailies to digitizing in Final Cut Pro. Sean quickly discovers sound problems stemming from the equipment and software that Kodak Cinelabs in Bucharest uses to do its telecine transfers. Cullen writes an email to Ramy inquiring about the Broadcast Wave audio file format the lab uses to prepare dailies. How can he get Final Cut Pro to read this kind of sound file, which isn't native to it? Dan Fort and John Taylor, two of DFT's house experts, provide Sean with a revised workflow that steps through the sound conversions he will need to make. This will not be the last time Cullen has to solve an audio-conversion problem on *Cold Mountain*.

Sean Cullen begins synching up first dailies in Bucharest.

The computer equipment DigitalFilm Tree ordered for Walter starts arriving at DFT on Sunset Boulevard, piling up in the halls and in the training room where Murch and Cullen sat just a few weeks earlier. DFT takes delivery of four Mac G4s and begins to set them up. Since it is a holiday weekend, however, the RAID storage drives from Rorke in Minnesota will not be shipped until Monday, July 8. This causes Ramy some anxiety since he knows he still has a lot to do before DFT can ship reliable gear to Murch. In an email to Rorke, Ramy requests shipment even if all the cables are not included; those he can find in Los Angeles. He signs off, "Sorry to be so 'grasping,' but this is the biggest thing we've ever done and the production starts shooting next week. — Festive regards, Ramy."

Reinforcements arrive at DFT the following day when Zed flies in from New York and takes the airport shuttle directly to DigitalFilm Tree. He puts his bags down and immediately gets to work with John Taylor, helping to prepare the *Cold Mountain* workflow for digitizing video into Final Cut Pro. "Ramy called me and said, 'It's on.' I literally walked out my door and didn't go back to even visit for months after," Zed says later. "Had somebody said at the time, 'Dude, one day you're going to be working right next to that man, Walter Murch,' I would have just shouted, 'You're out of your mind. It's just simply not possible!'"

Murch's Final Cut Pro gear at Digital Film Tree.

"The system we built for *Cold Mountain* really set the bar," Ramy says later. The capacity and reliability of the equipment DFT ordered for Walter "was like bringing a sledgehammer to the table. It was the one system we needed to work right, and it did. The same thing with the workflow. If we ever wanted a workflow to be perfect, that was when we needed it to be perfect." DFT prepares a document for Sean with the complete procedure for getting shot film safely and properly into Murch's edit system. It has 31 separate steps.

As Ramy and his staff prepare Murch's equipment, they take extra precautions. During this period, they are seeing a lot of problems with new Apple computers. "We'd had some Apple computers that just died. They just stop working, the processor, the motherboard, something, inordinately," Ramy recalls. He goes on to describe how DFT applied a special program to run on Walter's gear to test its limits. "We ran an application on all four systems that was intended to make the process fail. It used obscene computational activities that would literally heat the system and make it fail. But those systems passed muster."

Later Ramy reflects on that intense period during July 2002. He recalls how gossip and scuttlebutt began appearing on the Internet (some is still posted on various digital video and filmmaking Web sites) asserting that Apple paid the *Cold Mountain* production, or Miramax, to use its computers and its Final Cut Pro software. "The rumor that Apple paid Walter, Miramax, or us—BS!

They bought that bad boy. At the beginning there was talk of leasing the system through Apple Europe. But Apple Europe had never worked on a feature film like this, and the delays were putting real pressure on us. So then it was Bill Horberg who said, 'Screw it, we'll buy it on the spot.' And they did."

Over the July 4 holiday weekend and into the following Monday, Tim Serda and other DFT staff uncrate equipment, plug it together, and run a series of tests using digitized film material. Ramy, still a documentarian at heart despite his new role as systems supplier to *Cold Mountain*, picks up his DV camera and shoots footage of all the activity. At one point he walks into the training room amid all the equipment and finds Serda logging equipment serial numbers into a laptop. Ramy asks him if he has any helpful tidbits to pass on to Sean in Bucharest. "He shoulda used the Avid—that's the only advice I can give him," Tim says seriously. Then he turns to the camera and flashes a silly grin.

In Bucharest, meanwhile, Murch gets to see the first video transfers from film footage.

July 8, 2002, Murch's Journal
Here at Kodak, looking at telecine of Jude's tests. Look good.

"We tested the living shit out of those systems," Ramy says later. "We didn't want them to fail in Romania. But the systems held up. They never failed. And we went through everything we could think of in terms of what could go wrong."

"And built a margin of twice as much as was needed," Zed adds.

"Always assuming the worst, because, mind you," Ramy continues, "we are dealing with Final Cut. Final Cut as we know it, as we've applied it…"

"…does nothing but fail," Zed says.

"All the time," Ramy continues. "It was scary."

Ramy and Zed had worked with Final Cut Pro for years, beginning with its initial product release. They loved its flexibility and affordability, but they also knew the application as intimately as a lover, with all its blemishes and imperfections. After all, they made their living troubleshooting FCP for clients and applying it for all manner of film and HD post work.

"It was a scary proposition," Ramy continues, "that it would be in Romania, of all places, with bad electricity and all. We got the best power supplies, best components, and then all of that culminated in us tearing it down. We had no concern about it being rebuilt again in Romania. It was already detail by detail built here. Still, there was really just a sense of fear about it, that, my God, all this equipment is about to go to Romania."

July 9, 2:00 a.m., at DigitalFilm Tree. John Taylor (left) and Jim Foreman (right) finish reviewing the workflow for setting up Murch's Final Cut Pro system before Foreman flies off to Bucharest.

Ramy explains how DFT beefed up FCP's capability for accessing the digitized media that sits on the hard drives: "This is how we overshot the requirements. We provided Walter with the bandwidth so he could process data rates of 125 megabytes a second without a problem. And you know how much he needed? Two megabytes a second." This is like the difference between logging onto the Internet with an old 28.8 kilobit per second dial-up modem versus logging on with a DSL line. "It wasn't us being foolish. When you work on a project with that kind of complexity, you can't be robust enough. No one could have thought this back then, but in many ways Final Cut ended up being a better system. For whatever reason, Final Cut, the animal, was more suited for that kind of irregular environment, bad electricity and all."

"It wasn't as finicky as Avid," Zed adds.

JULY 9, 2002—LOS ANGELES, CALIFORNIA

By afternoon, DFT is ready to ship all the gear and software to Romania. Ramy phones the freight expediter for a 4:00 p.m. pickup. Even with the rush of getting everything packed up and prepared, he finds time to share the moment with Walt Shires, who had been part of the original orientation session with Murch and Cullen. Ramy sends Shires a collection of emails from the last several days, with this cover note:

Ramy Katrib seals the last box for shipment to Bucharest.

> Hey dude,
>
> This is to keep you in the loop on what is the craziest thing I and we have ever been a part of. This is THE THREAD to date.
>
> – hope you're good, I am in a state of controlled fear.
> – ramy

After he finishes taping up box number 13 for shipping—the last one—Ramy announces, "I think we're ready for him to come in." He walks out the door onto Sunset Boulevard and waves toward a white van that has been parked, waiting, in a metered spot. The driver for Packair Airfreight and Customs Brokers pulls up in front of DFT. The boxes are loaded, and at a few minutes past 6:00 p.m., the van pulls out into traffic and heads west into the pale summer sunset to Los Angeles International Airport. Ramy stands on the sidewalk, DV camera in hand, as $135,911 worth of editing gear begins its trip around the globe to Romania, where Walter Murch anxiously waits for its arrival, and where he will hold Final Cut Pro to the fire on the largest, most complex film project it's ever been used on.

The van with the *Cold Mountain* Final Cut Pro edit systems leaves DigitalFilm Tree for Los Angeles International Airport, and Bucharest, Romania.

With the last 72 hours of intense activity behind them, and the equipment out of the building, Ramy, Tim, Henry, Zed, and Edvin, can finally sit down and relax. Draped along a green office couch, they sit in front of the TV and watch the news.

Murch again writes a long email to Apple CEO Steve Jobs. He updates Jobs about arriving in Bucharest, his plans for the FCP editing setup, and his meeting with Bill Hudson and Brian Meaney in Berkeley before he left California. "We went over the major unresolved issues, which they may have reported to you: non-embedded OMF export & change lists being the major items. I gave B & B [Bill Hudson and Brian Meaney] a timeline of the shooting and post-production of *Cold Mountain*, and they were confident that the Cinema Tools and FCP software could be rewritten to get us what we need when we need it (around March of next year)."

Murch goes on to say he intends to convert from using Apple's System 9 during shooting to OS X once they move the editing to London, assuming Aurora's add-on cards for digitizing are also upgraded to the newer operating system.

"We are also ready and enthusiastic to make this leap," Murch continues, "even though not all of FCP's features are completely ready for a film as big as *Cold Mountain*, because we think it will ultimately all work out, and for the good of this specific film, for the film industry, and for Final Cut, which we think is the system that will come to dominate professional filmmaking in the years to come. We are excited to be playing an instrumental part in this adventure."

Then Murch broaches the idea of a barter: if Apple is willing to upgrade the computer hardware Murch is getting, he and Minghella are willing to plug the Final Cut Pro system. But Murch writes this under a false assumption that Apple is providing FCP software at no charge. Over the last few weeks there had been discussions between Melanie Laird at Miramax and Apple executives about a product placement deal—donating the software in return for promotional rights—but it never came together.

"Anthony Minghella and I would like you to know that we have been very happy with the progress that has been made so far," Murch writes to Jobs, "and would be glad to do promotional work for Apple and FCP whenever that would be suitable towards the conclusion of the project (summer of 2003 and on). The film is expected to be released in the fall of 2003."

Not being aware that Miramax actually paid for Final Cut Pro places Murch in an awkward position. Thinking the door is already open, Murch keeps on walking: "Apple has been generous with their time, and have given us the necessary software free of charge. I would like to request, if possible, some additional support in hardware. We will be using four G-4 2x1 GB machines. Perhaps something can be arranged through Miramax-Disney-Pixar if that would be a convenient channel."

There has been extraordinary pressure by Miramax and MGM on all departments within *Cold Mountain* to cut costs. This is typical for any film studio about to start a high-budget motion picture—and in the case of *Cold Mountain*, one of the big reasons it's been shot in Eastern Europe. Once filming begins, budgets only go up; they never go down. Only by setting their fixed costs as low as possible before production do the studios have any chance of holding the line against cost overruns caused by acts of God (weather, injuries, breakdowns, etc.) and flashes of creativity. For Minghella, this meant grueling preproduction meetings going over script, storyboards, and budgets looking for ways to save money by cutting down scenes, eliminating shooting days, removing locations, and reducing the shooting schedule. For Murch and other department heads, the financial squeeze means working with one less person than usual, or relying exclusively on lower-paid, less-experienced Romanian assistants. Even though Murch is ahead of the curve, having selected an editing platform that saves tens of thousands of dollars, he is trying to further economize his costs so he can bring on a needed third assistant editor, Dei Reynolds, from London. Saving money with Apple may give him the budget savings to have one extra body to work more comfortably.

"In any case," Murch concludes in his email to Jobs, "I am very happy with the situation we find ourselves in. It has just the right balance of certainty and unknown to be creatively energizing. I wish you well in whatever your endeavors are at the moment, and will report on our progress at decent intervals. All best wishes, Walter Murch."

JULY 10, 2003—BUCHAREST

The following day, film with test shots of actors in wardrobe and makeup is being printed. The second unit, a small-sized crew, is starting to film areas of the big battle scene. Assistant editor Sean Cullen sends emails to Ramy about sync sound problems he's having with this first set of dailies. Audio files that Cullen runs separately on an Akai digital sound player are not syncing up to the projected film workprint. He needs some way to convert these .wav files into either .aiff or Sound Designer 2 format. Characteristically, when he asks Ramy for advice, Sean seems calm and to the point. Just another workaround.

Later the same day, Sean sends another email to Ramy with a new question about the electrical power for the Akai machine providing audio playback. It is supposed to run on 120 volts at 60 Hz in the U.S. and Canada; 220-240 volts at 50 Hz in Europe. "Can I plug my (Akai) Dubbers into 240 V @ 50 Hz or will they fry? It is important to consider the downside of losing the dubbers: no dailies, then death." In the meantime Sean will use Murch's ProTools sound edit system, which had finally arrived from California. "Thanks for all the hard work," Sean writes to Ramy. "We started (second unit) shooting an hour ago, soon we will see what all this fuss is about. All the best, Sean."

As for the sound conversion problem, Zed puts Sean in touch with AVTransfer, an outfit in Australia that might be able to help him convert the audio files. However, they want $1,000 a day in consulting fees. It's a lot

THE SIX STAGES OF FILM PRODUCTION

1. Wild Enthusiasm

2. Total Confusion

3. Utter Despair

4. Search for the Guilty

5. Punishment of the Innocent

6. Reward of the Non-Involved

—an old movie industry adage recalled by Murch in his journal, July 9, 2003

Upstairs at Kodak Cinelabs in Bucharest.

of money and Sean wants to forestall unexpected financial expenditures like these because he and Walter are still trying to find room in their budget for Dei Reynolds to come on board. So, as an alternative, Ramy, Zed, and John Taylor (via telephone) review Taylor's previous workflow document to include a new conversion step. They tell Sean to use an AVTransfer application, which unfortunately is written to run only on a PC, not a Mac. But it will convert the Broadcast Wave files into Sound Designer II files so he can sync up sound for dailies projection. All Sean has to do now is find a copy of Virtual PC, a program that allows his Mac to imitate a PC.

Subject:	A book for Romania…
Date:	Wednesday, July 10, 2002 1:29 PM
From:	Sean Cullen
To:	Ramy Katrib

Ramy,

Walter has asked that we secure a copy of "Final Cut Pro 3 for Macintosh (Visual QuickPro Guide)" by Lisa Brenneis. Could you grab a copy and have Jim bring it along with him. You can't believe how much we envy your location. FedEx actually means something.

All the best,
Sean.

On Friday July 12, Ramy gives a sigh of relief: Miramax decided to forgo leasing the computer equipment and instead will make an outright purchase. This is a comfort, since DFT has by this time laid out $116,000 for hardware and $12,500 for software.

July 12, 2002, Murch's Journal

Birthday #59. Go out to battlefield for the "flag" shot. It had just rained, and was soggy muddy but shootable. Rode back to hotel in Dianne's car. Dailies good.

The "test footage" shakedown before the official first day of shooting on July 15 has escalated to include hundreds of soldiers. A camera crane executing a dramatic reveal of the Union soldiers lying on their stomachs, waiting for the tunnel dynamite to explode will later become one of the key moments in the film.

The Rorke hard drive array with 1.2 terabytes of storage capacity. It winds up holding all 113 miles of *Cold Mountain* film dailies, with room to spare.

By this time Walter's arrangements at the Kodak lab are in place. He knows Miramax signed off on paying DigitalFilm Tree for the Final Cut Pro systems still in transit. First day of principal photography is still four days away. It's a chance to breathe a little easier. Those who know Murch will not find it surprising that he connects with the two American photographers brought to Romania to take Civil War-era tintype photographs for the motion picture. These are important props in *Cold Mountain*, as Inman and Ada each give one to the other before Inman goes off to battle. While fascinated by new technology and how it can improve his daily work, Murch is simultaneously obsessed with older epochs, whether it's Civil War–period photography, what happened to the slaves after the sack of Rome, or Edison's attempts to play synchronous sound with projected film. So it's predictable that he finds kindred spirits in the tintypers, Stephen Berkman and Barrett Oliver. Their process replicates a long-forgotten 19th century photographic technique, and with their longish hair and muttonchop sideburns, they look like time travelers from the 1860s. They listen with equal interest to Murch's exposition of Bode's Law, a theory about the proportional distances of planets from the sun that has preoccupied Walter for many years. He actively works on a proof for the theorem, even while editing movies.

While the hubbub of filmmaking swirls around and the anticipation of full-on production grows to fever pitch, Murch takes refuge in "my planets," as he says, eager to share his theories with interested companions. In just two days the gates will open and the film footage will start to flood his days and nights. For now Walter can take comfort in the long view and the big picture.

German astronomer Johann Elert Bode (1747–1826). In his spare time Murch has been working on a proof for Bode's Law of planetary distances.

July 13, 2002, Murch's Journal

Lunch with Sean in Hotel, more about Bode.

Walter uses this tranquil moment before the storm to provide support for director Minghella on the eve of the first day of principal photography. This means receiving Walter's ritual gift of the director's prescription bottle: a genuine amber-colored plastic pill container (with child-proof cap) that Murch fills with fortunes—slips of typewritten messages, missives, maxims, and advisories all relating to the feat of directing a motion picture. Minghella's phial is labeled:

Murchway Pharmacy
One each day, AM or PM
Before or after shooting
Slight giddiness normal side effect
Do not operate heavy machinery
120 pastilles. Discard after 12/20/03

Among the fortunes inside:
- Find without seeking.
- Debussy himself used to play with the piano lid closed.
- Find, for each shot, a new pungency over and above what you imagined.
- Reorganize chance. That is the basis of your work.
- Those horrible days...when shooting film disgusts you, when you are exhausted, powerless in the face of so many obstacles...make them part of your method of work.

Director's medicine.

One legend has it that Murch's source for these epigrams is the French surrealist poet and filmmaker Jean Cocteau, or French film director Robert Bresson. Another says he's been collecting them from various places for years. At any rate, this third collaboration between Minghella and Murch provides the occasion for a third set of fortunes.

July 14, 2002, Murch's Journal

Eight mile run to the Botanical Gardens. I am attacked by a mangy dog who tries to nip my heel and keeps trying four or five times until I eventually move out of his orbit. Give fortunes to Ant in Prescription Bottle. It needs a label because transparent.

The first day of principal photography on a motion picture means high anxiety, exaltation, fear, madness, jubilation, and disbelief—and that's just during the first few minutes, and usually before sunrise. For Minghella and the *Cold Mountain* producers, this day has been six years in the making. But no matter how well prepared and professional the crew, how experienced and dedicated the actors, or how big or small the budget, the momentousness of the day quivers down in everyone's guts. The fact that on this same day, Walter's Final Cut Pro equipment arrives from halfway around the world, intact, sends an extra surge of electricity through the charged-up edit crew.

July 15, 2002, Murch's Journal

Official Start Shooting Cold Mountain. FCP Equipment from US arrives. Jim arrives to install it. Throw I Ching: good changing to very bad. Hmm…

Organizing Office. Run around Palace at 9:30 p.m.

Sean got LocPro to Synch Akai: thanks! And thanks that the Akai runs at 50hz— the only thing they said to watch out for was overheating.

Inevitably, the thrill of the first day's actual shooting gives way to the heaviness of grueling 14- or 16-hour days and the unrelenting demands of solving creative problems. For the edit team—Walter, Walter Jr., and Sean—the second day of production also means a similar sinking into the handling of actual film footage with all its wonderment and imperfection. Yes, the film runs properly, gets synced up, and will land on Walter's Final Cut desktop, and that's a relief. Just as it will be a comfort at the last preview come October 2003 in New Jersey, when the splices do indeed hold together. The physics of it all deserve recognition. But there isn't enough time to spend appreciating the wonder of technology, nor the fact this is a breakthrough moment. There's a movie to make, film to be evaluated, and a niggling storytelling problem that appears in the footage right away: why do the Union soldiers entrap themselves in the crater at the Battle of Petersburg?

July 16, 2002, Murch's Journal

Looked at second unit dailies and confer with Ant, John, and Darren afterwards. The problem is to explain visually why the northerners ran into a hole and trapped themselves. It is inherent problem in the script, but becomes more pointed visually. We screened dailies, limpingly with Mike's personal sound system, which was distorting. Help. And both channels weren't working. May tomorrow be a better day. I feel puffy and fat and shlubby.

Murch's desk on first day of principal photography.

The first film dailies of *Cold Mountain* were screened on July 17, third day of principal photography.

CHAPTER 6

Scenes I Can Cut!

A motion picture in the making is often more mysterious and complex than any one person can fathom, be it writer, producer, director, or editor. Luckily, movie directors who work with Walter Murch get an editor who wears more than one hat. Murch is a film editor and sound mixer, but he has also worked as a sound editor and designer, screenwriter, and director, so he can see a motion picture from many sides. His own varied interests—music, physics, translating Italian literature, history, astronomy, and beyond—likewise give Murch numerous entryways for discovering the secrets of a film. The material can tell filmmakers what to do, just as novelists say their characters often guide the plot, but you must know how to hear. Murch watches, listens, and contemplates, using a set of dependable tools he has acquired over 30 years.

For everyone involved in shooting the film, the screenplay is the front door, the portal to the story's interior. But for the editor, once closeted with actual footage, the written document doesn't remain useful for very long. It guides the editor's first assembly—all the scenes, as shot, put together in order, as written, but films are rarely released exactly as written. For one thing, most of them would be too long for audiences to tolerate. The rule of thumb is that one page of script equals one minute of screen time. But with certain directors, Anthony Minghella included, that formula isn't too reliable. The shooting script for *The English Patient*, for example, was 121 pages. Applying the one-page/one-minute equation, the first assembly should have been 2:01 hours. In fact, it was 4:20, more than twice as long. The final released version was 2:42.

Once a scene starts getting transformed from words on a page to film on the screen, all bets are off. Some directors, like Hitchcock and Spielberg, shoot exactly what's in the script as written; it's a way of working that suits their personalities. But they are the exceptions. Most directors find their conception for a particular scene changes once they're on the set. The tempo of actors' dialogue and the blocking of their movements, the vagaries of light and costume, can change the way a scene gets executed. New material might be added; planned shots may be jettisoned due to weather, schedule, or actors being unavailable; "coverage"—having multiple camera angles on the same action for the editor to choose from—might be compromised, causing a scene to be drastically re-imagined. The editor necessarily works with the material provided, rather than what was imagined but never shot.

AN EDITOR'S TOOLS

What does an editor use to think about the film? Every editor has his or her own methodology. For Murch, it's as if he builds himself a personal radio to tune in to the film using several different frequencies: picture boards with up to seven key images from each setup captured and mounted on black foamcore; two sets of script notes—one written on viewing dailies, a second on re-screening footage before editing a scene—which are embedded in his FileMaker log book; and handmade scene cards, coded by color and shape to delineate plot trajectory and the flow of characters.

So now, on the third day of filming in Romania, with Sean Cullen getting the Final Cut Pro systems plugged in and working upstairs at Kodak Cinelabs, Murch begins preparing his scene cards.

July 17, 2002, Murch's Journal
About 1/4 way through scene cards. I am doing them by hand this time, easier to look at. What color should Inman's trek be?

On his last few films Murch prepared the scene cards using FileMaker on the Macintosh. For *Cold Mountain* he goes back to making them by hand. "There is something appealing about the visual handcraftedness," Murch says later. "The personality of the handwriting is more engaging to the eye, especially if I'm going to stare at them for a year and a half."

July 18, 2002, Murch's Journal

Working still on scene cards. Amazing how long it takes always. But good I am doing them by hand this time, not computerized printing.

The scene cards, picture boards, and script notes are simple and uncomplicated tools. But they aren't just different methods of cataloging. Like composer and printmaker John Cage's throwing the *I Ching* to determine creative choices, these tools allow Murch to incorporate randomness into the edit process. If a scene isn't working for some reason that isn't readily apparent, a sideways glance at the picture boards might reveal a hiccup in the pattern of images that wasn't obvious before. Let's reshuffle the scene cards and see what color pattern emerges. Or, a simple script note ("alt line reading") made in dailies may turn out to unlock a solution—as the alternate line reading, "He'd kill *us* if he had the chance," did for *The Conversation*. But it requires forethought

DIGITALFILM TREE GETS PAID

Back in Los Angeles, the same day Murch begins making scene cards, DigitalFilm Tree finally receives reimbursement for purchasing Murch's Final Cut Pro systems. Ramy Katrib, in a digital home movie, turns the camera on himself and speaks with typical understated calm as he walks from the edit room to his office: "The Miramax wire transfer came in," he says in a close-up so extreme it distorts his face. "And just in the nick of time—we had $532 in our account."

"Blue with a yellow background means Inman is in a scene; plain blue means Inman is not in that scene. A lot of blue cards in a row means not much Inman— which makes me wonder 'is that a good idea?' A triangle indicates I feel it is a pivot scene. The size of card equals the approximate length of a scene."

Murch's scene cards in progress for *Cold Mountain*.

and effort to plan for the unplanned, to invite the unexpected, and to prepare these alternate tools for working on a film. Taking two days to prepare hand-made scene cards at the start of production may seem extravagant. But film directors who embrace Murch's style know that if they find him in his editing room cutting card stock into odd little shapes, what looks like child's play is really serving the best interests of their film.

Ironically, the more techno-centric film editing gets, the more powerful Murch's custom-made innovations become. The organic qualities of the scene cards and photo boards compensate for perspectives that are hidden in the digital world. The efficiency, speed, and increased choices of non-linear edit-ing all have their benefits. But systems like Avid or Final Cut Pro obliterate some film editing tasks that contribute to the editor's creative process. As Murch often points out, the simple act of having to rewind film on a flatbed

Murch assembles his picture boards as film dailies become available. These postcards from the film provide him another tool to see the movie.

editing machine gave him the chance to see footage in another context (high-speed, reverse) that could reveal a look, a gesture, or a completely forgotten shot. Likewise, the few moments he had to spend waiting for a reel to rewind injected a blank space into the process during which he could simply let his mind wander into subconscious areas. With random-access, computer-based editing, a mouse click instantly takes the editor right to a desired frame; there is no waiting, no downtime—and fewer happy accidents. The photo boards are one way to compensate for this.

Film-based editing is now referred to as "destructive editing" in contrast to the "non-destructive editing" of computers, also known as non-linear editing. When a scene is edited the old way—on film with taped splices—the only way to see if it might work better with, say, a different order of shots (the wide shot at the end of the scene instead of the beginning, for example) is to pull the scene apart at the splices and rejoin it in a different order. Not only does this take time to execute physically, the first version now no longer exists (unless a videotape copy was made along the way). In digital editing, the scene can be re-cut over and over again, and all the versions are preserved for later consideration. The computer program plays the footage by sending a request to the hard drives where the original media is stored: "play setup 293-take 4, from frame a to frame b." With a couple of keystrokes that command can be changed to: "play take 293-take 5, from frame c to frame d." Both versions still "exist" since no media has actually been touched (destroyed).

Digital editing, being so versatile and fast, provides film directors with many more choices than they have in film-based editing. When a director comes to the digital editing room to look at a newly re-cut scene, he or she can see the new version, the old version and—after a few clicks, have the editor play a third, recombined version of the other two.

Much of an editor's energy, and most of the assistant editor's, is spent organizing, logging, tracking, storing, and—like the sorcerer's apprentice—trying to stay in control of a huge volume of material. To get an idea of how much raw film footage is at the editor's disposal, recall the shooting ratio—the amount of film shot, compared to the amount of film used in the final theatrical release. It can range from 10:1 in low-budget independent films to 100:1 and more, depending on the style of the director. Stanley Kubrick, for example, was notorious for doing a hundred or more takes of the same shot. At the other extreme, Clint Eastwood is often satisfied after one or two takes. If a shooting ratio is 50:1, and the running time of the finished film is two hours, that means there will be 100 hours of raw footage, or 540,000 feet of film (16 frames of film equals one foot, or .66 seconds). That's just over 100 *miles* of film!

With so much footage to organize, it's no wonder that in film-based editing chunks of footage often get lost. The missing pieces are usually "trims," or

"With computer-based editing, there is no downtime—and fewer happy accidents."

A standard film trim bin.

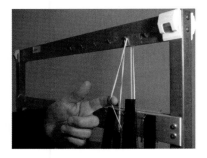

The "Murch bin" uses the ends of crochet hooks instead of straight metal pins. Rubber bands make trims even more secure. Bicycle wheel clamps allow an editor to raise or lower the cross-beam to suit her needs.

snippets of film only a few frames in length. These little bits multiply as a film is winnowed down to its essential self, shedding microseconds here and there as the editor finds the truest 1/24 of a second for a shot to begin or end on. The black hole that swallows film is called the *trim bin*, a square metal container the size of a shopping cart, lined with muslin to minimize film scratches, where the trims are hung on hooks.

But trims fall off their hooks in the commotion of editing and disappear into the hamper like socks in the laundry. Having to search around the bottom of the bins for a missing trim was an assistant's tortuous, painstaking job. One of Walter Murch's contributions to the film editor's tool kit, the Murch Bin, helps minimize this problem of footage vanishing from sight.

All editors use an accounting method to keep track of film footage. There is no one, industry-standard way to do it; each editor devises a system that suits his or her needs. Murch put his logbook together in FileMaker Pro, a database program that can search, find, calculate, and view by using multiple fields of information, customized to his preference. Each record represents one continuous camera take.

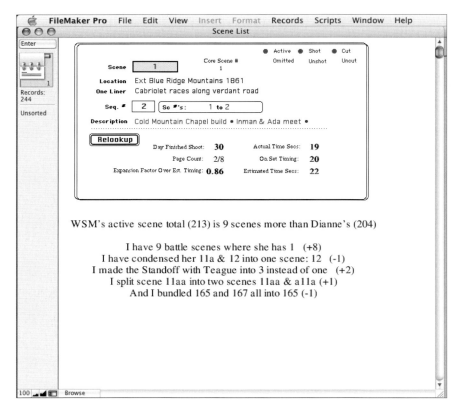

A page from Murch's *Cold Mountain* scene list kept in a FileMaker Pro database.

It is a week after principal photography began, and as film footage flies into the second floor at Kodak Bucharest, record keeping begins in earnest. Now that he has eight days' worth of material, Walter makes his first estimation about how much film volume he can expect, based on a shooting schedule of 110 total days.

July 23, 2002. Murch's Journal

354 Records as of today which represents 8 days of shooting. So 45 records per day x 110 days = 4955 or almost 5000 records at the present rate, first and second unit both using multiple cameras ¶ Tuesday, September 3, 2002 that rate is still holding: 45 a day, at 103 feet per take, so average 5000 feet of dailies a day. Grr. That would be 550,000 feet at the end of it all… ¶ 11/23/02 it's going to be close to that: around 520,000 feet ¶ 01/23/03 It was 4900 records and 597,000 feet!

Recalculations over the course of production, as indicated by the different dates in this journal entry, show that Murch's initial estimate for the total number of records is essentially correct. But the amount of footage—nearly 600,000 feet—turns out to be even higher than he projected. "This was the most amount of film for me to handle as an editor on my own, ever." There

Technicians at Kodak Bucharest assemble processed negative film before it is transferred to videotape on a telecine machine.

The telecine machine at the Kodak lab for transferring film to videotape.

was twice as much footage on *Apocalypse Now*—1,250,000 feet, or just over 230 hours—but on that film Murch was one of three film editors working simultaneously. And post production lasted over two years.

Why does the quantity matter so much? Is it simply a fact to be marveled at, a statistic to obsess about? Not at all. As Murch later explains, "It's in my job description. I should be able to tell a director—Anthony in this case—that at this pace of shooting the assembly will be over five hours long." The length of the assembly matters because it may determine whether the director, who is responsible for delivering a film on time and on budget, fulfills his or her contractual obligations. Other crew members and production executives keep track of production costs and scheduling issues; but only the editor can predict with any certainty if the schedule for editing is accurate, given the amount of work and footage to come. Moreover, the time it takes to edit a motion picture relates, in large part, to the length of the first assembly. The more footage an editor and his or her crew have to begin with, the longer it will take them to assemble it all, and then the longer it will take to pare it all back down to a releasable length. *Cold Mountain* was originally scheduled for 26 weeks of post production in London. While still in Romania, the producers adjusted this timetable upward; in the end, post production wound up lasting 46 weeks.

At this early stage, Murch also has his eye on what he calls the "30 percent factor"—a rule of thumb he developed that deals with the relationship between the length of a film and the "core content" of the story. In general, 30 percent of a first assembly can be trimmed away without affecting the essential features of the script: all characters, action, story beats will be preserved and probably, like a good stew, enhanced by the reduction in bulk. But passing beyond the 30 percent barrier can usually be accomplished only by major structural alterations: the reduction or elimination of a character, or whole sequences—removing vital organs rather than trimming fat. "It can be done," says Murch, "and I have done it on a number of films that turned out well in the end. But it is tricky, and the outcome is not guaranteed—like open-heart surgery. The patient is put at risk, and the further beyond 30 percent you go, the greater the risk."

In the case of *Cold Mountain,* a first assembly of five hours would mean that the 30 percent barrier would be encountered when the running time had been trimmed to three and a half hours: still too long, most likely, for theatrical release. To get below that length, the prognosis is for drastic surgery—unless some solution can be found now, during production, to cut the script or change the pace of shooting—very serious considerations.

But for now it's landmark day. The workflows, patches, plug-ins, and work-arounds that Sean Cullen and DigitalFilm Tree put together finally pay off: The first *Cold Mountain* footage pops out at the end of the pipeline, digitized, on Walter's Final Cut Pro desktop.

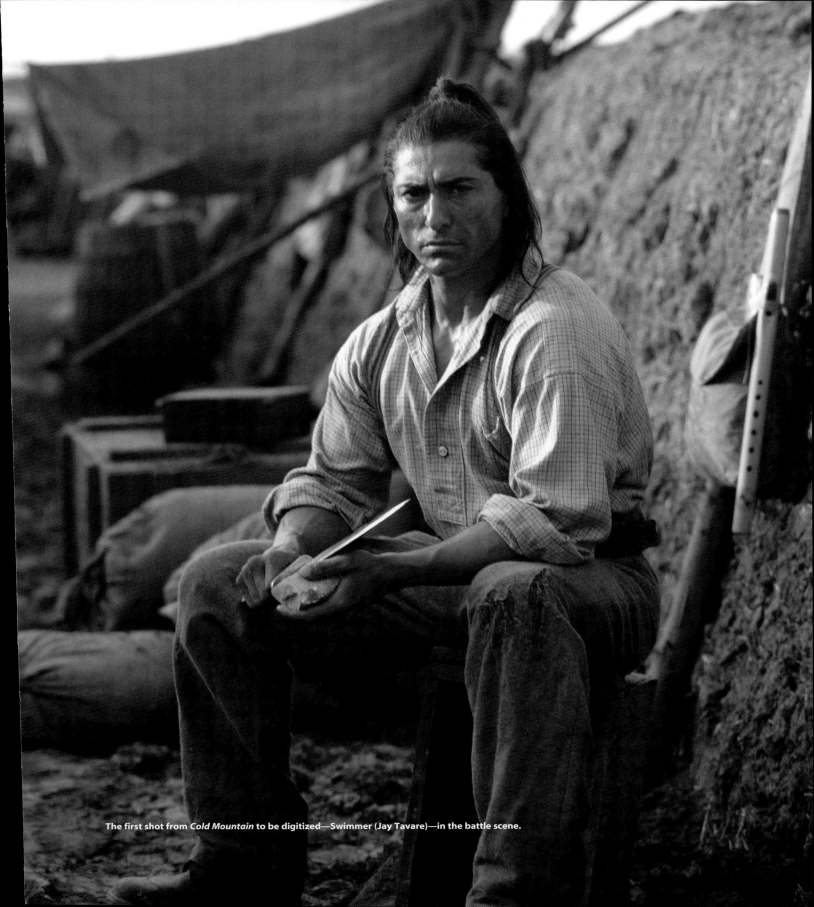

The first shot from *Cold Mountain* to be digitized—Swimmer (Jay Tavare)—in the battle scene.

First Digitize!! And we set the rate at two megabytes per second. Looking at a CU of Swimmer. It looks very good. Congratulations, we are beginning to be sort of up and running.

Once again, there isn't much time to celebrate. A movie is all about story, and the demands of story soon assume center stage. One of the Miramax executives, Bob Osher, visits the set and sits in on dailies screening. He takes note of the same troubling issue that Murch and the director of photography, John Seale, discussed earlier: will an audience understand how the Union army gets stuck in a pit they themselves created when they set off the massive explosion beneath the Confederates?

The opening shots of *Cold Mountain* show Union soldiers laying explosives under the Confederate fortifications. The huge explosion beneath the Confederate army's entrenchment momentarily buries Inman, the protagonist. The Union army's next move—a ferocious charge at the disrupted Confederate lines—occurs while a mushroom cloud rains dirt and mud down on all the fighters. It isn't easy to tell one side from the other, nor is it entirely clear that the Union's charge into the crater wasn't deliberate. How will the film be able to show events clearly enough for the audience to understand what is happening, yet not so clearly that the Union soldiers look foolish for trapping themselves? It's a proper question for Murch to have on his radar, but it won't truly be addressed until he begins cutting the scene.

Meanwhile, Murch's request to bring on a third film assistant has been approved. Final Cut provides digital film sound that can easily be played back from a portable Akai digital dubber, so location dailies will be screened using a portable Arriflex Loc-Pro projector linked to the Akai—a system that any production assistant can operate. Consequently, the money budgeted to hire a projectionist is freed up to bring Dei Reynolds to Bucharest from London. But Reynolds hasn't yet arrived and pressure mounts. Being shorthanded and under the gun, Walter works with his son and with Sean Cullen to prep film dailies. The job of ushering film through the lab, rearranging the footage in the order Anthony wants to see it, and getting it synched up with sound on the ProTools system—all in a morning—is usually handled solely by assistants. But as the footage piles up Murch must step in to help. In his journal he simply writes, "Too frantic dailies prep."

During the battle scenes, the first and second camera units are both shooting at the same time, each with up to four cameras. Plus there are five Eyemo cameras, 60-year-old refurbished hand-held movie cameras originally used during World War II. The amount of film being processed every day averages 5,000 feet, or almost one hour, though on certain days that balloons to two hours or more.

MINGHELLA ON FILMING THE BATTLE SCENE

When we were shooting, there was a moment of it being absolutely overwhelming. We were right down in the crater, hand-holding the cameras with a thousand people milling around us, and for a second I got some sense of what it must be like in a war when you can't hear, you can't think, and you can't see, and you're just falling. It was 105 degrees, and the actors wore prickling wool uniforms and were just passing out. There's nowhere to go, nowhere to hide. I thought if I could get it right— obviously I'm not noted for my action sequences—it would be indelible in the film.

—from an interview in the February/March issue of *Written By*, published by the Writer's Guild of America

Inman (Jude Law) buried after the explosion underneath the Confederate's position at Petersburg.

Minghella requested that the dailies be broken down into "selects" and "non-selects"—select rolls being made up of just one good take from each camera setup, in shooting order. This gives him the flexibility (after a long day's shooting) to see a short but essentially complete selection of dailies—20 minutes of film on an average day. But the non-selects (the other forty minutes of dailies) have to be available, just in case. A camera setup is literally that. If the camera is moved—or even a lens changed—for the purpose of getting a closeup angle of what was just shot from a medium angle, for example, that is considered a different setup, and given a new identifying number. The actor's dialogue and movements may be exactly the same, but the shot is regarded as distinct.

Preparing a "selects roll" that samples each setup adds an extra side-step to the preparation of dailies. The lab processes and prints in "camera rolls," in the order footage actually goes through the camera. So the assistants must break down the film print from each camera roll into individual shots, pull out the proper ones, splice these together for projecting dailies, and then find the sound to go with them.

The day after Murch's Final Cut Pro system finally receives its first digitized material, ready to cut, just when the road ahead seems clear, the external world intrudes with some disheartening news. Walter unexpectedly receives a long letter from Will Stein, the senior executive at Apple managing the Professional Applications Development group ("Pro Apps"), which includes Final Cut Pro.

Stein first acknowledges the July 7 email message Murch sent to Steve Jobs updating him about how well everything seemed to be going on *Cold Mountain*. Stein writes that editing *Cold Mountain* on FCP, "has a lot of visibility inside Apple, and we are very excited to see Final Cut Pro proposed for such a significant production." Stein looks forward to Murch's "feedback" about working with FCP.

Stein also responds to Murch's earlier communication with Brian Meaney about director Minghella being "a little surprised" at Apple's "lack of enthusiasm in the *Cold Mountain* project." Stein writes that Apple's Final Cut Pro team has "a long-term strategy to push into the high-end film market only when our product and support team are ready to provide a great experience to the feature film production community. What may appear to be a lack of enthusiasm," he writes, "is actually concern over the quality of experience" given FCP's missing change list feature, possible rough edges in trim mode, and the issue of OS X not supporting SAN (shared area network) storage—linking editing stations to a central hard drive array through a fiber connection. "Speaking for the team," he writes, "we would rather encourage you to be a happy partner later than a less-than-happy partner now," a turn of phrase that had a somewhat ominous ring, given that production was already underway.

Young Walter Murch prepares rolls for a screening of dailies.

Stein goes on to write that advances and improvements to FCP are still in progress. "Based on our project plans," he continues, "and what I understand to be your production schedule, there is **almost no chance** [Stein's emphasis] that any of these changes will make it into a stable and shipping version of Final Cut Pro or Cinema Tools in time to be used on *Cold Mountain*."

Then Stein says that if Murch is "reasonably confident that our applications (and third-party tools), as they are shipping now, will be sufficient for your needs (and you are looking for that 'early adopter' type of experience)—I will be very happy to work with you to extend our support of your project. The types of collaborative efforts you outlined in your message to Steve are exactly the type of thing we look for to help drive Final Cut Pro to the next level in the Hollywood community. I hope all is going well at the shoot, and look forward to hearing from you. Best regards, Will Stein."

Murch genuinely believed that once he was "in country" and actually using Final Cut, Apple would come through and work directly with him on *Cold Mountain*. With this letter Murch knows that door is now closed. Later he describes feeling like a trapeze artist caught off-guard when the master of ceremonies announces, with no warning, that tonight's performance will be done without a net. There's nothing else to do but swallow hard, trust one's instincts, and not look down. The show must go on!

Instead of agreeing they've reached the end of the road, Murch writes back to Will Stein reiterating their common interests, while also acknowledging the current incomplete state of Final Cut's version 3.

COLD MOUNTAIN • KODAK • BUCHAREST

TO: Will Stein
FROM: Walter Murch
DATE: July 26, 2002
RE: Apple Cold Mountain

Dear Will Stein:

Good hearing from you, and I'm sorry we couldn't have linked up back in June.

Thank you for your encouragement and your words of caution. We are fully aware that there will be no shippable fixes for FCP by early next year, and we have – or will have by the time we need them – our own solutions for the outstanding concerns, such as Change Lists and OMF export. The smaller issues – such as 4 hour project length, asymmetric trim, ink & key number fields, etc. – I would categorize as desirable but non-essential.

We actually welcome the current state of FCP, in a way, because we hope that some of what we learn on this film can perhaps be integrated into later versions of the software. In fact, other than the excellence of FCP, one of the central reasons for embarking down this road, as I hoped I indicated in my letters to Brian and Steve, is to promote a creative exchange between you at Apple/FCP and us on Cold Mountain.

I am intensely interested in furthering the evolution of cinema post-production, and I see it taking the FCP path. I am, and have always been, in my thirty-seven years of working in film, an "early adopter" personality (to use your words) and fully prepared for the smooth as well as the sometimes rough patches that are part of the territory.

At any rate, we are "in country" in Romania with four FCP stations, happily digitizing and working away – Cold Mountain started shooting two weeks ago – and I would like to reiterate my belief that we both have things to offer each other, and hope that this project can be the field on which the exchange takes place.

Best wishes from sunny/rainy Bucharest,

Walter Murch

The same day Murch writes his response to Stein, he finally gets underway editing *Cold Mountain* using Final Cut Pro.

July 26, 2002, Murch's Journal

Response to Will Stein.

First really prowling around on FPC and although slightly awkward, there are some good things. I am keeping lists of things to improve.

Feeling weird—just overwhelmed by things in general—that slightly levitated feel I remember from the first day shooting on OZ after I was brought back on again, in the tower room.

Murch's Final Cut Pro workstation in Bucharest.

On July 27 Stein writes back with a follow-up: "All required cautions now out of the way, I can reiterate that we are very excited by the project, and will try to be actively involved in smoothing the way for you where possible... Brian [Meaney] and Bill Hudson will also be the leads in terms of organizing technical support where required during your production."

In Murch's view, Stein's initial July 26 letter was the fallback position. Murch reflects a year later: "If, say, two months down the road, everything blew up and we were running around with our hair on fire in Romania, Apple would be able to pull this letter out and say, 'Listen, we told them this was our position, and they went ahead anyway.' It was written as a documented record in case there were troubles down the road. *Full Frontal*, which was also edited in Final Cut Pro, was a qualified experience on both sides; neither party enjoyed it the way they had hoped, and yet that was a low-profile, low-budget film with a very quick turnaround—two weeks of shooting and only a few weeks of post production. *Cold Mountain* is a different animal and much more visible, so if there was a calamity of some kind, Final Cut's reputation would be damaged. It would not be their fault but nonetheless they'd be damaged. So it made a lot of people at Apple nervous."

The Stein letter means the company isn't going to partner with Murch in any official capacity. Murch had been hoping Apple would be a companion to climb *Cold Mountain*—together they might take Final Cut Pro to a higher level, working in a mutually supportive way. Murch offered Apple an applied laboratory, so to speak, for testing and improving more advanced uses of its application, and at the end of the process, a high-visibility film Apple could point to as a success. He assumed Apple would openly embrace the chance to put the application to task, with the company stepping in to provide needed solutions and improvements as they arose. He imagined a give-and-take, we're-in-this-together spirit that defined Murch's association with Ramy Katrib and DigitalFilm Tree. Instead, Murch will go up the mountain with his own team: Sean, the assistants, DigitalFilm Tree, and Aurora. Apple will stay at base camp, wish them well, and occasionally send up a few supplies and fervent prayers.

Still, Murch doesn't give up on Apple. Even if FCP is not yet fully developed to accommodate the needs of a major feature film and doesn't have all the functions he'd like, Murch is becoming a fan.

July 27, 2002, Murch's Journal

More working with FCP: in a sketch-pad mode, understanding the clips, sequences, projects, etc. Navigating around the controls, which are good—sometimes very good—and sometimes just different and sometimes not as good (no asymmetric trimming). I am keeping a running list of things to send to Brian and Bill.

This dance between Murch and Apple will continue until Cold Mountain *is finished.*

This dance between Murch and Apple, a tango of overlapping interests, will continue until *Cold Mountain* is finished. Coming as they do from two different worlds, the creative and the corporate, the editor and the computer company move in different rhythms. Walter is drawn to the Final Cut Pro application and is willing to use it, even in its present imperfect state. Apple looks at a high-profile project and wants to proceed cautiously, lest its new baby be running before it safely walks. Nevertheless, when Murch writes to Ramy back in Los Angeles about his exchange with Will Stein, he reveals an unwavering optimism, a belief that the natural symbiosis between *Cold Mountain* and Apple is self-evident and might still prevail.

> **Date:** July 28, 2002
> **From:** Walter Murch
> **To:** Ramy Katrib
>
> Will S. has opened the door a crack, and I am writing him today to tell him that I would like him (Apple) to work with DFT and give you what you need to proceed. Our main focus, as I outlined in my letter to Will, should be change lists and non-embedded OMF export (for sound files). I am happy with how this has all turned out—perhaps a month late, but the essential fact that we are in Bucharest and working with FCP on Cold Mountain, already two weeks into production, is a major "convincer" of the seriousness of our intent. Sydney Pollack just arrived today, and is happy that we are using FCP. He has it on his laptop.

> **Date:** July 29, 2002
> **From:** Walter Murch
> **To:** Ramy Katrib
>
> Jim Foreman [Aurora's and DFT's man in Bucharest] left this morning. All worked out very well and I think he enjoyed himself. We kept a clipping of his hair to bring near the hard drives and the CPUs if something begins to go wrong—a kind of editorial voodoo.

July 31, 2002, Murch's Journal

Article in Herald Tribune about nerve systems. We have two: a thick fast fiber, giving us the 'hard' information about when, where, impact, etc. and another, thin slow fiber system giving us emotional information about the nature of the touch, love, etc. The signals for this second system are processed in the visual part of the cortex .

Don't forget little people for the monitor here. Tomorrow.

The "little people" are another one of Walter's handmade edit room tools. These are paper cutouts in the shapes of a man and a woman that he affixes to each side of his large screening monitor. They are his way of dealing with the problem of scale.

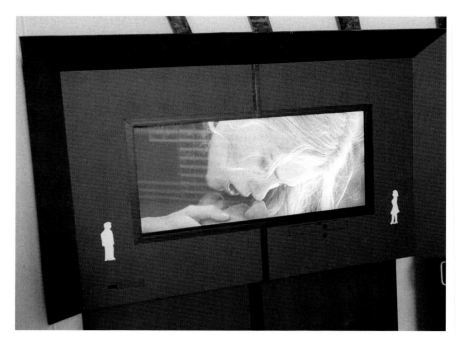

Murch's "little people" next to his viewing monitor remind him that this image will eventually be 13 feet tall.

As an editor, Murch must remember that images in the edit room are only 1/240 the square footage of what the audience will eventually see on a 30-foot-wide screen. The large TV Murch uses for viewing—the "client" monitor—is masked off to the proper aspect ratio, (the width 2.35 times the height in the case of CinemaScope, the wide-screen projection format for *Cold Mountain*). But it's still easy to forget the size of projected film, which can trick an editor into pacing a film too quickly, or using too many close-ups—styles more akin to television. The eye rapidly apprehends the relatively small, low-detail images on a TV. Large-scale faces help hold the attention of an audience sitting in a living room with lots of distractions and ambient light. But in movies, images are larger than life and more detailed, so the opposite is true. The eye needs time to peruse the movie screen and take it all in. But for many months, except for projected film dailies, the film editor works at TV scale. The solution for Murch is to have these two human cutouts stand sentry on his monitor, reminding him of the film's eventual huge proportions.

August 1, 2002, Murch's Journal

August first—new month. Let it be blessed with good luck and productivity.
Amen. Cutting "soldiers" tape.

Problems arise almost immediately as Murch begins to use Final Cut to actually begin editing footage on *Cold Mountain*. Never one to panic, he casually mentions this at the end of an email to Ramy, almost as an afterthought: "We are still getting the occasional stutter in the Canvas screen, so if you have any brainwaves in that department, let us know. All best wishes from Bucharest. Walter." The Canvas is the screen in the FCP interface that shows the results of an edit. Those faltering images are annoying, even if the edited material isn't itself flawed.

DFT and its network get to work searching for solutions to the stuttering image problem among software engineers, developers, and Final Cut users. The problem makes its way from Bucharest to Zed Saeed at DFT in Los Angeles and then to Michigan, headquarters for Aurora, the company that makes the Igniter add-on card for digitizing video into FCP. The issue turns out to be simple to resolve; it's not unlike the set-up problems any computer user has with new equipment, setting preferences and defaults to work optimally with a system's associated hardware and software. All computer monitors have settings for resolution (the size and density of the screen pixels), brightness, and color depth (number of colors). Aurora suggests that Jim Foreman, who is providing on-site tech support, reset the pixel resolution on Murch's monitor and change the color depth to "thousands of colors" instead of "millions of colors." That does the trick; the stutter goes away.

The Mac OS 9 Display control panel for setting numbers of colors for the monitor. Until Murch reset this to "thousands" he had problems with image stutter.

The next hurdle that shows up isn't so easy to get over. Sean reports to Ramy that when Walter works with color-corrected digital video footage, he can't get his preferred edit-on-the-fly technique to work accurately. If he taps the spacebar (stop), or the K or Enter keys (pause) while watching a scene play back on the monitor, the scene plays on for several frames, instead of stopping immediately. This negates Murch's intuitive frame-marking method.

On July 30, Walt Shires weighs in on the problem of frame-accurate stopping with an email to Sean. The news isn't good: "The problem you are referring to has been a common problem with FCP. There is a certain mount of CPU time necessary for FCP to process the keystroke for stop and then make the call to QuickTime to stop the video playback. I suspect that when working with real-time color correction the load on the CPU is causing the stop playback to occur later than usual. Unfortunately, there is really no way around it." This function was one of Walter and Sean's deal-breakers when they first went to see DigitalFilm Tree about Final Cut Pro. Murch continues working, however, bypassing the color-correction mode until it can be fixed at some later date. The telecine transfers of the film to video, done by a Romanian technician just down the hall at Kodak, are extremely good, and generally no extra color correction is needed. With confidence in Sean and DigitalFilm Tree, tolerance for the ups and downs of technology, and a deep-seated faith that things work out eventually, Murch is just satisfied to be underway.

MAKING IT WORK

Robert Grahamjones: "After [Walter] got settled in Romania, I got emails from him saying everything was going really well. He was really happy with the things he was able to do. What I was hearing back here, from friends and colleagues in the film business, was 'I wonder what his assistants are saying now?' Because they're the ones who have to make it work as a system."

Finished the "soldiers" tape and put music on it, gave it to Huw [Cold Mountain liaison to the Romanian army]. My first cut sequence on FCP! worked out well Anthony viewed the tape, and liked it—"good to see some Walter cutting"— thought that the interaction between Oakley and Inman is an indication of how it will be. He liked the music—wondered if I had come upon that decision myself. I told him Dianne had told me what he was thinking.

Walter's August 2 Journal entry reveals something very telling about relationships and communications within the *Cold Mountain* film community. Minghella is much admired and respected by his cast and crew, in part because he creates a working environment that is open, creative, and collegial. Many high-caliber people keep working with him—in front of and behind the camera—because Minghella encourages contributions from all quarters, and conversations about creative choices, which isn't the rule among many film directors. The collaborative environment, his directorial sensibilities, and the kinds of material he finds attractive are reasons some of the best people in the film business stick with him on one film after another: cinematographer John Seale, costume designer Ann Roth, composer Gabriel Yared, top producers— and Walter Murch. Minghella encourages his film family to engage in cross-talk and to share ideas and information even if he's not always aware of what's under discussion.

Director of photography John Seale (behind the camera) on the set of *Cold Mountain*.

Screening all unscreened material. Trying to catch up

Sean still needs to find a solution to the audio file conversion problem that arose before the Final Cut Pro systems arrived from Los Angeles. This bottleneck costs him precious hours syncing up sound in time for the next day's screening of dailies. Ramy reports to Sean that he is trying to work something out with AVTransfer, the company in Australia. Sean writes back to Ramy, pleased that DFT is putting out another call for help on sound: "Thank you, thank you. We are in this weekend, catching up and lying low. Walter continues to be a happy camper, so at least we're doing something right."

Two unsolved problems remain with the Final Cut Pro workflow: 1) converting sound files from .wav format (required by the telecine in the Kodak lab) into a format that can be recognized by FCP and ProTools; and 2) Walter's inability to get accurate results using his preferred edit-on-the-fly technique on color-corrected clips. Two longer-range problems are on the back burner: getting audio files from Final Cut Pro out to ProTools for sound editing; and getting reliable change lists to conform the 35mm picture when the film workprint is cut and recut over the course of post production.

On the other hand, by early August, the DVD authoring feature of Final Cut has been put into operation, and copies of the dailies are made into DVDs

Murch works on the battle sequence.

and sent to Anthony, Sydney Pollack, and the other producers. Minghella starts building a folder containing a disc with each day's work. This means he can review shots anytime and anywhere using his PowerBook.

A few days later, as the battle sequence Murch puts together reaches 16 minutes, he suspects another long-term problem may be lurking: FCP seems to have a hard time ingesting long sequences—a concern that came up in Los Angeles but was never fully tested. It's taking over a minute for each version of the battle sequence to load into FCP. Since Murch is working with several versions at the same time, "that means 3-4 minutes of video prep as the FCP unit is firing up," he writes Ramy. Is this a smoldering fire that might burst into flames? Will Final Cut be able to load a five-hour assembly when the time comes, three months from now?

On this basic function, Avid systems work on a completely opposite principle from Final Cut Pro. When Avid is loading a project, regardless of its length— an entire two-hour film, say—Avid only loads small sections of media, the idea being that Avid provides the editor with just the media he or she needs for the part of a show that is under construction. Normally an Avid editor adjusts this setting so the machine loads a single three- or four-minute chunk of digitized video and sound at a time. Within that section, operations such as edits, trims, saves, etc. happen quickly and efficiently. However, if he or she wants to jump to material that exists outside that short swatch, the Avid editor will have to wait on the machine. Final Cut Pro has no similar adjustable setting to control the amount of media the editor wants to load; it simply loads an entire sequence from beginning to end. Murch knows this is a structural problem that goes to the basic engineering of FCP that may eventually get fixed. So he asks Ramy, "Any procedural suggestions in the meantime?"

There is no immediate solution forthcoming from DFT, but Walter remains unruffled. In fact, he flies to Paris three days later to meet Aggie and celebrate their 37th anniversary over a four-day weekend. On Murch's return, he learns that Mihai Bogdan, the Romanian driver assigned to the edit crew, has hepatitis. The whole edit group must get gamma globulin shots, on top of the anti-rabies vaccine recommended for Romania.

Murch was happy with Final Cut Pro's jog wheel, which moves images backward or forward at varying speeds.

Murch gets back in contact with Ramy. Before reminding him about the FCP load-in problem, Walter delivers an upbeat report: "FCP performed very well. I am particularly happy with the jog wheel, which is the most 'film-like' digital scrolling device I have experienced. I can really convince myself that I am looking at film going backward and forward at various speeds." But the problem of how FCP handles media has just cropped up in another function. When Murch performed a routine deletion—removing an unused empty soundtrack from his Timeline, the graphic representation for a sequence—

and FCP took 45 seconds to execute the command. What was a smoke alarm is now a bell-ringer. Walter knows if such a simple action takes that much time (it doesn't even involve actual digitized video material) he might be in for some *really* long waits once he tries to load hours of material into Final Cut's memory.

Walt Shires follows up for DFT by email. He tells Murch that Final Cut Pro plays back an edited sequence by building a virtual movie (called a .moov) that is held in its memory cache, not written onto a hard drive. "You are right," Shires writes, "the longer and more complex the edited sequence gets, the longer it will take to build the .moov. The length of time it takes to organize the .moov gets exponentially longer as the sequence gets more complex. Final Cut builds the whole movie at once so you can review any portion at any time." One can feel Shire's anxiety on Walter's behalf: "There is a trade-off. Perhaps good, perhaps not. Hope your experience continues to be a good one. Walt."

Murch appreciates Shire's explanation, but he is blunt: "This is the one aspect of FCP that I have my eye on as being a potential troublemaker down the line—the [first assembly of the] film will eventually be over four hours long [over five, as it turns out]—the wait is going to become increasingly frustrating." Murch says this issue is high on his list of "musts" for Apple to work out in subsequent FCP versions. It should be able to use buffers, like a computer printer, or an online media player, to absorb chunks of data and spool it out as needed. "Certainly," Murch continues, "something as procedurally brainless as deleting an empty audio track should not take 45 seconds to accomplish. Otherwise, all is well. How are we moving on the change lists and OMF output fronts?"

Aside from fretting about the capacity of his editing system Murch must attend to standard editor's duties: informing Anthony and the producers about "negative scratches—not too serious;" providing notes to help guide the chapel-building scene which is being re-shot due to weather; and an email to producer Bill Horberg about the lead actors. "Two worry beads for me: Ada's accent (nasal, hard to understand, very few consonants) and Inman's hat (not cool, like Oakley's)—it makes him skulk, if worn too low on the brow, too Hobbit-like. A girl would wonder about a guy who wore a hat like that. And a guy would wonder about a girl with a voice like that. Hmm... I have talked to Anthony about these things."

Anthony has a chat with the dialogue coach. Afterward, when he screens new dailies of Ada, Murch's concerns about Kidman's accent and speaking style are allayed. As for the hat Jude Law wears, Horberg writes, "Hats are Ann Roth's domain—tread there at your own personal risk!!!"

Romanian crew member Mihai Bogdan who was promoted from driver for the edit crew to syncing up dailies.

MURCH EMAIL TO MINGHELLA AUGUST 14, 2002

I am struggling a bit, just with the amount of material and keeping all the other pots on the boil, but stirring away gaily.

Finished the battle "work-in-progress" and sent it off to Anthony with the dailies. Let's see what his reaction is. Screened some dailies to catch up. Need to screen two days worth each day at least to get up to speed. When will Sean be ready to give me more scenes I can cut!!

Murch is impatient. Although he has begun cutting the battle scene, he's ready to do more. And footage is really beginning to accumulate. Getting started two weeks late is having its effect. The equipment from DigitalFilm Tree arrived safe and sound on July 15, the first day of principal photography. But in Murch's ideal universe it should have been in Romania in time to be plugged in, tweaked, and operating—all set to go for first day of dailies. Sean Cullen later describes how restless Murch felt as Cullen put the system through all the necessary tests, methodically taking a piece of edited film through the entire system: "I still had to wring out the system and then wring out our workflow. This meant digitizing material, cutting a sample together on another machine (to simulate Walter's), making tapes and outputting cut lists to check that the whole system would work in post. Walter got to see *me* cutting material together but *he* couldn't start yet." To allow Murch to begin editing something—the battle scene—Cullen gave him a series of one-hour QuickTime movie files. Each QuickTime movie represented one complete reel

Assistant Sean Cullen preparing digitized film footage for Murch to cut.

of film telecined to videotape. Even though these one-hour QuickTime files let Murch get started, it would turn out later that they were the cause of his frustration with the long load-in time he was now experiencing on Final Cut.

Up in Brasov, on the set, Minghella looks at the DVD on his laptop with the battle scene Murch has edited. He sends an email:

Date:	8/17/02 9:14 PM
From:	Anthony Minghella
To:	Walter Murch

Thanks, Walter

just had some time to look at the battle sequence, for which many thanks. It has, of course, your beautiful taste and touch, and is encouraging. I hate myself, as you would expect, and my failings, and I also see how much we will have to do to get the sequence right, and how much I have ahead to make the film work between that stuff and what I'm doing now. I can't really look at it now with a sane eye, and - naturally - mourn what isn't there yet as much as I do what is already there, with its frailties. But I also can't wait to stop collecting the material and sit with you in Hampstead and begin the fun.

thanks, dear friend
from rainy Brasov
ant

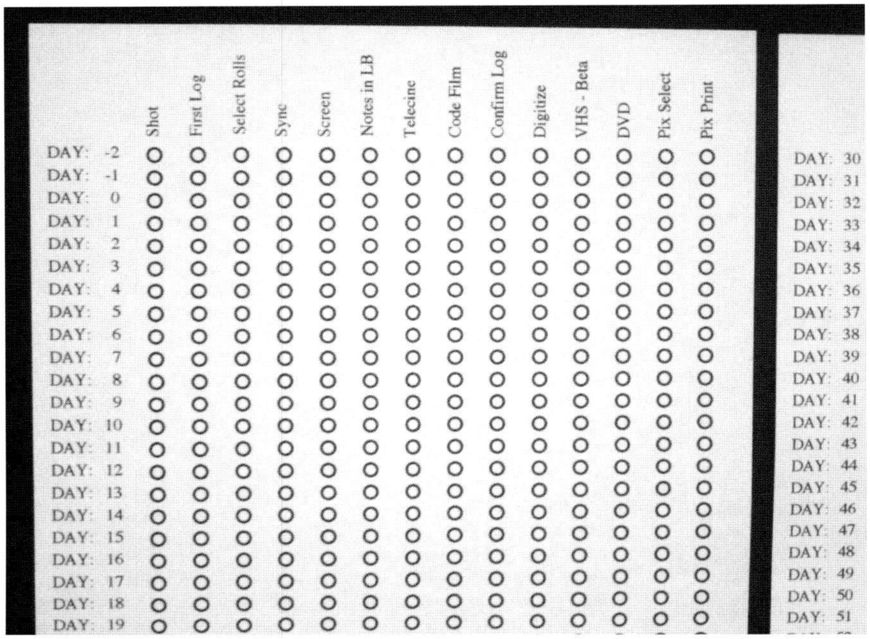

Cullen's workflow for getting shot film onto Murch's desktop for editing.

"Anthony sent a sad email after looking at the sketch of the battle," Walter writes in his Journal on August 18. "I thought somewhere it would make him happy, but it just seemed to depress him more."

If Murch's spirit is dampened by Minghella's response, it doesn't last long. The next day Sean solves the problem with loading media. On advice from DFT—"Don't put your entire project in one FCP file"—Sean breaks the media down into bite-sized pieces for Final Cut Pro to digest.

August 19, 2002, Murch's Journal

Hooray! Clips are in FCP. And when a sequence is opened up, it does so 150 times faster. An hour-long sequence opens in two seconds as opposed to four minutes. Why? Probably because the sequence is assembling from short clips of shots rather than long clips of tapes. A huge relief, that it functions so well now—that was a thundercloud bearing down on me as I thought of the problems further along in the process.

"This was a huge turning point, in retrospect," Murch says afterward. "It wouldn't have been possible to keep going if it hadn't worked out this way." Without this workaround, Murch would be waiting longer and longer—up to a half hour or more—for his project to load into Final Cut Pro as the assembly grew in size. That kind of delay would be unacceptable in the rush to finish a major motion picture.

The problem with large amounts of media and Final Cut Pro wasn't an issue on previous feature films, such as *The Rules of Attraction* and *Full Frontal*, because, according to Ramy, "they got used to it." As with many off-the-shelf features in FCP, editors simply accept the default settings, so to speak. But Murch wasn't going to be satisfied waiting on the equipment. Sean ran with DFT's suggestion by making separate QuickTime movies for each "flash-to-flash" take. These are discrete camera takes marked at the beginning by one or two frames of unusable bright images when the camera starts. The motor isn't yet up to speed, so the film gets overexposed for a brief moment. A similar bright flash occurs at the end of a take when the camera is turned off and two or three frames of film are overexposed as the motor slows to a stop. By using a QuickTime movie for each flash-to-flash segment, and then linking all the adjacent QuickTime movies back together, FCP could play them seamlessly. The whole equaled its parts. Walter's faith is rewarded after all. There was a better method for loading media; it was just a matter of discovering it.

Murch had started projecting the total amount of footage to expect on *Cold Mountain* one week after principal photography began. His yardstick then was the average length of each take compared to its projected length when those script pages were read aloud. At that point, take timing exceeded read-script timing by an expansion factor of 1.38. He projected the first assembly to be just over 3½ hours.

MURCH'S CALCULATIONS TIMING *COLD MOUNTAIN*	
Script Pages/ Timing	129/ 2:09
WM 1st script reading	2:48
WM 2nd script reading	3:05
Script supervisor reading	2:20
Average script timing	2:44
On-set timing (master shots)	3:37
Expansion of on-set timing over average script timing	1.38

Now, four weeks later, Murch can use a more precise tool to make his estimate—an expansion factor that uses the relationship between the timing of an edited scene and the timing of that scene when it was read aloud.

Scene 12 all cut together is 144 seconds long, or exactly twice what it timed out at. So the first assembly of this film could be five and a half hours long. Read this in five months and tell me what happened.

For Murch, this is further proof that *Cold Mountain* is going to have a long first assembly—longer than either *English Patient* or *The Talented Mr. Ripley.* He had hoped that after the first three weeks of filming the 12-camera action scenes of the Battle of the Crater, *Cold Mountain*'s expansion factor would shrink as Minghella moved into more conventional dialogue scenes. But the early indications are that this is not happening: the expansion rate stays the same.

This means that the assembly will most likely be over five hours, and that consequently the 30 percent barrier—and its implications of open-heart surgery—will indeed have to be crossed somewhere down the line in London, during editing.

The ultimate scheduling question is: Can he and Minghella get the film edited in time for a Christmas, 2003 release? But the high expansion rate has short-term consequences as well. Can the assistants prepare dailies for Minghella and the producers on a timely basis? Does Murch have enough time to screen and take notes on all the footage? Will he be able to prepare a first assembly by the time production wraps in mid-December? With all these demands, will Murch also be able to have a creative connection with the material so he can adequately advise Minghella about story or character issues while still in production?

The question of keeping up with the amount of shot footage, and the inevitability of crossing the 30 percent threshold both lie on top of the fact that Murch, Cullen, and DigitalFilm Tree have just shaken out a new editing platform with several key functions that are still unproven. That should certainly be enough. But there are other, more unwelcome surprises.

August 27, 2002, Murch's Journal

Driver crashed on way back from Brashov and the negative scattered all over the road. All ok, though—the cans didn't open up.

To be followed by agreeable arrivals.

August 30, 2002, Murch's Journal

Aggie arrives today she is just getting on the plane as I write this!

Aggie arrived! At 6.30—great to see her—she brought gifts for everyone (tea and Marmite) and everyone loved to see her. Especially me.

At the end of August, the *Cold Mountain* production moves to North Carolina for three weeks to shoot various scenes there: Inman's walk from sea to mountains; the hospital and the peanut seller; Veaseytown; the ferry crossing; and Veasey's discovery of the saw. Murch and the edit crew stay in Romania, so this is a chance to get caught up with logging, digitizing, and other housekeeping duties, since it will be two weeks before dailies footage from the U.S. arrives in Bucharest.

Minghella sends Murch an email report from the U.S.:

Date: 9/2/02 4:04 PM
From: Anthony Minghella
To: Walter Murch
Subject: Charleston

…where, apparently, the drought they're suffering is about to be solved by a huge tropical storm! I am plagued.

Happy to get some dailies on DVD although they don't all play well. Kiss interrupted by skipping disk.

[*Cold Mountain* author Charles] Frazier saw some stuff and seemed cheered.

Should I try and get a close-up of Butcher lying dead on the ground in the night raid? He lives in Charleston.

Having a free day here for Labor Day after an interminable journey immediately followed by a day's scouting. Relentless.

Very prone to depression on this movie. Which was also the case shooting The English Patient. What is it? Why is it? Just tired, I suppose. But trying to find a way to take pleasure from the challenge of collecting the material and not just to be ground down.

Love to you. Very glad you're out there helping
xa

From: Walter Murch
Subject: Re: Charleston
Date: 9/2/02 4:41 PM
To: Anthony Minghella

Caro Ant:

Coraggio! The material is going together very well. Aggie was here over the weekend and very moved and impressed with what she saw. Muriel and Ann as well.

The coming into the world of the new is never easy because there are no guidelines.

The Furies are jealous of such beauty and attack with weather.

Perseverance Furthers.

KYPU

Etc.

or as Stein put it in "Lord Jim":

"A man that is born falls into a dream like a man who falls into the sea. If he
tries to climb out into the air as inexperienced people endeavor to do, he
drowns—nicht wahr? … No! I tell you! The way is to the destructive element
submit yourself, and with the exertions of your hands and feet in the water
make the deep, deep sea keep you up. So if you ask me—how to be? …
I will tell you! … In the destructive element immerse."

Butcher … Hmm … You could, but I think a wild line would do more to
identify him. In the hurry of escaping, and him on the ground at night, I don't
think that we would know who we were looking at.

Your pal in Bucharest,
W. xox

September 2, 2002, Murch's Journal

*Sad email from Ant about woes—tropical storm Edouard is on its way to meet
them.*

Just then, an unexpected producing crisis strikes that will demand Murch's
attention. Whether for its own financial reasons or because of the size of
the total budget, MGM pulls out of its financing deal for *Cold Mountain*.
Miramax, left holding a half-empty bag, needs to find a partner with $40
million to complete the movie.

September 10, 2002, Murch's Journal

*Anthony wants to make a demo DVD of key scenes from the film for extra
financing. Can I do this somehow in the time available? Can you give me help?*

ORIGINS OF THE
COLD MOUNTAIN PROJECT

Cold Mountain originated as a United Artists/MGM motion picture. The
initial producers, Ron Yerxa and Albert Berger (Bona Fide Productions), took
the book to Mirage Enterprises, the company partnered by Sydney Pollack
and Minghella, for Pollack to consider directing. Pollack wanted Minghella
to direct. The two entities connected with Lindsay Doran at United Artists/
MGM, who'd worked with Pollack on previous pictures. Meanwhile *Cold
Mountain* had become a best-seller and a hot property. The Bona Fide/
Mirage/United Artists group bid for the film rights in an auction among

several producers, including actor Brad Pitt's company. Author Charles Frazier liked what Minghella said in their phone conversation about how he'd adapt and realize the novel for screen, and the Bona Fide/Mirage group won the rights with their $1.5 million offer. Harvey Weinstein, Miramax co-chairman, loved the story and the screenplay, so Miramax Films came on as a co-producing distributor, committing itself to 50 percent financing of the $80 million project. All was going along as planned until MGM executives decided that weather conditions and other difficulties were sending costs uncontrollably higher, and backed out.

Murch and Minghella had been through this kind of thing before. It's not that unusual for major studio films, like their low-budget independent cousins, to have last-minute fiscal crises. Minghella's first picture with Miramax, *The English Patient*, started off with just such drama. Fox Studios put up production financing after producer Saul Zaentz had developed the project to the takeoff point. As crew and cast were assembling in Italy, and sets were being built, Fox got cold feet and pulled out. Minghella asked the cast and crew not to leave, he was that confident in the project's viability. Minghella and Zaentz quickly shopped the project around, got Harvey Weinstein to put up the $30 million budget, and Minghella was shooting two weeks later.

The only benefit of MGM pulling out of *Cold Mountain* at this late date is there is some film footage in the can, and it can be shown to attract interest. So Miramax, through Minghella, asks Murch to cut together a promotional sequence—a selling tool with sample scenes to attract a new studio partner. Murch gets right to work and makes another footage calculation:

September 11, 2002, Murch's Journal

Estimate Length:
Of the scenes I have cut together so far, forgetting the battle = 34.45
These were estimated to be = 18.14
So expansion rate = 1.9
For an estimated 2.48 length x 1.9 = 5.20.
Five hours and twenty minutes…..
How can I best break the news to Anthony? For I must…

One week later Murch completes the first draft of a 25-minute sample sequence on DVD. And with a memo to the files he reminds himself about taking useful editing notes—never to forget that lesson of rediscovering the alternate line reading, "He'd kill *us* if he had the chance," from *The Conversation*.

September 20, 2002, Murch's Journal

*In taking editing notes the skill is to think that every line reading might have
a context in which it could be good. Imagine the cuts, and the good might lie
right next to the bad. Don't under any circumstances write off a take as being
throughout no good. If you must, then say WHY it is no good. This sharpens your
perception as well as being a good reference later on.*

Murch put scenes together in conjunction with each other for the first time in
cutting the sample DVD. Now, by editing actual scenes, the expansion factor
is no longer theoretical. How will he ever bring the film in with a releasable
running time? Working under the stress of a deadline to finish the sample
DVD, Murch gets more comfortable with Final Cut Pro, and like Minghella
and the producers, also contemplates wholesale scene removals.

September 22, 2002, Murch's Journal

Left eye seeing double.

*Where can script be cut: Inman start on his journey faster, and the area around
Maddy, Junior redux, Sarah. Sarah could go if you were being brutal. Feel more
and more comfortable with Final Cut, especially since QuicKeys can work with it.
Make more use of duplicated keys and the f keys.*

"Junior redux" is a scene Minghella added to the screenplay late in the game.
On his journey back to Cold Mountain Inman meets up with Reverend Veasey
(Phillip Seymour Hoffman). The two fugitives take shelter with Junior, a
backwoods moonshiner with questionable motives and a house full of sirens.
Junior uses these available women to lure Inman and Veasey into his trap:
turning Inman and Veasey over to the Home Guard for a bounty. In the
added scene, Inman returns to Junior's farm after his encounter with Maddy,
and kills Junior in revenge, retrieving his LeMats pistol and the book Ada gave
him. Faced with the fact that the first assembly is likely to be over five hours
long, with all the attending financial, scheduling, and editing consequences,
Minghella decides to abandon the Junior killing scene, and it is not filmed.

Meanwhile, executives at Miramax see the DVD with the sample scenes and
send word back to Murch through producer Bill Horberg that they are happy.
Already there is a feeling at the studio that Renée Zellweger's performance as
Ruby is dazzling, that she will be an important element in the film's success,
and that Murch should adjust the sample reels accordingly.

September 25, 2002, Murch's Journal

*Anthony came to cutting rooms [on his return from filming in the US] and liked
what he saw—the cut footage and the facility. A refuge. He thought that I had
put together a lot of stuff, despite that it seems to me that I haven't. That funny
perspective we have of what we do. Anthony finishes each day thinking that he
hasn't gotten anything—I remember it well from Return to Oz.*

Renée Zellweger as Ruby in *Cold Mountain*.

October 5, 2002, Murch's Journal

Call from Bill H. about Tape for MMX. They want to include more Renée and have less battle, keep it at 25 minutes. He said Anthony would phone.

At last, the Final Cut Pro system is running smoothly. The hardware, software, and workflow hums along; footage from the North Carolina shoot is screened and logged; the DVD demo is out the door; Murch can breathe relatively easy for the moment. It's a good time to introduce an innovation made possible only by virtue of Final Cut Pro: giving assistants a chance to do some real editing.

A scene for everyone to cut: put them to work! Now that we have almost caught up.

Up until the early 1970s, when film editors began switching from upright Moviolas to flatbed Steenbecks and KEMs, assistants worked in closer proximity with their editors—more like apprentices at their sides. But new editing systems began to push apprentices out the door, literally. An editor no longer needed an assistant right there, handing up film rolls and filing trims. Gone, too, was the chance for an assistant to learn the craft by watching and participating in editing moment by moment. The move to Avid accelerated the process of estrangement. Assistants began to work at their own edit stations doing file management, or on the film conform bench, away in other rooms. Murch seizes on Final Cut Pro's inherent pluralism to make film editing more accessible. "Another upward twist of the spiral," as he puts it.

October 11, 2002, Murch's Journal

The guys have installed FCP on their machines and are getting ready to start cutting. Sean is helping them and they are excited.

Murch seems to be in the zone. There's joy in the work, being fully engaged, pushing the technical limits. He's signing emails to Ramy: "Narok!! Valter Murcescu."

Assistant editors before biking to work on *Cold Mountain* in Bucharest.

The eye on the pole.

CHAPTER 7

The
Flow of It

Three months into production, Murch is working 12 to 14 hours a day, six days out of every seven. But he faithfully takes an eight-mile run once a week, on Sunday, his one day off. He throws a coin onto a city map, then heads off in that direction from the hotel. Bucharest is a wonderfully strange city, with much to take in, so he brings along two tools of the trade: a digital still camera and a microcassette audio recorder. Today, a fine fall Sunday, is particularly plentiful:

The Story of the Eye on the Pole

"It was in a bleak industrial boulevard and I was the only pedestrian. I had a creepy sensation someone was looking at me. I went back a few yards and found this eye looking at me from an old political poster. It was on a huge power pylon that had been painted over, but some of the paint had flaked off, revealing the eye. It was alternately frowning and encouraging at the same time, depending on where you imagined the nose to be. I made it my computer screen background—a talisman for the rest of *Cold Mountain*. It represented the ambiguous position I found myself in—doing this unusual thing with Final Cut Pro on such a large budget film in such a place as Romania."

October 13, 2002, Murch's Journal

Good Run out Plevnei Boulevard to the pedestrian overpass across the RR tracks.

Main entrance of Cotroceni Palace, passing it just now.

Took a picture of an eye on a telephone post—beautiful.

An older woman in an orange overcoat: talked to me about "sports" as I ran by on Plevnei.

On Giuleshti—why does this all feel familiar in some strange way? The northern part of Manhattan, southern part of the Bronx when I was growing up.

Grand Overpass: you can drive onto it from Giuleshti, but how do you get off it onto Grivitsei? It seemed like you could from the street map I just passed.

The halfway point is the little pizza place on Grivitsei that they were painting up about a month ago.

A wedding at St. George's: with an accordion player outside welcoming them in.

Next day, it's back to work upstairs at Kodak Cinelabs. At this stage in the filmmaking process Murch organizes his editing activities into what he calls "groups." He defines a group as the amount of film he can "put on my plate at any one time." Ideally, it is also a sequence, a succession of connected scenes.

Earlier, Murch broke the script down into numbered sequences before shooting began, based on his feeling for the dramatic "clustering" of scenes. For example, group 16, as Murch catalogs it, consists of part of sequence 18 and part of sequence 19, four scenes in all: Inman and Reverend Veasey leaving the river where they hid from the Home Guard; the two of them coming upon Junior (Giovanni Ribisi) and a dead bull; helping Junior dispose of the bull; Junior inviting them back to his place; and the men being greeted by the women at the cabin. In the screenplay these are part of scene 93 and all of scenes 94, 95, and 96. Murch's one-line description for the sequence is: "Inman & V: find saw, meet Junior, 'There'll be tang.'" There are a total of 45 sequences in the film, and they consist of 213 scenes.

October 14, 2002, Murch's Journal

If I finish Group 12 today, God willing then I will have cut 12½ minutes in three working days from start to finish, which would be 25 minutes a six-day week. If I could maintain that… I would be done cutting the film three days after they finish shooting… Inshallah. 01/14/03: I did not even come close. 02/14/03: I hope to be all finished by Monday Feb 17th.

During production, selecting a group to work on is simply a function of what sections are available in their entirety—what's been shot. A scene that has been shot has its card marked with a yellow tag, so when Murch looks over his scene boards and spots an adjacent set, all with yellow tags, he'll designate that as a group. But group 15, for example, was made up of four disconnected scenes: 56–Rooster attacks Ada; 67–Ada looks into the well; 86–Ruby and Ada build a fence; and the main part of 93–Veasey finds a saw. A group averages 15,000 feet of film dailies, or three hours. By working in these hunks, Murch's notes can be "proportional and useful," he says. "Any smaller and I'd be too picky and detailed; any longer and I'd be overwhelmed."

Murch views each shot from the group, making a second set of notes about what he sees. He made the first set of notes during dailies, the day after shooting. Murch puts notes into the logbook on his laptop. It's a record-keeping system set up in FileMaker Pro that he designed for this purpose, first used on *The Unbearable Lightness of Being*. The single record (shown on the next page) contains all the editing information for one camera take: a wide shot in group 16/sequence 18—Inman, Veasey, and Junior stand in the creek; Inman and Veasey help Junior with the dead bull.

Murch's first set of notes from dailies screenings are simple, descriptive, and record his immediate emotional reactions—all that's really required at this point in the process. The notes from his second viewing will be more detailed and analytical, go deeper, and record the footage counts for each of the 20 "beats," or dramatic moments, that Murch feels in this single shot. "The first set of notes are a lover's first impression of the beloved," Murch says later. "The second set are a surgeon's notes before making the first incision."

MURCH'S FIRST VIEWING NOTES OF SHOT #459-B17

Angle up the creek with calm water in foreground, Junior pulls the Bull and then both hands up when turn to Veasey, good see him get the liquor. Inman enters on Tassel. Good Inman kneeling by stream for dialogue.

ON NOTE TAKING

He uses very base language in the description of shots when he first sees them. He'll say things like, "Her forehead looks like a washboard." It's very simple language. He'll know exactly what the first viewing meant to him.

—Edie Ichioka, Murch's assistant editor on *The English Patient*

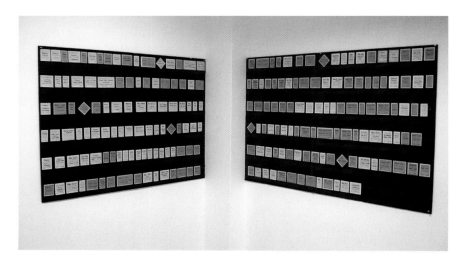

Murch makes these scene cards by hand. When a group is marked with a yellow tag, it means the scenes have been shot and they're ready for editing.

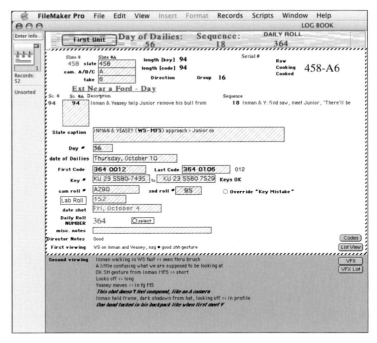

A page from Murch's logbook for the scene of Veasey, Inman, Junior, and the bull.

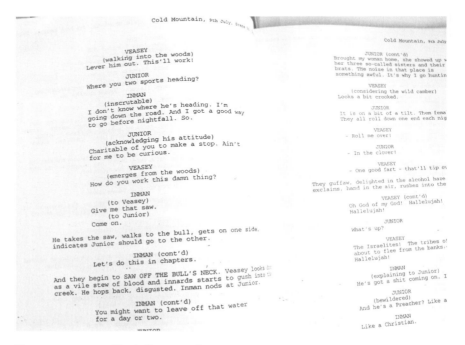

The same scene as written in the screenplay.

As he is writing his "surgeon's" notes, Murch hasn't yet looked at Minghella's shooting comments, which come with script supervisor Dianne Dreyer's notes as well. Interestingly, there is no distinction between Minghella's and Dreyer's comments. When Murch finally toggles FileMaker to reveal Minghella/Dreyer's comments for this particular take, he finds simply, "With Hallelujah." The note means there was an extra line recorded for this take: Veasey's exclamation as he runs into the woods to defecate.

Work on a group normally takes three days. On the first day, Murch screens and takes notes. If a group consists of three hours of film (a typical amount), it will take Murch nine hours to watch it, stopping as necessary to make notes. On the second day, he'll use FCP to assemble the material into scenes—the first time the material has been joined together editorially. He will do this with the sound turned off, even if it is a dialogue scene, treating everything as if it were a silent movie. On his third day with a group, Murch turns on the sound and refines his work of the previous day—trimming beginnings and endings of shots, moving dialogue around, overlapping picture and sound. He is finding the film's rhythm and getting shots to work more precisely with each other. Larger structural issues that may arise are noted but left undone. It's not yet time for those kinds of decisions. As Murch describes it, he "doesn't know enough yet, and I'm only the editor." So he works with "eyes half-closed, not expressing opinions unreservedly." Until the first assembly is completed, every scene gets the benefit of the doubt.

Working six-day weeks, Murch can complete two groups a week. The amount of film shot on *Cold Mountain* already surpasses 300,000 feet, or 55 hours. Having passed the halfway point in the shooting schedule, Murch is rethinking his note-taking system, pondering how best to keep up with the regular flood of footage, yet adequately annotate so he has a useful reference.

October 19, 2002, Murch's Journal

Finished group 14 sound and revisions and got 4,000 feet into notes on 16 (12,000 feet) so a third of the way. Also caught up on dailies looked at four reels from day 61. How can I speed up the note-taking process? I have tried doing selects only… "Be a star in three scenes and adequate in everything else," as John Ford said. The trick is to define adequate.

Back in the U.S., word that Murch is using Final Cut Pro to edit *Cold Mountain* begins to get around the filmmaking community. A technology reporter for *The Hollywood Reporter*, the entertainment industry trade paper, inquires about doing a story. Walter has an exchange of emails with Ramy at DigitalFilm Tree about whether it's a good idea to be interviewed for the story while technical issues are still being worked out. How should he explain the "known unknowns"—especially the uncertainties of having reliable change lists and the audio export protocol needed for sound editing? He doesn't want to come out with anything that might embarrass Apple.

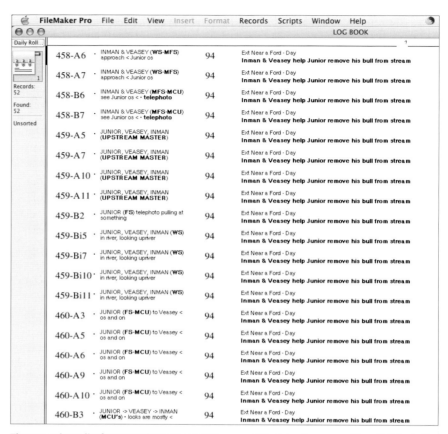

The two-column list from Murch's logbook with some of the takes for scenes 93 and 94, including shot #459-Bi7.

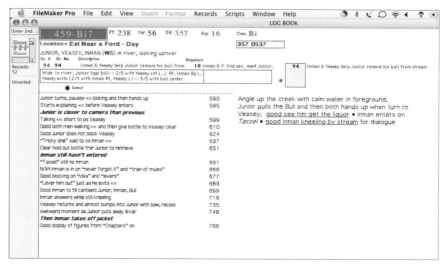

Murch's second viewing notes for shot #459-Bi7.

"I don't want Apple to have a fit," he writes to Ramy. "On the other hand I don't want Miramax to have a fit either. The truth is, it will all work out, but it is a delicate political situation."

Ramy answers by encouraging Walter to go forward with the interview; DFT will be happy to supply *The Hollywood Reporter* with any background or technical information for the story. In this same email, perhaps of more immediate significance, Ramy also writes about new developments with change lists: "We are providing Apple with workflow notes for Loran Kary who is leading the creation of Cinema Tools' change list functionality due out around April… it is public knowledge that Apple recently purchased EMagic, a large European audio software/hardware company. Clearly Apple is 'going in the direction' of professional software/hardware." Since its inception, Apple has branded itself as making computers "for the rest of us"—suggesting that it focuses primarily on serving consumers. But as more highly regarded professionals like Murch pick up applications such as Final Cut Pro and run with them, Apple becomes an even stronger force in the creative community, where it has always been the favored platform.

The news about positive developments with change lists for Final Cut Pro is soon confirmed when Ramy gets an eyewitness demonstration at Apple headquarters, which Walter notes in his journal:

October 22, 2002, Murch's Journal

Great email from Ramy: "I just saw a change list print out. It looks really good. In short, change lists will not be an issue. Loran did well, he surprised us. Just wanted to let you know. Please keep this sealed." That is great, great news—another ogre waiting for us down the hall just disappeared. Inshallah.

Murch decides to do the interview with *The Hollywood Reporter.*

By this time, Murch's assistants are going strong on their Final Cut Pro systems, cutting away on their scenes. In a follow-up email to *The Hollywood Reporter* writer, Sheigh Crabtree, Murch proudly explains how the apprentice editors are working: "G4 laptops (even an old clamshell iBook) can become satellite stations, not linked to FibreChannel." Murch is saying that Final Cut can be configured to run more simply on laptops than when it is networked among several workstations and must use an external viewing monitor, as it is configured for his edit room. "You download the selected media to each laptop, which is equipped with just FCP (no Aurora card needed if no NTSC monitor)." The assistants can then export their edited scenes back to the main system—as sequence information only—"where it is relinked to the media on the FibreChannel. If you include these laptops, we have *seven* stations working on the film."

November 2, 2002, Murch's Journal

Sean and Dei's scenes are done, recut, and in the film. They turned out well and just needed a little "Murching." We may catch up some time. Saw Walter's scenes in progress. There is something very considerate and precise about his work and the way he is doing it. God bless. Ilinca and Susanna's scenes yet to come: Wuthering Heights and "Cut my hair once." Five assistants learning to edit by actually doing it, and then showing the material to me, getting notes, and revising. What other system would have made doing this so easy?

Having passed the two-thirds point in the shooting schedule, Murch begins to share a common concern among crew, cast, and producers: Will Minghella finish filming on time, which is scheduled for December 7? Going overtime on a motion picture can cause all sorts of problems. Just being permitted to film for extra days can be a major struggle between director and studio. It may even be forbidden by contract or by the completion guaranty company that issues the insurance bond against just such a contingency.

November 6, 2002, Murch's Journal

In any ten-day period Ant has shot 20 scenes, sometimes 19, once 18. EXCEPT for the first ten days, when he shot seven, and days 61-70, when he shot 11 (Chain gang escaping from Brown and killed). Otherwise it is 20, 18, 19, 20, 20, 19. If he can keep up that rate, he needs 35 more shooting days, and he has 28. So seven is the magic number.

Film production can be exhausting.

Murch determines from Dianne Dreyer's reports that Minghella begins picking up the pace: He writes in he journal: "In the last ten days: Ant has shot 23 scenes, including all of the Sara stuff, or 2.3 scenes a day. He has 60 scenes to shoot in 26 days, which is 2.3 scenes a day. So maintaining the current pace, he can finish on time. Congratulations!"

Later in November Murch has dinner with Steve Andrews, the first assistant director. (Andrews, Murch, and Minghella all worked together in their same capacities on *The Talented Mr. Ripley* and *The English Patient*.) As first assistant director, Andrews is primarily responsible for keeping director and crew on schedule, and for getting each day's designated script pages shot in the time allotted—"making the day." Murch and Andrews discuss what this takes, and what can drag it down.

"Will we finish on time?" Andrews asks.

Murch tells him they will if the rate of 2.3 scenes a day established over the last ten days continues.

"Do you have enough time to cut the film?" Andrews asks.

"It is about the same as *Ripley*," Murch responds, "with a little more wiggle room because of intercutting the two stories. The weak spot will probably be from the end of the battle until Inman gets on the road and Ruby appears." There will be tremendous pressure to resolve this as soon as possible, he says.

Film dailies being processed in the "bath" at Kodak Bucharest.

In addition to being a beehive of activity, Murch's editing room has now become a preferred destination for anyone who visits *Cold Mountain* in Romania, according to producer Albert Berger. "Normally you'd just high-tail it to the set, but this was a must-stop, to go to his domain. He was like a mad scientist up there doing all these experiments." Producers, movie executives, press, friends of the cast and crew—even *Cold Mountain* author Charles Frazier—all climb the stairs to the second floor of Kodak Cinelab. They know Murch's credits and awards, of course, but are drawn because they hear that Murch is up to something special using the Final Cut Pro system.

November 11, 2002, Murch's Journal
Reviewed Sean's new scene: very good, just one or two changes… and also Dei's scene, same thing—the scene at the door with Sally and the girls he did very well. Charles Frazier and wife Katherine came to visit—very nice, spent an hour or so with them, talking about the film and the process.

Gave Ilinca her scene.

Having assistants able to cut scenes is one aspect of Final Cut Pro's potential for egalitarianism. Ilinca Nanoveanu, the Romanian apprentice editor, cuts the scene of Ada reading *Wuthering Heights* to Ruby, and she later mentions this to Anthony at a crew and cast party.

"I heard you liked my scene," she says.

"What?" Anthony says, astonished.

As young Walter later tells the story: "Dad sat us down at breakfast. No one was supposed to know that we were working on scenes. Ilinca came into our edit room later and cried her eyes out because she thought she had done something terrible. I told her to go in and tell Dad. 'You'll feel better,' I said. She came back in tears."

Later Murch explains to Minghella that he is giving the assistants rare editing experience, something Final Cut alone makes possible. He makes it clear that he reviews and re-edits those scenes as necessary. Minghella supports the experiment—another testament to his faith in Murch.

December 10, 2002, Murch's Journal
Ilinca upset that she told Anthony that she cut the Heathcliff scene. Tears and self-recrimination. I console her, but tell her to take the lesson to heart. But not so much to heart that it becomes a black hole.

Despite the contretemps, Murch later looks back on it proudly. "Seeing Ilinca cut that scene makes Final Cut Pro worth the price of admission," he says. "It's the first time the assistants had access to the editing experience on a film

Ruby reads *Wuthering Heights* after Ada falls asleep—"Ilinca's scene."

like this, where they can work with professionally shot material and be able to bounce their work off me. Something like that just hasn't been economically or logistically possible before FCP."

The time is soon approaching when production will end, the editing crew will move to London to finish the film, and the sound conversion issue becomes more urgent. An email from Ramy gives Murch hope for a new solution. Ramy proposes a working relationship between Murch and Mark Gilbert, an audio software developer with the London firm, Gallery. "There is the potential of him playing a part in addressing 'unknown sound post' issues facing us," Ramy writes to Walter on November 19, 2002.

Like DFT's friend, Brooks Harris, Mark Gilbert develops software solutions for difficult audio-transfer problems. As it happens, Gilbert has worked for George Lucas on *Star Wars Episode I* and met Murch, who was visiting a dialogue recording session for *Episode I* at Abbey Road Studios in London. Gallery has a pioneering OMF technology called MetaFlow, which takes 24-bit film sound recorded on location, converts it into 16-bit files readable by an Avid, and then exports these edited soundtracks into ProTools for refined sound editing. Movies such as *Die Another Day*, *The Matrix*, and *Jersey Girl* all used MetaFlow. Gilbert tells Ramy he's "really keen" to see if he can adapt MetaFlow to help Walter with Final Cut.

Once again the question of Apple's operating systems arises. Ramy engages Murch in an email dialogue about upgrading all of Murch's Final Cut Pro systems from Mac OS 9.2 to Mac OS X (aka "System 10"). By making this change Murch could step onto Apple's chosen playing field, and be in a better position to receive official support. Two companies whose gear Murch uses are already preparing for the new OS. Aurora, which makes his Igniter video digitizing card, is coming out with a beta version for OS X. Rorke, which makes his shared area network (SAN) media storage system, is also unveiling an OS X beta test version of its networking software for the 1.2 terabyte hard drive array. Murch is game for converting to OS X when he moves to London. Two days later Ramy shares this information with Bill Hudson at Apple: "There are some important issues that need to be addressed now, including their [*Cold Mountain*] migration to OS X. I am assuming this is something everyone will want. In my last communication with Walter, he was open to migrating to OS X if done properly and safely. So let's strategize our next step here as they will be going to London and start post soon. Call me at the next opportunity as we want to be on the ball."

Two weeks later Hudson replies in an email to Ramy that converting *Cold Mountain* to Mac OS X, "scares the hell out of me—especially since they are working so well now with what they have." Separately, Brian Meaney concurs: "I think moving them to OS X will be very hard right now without a known SAN solution." Apple is once again caught in a dilemma. Getting Murch on

Mac OS X would allow the company to be more on-the-record helpful with software solutions and general troubleshooting. But changing operating systems in the middle of a film does not seem wise. It could put the film at risk. Apple advises to stand pat. Cautious as that may sound, Apple has Murch and *Cold Mountain*'s best interests at heart.

On Thanksgiving Day Ramy receives bad, but not quite terminal, news from Mark Gilbert in London about his MetaFlow program for sound export: Gilbert may not be able to solve Murch's audio export problem after all. "FCP can only do embedded OMF," Gilbert tells Ramy, "rather than compositions only. This seems to be what Walter is asking for. In fact, that's not something we will be able to assist with, I am afraid. I will look into other ways of getting the events list out of FCP. I know there is a hack to do this which might be exploitable." Should Murch and Cullen fail to get a solution from either Mark Gilbert or Brooks Harris to overcome Final Cut Pro's sound export limitations, they will be forced to create their own multi-step workaround—an extra task they hoped to avoid but are ready to do if necessary.

November 23, 2002, Murch's Journal

Party for "Thanksgiving" here in Brashov—thrown by Nicole, Jude, Renée. Jack White and the White Stripes performed (he plays the character, Georgia). Very loud but good—but I couldn't take too much of it. I sat and talked to Ilinca at the coffee bar and Jude came over, and Ilinca was very happy to meet and be introduced to him. He talked about his work on this film, and how meeting this character has been a revelation to him, has forced him to be a better person.

There is one month left until production wraps in Romania. Having cut together more and more film, Murch begins to find *Cold Mountain*'s rhythms and patterns. He senses how some separate scenes might work better intermingled.

November 16, 2002, Murch's Journal

Finished Swanger killing and torture, group 20, turned out well, I think— interesting sounds (breathing and squeaks)—and good surprising intercuts of Ada and Ruby after the shotgun blast goes off. I thought it would be one intercut, but it turned out to be three: "what's that" :: then return to Esco killing and Sally collapse :: back to Ruby running off leaving Ada :: move in on Teague looking and listening to the struggle :: back to Ada running off.

Four months later, when he edits this scene again in London, Murch will write in his journal, "Now it is just, 'what's that?' without either of them running off."

The dogs of time keep nipping at his heels. On Sunday, November 17, Murch writes about his progress putting the first assembly together: "Today I have been cutting for three and a half months and am just coming up to three

IF JOHN CAGE WAS A FILM EDITOR

When Aggie goes to a party, she's very social. Walter can be—yes or no. He sometimes gets a cocktail stick and a paper plate and draws an arrow on the paper plate, puts it on top of the stick, spins it, and goes as far in the direction of the arrow as he can. When he stops, he spins it again, and goes as far in that direction as he can. And he spins it again.

It's a Walter thing. And that's how he edits—the paper plate on the stick—sometimes. He goes with a belief until it stops and then he hooks up with another idea. I think that's part of the mindset. It's a "created randomness" that leads you to discover how you want to put everything together.

—Edie Ichioka, Murch's assistant editor on *The English Patient*

December 6, 2002, Murch's Journal

22,000 feet of film came in last night. Nine lab rolls. A new record. So we have well and truly crossed the 500,000 equator—probably at 520,000 feet including today's dailies.

hours, which is not quite fifteen minutes a week. How to improve, move faster, keep the work at a high level?"

A makeshift sound stage has been constructed in an abandoned helicopter factory up in the mountains. This is where the first camera unit will film crucial scenes between Inman and Ada by the campfire, their subsequent love-making, and the forest scene where Teague and his gang find deserters Pangle and Stobrod and shoot them.

Weather permitting, a day must also be found to film the exterior scene of Inman's death—the final scene in the film except for the coda, which was shot months ago at the height of summer.

At this point there are often more than three hours of dailies to be screened and logged each day, which eats up time that would otherwise be spent assembling material. Aggie flies in from London the afternoon of December 6 and hangs out in the editing rooms until Murch finishes screening selects at 10 p.m. This week 56,000 feet of film dailies are printed, more than double the average week's volume.

Any equipment not immediately necessary to the task at hand is boxed up to be shipped in advance to London. The edit rooms begin to have a transient look to them.

The plan is now to extend the shooting an extra six days past the original wrap, with Saturday, December 14, being the final cutoff. Anything not done by that date will not be shot.

Ilinca marks sync on the last *Cold Mountain* daily roll using "the electro-muscular-mechanical process," as Murch calls it.

On December 9, Aggie flies back to London after a final weekend in Bucharest, with a last celebratory dinner for the whole editorial crew on Saturday.

More footage is shot in the final six days than in any other week of production—59,000 feet, almost 10 percent of the entire amount of workprint over the 113 shooting days.

The last take on the last day of filming (setup number 954) is Georgia's point-of-view of Teague shooting Pangle and Stobrod. And with that gunshot, production comes to an end.

Activity at Cinelabs continues for another day, however. Saturday's material has to be developed and printed, and then screened on Sunday before the actors and crew can be released. If the film has been scratched or damaged, the scene must be redone. The lab is kept open and busy over the weekend.

DECEMBER 12, 2002, MURCH'S JOURNAL

English Patient x 2 today: this is the day that we cross the 564,000 foot threshold, which is double the workprint on EP.

December 15, 2002, Murch's Journal

Finished looking at dailies from the last day's filming. All ok. 4,900 records in the Log Book. 597,000 feet of dailies. 33,000 in the last three days. There are some MIA's I have to catch up on, but that's all… Congratulations to everybody… Packing UP!

On Monday, Murch and Cullen, and Cullen's wife Juliette and baby Ora, leave Romania for London to set up the editing rooms at Minghella's Old Chapel Studios. Young Walter, Dei Reynolds, and the Romanian apprentices, Mihai and Ilinca, stay on to finish the final boxing up of equipment and film.

December 16, 2002, Murch's Journal

Flying out of Bucharest to London with most of the crew—Anthony sitting across the aisle, Ian in front of me, Sean and Juliette and Ora up the by the bulkhead. Farewell Romania. You were good to us and we thank you.

Arrived safely at PH. Aggie was home, and we spent a lovely afternoon evening.

When British film directors choose to live and work in London rather than migrate to Hollywood, they are saying something about who they are and the kinds of films they want to make—and that's true for Anthony Minghella, who was born on the Isle of Wight. There is an active moviemaking community in the United Kingdom, and some wonderfully original and independent voices. Think of Mike Leigh, Mike Newell, Stephen Frears, and Neil Jordan. Normally they work on smallish budget films with backing from various U.K. government funds and tax-benefit programs; only rarely do American studios support their work. So when an Academy Award-winning director decides to stay home and not relocate to Los Angeles, that's news—especially when his

Murch and the edit team moved to London from Bucharest in mid-December 2002 to complete the film.

current movie is the high-profile *Cold Mountain,* financed and distributed by Miramax Films. Recognizing this, along with Minghella's vision, leadership, and ambitious ideas for the industry, the British Film Council appoints him chairman of the prestigious British Film Institute at the end of 2002.

Minghella will complete *Cold Mountain* working from the London production office of Mirage Enterprises, a company he runs with his partner, Sydney Pollack. Mirage is located in a former Baptist chapel near Hampstead Heath in North London; it was previously a studio space for rock-and-roll photographer Gered Mankowitz. The Old Chapel studio, as it's called, is a convenient ten-minute walk from Minghella's house. Murch's edit suite will be located on the second floor in four small, cozy rooms. Downstairs in his office, Minghella will have his own Final Cut Pro edit station. Like the other four stations upstairs, it will be linked to the Rorke RAID system over a FibreChannel.

The Old Chapel Studio near Hampstead Heath in London.

Minghella at his own Final Cut Pro workstation in the Old Chapel.

Meeting with Anthony to discuss preliminary scheduling. I said I wouldn't be done at least before the 27th of January, God willing.

Half of the *Cold Mountain* Romanian edit rooms were disassembled two weeks prior, crated up, and shipped to London so Walter could arrive and continue working unabated.

Trying to do notes on 30 and did some, but felt exhausted, hopeless. Rest of our equipment didn't arrive today and now will sit in storage until Monday the 6th.

The holidays are here, time for a break: two weeks off. Fortunately for Murch, he is well acquainted with London and enjoys living and working here. In the mid-1980s, not far from the Old Chapel, he oversaw work done by the Jim Henson Studios for *Return to Oz*. He edited *Julia* for director Fred Zinneman in London. His wife, Aggie, is English, and they have a cottage in Primrose Hill, a pleasant 20-minute walk from the Mirage offices.

It's been five months since Murch passed through London on his way to Romania to begin work on *Cold Mountain*. The film is now scheduled to open in one year's time, on Christmas Day, 2003. In an ideal world, after this holiday hiatus Murch would be screening the first assembly for Minghella. Instead, he estimates he's at least four weeks behind schedule. Standing down now for two weeks provides much needed rest, recuperation, and resettling for him and his assistants. But this interval is like intermittent slumber with troubled dreams of big things left undone. After the break, when Murch arrives at the Old Chapel to resume work, it's the middle of winter and threatening to snow.

January 6, 2003, Murch's Journal

I am grumpy and nervous, scared, tired, disoriented. Walk to the Chapel and have a meeting with Sean, Walter, Dei—what needs to get done this week.

Is Final Cut Pro to blame for Murch being behind? Would the edit schedule have been any different using Avid? Recall that Murch did not start assembling footage until the end of July, two weeks later than he originally hoped. There were delays getting the conventional editing equipment through Romanian customs: benches, rewinds, bins. A lot of time and energy was spent early on with Final Cut Pro issues: getting audio conversions figured out, refining the workflow, and communicating with DigitalFilm Tree. All that effort, to some undetermined extent, cost precious time.

On the other hand, FCP never seized up. Ingenious workarounds kept everything running. It may have simply been the deluge of film footage that weighed down the schedule, on top of not having second assistant Dei Reynolds on board until the end of July.

It snowed all that week of January 6 in London—the heaviest in a decade. By Friday the snow is gone, Walter's edit room is fully set up, and his spirits lift.

January 9, 2003, Murch's Journal

Harvey W visits the Chapel and we screen some material for him: Junior's, Sara's, Stobrod, and Ruby. He likes it, laughs at the right places.

Once again the journal is replete with footage calculations, schedule projections for the remaining groups, a new three act division of the entire film, and a measurement of the walking distance from Murch's cottage to the edit rooms at the Old Chapel: 1,280 paces. And a meditation: "May I ask your help to find out what the best path is to get the assembly together, in the best shape."

The pace picks up, from a brisk walk to a healthy jog.

January 13, 2003, Murch's Journal

It feels good to be cutting again: like grandma playing her piano: "If I didn't do this every day, I would have died long ago," she said to me once, aged 97, as she was pounding it out in the front room of her house. There is something about it, the music of it, which is enhancing.

Minghella on the stairway at the Old Chapel.

Everything about the edit is now directed at the intermediate finish line of completing the first assembly. Only when Murch has all the scenes laid out according to the script can Minghella re-engage with the work and make his transition from director shooting to director editing. Once a first assembly is screened, the director can truly fathom what he has to work with and start getting the film down to a releasable length. Minghella and Murch will start searching for the movie that lies beneath the surface, like Michelangelo, finding the figure that exists within the marble, waiting to be revealed.

As Walter sees it, the break a director is forced to take between filming and editing is a good thing, a necessary transition. Film directors should come down off the emotional roller coaster of shooting a movie before they enter the quiet, deliberative environment of the editing room. From production's white-hot, highly social milieu of a large crew and top-notch cast, Minghella now joins Murch where a quieter, cooler, and more dispassionate viewpoint prevails. A director must now be prepared to judge a shot for what it is on the screen, not for particular events or emotions involved in filming it. Associations recalled from that particular day on location, positive or negative, are memories to be left behind. Such withdrawal takes time. The further the director distances himself from the shooting, the more helpful he will be in the editing room. On *Julia*, the 1977 film with Jane Fonda and Vanessa Redgrave that Murch edited, 70 year-old director Fred Zinneman went off to the Alps to scale some mountains, to put himself in life-threatening situations where he *had* to forget about shooting. For Minghella, a director who relishes the editing process and feels completely at home inside the edit room, coming down off that mountain is a good thing. But the first assembly of *Cold Mountain* is not yet ready. It is a matter of professional pride for editors to be done with the assembly as quickly as possible after shooting—usually two weeks—and Murch feels guilty that this is not the case. He hopes Minghella will be sympathetic to the facts of the schedule.

January 16, 2003, Murch's Journal

Answer from Anthony who was calming—talked about being finished when I am finished. "I know you'll be ready with the assembly as soon as you can be, and that's the beginning and end of the matter. If there's anything I can do to help then let me know. I meet with Miramax and the producers on Friday and will explain the delay and why there is one. Obviously, we need to get going on a cut, but the failings are mine, I think, rather than yours."

However patient he might be, Minghella is champing to get underway with the editing. He's spent the past two weeks getting familiar with Final Cut Pro and he wants to put it to work reviewing scenes on his own, thinking about changes, making notes, and engaging with Murch in the process. So now, at the end of January 2003, not wanting to keep Minghella waiting any longer, Murch screens a nearly completed first assembly that runs just under four hours. Murch, Minghella, his wife Carolyn and son Max, and Cassius Matthias, one of the Mirage staff producers, gather in Walter's edit room on a Saturday afternoon. Murch turns down the dimmer, the track lights go out, and he hits play. The Panasonic 50-inch plasma display lights up and the film begins. A few moments into the battle scene there's a problem: "It kept freezing," Murch writes later, "something about the complexity of layered and filtered sound when the film is that long… it was frustrating, but ultimately Ant was generous about the situation. We will reconvene on Monday afternoon."

Sean and Walter stay late to figure out the nature of the problem. They can see that the playhead on the Final Cut timeline acts fragile and sticky even when they reduce the amount of media they ask FCP to play from 2½ hours to half an hour. An important viewing for the director was cancelled, and the solution was not yet in sight.

January 25, 2003, Murch's Journal

After the screening, walking home, I feel as if my head is coming unscrewed.

The following day Murch shares his frustration with Ramy in an email with a subject line, Difficulties: "You can imagine the disappointment all around, particularly for me. The editor has only one chance to show the director his version of the film, and this is now gone."

Over the weekend, Murch and Cullen discover Final Cut's problem: the software can't handle the quantity of audio equalization filtering that Murch had added to the soundtracks. He was using multiple filters to improve the sound of some sections of dialogue. They were playing in real time, as opposed to being rendered, or permanently embedded in the saved file. If more of these audio effects are rendered ahead of time, it's easier for FCP to play long sequences. A bug in FCP 3.0 overestimated the complexity of audio filtering, acting like a software traffic cop telling it, "Slow down, slippery road ahead," when in fact the road was clear and dry. Murch learns that FCP can be ungainly when it moves, copies, and renders large amount of digitized footage. It all takes longer than it would in Avid. The frustration level rises. "How will the schedule work out with so much still to edit?" Murch writes a few days later in his journal. "God bless this situation and may it resolve itself happily and creatively."

The second attempt to screen the four-hour assembly using newly rendered audio material goes fine. Not yet being the entire assembly, it ends with Inman cresting the mountain and seeing the town of Cold Mountain below.

January 27, 2003, Murch's Journal

The motto on Tower Cottage [an old house Murch passes every day on his way to work]: is "Strength and Patience"—Fortis et Patiens. Let that be your motto now. Successfully screened the film twice—once for me to see that it all went smoothly, once for Anthony and me. We finished about nine thirty. Well done! You got through it—at least this part.

There is much to think about in that four-hour assembly, but firm opinions have still to be put on hold until the whole film can be seen in one piece from beginning to end.

Plans are made to staff up the sound editing crew. Walter and Anthony meet with Eddy Joseph, the supervising sound editor, a 50-something Englishman who's worked in that capacity on *Harry Potter and the Sorcerer's Stone*, many of director Alan Parker's movies, and has 25 years experience with sound and movies. In addition to editing sound himself, Eddy will manage a six-man crew of sound editors and assistants who each specialize in various sub-fields: dialogue, ADR (automatic dialogue replacement), atmospheres (like birds chirping, wind blowing), "hard" effects (gunshots, horses, etc.), and Foley (footsteps and character movement). He'll be responsible for bringing all the sound elements together in the sound mixing theater, first in temporary mixes for preview screenings, and at the end, for a final sound mix that Murch will manage, and co-mix.

Cold Mountain **sound supervisor, Eddy Joseph, has worked on sound for major motion pictures for over 25 years.**

Anthony explains to Eddy how he and Murch will be making "enormous changes at the last minute," which can be a nightmare for the sound department. Anthony likes to work on films until the very last possible moment, tweaking the cuts, replacing lines of dialogue, dropping or adding scenes, or trying a new music cue. It comes from his live theater experience and a writer's never-ending need to revise. It's difficult for Minghella to see the enterprise as really ever done, finished and impervious, like cured concrete. Murch shares this same drive to find perfection. Eddy says he is ready to be flexible and "pro-actively creative." There is one potential hitch: Eddy says he doesn't really like the ProTools sound editing system. He doesn't have that much personal experience with it, but is "willing to give it a go."

February 13, 2003, Murch's Journal

I finished the campfire killing grounds scene—whew. But that puts me behind the eight ball for the remaining scenes with Inman and Ada. Guidance and wisdom and assistance, please…

The day before Murch completes the full first assembly, he steps back for a moment and asks rhetorically, "Why are we screening the film two months after the end of principal photography? Because the load of film—600,000 feet—is just beyond what I can process and keep up with working six days a week. It means that the slightest wrinkle sets me over the edge and I lose time that I cannot retrieve."

Murch makes a list of what might have kept things on schedule, and what could be done differently next time.

1. Shoot less film

2. Anthony make selections and give me detailed notes

3. Hire an additional editor to work with me

4. Hire a different editor, one who works faster than I do

5. Not have delays at the beginning that made it impossible for me to start editing until two weeks after start of shooting

6. Not move into a facility (the Chapel) that had never had a film edited in it (also applies to Kodak)

7. Not move location until the first assembly is finished

8. Have a "Man in Havana" here in London setting things up before we came back

What may appear on the surface to be an aggressive, even cold-hearted attitude, is really a matter of feeling bad about being late, Murch admits later. "Editors often strike a macho posture," he says, "proving to their directors how good they are by delivering a first assembly as soon as one week after production ends."

Murch will screen the entire first assembly on February 18. He refers to this volume reduction—compiling the first assembly from all the raw footage—as "the crush ratio," a term in winemaking that measures the first pressing against the original volume of picked grapes. A second pressing will get the first assembly down to a release print. Murch already looks beyond the first crush to the second pressing: getting a five hour-plus assembly to a releasable length.

February 15, 2003, Murch's Journal

Crush ratio on CM is 22:1.On EP it was 11:1. Julia had a CR of 12, but only shot 180,000 feet. Then there is the second pressing, which is how much of the assembly do you throw away? On Ripley it was 55%. On Julia it was 30%. On EP it was 40%. On K-19 it was 43% ¶ 03/15/03 on Apocalypse the crush ratio was 11% and the second pressing was 55%

February 16, 2003, Murch's Journal

Finished this assembly 11pm Sunday night. Five hours four minutes seventeen seconds. Congratulations! Exactly two months since we returned to England, and seven months since the first day's dailies.

One of the limitations of Final Cut 3.0 is an arbitrary time cutoff: no sequence can be longer than four hours. So, as with old-fashioned road-show movies of the fifties, the *Cold Mountain* first assembly must be shown in two parts, with an intermission.

Beautiful sunny frosty day and I'm off to screen the film.

Successful screening of the film, no technical glitches—in two 2.5-hour parts. First impressions: It is long and has an eccentric beginning. The film hits the tracks when Ruby arrives (and Veasey soon after). Solve the beginning, cut it down but keep the two stories balanced, find the most efficient path.

Taking tomorrow off…

There is nothing more important to humanity's physical, psychic, social, and political survival and well-being than the conversion to hydrogen fuel.

A new phase of editing begins—refining the story, clarifying the emotions, making the first steps at reducing the first assembly to an acceptable running time. The orientation over the last six months has been one of accumulation, a building-up of material. Now the engines are suddenly thrown into full reverse. The enterprise will head in the opposite direction, shedding material as expeditiously as possible. Murch may be more than five weeks behind schedule, but before he turns up the speed it's time to make inquiries to Apple in Cupertino about acquiring Final Cut Pro version 4.0. Among other features, the new software release is rumored to include support for making reliable change lists and a function for exporting edited audio files to ProTools for further sound editing. These two functions could help Murch make up for time lost, or at least prevent further delays.

FEBRUARY 24, 2003—LONDON

Murch sends Brian Meaney, Apple's Final Cut Pro product designer, an email update on progress with *Cold Mountain* and the successful first assembly screening. "Anthony Minghella said that he had 'absolute confidence' in the fidelity of the FCP image compared to what he remembers from the projected 35mm film dailies, and would be delighted to show the film to Miramax on an FCP output." Murch mentions the "teething problems" he experienced with slowed-down playback caused by the audio filters. Then he invites Meaney to come visit the edit room in London, in part so he can discuss "a running list of suggestions for operational improvements in FCP as well as features in the present system that I think are particularly successful. Toward the end of March we would like to begin the process of conforming the 35mm workprint," that is, preparing a version in film that mirrors his FCP cut—a projectable film print for theater screenings. Then Murch pops the question: "To that end, when a beta of the next version of FCP is available, we would love to be able to test-drive it on the one CM workstation that we have already converted to OS X." Murch encourages continued dialogue between Apple and DigitalFilm Tree regarding OMF sound export. He then concludes, writing about the whole *Cold Mountain*/Final Cut Pro endeavor:

"Congratulations to everyone on the FCP team whose efforts made this achievement not only possible but eminently pleasurable."

Two days later Meaney responds to Murch. It's a friendly, positive email but it needs some decoding: "Thanks for the good word! I'm glad things are moving along so well with your project... And most definitely when a new version of FCP is available, I would be very interested in getting your thoughts." Not exactly a commitment for a tangible piece of software Murch hoped to get, but Meaney does offer to send Walter the beta copy of Cinema Tools, "which has preliminary change list support inside of it."

This is very good news. Murch and Cullen will at least get one piece they need to finish the puzzle: the change list function. Revisions to the picture that Murch makes will be accurately and efficiently transmitted to the sound editors. For now, it's back to the task at hand: finding fat, cutting it, and rearranging the essence.

Murch wrote to Apple manager Brian Meaney in Cupertino, California, to request the beta version of Final Cut Pro 4.0.

March 4, 2003, Murch's Journal

Revising the battle and pre-battle nips tucks transpositions. Connected up the rabbit in the tunnel with the rabbit in the trench, and all the associated restructuring.

Murch and Minghella settle into what will become their editing routine for the next 12 weeks. This process began with the February 18 showing of the first assembly. The work will revolve in three-week cycles, each interval marked by a screening in Murch's second floor edit room using Final Cut Pro on the 50-inch plasma monitor for an invited audience of up to ten people, which is all that the room can comfortably contain. After each screening, having debriefed together immediately afterward, editor and director collate their own notes with comments from the others who attended. They review that list, decide priorities, and establish goals for the next screening. Significantly, the entire assembly is not up for grabs each pass; some sections are put aside for a later date while others become the immediate focus. As Murch tries out ideas, makes discoveries, and tightens things up, Minghella is downstairs on his FCP workstation re-examining material, looking at the choice of takes, and otherwise getting himself oriented to the material that Murch reworks upstairs. As Murch gets scenes or sequences sketched out, Minghella goes upstairs to watch, review, discuss, and make decisions. The upstairs-downstairs pattern continues on a daily basis, whenever Minghella is available.

From here on out, editing is, for the most part, all about story, structure, character, and length. There were hints, clues, and portents about these big issues as the dailies flew by over the last six months. But now the material has been "crushed" (first assembly), so the process of revision and reordering can begin in earnest. In film editing, however, unlike the winemaking process, none of the raw material is ever really discarded.

Feeling good today though a little tired. Good Chi—thank you!

On a subconscious level, the mass of film, all 111 hours of it, is rooted in Walter Murch's memory/dream bank, not as an objective database, but as a living organism. A film editor draws on this subliminal source for creative thought and discovery much as a musician does. It is said that musical performers "work" on a piece even when they are away from their instruments, not actually practicing in the corporeal sense. The mind somehow keeps on playing the music surreptitiously, of its own volition, preparing for the next performance while the musician goes about other business, or is asleep. This Jungian stew, these *Cold Mountain* sounds and images, cooks night and day whether Murch is aware of it or not. Elements reshape and rearrange themselves of their own volition, boiling up into consciousness, sometimes uninvited but always welcomed.

March 5, 2003, Murch's Journal

Screen for Gabriel, Dennis, Eddie, Alan (Music, VFX, SFX). Went well, but a few miscuts because of improper relinking. Sean says will be fixed by tomorrow.

MARCH 19, 2003—LONDON

Exactly one month after screening the first assembly, Murch and Minghella have cut out 53 minutes, or 17 percent. But removing unnecessary shots isn't even half the battle. The tricky part is connecting what remains, having shots and scenes work together that were not written to coexist. With new juxtapositions come insights and revelations about characters and meaning. Economical ways to move the story forward are discovered. Remove the wrong support beam, however, and the structure tilts dangerously. Alone together now, upstairs in the Old Chapel, Minghella and Murch play their familiar tune, one they practiced to perfection on two previous motion pictures. The lines between director and editor, editor and writer, writer and director become transparent. With trust, openness, and a Socratic method of inquiry, the duet begins.

"I write notes to Walter as well as discuss things with him," Minghella says later, sitting on the couch in his roomy office, which is decorated with framed black-and-white production stills from *Cold Mountain*. "I find that both of us operate on different levels, and sometimes we like to read ideas, sometimes we like to speak ideas. I've fallen in with Walter's requirements. And part of the way he likes to work is to catalog and list and order."

March 22, 2003, Murch's Journal

Cut out six and a half minutes from first hour. We made an important connection between the line "store hours" and the match being struck, leading to the "flag" shot—definitely not store hours. Anthony said that he saw how the beginning would work now…

MARCH 10, 2003
MURCH'S JOURNAL

We start putting pressure on Veasey scenes. Cut about four + minutes.

When Minghella and Murch work together, divisions disappear between director and editor, editor and writer, writer and director.

What is it like for to work with Murch? "In the middle of a conversation, Walter will suddenly walk over to a screen and start looking at the rhythms of prime numbers," says Minghella. "I mean, literally, he will suddenly be examining the logarithmic relationships of one prime number to another. It's not accidental that his mind is intrigued by patterns at a point when the film is so obsessed with its pattern. And so he finds it important to have lists, and so what we tend to do is both talk around the film, talk of the film, but also to make lists. And those lists of impressions are very significant. He stores them all, catalogs them all." If Murch wanted to, he could even bring up the *English Patient* lists now, says Minghella.

"I never discuss with Walter what I think the best take is," Minghella continues. "I never discuss with him what I think the shot sequence should be. I realize I would miss out on his own creative reaction if he was simply following my instructions. It's one of the reasons why I don't like to dictate to him how to solve a problem."

"People I work with have proved themselves and they play their instruments in a particular way"—Minghella is speaking of Murch, director of photography John Seale, wardrobe designer Ann Roth, first assistant director Steve Andrews, and others. "They are a handful. They are extremely experienced, extremely successful, arguably each of them is the best in their field. They bring with them an enormous amount of baggage. They're not eager to prove anything. If you're not interested in that way of playing, then don't work with them."

"Of all of them, Walter's idiosyncrasies are the most pronounced. I'm about to spend a year with Walter, and I know that year will be as defined by his personality and requirements as it will be by mine—an intense, relentless, feast-or-famine experience. Walter can either be closed and silent and remote, or the exact opposite, overwhelmingly warm and embracing and loquacious. If you're not prepared for the inexplicable changes in temperature in the room, if you're not prepared for the sudden excursion into issues of the nature of the rotation of the planets, of the derivation of certain words, if you're not in the market for his particular intellectual and emotional gymnasium, then find somebody else to work with. He has much more to contribute in terms of the atmosphere of the editing process than I do. I don't see it as my job to control that. I approach it as he says he approaches the film, which is to surrender to the flow of it."

"Part of the process of making a film, to me, is a process of enabling. It's about passing on empowerment. The more you can empower everybody, the more likely you are to get the best result. Certainly with Walter, a disempowered Walter is a waste of a huge, huge mind and a huge talent. So I just try to understand his particular requirements and respect them and nourish them, because he is easily destabilized. He has an enormous amount of pride, an appropriate pride. And it simply doesn't do to mess with that."

"Walter can either be closed and silent and remote, or the exact opposite, overwhelmingly warm and embracing and loquacious."

The Old Chapel Studio in north London, offices of Mirage Enterprises, where *Cold Mountain* was edited.

Chapter 8

The Hemidemisemiquaver

MARCH 31, 2003—LONDON, ENGLAND

Walter Murch walks to work over Primrose Hill and notices that the morning shadows seem longer; daylight savings time is in effect. The trees are bare, but buds are visible, about to burst. The war in Iraq is ten days old and anti-war signs flutter along the iron fence of Primrose Hill Park.

Twenty minutes later Murch reaches the end of Parkhill Road where it meets Fleet Road. Here, set back from the gently curving corner, is the Old Chapel Studio. He lets himself into the stone building and goes upstairs to the second floor to begin the 255th day of editing *Cold Mountain*. The landing at the top of the stairs is a slab of translucent green glass. One doesn't walk so much as float across it into the realm of film editing. Murch waves a greeting through the window to Sean Cullen, already at work inside his narrow rectangular room. The cubicle on the left, with its rewinds

Susannah Reid in one of the edit rooms at the Old Chapel.

The brass B on the back wall of Murch's edit room in London.

and other film accessories, is empty—neither of the two film assistants, Walter nor Dei, is in yet. They had a late night at the edit bench. Further down the main hallway is a closet-sized room that barely accommodates a four-plate Steenbeck editing table and a Final Cut Pro workstation. Floor-to-ceiling bookshelves are filled with boxes of film dailies. The trainee Susannah Reid, works out of this space.

Murch opens the heavy wooden door to his room at the end of the hall and goes inside. With a sharply peaked exposed-beam ceiling and white walls, this uncluttered space seems more like an architect's studio than an editing room. The Final Cut Pro system sits on a chest-high drafting table. Not one frame of film is in sight. Only Murch's picture boards tell the story of what goes on in here. He turns on the Mac, and crosses the rough wooden plank floor to his simple desk at the rear of the room. Murch takes his Mac PowerBook out of its black carrying case, wakens it, and makes a journal entry while his workstation comes to life.

Behind him, hanging on the wall, is a shiny brass "B." Curious. Ask Walter about it, and he'll tell you about aiming for a "B." Work hard to get the best grade you can—in this world, a B is all that is humanly attainable. One can be happy with that. Getting an A? That depends on good timing and whims of the gods—it's beyond your control. If you start to think that the gods are smiling, they will take their revenge. Keep your blade sharp. Make as good a film as you know how. It's an Eastern-oriented philosophy, characteristic of Murch, as differentiated from the Western outlook, as expressed by the American writer and philosopher, Ralph Waldo Emerson: "We aim above the mark to hit the mark."

Over the last six weeks, since Murch finished the first assembly, he and Minghella have removed 53 minutes of material from the film. The current edited version of *Cold Mountain*, 4 hours and 14 minutes, is still a huge amount of footage—equal to the entire first assembly for *The English Patient*, which was itself considered a high-volume motion picture. In his journal Murch describes this revealing statistic as "sobering."

Back at his drafting table, Murch opens up the Final Cut Pro application. The splash screen comes on for a moment with its film clapboard logo and green eye, sister to the screen saver on Murch's PowerBook—the "eye on the pole" photo he took in Bucharest.

Like most days now, this one will be devoted to structural issues in the film, one of three strands in Murch's editorial process. First there is the logistical wrangling of all the footage—getting it into the system correctly, in sync, properly logged, and then getting it out the other end when the creative work is finished. "Even if there were no creative job at all," Murch says, "it would still be a challenge to do that. How do you get this load of material from one port, across the ocean, to that port, intact and in good condition? I spend a

Murch describes editing as wrangling, performance, and analysis.

good part of my brain thinking about that. Sean spends an even bigger part of his brain thinking about it."

The second strand is what Walter calls the "performance" of editing, that is, selecting takes with the right line readings, putting them in their proper places relative to each other, and intuiting how long to hold each one before cutting to the next. "You can be a perfectly good logistical editor, but if you don't have the feel for the right choices and the right rhythms, it's like somebody playing a musical instrument who gets the notes all right, but something somehow just doesn't feel right."

The third element is the analytical part, the things Murch says a book editor might tell an author about basic structure: "Well, this is a great chapter, but it may be too long relative to the other chapters. Why don't you try dividing it in half and take the first half and put it ahead of the other chapter? And this here? Maybe you don't need it. Maybe it should be in a different place." Structure, for Murch, is distinct from either the "tone or touch" of performance, or the "systems functions" of managing film inventory. "You can't survive without all of them interweaving," Murch says, "although various editors have more talent in one area than in another. The impossible goal is to be equally good at all three."

February 24, 2003, Murch's Journal

Bill Horberg and Elena and Jude screen the film [in FCP] downstairs in Anthony's office. Jude comes at the halfway point. They like it, are excited and overwhelmed at the vastness: "where do you begin?"

Murch starts at the beginning, with the opening battle scene. He is on the prowl for redundancies: where is there fat to cut out? He plays the scene. There. A shot of the Union charge feels like it goes on too long. He'll remember that. There. The Confederates are slow to move their cannon into place. After watching the entire sequence play, noting all the possibilities for trimming shots, he returns to the beginning. Now he sets Final Cut Pro into trim mode so it will loop, or replay, the same shot over and over. Murch holds his index finger over the "K" key and watches the shot play on the large widescreen monitor on his left. As he feels the moment where it ought to end, he presses the key. The shot is trimmed by six frames, and a small readout "−6" appears. The shot replays. Again he feels the moment and presses the "K" key: the readout again reads "−6" which means he hit the same frame twice in a row. "You have to feel the musicality of it," Murch says later, speaking about this edit-on-the-fly technique, for making outgoing edits.

Other editors may freeze the two sides of an edit (with the outgoing frame in one window, the incoming frame in the other window) to carefully study how they relate. But this isn't Murch's way. At the crucial moment of the cut, he insists on working from instincts to give him the kind of emotional connection to the film he wants. "I started this on the KEM when I was editing *The Conversation*, and I used the mechanical frame counter. I would set it to 000 at some arbitrary point upstream from a potential cut point, run the film, and would hit the stop button where it felt right, and read the frame counter; let's say it was 145. And then do it all over again a couple more times, hoping for the same 145. The Avid was very efficient at this—better than the KEM, in fact. One of the first things I asked about Final Cut Pro was its ability to do editing on the fly."

February 9, 2003, Murch's Journal

It is a miracle: the ability—more often than not—to think this shot needs a one-frame trim at the tail. And then be able on the first try to run the shot and hit the trim marker, and get a reading of −1. How is it done? It is mysterious to me. By looking at the rhythms of the image as a kind of visual music, I guess, and then hitting the mark when the new instrument (the new shot) should enter. Musicians do it all the time. Not coincidentally, the frame corresponds to the smallest interval in music: the hemidemisemiquaver.The hdsq *is 1/32 note, and it would correspond to a film frame at a metronomic setting of 180.*

"If I can't do this," Murch wrote in *In the Blink of an Eye*, "if I can't hit the same frame repeatedly at 24 frames per second, I know there is something wrong in my approach to the shot, and I adjust my thinking until I find a frame I *can* hit."

Murch's on-the-fly technique derives from his theory of "the blink." The edit in film—"a total and instantaneous displacement of one field of vision with another"—isn't so different from what we do thousands of times every day in real life when we blink our eyes. While editing Francis Ford Coppola's *The Conversation*, Murch realized his decisions about where to cut shots were coinciding with actor Gene Hackman's eye blinks. Early one morning, after staying up all night working on *The Conversation*, Murch walked up from Folsom to Market Street in San Francisco for breakfast. He passed a Christian Science Reading Room with a display copy of that day's newspaper in the window. It featured a story about film director John Huston, who had just directed *Fat City*. Murch stopped to read the interview. Huston said an ideal film seems to be like thought itself; the viewer's eyes seem to project the images. Huston observed that we regularly cut out unnecessary information by blinking as our gaze adjusts, say, from a person sitting next us to a lamp across the room. Huston's idea connected to what Murch had himself just experienced editing scenes of Harry Caul in *The Conversation.*

Murch's edit-on-the fly technique makes a cut in the blink of an eye.

Murch took the idea one step further by noticing that we also blink when separating thoughts and sorting things out. "Start a conversation with somebody and watch when they blink," he says. "I believe you will find the listener will blink at the precise moment he or she 'gets' the idea of what you are saying, not an instant earlier or later." Murch now understood why his edit points were aligning so closely with Gene Hackman's eye blinks in *The Conversation*. The actor had so thoroughly become Harry Caul he was demonstrating his completed thoughts and feelings in this specific, instinctually physiological way.

For several hours Murch proceeds with the *Cold Mountain* battle sequence. He advances through the Final Cut timeline by "scrubbing" back and forth to locate each shot in the battle scene that had felt excessive on that earlier pass. Using his reflexive technique to intuit a new cut point, he marks then removes the superfluous frames. After finishing this pass Murch sets the playhead back to the beginning of the revised sequence. He cracks his knuckles one by one, turns to his left, still standing, crosses one leg over the other, puts one hand on his hip and rests an elbow on the drafting table. He presses play and watches the results on the big monitor. How does it feel? Does it move along properly? Is there a rhythm to it? Did he drop anything important? Were any telling moments compromised? No, it looks fine for now. The battle is now shorter by one minute and a half. He will show it to Anthony later in the day, when he returns from a meeting at the British Film Institute. For now, he sets it aside.

An editor's responsibility, as Murch sees it, is "partly to anticipate, partly to control the thought processes of the audience. To give them what they want and/or what they need just before they have to 'ask' for it—to be surprising yet self-evident at the same time."

There's another reason Murch edits in real time—why he doesn't stop frames on his monitor to make decisions about where to end a shot. This stems from his "rule of six," a hierarchy of what constitutes a good edit. The list upends a traditional film-school approach that normally puts "continuity of three-dimensional space" as the top priority of editing. For example, you see a woman open a door and walk halfway across the room in shot A. In closer shot B, you find her at that same halfway point as she continues across the room to sit on a sofa. Not maintaining that spatial logic, "was seen as a failure of rigor or skill," as Murch writes in his book, *In the Blink of an Eye*. Murch puts this objective at the bottom of his list. Instead, emotion, "the hardest thing to define and deal with," is at the top. "How do you want the audience to feel? What they finally remember is not the editing, not the camerawork, not the performances, not even the story—it's how they felt."

Film editing means aiming at a moving target. A shot length that feels appropriate today might not seem that way later when adjacent scenes and sequences

FROM *IN THE BLINK OF AN EYE*

The Rule of Six

1. Emotion	51%
2. Story	23%
3. Rhythm	10%
4. Eye-trace	7%
5. Two-dimensional plane of screen	5%
6. Three-dimensional space of action	4%

An ideal cut (for me) is the one that satisfies all the following six criteria at once: 1) it is true to the emotion of the moment; 2) it advances the story; 3) it occurs at a moment that is rhythmically interesting and "right"; 4) it acknowledges what you might call "eye-trace"—the concern with the location and movement of the audience's focus of interest within the frame; 5) it respects "planarity"—the grammar of three dimensions transposed by photography to two (the dimensions of stage-line, etc.); 6) and it respects the three-dimensional continuity of the actual space (where people are in the room and in relation to one another).

Emotion, at the top of the list, is the thing that you should try to preserve at all costs. If you find you have to sacrifice certain of those six things to make a cut, sacrifice your way up, item by item, from the bottom. The values I put after each item are slightly tongue in cheek, but not completely… emotion is worth more than all five of the things underneath it… there is a practical side to this, which is that if the emotion is right and the story is advanced in a unique, interesting way, in the right rhythm, the audience will tend to be unaware of (or unconcerned about) editorial problems with lower-order items like eye-trace, stage-line, spatial continuity, etc. The general principle seems to be that satisfying the criteria of items higher on the list tends to obscure problems with items lower on the list, but not vice versa.

have been changed or reordered. Every edit decision, no matter how trivial it seems or how few frames it involves, throws a pebble into a placid pond. It ripples all the surrounding material. That's why there is a constancy and perseverance to film editing—viewing, reviewing, and rethinking. Through it, the work itself takes on a persistent rhythm.

Examining structure, not just of individual shots, but of the entire film, is Murch and Minghella's principal task now. They gaze at the overall narrative arc of the film's architecture. Naturally, its overarching forms are most apparent when seeing the work in its entirety. So it's not surprising that

Ruby's (Renée Zellweger) arrival at Black Cove Farm.

after screening the first assembly in mid-February, Murch and Minghella now focus on the "two stories"—those of the protagonists, Ada and Inman, whose narratives alternate on screen throughout most of the film. The characters only appear together for a short time at the beginning and the end of the story. This "double-helix" structure, as Murch calls it, comparing the narrative to the shape of DNA, is a difficulty inherent in the premise of the book *Cold Mountain*. Minghella had no choice but to carry over this configuration in the film adaptation. The movie's shape must accommodate that fact, yet also find a rhythmic equilibrium that keeps the Ada-Inman relationship in the forefront of the audience's mind. Their romance has barely begun when they are separated by the onset of the Civil War. They remain separated by place and by the dramatically different consequences of the same war. Their desire for each other must be present, accessible to the filmgoer, yet remain unfulfilled until the end of *Cold Mountain*. This is a formidable storytelling challenge. And one that Minghella and Murch felt from the start.

In his post-first-assembly journal entry, Murch called the opening "long and eccentric." He meant there are two different problems in the beginning section: 1) two principal characters, Ruby and Reverend Veasey, don't show up until the end of the first act, approximately 50 minutes from the start; and 2) asynchronous shifts in time and place between Cold Mountain in 1861 and the Battle of Petersburg in 1864 may be too demanding.

Shortly after screening the first assembly, Murch and Minghella discovered a possible solution to these problems in the first act: Ada's letter-writing to Inman.

February 25, 2003, Murch's Journal
We go over the 'bungee cord' section during the letter writing, and see what we can restructure to make the 'tenses' of the film (past-present) lie easier next to each other.

Ada's difficulties at the beginning of the film, after her father dies and before Ruby arrives, could be condensed by adding material to her letters in a voice-over narration that is "expandable and contractible." This "bungee-cord" section is one of those "hinge" scenes that Murch expects and needs in every film—a section capable of absorbing major structural changes that occur before and/or after it, while also being malleable enough to enlarge and shrink as necessary over the course of editing.

Originally, a series of scenes were linked to each other in real time: Ada's father dies, she tries to cope with Black Cove Farm on her own, she suffers in the winter, she is threatened by Major Teague. But these scenes seem to drag. They could be used, however, more as fragments if they become elements within Ada's letters to Inman. Production-wise, augmenting Ada's letters beyond the original screenplay (and what was shot on location) is relatively painless and affordable: Minghella sends Kidman more letter text to read; she records the new voiceover in a sound studio in New York; a sound file of the material is emailed to Murch in London; Sean Cullen integrates it into the audio flow of FCP; and Murch can now start to sketch out a structure, relating the new audio to the appropriate scene fragments. Some directors hate the process of adding new dialogue to their films. Minghella loves the opportunity to record newly written lines that either deepen his original intentions, or revise them completely. Like the editing itself, it's another opportunity to rewrite the film.

Ada's (Nicole Kidman) letters to Inman prove to be an important structural opportunity for Minghella and Murch to solve story problems.

Expanding Ada's letters may also smooth out the problematic shifts in time and place that Murch noted in his journal entry. Even before leaving for Romania, Walter wrote about this issue in his script notes to Minghella: "Time/space transitions in which the story leaps back and forth with an accelerating time scale; there is a tricky area between page 20 and 34." It's not a problem of simply using flashbacks—a device some directors and screenwriters consider a cliché and refuse to use—and it's not a problem of parallel locations (Cold Mountain/Inman's walking). It's the complicated way those two dimensions interact.

Cold Mountain begins in 1864 at the Battle of Petersburg. After a big explosion under their trenches, Inman and his fellow Confederates fight the Federal army troops who are trapped in a death pit created by the blast they themselves set. Then the movie goes back in time to 1861, when Ada first arrives at Cold Mountain and meets Inman. After their love interest is established, the story returns to the aftermath at Petersburg. We see Inman get a bullet in the neck while on a night mission across enemy lines. When the story returns again to Cold Mountain, it doesn't pick up where we left off. Time has passed, several days at least. And as the story progresses with Ada and Inman together at Cold Mountain during 1861, it makes internal leaps forward in time. Minghella likes this structural motif. He tells non-linear stories and expects an audience to work a little harder to follow them.

The big explosion at the Battle of Petersburg, 1864. After this scene the film shifts locations to North Carolina and goes back in time to the year 1861.

In the first 33 pages of the August 2001 version of the *Cold Mountain* screenplay (essentially Act I) there are 11 time shifts and 6 location changes. Some of these movements shift both dimensions simultaneously. And time moves at a different, quicker pace in Ada's Cold Mountain scenes than it does in Inman's war and recovery scenes. Eventually, about an hour into the film, at page 34, when Inman encounters Reverend Veasey (Philip Seymour Hoffman), Inman and Ada's stories have caught up with each other. Both characters now occupy the same time frame. Thereafter the two main characters are intercut by location. After showing the lovers in parallel time, they finally converge in space at the film's climax, in the Rocky Gorge on Cold Mountain.

Minghella and Murch conclude that asymmetrical shifts in space and time at the beginning of *Cold Mountain* might be too complex for the good of the overall story. Having Ada recount more about her plight in a longer letter would simplify the story arc without giving up important information or dramatic scenes. "This allows us to be brief and succinct," Murch says about the structural change. "We will hear her voice reading the letter and then there will be a scenelette, then she'll read some more, then there's another scenelette. That gives us a well-defined area where time can be freely elastic. She's bringing Inman (and us) up to date on everything that happened to her over a three- or four-year period, 1861 to 1864." The volunteer at the hospital finishes reading the letter to Inman, who hears the final lines from Ada, "Come back to me." We follow him briefly in his recovery, talking to the peanut vendor outside the hospital. When Inman escapes through the hospital window at dawn and begins his journey home, he's now caught up in time with Ada. "That morning he's hitting the beach," Murch says, "is the same morning that Ada goes to sell her father's watch at the store, so all the acceleration in time— the bungee cord—happens in the turbulence of the letter."

Expanding the letter has another unexpected benefit: it strengthens a connection the film wants to make between Ada and Inman even while they are away from each other. She writes and he reads; they are intimately together, at least in spirit, while being apart physically. And it's believable that letter writing nurtures their bond—it's in keeping with the reality of the Civil War, as Ken Burns drove home with his PBS series on the Civil War.

Finally, the open structure to the newly edited letter scene allows Murch to find a home for a fragment of a longer scene between Ada and Captain Teague (Ray Winstone). Ada sits alone in the chapel that her recently deceased father (Donald Sutherland) had built when he came to Cold Mountain. Teague follows Ada inside, sits down behind her, and alternately threatens and woos her. In a beautifully Minghellian moment, not originally part of the book, Teague tells Ada to look him in the eye. Then, with a slight tremor he whispers, "I'm not nothing." Minghella wrote the scene at the last moment, in desperation, as backup ("weather cover") that could be shot indoors during a particularly rainy

Captain Teague (Ray Winstone) tells Ada, "I'm not nothing."

Once Inman escapes from the military hospital to begin his journey back to Cold Mountain, his "film time" matches Ada's.

period on location. Miramax co-chairman Harvey Weinstein had his doubts about the scene. Yet it's one of those wonderfully revealing scenes that lets the audience understand, even sympathize, with the bad guy—always a very difficult storytelling sleight of hand. The fragment plays just right inside the augmented letter sequence, without needing a beginning to set it up, or much of a middle for development.

To get the film down from four hours to a releasable length, Murch and Minghella will have to do more than trim fat from specific shots, as in the battle scene, and restructure to compress time, as with Ada's expanded letters. They must look for whole scenes that might be dropped. No magic number for *Cold Mountain*'s running time was pre-established. When Bill Horberg, one of the film's producers, comes to visit in London, Murch notes Minghella's aversion to being tied down.

February 26, 2003, Murch's Journal

Bill Horberg visits: meeting with Anthony and me; discuss approach to film, how to make it better at the beginning, then how to cut it down. Anthony rejects idea of aiming for a particular length, quotes Godfather II in support.

Murch and Minghella know full well that Miramax doesn't want its showcase Christmas release, the film being positioned for top Oscar contention, to be three hours long. It's largely a matter of economics. Theater owners and

Captain Teague brings rabbits to Ada for her to cook and eat. This scene was dropped, in part because it did not have continuity with the sequence of seasons.

distributors hate it when a movie is so lengthy it can only have one decent evening showing. The cut-off point is about two and a half hours. To avoid conflict with the studio about the running time, Minghella and Murch would rather stay in control of the edit by making the cuts and rearrangements they choose for getting the film shorter. Weinstein is known for asking directors to make last-minute changes to their films. So the more Murch and Minghella do now to get ahead of the curve, the better.

Now, at the end of March, the running time of the film is just under four hours. The amount of material cut out since the first assembly is approaching the 30 percent threshold—that borderline where Murch says further cutting can endanger "the patient." So far, only two major scenes have been dropped entirely. Soon after Ada's father dies, Captain Teague brings dead rabbits to Ada for her to cook and eat. Teague helps her with a few chores as he toys with her aggressively. She takes the rabbits but can't bear to cook them, and buries them in the yard. In part the scene didn't work because it was supposed to take place in winter yet it was shot when there was no snow. Also, the "tang" and double-entendre of Teague's lines as written in the shooting script feel heavy: "Need a hand with that pump?" "If it don't yield meat, or you don't sit on it, or suck on it, it don't have much value...and you're sleeping all right?" Removing "the rabbits," as the edit crew refers to the scene, would cut out two and a half minutes. Another complete scene featuring Teague near the end of the film was also cut. In it, the Captain and his Home

Guard posse spend a night at Black Cove Farm while Ada is away, up on Cold Mountain with Inman. It may have said more than necessary about Teague's sexual predilections when he lies down on Ada's bed with her scarf draped over him.

These cuts bring the film below four hours, so the next screening will be a significant first: the whole film can be seen from start to finish without a break, since it falls within FCP's limits.

Murch goes back to the beginning, looking for wholesale cuts. The first prospect is a scene between Inman and Swimmer, a Cherokee from Cold Mountain, that was designed to open the film. The two soldiers sit together behind the Confederate lines and Swimmer recites a Cherokee battle curse to Inman, in Cherokee. The novel has a more elaborate version of this scene, which takes place in Inman's mind, as a flashback, just before he writes to Ada saying he's decided to abandon the army and walk home to her. Minghella added this scene to the shooting script late in the game. It hadn't been in the August 2001 screenplay that Murch read back home before production.

April 1, 2003, Murch's Journal

Still wrestling with the curse at beginning. The problem is that the opening in Cherokee puts everyone's brain to sleep, and so they don't listen when he translates it.

One of Anthony Minghella's methods for taking his film's temperature is to invite some peers from the filmmaking, literary, and theatre communities to the work-in-progress screenings being held every three weeks. Respect among them is mutual and thorough going, so Minghella expects to hear the truth, regardless of its implications. These trial showings, like any preview, can be bracing. But this is what helps Minghella and Murch confront the film's opening. "It was just sailing over people's heads," Murch says later. "Even very bright filmmakers couldn't get what was going on. There's something about beginning a film in a foreign language without subtitles that says, 'What people say in this film, isn't important. It's just syllables and sounds.'"

The scene is cut.

A week later Murch is midway through this same round of revisions when Minghella recommends another scene for removal: Ada and Ruby at Black Cove Farm talking as they fix each other's hair. It's an intimate tableau with moments that flash with humor. For the most part, however, this episode reveals class and cultural differences between the two women we know already.

Lost the hairdo scene and are starting to group in bigger chunks—Veasey is continuous from discovery through end of Ferrygirl, and Ada-Ruby is continuous from "what's this wood" through "He left you?"

At times, pleasant surprises await filmmakers after they lift a scene and join together what remains: two scenes never designed to lie next to each other suddenly make a perfect fit, enhancing one another and the flow of the story. After Minghella and Murch take out the hairdo scene, two scenes remain that each work better in this new structure. The scene of Ada playing Inman's song on the piano while Ruby listens now immediately precedes the sale of the piano for a flock of sheep. The intervening hairdo scene implied that it was Ruby's idea to sell the piano, with Ada reluctant. Now it implicitly seems to be Ada's idea, and playing Inman's song was also her farewell to the piano the night before selling it. The scenes now do double duty; always a good thing to keep the audience from getting ahead of the story.

A few days later, while going through the last reel of the film, Murch tries removing another major sequence, perhaps the largest so far: a series of scenes in which Inman finally arrives at Cold Mountain town, goes to Black Cove Farm, then walks back up the mountain looking for Ada and Ruby. It's nearly three pages in the screenplay.

April 11, 2003, Murch's Journal

We cut out the Inman detour through Cold Mountain and Black Cove farm. Now he simply comes across Ada as she is shooting turkeys. A saving of 4 minutes, which is significant at this stage of the film, but more specifically it cuts out a loop and the energy-draining feeling that comes with "I've been on a long walk." As long as he (and we) have walked, and reached his (our) destination, he now has to resume walking and go back up the mountain, and the audience would be forgiven for thinking, so long into the story, "Isn't this film ever going to be over?"

Lifting the Inman sequence improves the final act's pacing. The culminating Rocky Gorge encounter with Ada plays more powerfully and emotionally. Meanwhile, Murch can't avoid a scientific analogy for the creative act he's just performed.

April 11, 2003, Murch's Journal (continued)

Organic molecule building is the folding of proteins into each other in particular and energy-efficient ways, facilitated by enzymes. The film editor is similarly a kind of enzyme, facilitating folding the giant molecule of the film into particular and energy-efficient patterns.

THE BENEFITS (AND RISK) OF REDUCTION

Major removals, or an accumulation of minor lifts, can disable a film. Murch uses a racing car analogy: "The goal is maximum power with minimum weight. In altering the car you must do nothing to harm its structure. So to drill out space in the wheels, for example, may reduce the weight by two ounces. And you keep doing that around the wheel and other wheels. Eventually, in the turbulence of the race, however, the wheel buckles and goes awry."

The watchword for this second round of revisions has been large-scale removals, but Murch also continues to make subtle adjustments as they present themselves—the moving-target phenomenon. For example, something now feels out of order in the Rocky Gorge scene. Maybe Ada and Inman's reunion is more in the clear now, and without Inman's walkabout, the rough surface of this scene is better exposed for polishing.

April 12, 2003, Murch's Journal

> *Working on Saturday recutting Ada and Inman meet. Changing the POV to include Inman as well, and Inman's incredulity at seeing Ada—is that Ada? Something didn't seem right, though, and I eventually figured out it was the placement of her shooting the gun, which now comes after the "Ada Monroe?" dialogue rather than at the beginning. It seems better because he is also put off by the sound of the gun and a great image following it of Ada the black spike with smoke swirling around her—definitely not the girl he left.*

A few days later Minghella and Murch agree that this new version is ready. The film is now 3 hours, 26 minutes: poised on the brink of the 30 percent barrier. In the two months since completing the first assembly, they have cut out 1 hour and 40 minutes. Coincidentally, this rate of cutting, which averages 13 minutes a week, is exactly the same rate at which Murch first assembled dailies as they became available during production.

If the film editor seems fated, like Sisyphus, to keep repeating his or her work endlessly, well, there's some truth to that. Each round of revisions leaves material in new arrangements, which in turn requires revision. And so it goes, for weeks and months. Get to the end and start over from the beginning. Murch describes this process as a requisite way for finding the film. "The first assembly, like all subsequent versions of the film, is a lens through which we can glimpse the film itself. And in its transubstantiation, it not only gives us a way of seeing, an approach, but the image in the lens eventually becomes that thing itself." At its extreme, this formulation helps explain why many filmmakers (and other artists) can't bear seeing their work once it's finished. When the tinkering comes to an end and the work is no longer pliant in the creator's hands, it might as well not exist anymore. The process is a reward. And it's the incentive to keep showing up for work.

Before plunging into the potentially treacherous "open-heart" territory below three-and-a-half hours, Murch and Minghella now decide to take stock by trying two completely new and different structures for the opening. It's the only way to "see where the film leads us." That non-linear digital film editing is non-destructive allows for this sort of playful, "Let's see what it looks like" approach, and it takes only a couple of hours to execute.

The first new structure lets the Battle of the Crater at Petersburg continue unabated with no interruptions. It runs from the opening frames until Inman's

Ada, definitely not the girl Inman left.

buddy, Oakley, lies dying while Stobrod the fiddler plays a tune for him. Only then does Inman recall earlier days in Cold Mountain. The story flashes back to the chapel being built and Inman meeting Ada for the first time.

A second trial opening uses a purely chronological approach: the film begins in Cold Mountain in 1861 with Ada's arrival and remains there until Secession is announced and Inman goes off to battle. At that point we see the war itself, beginning at dawn when the Federals lay out barrels of gunpowder for the impending explosion.

Neither restructuring attempt is very satisfying. Yet the doing of it, having new lenses through which to understand the film, reveals insights.

April 29, 2003, Murch's Journal

Screened the beginning restructure and it seemed all right. A little flat-footed— too Merchant-Ivory and not enough spin. The problem the other way was that there was too much spin. How to find the middle ground.

The two have a revelation: after Inman gets injured, he languishes as a character. It's still early in the story, and Minghella and Murch decide it would be better if somehow Inman was up and walking back to Cold Mountain sooner. They had already removed the intervening scene of Teague coming to Ada's with the rabbits. The expanded letter compressed other material in that area, showing Ada struggling after her father's death. Now it's a matter of stitching together the surviving scenes; the results inadvertently help advance Ruby's arrival at Black Cove Farm.

April 30, 2003, Murch's Journal

Tried new structure for after the letter: staying with Inman through to his going out the window, then go to Ada. Better, I think, because it gets Inman walking earlier, it separates his walking (big moment) from Ruby's arrival (big moment), which were right on top of each other in the previous version. Shows the strong effect of the words "come back to me" on him, almost biblical healing. Puts a strong section of Inman where we need it, after a long time "away" from him, scenes where he is just a piece of suffering flotsam. We get that good superimposition of Inman running away with Bosie saying, "any man who deserts is a traitor." Nice dissolve from well to tunnel of trees.

It's a good day at the Old Chapel for analysis and structure. The two second assistants achieve their own distinction in film wrangling: Walter and Dei conform the first reel (approximately 2,000 feet, or 22 minutes) of 35mm work-print on the edit bench. This is the initial step for having a projectable film version of *Cold Mountain* to screen in a theater for producers and eventually for preview audiences. It's the first full-on test of a cut list, or film assembly list, that Sean Cullen generates using FCP and CinemaTools. The 300-odd film splices in this first of nine reels must match, frame for frame, the version of reel one Walter edited on Final Cut Pro. Murch and his assistants squeeze into the tiny room with the Steenbeck editing table to watch and listen. Dei puts the reel on a spindle, threads it up through the viewing prism and Murch sits down at the machine. He runs the film, with the sound coming from a ProTools sound file. It's in sync. There is much to celebrate. The digital alchemy of getting 24-frame-per-second film footage into 30-frame-per-second video, then back out with 24-frame information for the assistants to use has succeeded. The workflow works. The assistants are now confident that they will be able to get the workprint prepared for its debut screening on time and accurately.

On the other side of the equation, however, the sound situation remains unsettled, especially getting sound from Final Cut Pro into ProTools and back out again for the sound mixes. The sound editors have been working with Walter's edited soundtracks as Sean exports them, so that part of the journey is accomplished. But it's a roundabout route that uses another application called Titan. The question bothering Murch is how long the audio conversions will take once he locks the picture and then must turn right around to mix the sound. He will probably make changes to the picture at the last minute, just before beginning the mix. Might a lag in getting up-to-date sound files prepared in time delay the mix? That would mean not being ready in time for the first public screenings.

Film assistants Dei Reynolds, left, and Walter Murch, right, at the Old Chapel.

But an even higher tide is rising just over the horizon.

Since arriving in London from the film sets in Romania at the end of 2002, Minghella and Murch have been left to their own devices, editing on the equivalent of a desert island—screening, thinking, editing, and thinking again. They are free to try things without having to be accountable. Difficult and intense as it's been to get *Cold Mountain* reshaped into 3 hours and 20 minutes, these two and a half months in the Old Chapel have been a lush life. The pair's creative sanctuary is about to be invaded.

May 7, 2003, Murch's Journal

Ready to show the film to Sydney [Pollack] this afternoon. Put the narration and Ada snow back in the film, followed by Stobrod and Pangle leaving footprints. Keep the "catastrophe"—Sara cut.

I feel as if the wind is at my back today. Thank you.

Tim [Bricknell, Minghella's assistant] comes in looking sheepish: Harvey [Weinstein] is in town and wants to see as much as he can.

It's not as if Minghella and Murch forgot they're making a major studio motion picture. Having creative freedom in seclusion is just what the film needed at this stage. Smart producers know when to let filmmakers do their work uninterrupted. Like kids left home alone to play, they know Mom and Dad are coming back. But it's still a shock when the door opens and there they are.

It's right on schedule for Weinstein and Sydney Pollack, Minghella's Mirage producing partner, to go up to the editing room to see the work-in-progress. The producers have obligations to make sure the enterprise stays on budget, on schedule, and arrives in theaters being the film they wanted to make. Minghella and Murch have done two pictures with Weinstein, so he's not a stranger. Pollack is himself a fellow filmmaker, and Minghella has co-produced two award-winning films with him (*Iris* and *The Quiet American*). Nevertheless, Minghella and Murch are still figuring out *Cold Mountain* themselves. They may not be "skinless," as Murch described Minghella at preview screenings, but their flesh is tender as the director and editor make space in the editing room for new onlooker/participants.

Screening for HW: ok but not great. It ended well, but he dozed off briefly in the first hour. Felt that the opening structure was wrong and that the film really begins with Ruby's entrance. When will we not hear that comment? Probably never. As it was on K-19: the film really begins when the reactor melts down.

Why did Ant ask Harvey how short the film should be? Couldn't he guess? Was it a real question? He prefaced it with "make things difficult for me"—and he did, saying 2.30, which is fifty minutes less than currently.

Harvey wanted to cut out the Rebecca meeting in Veaseytown: "you've got your production value, just get in and get out."

By this point in his career Murch is used to getting comments, or notes, from producers. It comes with the territory of being a film editor. He's philosophical about it: "I transcribe the notes without prejudice. If they said it, I put it down, make of it what we will. Sometimes there are great ideas in there. Sometimes even a bad note is productive, because it makes you think, what caused them to say that? It's like referred pain: 'Doc, my elbow hurts.' And the doctor says, 'The problem in your elbow is a pinched nerve in your shoulder.' So it frequently happens that third parties can see things we can't. They're freer in a sense, but at the same time they also don't know the code as well as we do. So you have to listen carefully to what people say. You can't take everything on board. But you have to be willing to give every question the benefit of the doubt. One person's comment might shed light on the other's."

Despite their notes and comments, Weinstein and Pollack agree that this assembly, with some changes still under discussion, should have its first theatrical showing at the National Film Theatre in London to an invited audience of Minghella's film friends and associates, and then in New York for a similar Miramax-invited group. These screenings will be held in mid-June. The picture editing of this version must therefore be completed, or "locked," the first week of June to allow one week for a temporary sound mix to be done.

For the next four days, Pollack stays in London to go through the entire film scene by scene with Minghella and Murch, discussing and trying out ideas. As Murch says later about Pollack, "I have a lot of time for Sydney. It was intense, but enjoyable. He's got a very good bedside manner about him."

Working with Sydney: got halfway through reel eight, the raiders arrive at Sara's.

This is the week that we need the beta of FCP and figure out an exit strategy. Canadian geese honking overhead as I walk home at night.

Within the month, the crucial period begins for sound editing. Murch, Cullen, and the guys at DigitalFilm Tree have had their eyes on XML (eXtensible Markup Language), which may allow a developer to create just the custom software they need to move sound files without any clumsy reformatting or file conversions. Although Cullen now has the upgraded Final Cut Pro application, version 4.0, on his workstation, it doesn't contain such a plug-in. And up to now Apple has not been willing to let Murch and Cullen have a trial version of XML, even though DFT believes it will probably work based on the beta testing they are doing. Murch sent emails about XML to Hudson and Meaney at Apple, and to their boss, Will Stein, and to Steve Jobs. Up to now, there have been no replies.

John Taylor, a Final Cut editor working with DFT at this time, is in email contact with Sean Cullen about the sound transfer issue. Taylor confirms that Brooks Harris, an original designer of the OMF protocol, can create what Sean needs with the XML plug-in, if Apple gives permission: "It becomes more of a question for Ramy on how to make this a go."

Ramy gets in touch with Brian Meaney at Apple to make a request on Walter and Sean's behalf: "They will be starting to hand over to sound department in two weeks. Again, this is a critical juncture. Can we authorize Brooks to see what he can discover/do with an XML export from our Beta FCP 4? Brooks is willing to allocate time to do this."

Meaney does not want to jump the gun on an Apple developers' conference on June 23 when XML will be officially unveiled. Meaney writes to Ramy: "There is no way to do anything before the conference… I'm afraid the answer is still no, as we do not have the resources to do this. I know that it all sounds very enticing, but really don't have the ability to do this. I would not recommend waiting or scheduling anything based upon things that are not finished being developed, there are too many unknowns in that process."

Cullen must move forward and prepare sound files for the sound editors using the clumsy Titan system translation. He and Ramy Katrib decide to make one more attempt to convince Apple to provide the XML plug-in. On May 14 Cullen writes a three-page background email to Ramy with all the information Ramy might need to take another run at Apple. Cullen summarizes the set-up, workflow, and achievements editing *Cold Mountain* on Final Cut Pro. He concludes with a plea that Ramy can pass on to Hudson, Meaney, and their boss, the director of professional applications at Apple, Will Stein: "It takes days to rebuild the sequence in ProTools when it could take less than an hour. If we had some idea about the timeframes involved for XML output: weeks, months or years, we could start making educated guesses about how to proceed. Without any hint of information, it leaves us out in the cold and we had hoped that Apple would provide a little more warmth. We are not asking Apple to take responsibility for any aspect of our show, we are only looking for information. We are not looking for a scapegoat, we are looking for a partner."

Ramy and Zed later describe the ironic situation DFT faced, since they already had the XML plug-in from Apple on their computers. It was included in the FCP 4 beta test version Apple provided to them. One of DFT's roles as an Apple development site is to help test just such new software. DFT could have emailed a file with the XML plug-in to London, surreptitiously, in a matter of seconds. "Instead we basically played it above board," Ramy says later. "We appealed to Apple at the highest level—just short of Steve—saying we would like to have your permission to explore this new functionality with Brooks Harris, who's world class, renowned."

Murch keeps his eye on the XML issue and follows the email thread. For him and Cullen the sound transfer problem is the last Final Cut Pro hurdle standing between them and the finish line. Perhaps they will be able to get there without Apple's help after all? Nevertheless, Murch offers to contact Will Stein.

Composer Gabriel Yared began working on music for *Cold Mountain* during production in 2002.

In emails to Walter, Ramy expresses his anxiety about pushing forward with the XML solution in the face of Apple's discouragement: "Knowing what Apple has done to those who've broken their nondisclosure agreements has me concerned about what they will do to our Tree. They're in a position to slice our throat regardless of how good-looking we are."

Meanwhile, a new creative demand arises in the Old Chapel. It's time that music for *Cold Mountain* be further developed. Composer Gabriel Yared— like Murch, a veteran of *The English Patient* and *The Talented Mr. Ripley*— had earlier prepared sketches of musical ideas and given them to Murch for placeholders. This is the best way to work with music while editing movies, since anything composed, orchestrated, and performed too early in the process is unlikely to fit the rhythmic needs of the picture, which is ever-changing. Whole scenes and sequences fall away in the early part of editing so it's a waste of resources to prepare music too soon. But there comes a point when an assembly is far enough along that scoring and recording can safely begin. Minghella will work closely with Yared on the music over the next six months, spend many long days in Yared's studio generating completely usable music tracks from samples, and attend the final recording sessions with the London Symphony Orchestra at nearby Abbey Road Studios. Minghella is himself a musician, a singer-songwriter who performed and recorded as a young man before getting involved in theatre and film. When he and Yared get to work, it's a deep collaboration—more so, perhaps, even than Minghella's relationship with Murch because of all the facets in filmmaking, music is Minghella's métier.

A beautiful morning. Another backwards-walking person: a girl this time, going up Primrose Hill. Gabriel is hungry for Anthony and can't write music without Anthony being there. An eclipse of the moon tonight at 3am.

Murch, too, feels strongly about music. He is the one who has to braid the music with his edits, and music choices shape a film's personality. Moreover, Murch can make magic happen at the intersection of film and music by working a music cue into an existing scene so it fits comfortably. He will mix and match musical moments to support a sequence; or even steal music designated for one scene and find a better home for it elsewhere in the film. As lead sound mixer, Murch will also be handling duties with music volume, EQ, and its blending with other sound elements. Murch knows that writing and recording music, especially large orchestral sounds, takes time.

Murch begins anticipating the first temporary sound mix, which is only a few weeks away. He has kept his ears open to what the sound editors are doing. As a former sound editor himself, it's second nature. He sends the sound department his revised scenes for sprucing up as soon as they become available. They send him back QuickTime files with rough drafts of their work. He incorporates those files into his Final Cut Pro system and links his version to their new soundtracks. So it goes, back and forth between Murch and the sound department, all aiming at the day when Walter will sit down at the sound mixing console. By that time he will have previewed and many of the key sound elements, including the music, so he can concentrate solely on blending them together into an artistic whole—itself a hugely demanding job.

A full-length motion picture has thousands of sound effects. An axiom for sound editors, as for picture editors, is that their work should be invisible. Moviegoers should only rarely notice a specific sound. Instead, the cumulative effect of the soundtrack should take the audience further inside the movie. Sound editors and sound designers describe their task as "sculpting" an audio environment. And if a particular sound isn't already in their library of effects, sound editors will either go into the field and record it live, or recreate it using whatever object or tool gets the job done. Murch, like most of his colleagues, does whatever is necessary to capture a particular audio moment, and is wildly inventive at coming up with the proper facsimiles to create it if the real thing does not exist or doesn't sound quite right for the movies.

One sound cue in the first part of *Cold Mountain* is a particular challenge. Having just arrived in Cold Mountain, Ada Monroe takes delivery of her much-loved piano. It arrives from Charleston in the back of a horse-drawn wagon, and Ada sits alongside it as the instrument is jostled up the road to Black Cove Farm. She stops the wagon at the Swanger Farm where she sees Inman at work, as she had requested, plowing Swanger's fields as a favor. As

Ada brings her beloved piano to Cold Mountain.

the wagon jerks to a stop, the piano emits a clunking sound of jumbling notes. "That's a fine-sounding thing," Sally Swanger says sardonically. Murch is not happy with the sound the piano is making.

May 16, 2003, Murch's Journal

The piano sound doesn't work: "that's a fine sounding thing." It sounds like somebody is playing the piano badly. What would work best? A chattering kind of sound, with the hammers loose on the strings, dampened a bit. Bolt a paint shaker to the frame of a piano and let it go.

Sound editor Martin Cantwell eventually found a wrecked piano, extracted the harp, and coiled and uncoiled a thick rope across the strings. It gives a proper soft dissonance without sounding as if someone was playing the keys randomly.

Now that the first screening deadline is set, Final Cut Pro starts acting up. In part it's a logical consequence of having a more evolved show for Final Cut to digest. The assembly now has more of Walter's color corrections to the picture and his fine-tuned adjustments to the soundtracks. In a May 17 email to Ramy and to Aurora Video Systems, which provided the circuit card to digitize the video, Murch writes, "I am going through a bad patch right now with crashes—at least a couple a day—from trimming with color correction. The amount of color-corrected clips is increasing as we get more 'presentational' with the film. So this was always a problem lurking in the background but now it has come into the foreground. Especially foreground when Anthony and Sydney Pollack are in the room with me."

"The Aurora guys were great," Sean recalls later. "After a few phone calls and some late hours on their part, they fixed the problem, made it go away completely." Aurora made a new software build of their driver to help reduce crashing with color-corrected clips when using Final Cut Pro's trim window. Not only that, but they quickly posted the *Cold Mountain* fixes on their website for everyone to use.

The following week the other producers, Albert Berger and Ron Yerxa, arrive at Old Chapel to screen the assembly along with music producer T-Bone Burnett, who, with Minghella, had recorded period music prior to filming. Berger and Yerxa spend the next three days with Murch and Minghella going through the show scene by scene, just as Pollack had ten days earlier: critiquing the film, providing notes, and having Murch try out new things, such as having Oakley's dying scene after the battle play out in real time, instead of intercutting it with the scene where Ada plays the piano as Inman plows Sally Swanger's field.

During his second day working with Berger and Yerxa, Murch realizes Ramy has not replied to his last two emails. This is uncharacteristic.

Subject:	All right?
Date:	May 20, 2003
From:	Walter Murch
To:	Ramy Katrib

Dear Ramy:

Haven't heard any answer from last two emails I sent you. Is everything all right?

Concerned in London,
W.

"There was only one time where I exited the scene for a few days," Ramy recalls later. "And Walter sent me an email saying, 'Is anything wrong?' It's almost like he sensed it. He picked it up. I never said anything, that my dad had passed away. I didn't make a big deal about it.

"I wrote back that I was with him at his deathbed for the last week," Ramy continues. "He writes a response which really helped me process it. I got blown away by this. It's just something I'll never forget from Walter, of all people. To even take the time. It wasn't just taking the time, he related it to his experience."

Subject:	The lens
Date:	May 20, 2003
From:	Walter Murch
To:	Ramy Katrib

Dear Ramy:

Truly sorry to hear about your father.

My dad died many years ago, when I was 24, and it still continues to hit me in unexpected ways, 36 years later.

The image to keep in mind is a slide projector with the lens suddenly removed. The slide is still in the gate, and the image is still projecting but in a diffuse way. Our bodies are lenses that allow "us-ness" to achieve a particular focus and presence on the screen of this world. But the slide—the soul, the spirit—is still where it was, throwing out its particular colors and tonalities, and tinting the objects that its light falls upon, waiting for a new lens.

When your "eyes" accustom themselves to the lack of sharpness, you will be able to discern the familiar shapes and presences.

Love,
Walter.

A week later Zed informs Walter that DFT has not heard back from Will Stein about the XML plug-in request. Murch quickly sends an email to Stein—himself.

Subject:	FCP 4
Date:	May 26, 2003
From:	Walter Murch
To:	Will Stein

Dear Will:

We have had successful screenings (plasma screen of direct FCP output) for Harvey Weinstein of Miramax (studio) and Sydney Pollack (producer). We are now headed for an official digital-image showing to Miramax in New York towards the end of June, followed by a 35mm audience preview in New York on July 20.

> As happy as we are with FCP, we are still searching for a way to convey our sequence and media information to the sound department in a quick and complete way that includes all the metadata and that can be accomplished in hours and not days.
>
> **To that end, I would like to ask your permission to allow DigitalFilm Tree (Ramy Katrib) to show the XML output of FCP 4 beta to Brooks Harris, one of the original designers of the OMF export protocol. Brooks feels he can put together a utility for us that will speed our plow, so to speak, in the next few weeks.**
>
> Thank you in advance for the help you might give us,
>
> Sincerely,
> Walter M.

Stein relies promptly to Murch the next day, but the news is not good. He takes a firm position, saying the XML "is not as far advanced as the rest of the (FCP 4.0) application... it has known problems at this time that will prevent Brooks from being successful." Stein goes on to acknowledge Murch is stuck with "an inefficiency... the current work-around process for audio is tedious, but I'm hoping it won't slow you down too much. This was the one area we were most concerned about when you started *Cold Mountain*, and the biggest obstacle we were aware of for using FCP in a major film production. The XML interface should allow us to clean up this workflow in the future [probably July], but the timing is unfortunate for your current project. Best regards—Will."

Murch is not easily discouraged. He sends an email back to Will Stein appealing the decision: "I appreciate the dilemma and understand your position, but I would ask you to please reconsider... We have gotten this far—ten months from the start of shooting—with very little in the way of hand-holding, and I wouldn't want to stumble unnecessarily at this late stage... Please would you see if there is some way to grant my request."

But Murch doesn't stop there. He sends Steve Jobs a long email, restating the *Cold Mountain* update he provided Will Stein, and informing Jobs of Stein's decision to turn down the XMl request. "Thank you in advance for any help you might give us," Murch concludes, "and congratulations on the thorough reworking of FCP in version 4."

Meanwhile, there's a film that needs Murch's attention. Along with music, sound effects, producer's notes, and preparing to lock the picture for the June screenings, it's time for Murch to take up a new post-production task: visual effects. Although it's a period film, *Cold Mountain*, like most major films, requires a number of computer-generated special effects to either fix problems with the images, or supplement what's there. Not enough stars are visible in a nighttime shot: add stars. A modern-day sailboat appears, a speck on the horizon in Charleston Bay: remove it digitally. When the Home Guard garrotes Esco Swanger, the fake sword can be seen bending slightly in the last few frames: touch it up digitally. Inman reaches the snowy ridge above Cold Mountain town and in his close-up we ought to see his breath: draw it in. And so on. One of Murch's jobs is to spot, or call out, each shot that needs a visual effect. Dennis Lowe is the visual effects supervisor; he was on location in Romania offering advice and will produce the final effects, doing many of them himself.

May 30, 2003, Murch's Journal

Finish going through film with Dennis and there are around 230 effects shots which Dennis thought was in the ballpark for what he expected. A lot of breath and snow shots as befits Cold Mountain.

At the beginning of June, with their first major deadline looming, Murch and Minghella are locking one reel a day. Working out of order, which is typical in film editing, they finally lock the last reel—number one, the battle. Murch considers it, "semi-refined… more work to do, but at least it is all on the table."

The film is well below three-and-a-half-hours, and Murch is amazed that it still has most of its internal organs, despite the fact that they have cut out more than 30 percent of the original assembly.

June 3, 2003, Murch's Journal

Total length of film is three hours six mins and two seconds, allowing two minutes for titles at the end of the tree shot, which is a fudge—it is really a minute and a half. But we have cut out just over two hours, which means 40% of the assembly. No main character is gone. Swimmer is hostage to this version, and barely there, and no extra loop down to Black Cove. That is a significant plot moment, but it was arguable that it was a mistake to begin with, since the book treated it as a flashback.

This latest assembly of *Cold Mountain* is done just in time. Murch has another milestone to attend to: back in California, his daughter Beatrice is getting married.

June 4, 2003, Murch's Journal

Flying home: Walter came to Primrose Hill Cottage at 11, and we rode to the airport together. He is on this flight, though in economy and I am in business.

Bought Rise and Fall of Third Chimpanzee: by Jared Diamond. He wrote this in 1991 and it is good, and reminds me of Mysteries of Modern Science by Stableford—a remarkable book.

Have neglected this journal for the last three weeks, as the crunch intensified. Also neglected my morning exercises. Start up again. Cleaned up the house and put the dishwasher on—has not been on since Aggie left a month ago. The dishes in there were full of mold.

The Murch family at Beatrice's wedding.

CHAPTER 9

Another Rubicon Crossed

JUNE 7, 2003—BLACKBERRY FARM, CALIFORNIA

On a warm, overcast afternoon on the expansive front deck, Walter Murch's daughter Beatrice marries Kragen Sitaker. Two days later, still home, Walter gets back to the business of finishing *Cold Mountain*. It's coming down to the wire with Apple about getting the beta, or even alpha, version of the XML software that could be used to transfer sound information from Final Cut Pro to Pro Tools, the sound editing application. If they are going to receive it (Apple's Will Stein initially said no) Murch and Cullen must put it right to work, though it may already be too late. A temporary sound mix to prepare the soundtrack for the first screenings outside the edit room, begins Saturday, June 14, three days after Murch's return to London.

Date: Mon, 09 Jun 2003 16:26
Subject: Checking IN
From: Ramy Katrib
To: Walter Murch

Hello Walter,

Have you heard anything in regard to the last round of threads? FCP 4 is supposed to release this week, and it appears things are more chaotic than usual in Cupertino.

Regards,
ramy

From: Walter Murch
Subject: Re: Checking IN
Date: 6/9/03 11:21 PM
To: Ramy Katrib

Dear Ramy:

Thanks for the letter.

No, I haven't heard anything from Will or Steve, or Brian. I did get an automatic mailing from Apple that urged me to be the first to own FCP 4! I am just about to get on a plane back to London. Daughter's wedding last Saturday which went very well.

I wonder what our next step should be?

We are doing a temp mix starting on Saturday, so for the time being, the EDL-Titan pathway seems to have done the job. But it is clumsy and incomplete compared to what is just out of our reach.

Despite the probable chaos, I am a little cheesed off at Will S. for not answering or even acknowledging my last letter.

Best wishes,
Walter

The workaround Murch and Cullen use for getting unembedded sound information from Murch's editing system to the sound editors is cumbersome and requires several time-consuming steps using two different, specially written applications (MetaFlow and Titan) and a file transfer using the OMF protocol. At the upcoming sound mix, they will discover whether the process did its job and kept audio tracks in sync with the picture. If not, if somehow sync got lost during all the conversions and reconversions, then an unavoidable pothole lies ahead that will require precious time and labor to pave over.

All during the last 12 months, beginning with that June 2002 conference call among Katrib, Murch, Cullen, and Brooks Harris at DFT's offices, the group has been expecting the XML plug-in Apple was developing, to permit a transparent data transfer of sound information. At the end of May 2003, before leaving for the wedding in California, Murch had appealed to Will Stein and Steve Jobs. He asked if they would reconsider Stein's initial decision to deny access to a test version already sitting on Ramy's computer in LA; it had inadvertently been included within a beta version of Final Cut Pro 4.0 that Apple gave to developers for testing, DFT included.

According to Ramy, talking later at DigitalFilm Tree, "Without even lifting a finger, they [Apple] could have helped tremendously our effort, our cause."

Zed jumps in: "Walter and Sean, they really needed this one, man."

Expressing Apple's position about XML a year later, Brian Meaney says, "I understood their need for wanting it. It wasn't finished. It was still being worked on. There were many people in the industry who wanted it. It was difficult to have to say no, but we simply can't deliver what we don't have. XML wasn't in a state to pass off for anyone to do anything with it."

"We always had the production's best interests in mind," Bill Hudson adds. "That's why we gave them Cinema Tools. We knew it wasn't going to expose them to anything that could potentially be damaging to the production."

"Here we were," Ramy recalls, "*knowing* it will work because Brooks saw it, saw it right there with his eyes. So we're asking permission instead of just doing it. That was one of the critical moments in the whole *Cold Mountain* experience."

Neither Murch nor Katrib ever hear back from either Will Stein or Steve Jobs about their appeal to have access to XML. But DFT and Murch have one last hope for getting the XML plug-in: an earlier email from Apple's Brian Meaney to Ramy Katrib indicated that Apple would "engage" Brooks Harris, representing DigitalFilm Tree, at Apple's upcoming World Wide Developers' Conference on June 23. Ramy has it on good authority that Apple will unveil the new XML software at that event. By following Meaney's willingness to "engage" at the conference, Harris might get access to the program—not in time to put to work on the first sound mix for *Cold Mountain*—but if the Titan-EDL workaround fails, it still might be needed to rescue a loss. What Meaney intends by "engage," however, is uncertain.

June 11, 2003, Murch's Journal
Arrive in London all ok. Had a bath and lay down for a bit—now at the office where all is well. Saw Anthony in Tim's office—he looked tired.

Back in London, Murch had email from Ramy about the XML situation:

Date: Wed, 11 Jun 2003 15:36
Subject: Re: Checking IN
From: Ramy Katrib
To: Walter Murch

Hello Walter,

As of now, I'm working on Brooks going to the developers conference where Apple is going to make major announcements, including XML. The tickets are $1200, so I'm working on getting free passes for him, as we are not quite rich yet. I've arranged for Brooks to meet one of the principal FCP programmers at the conference, so they can talk and cover major ground. Brooks would be going on his own time/money, but we're doing everything we can to make it happen. Will keep you updated, regards,

ramy

Four major screening milestones define the near-term schedule for *Cold Mountain*, each a work-in-progress preview:

- National Film Theatre, friends/family screening, London, June 20, 2003

- Miramax Films, internal screening, New York, June 26, 2003

- First test preview screening, New Jersey, July 21, 2003

- Second test preview screening, New Jersey, August 20, 2003

The studio has the option of holding one additional test preview screening on the East Coast at the end of September.

These showings, roughly a month apart, set a new tempo by which time gets measured at the Old Chapel and throughout the rest of *Cold Mountain* post production, which comprises music recording, ADR (automated dialogue replacement), sound editing, temporary sound mixes, opening and closing titles, visual effects, and picture editing. While these functions all continue toward completion, each with its own pacing and steps, they are all driven by the demands of the screening schedule. Each screening requires a deliverable version of the movie that can be shown in a theater and stand up to an audience's expectations for what a major film looks and sounds like.

Showing the film in a theater environment means another hurdle for Final Cut Pro to get over. The conforming process—by which the 35mm film print version of *Cold Mountain* is kept up-to-date with changes made in digital editing—depends on all-important change lists. When Dei and young Walter, the second assistant editors, began the conforming process at the end of April, they used Cinema Tools to produce an accurate conform list to make their first round of film edits, and it worked fine. But to keep up with hundreds of changes since then requires a change list function that only became available when Apple provided it to Murch in the Beta version of Final Cut Pro 4.0. Back in California, when Murch and Cullen first decided to use Final Cut Pro, they proceeded knowing the system could not yet make reliable change lists. Very shortly they will discover if the gamble pays off—if this new piece of software gives the film assistants the tool they need to generate a 35mm print that matches the version Murch edits in Final Cut Pro, and whether it plays in sync when projected.

Each new version of *Cold Mountain* that gets screened from this point on emerges from the molting of its previous version. After first absorbing the emotional consequences that come with each public showing, Minghella, Murch, and the team must take into account and somehow incorporate—or reject—the comments, reactions, and suggestions generated from the preceding screening—be they from audience, attending producers, or Minghella himself. They must sift through it all, decide what adjustments must be made and how to make them, and get back to work in the edit room. With each new redaction, the film must also get progressively shorter in length.

De Lane Lea, where the sound for *Cold Mountain* was mixed in London.

Saturday, June 14, 2003, Murch's Journal

Get up at 7:30 and be at work before nine.

With that entry, on the first day of sound mixing at De Lane Lea studios in Soho, Murch goes off-journal for the next week and a half. Like the Apollo I circling behind the moon, he'll be out of radio contact before beginning the trip home to Earth. "It was a scattered time," Murch recalls later, "with Aggie's mother dying and lots of cross-Atlantic flying and cutting and mixing, etc."

There are several top-notch facilities for sound mixing in and around London. Miramax, in consultation with Murch and Minghella, had selected the re-recording theater at De Lane Lea in London's West End. They chose it over either the Pinewood or Shepperton studios, both of which are on the outskirts of London, due in part to its location, being reasonably close to Murch and Minghella's base of operations at the Old Chapel—about 20 minutes by taxi or tube, or a 45 minute walk from Murch's house in Primrose Hill. Mixing there, within the vibrant narrow streets of Soho, also means every kind of motion picture and media post-production service or supplier is in walking distance. The *Cold Mountain* sound editors are set up nearby at Goldcrest, a long-standing sound studio; Double Negative, which is doing visual effects, is two blocks away; and the film lab, FrameStore/CFC, is also close by.

De Lane Lea contains three floors with editing rooms, a screening theater, a large music recording studio, offices, a café, and, on the first floor, a sound-mixing theater, (or mix stage), where Murch, Minghella, and the sound crew will spend much of the next six months preparing the soundtrack.

Among films using DLL-Soho for ADR and other sound services over the last few years are *Pirates of the Caribbean, Master and Commander, Spider-Man, The Hours,* and *Gangs of New York.* The second *Harry Potter* movie was mixed there after *Cold Mountain.*

A movie soundtrack blends three kinds of sound: dialogue, music, and effects. For filmmakers, this process of mixing sound is their final chance to shape a film. What filmgoers hear inside the theater is every bit as complex and emotionally important to storytelling as the images they watch—maybe more so, because sound should do its job at a subconscious level.

Every sound mix has its own personality and should properly complement the story being told. A soundtrack for a romantic comedy like *Down with Love* should be "bright"—it features contemporary pop songs, and brings intimate dialogue to the forefront. A thriller like *Fight Club* should sound "dark," contain lots of jarring, spooky sound effects, and use a brooding musical bed. The soundtrack's character is defined early on with discussions among the director, composer, location sound recordist, sound supervisor, sound designer (if separate from the supervisor), and sound editors. Before the picture is even finished being filmed, sound effects are found or recorded—on location, from existing effects collections, off location, and in the recording studio. In *Cold Mountain,* for example, sound supervisor Eddy Joseph and sound effects editor Martin Cantwell, spent two days recording gun collectors firing authentic Civil War munitions in the countryside north of London, an event specially arranged for this purpose.

Even at the script stage (and certainly by the time the first assembly is completed), the director and sound supervisor will "spot" the film, deciding which spots in the film should have which kinds of effects. Likewise, the director and the composer of the musical score together plan what sorts of music belong in which scenes. Even though the best quality recording of the actors' words is taken on location, that "production sound" is often replaced later in the studio with ADR—because the quality on set was compromised by unwanted ambient sounds, technical problems, or faulty line readings. With Minghella, even more than with most film directors, ADR is an opportunity to rewrite the film one more time—replacing lines, rewriting phrases, adding voiceover—all for the purpose of sharpening story, character, and emotion. ADR is also used to obtain background conversation and off-camera dialogue color using "loop groups," actors who, in a battle scene for example, articulate sounds such as grunts, cries, yells, and occasionally actual words, none of which were recorded during location filming.

There are four components to the mix: 1) the sound itself, created on a digital audio workstation (DAW) such as Pro Tools, and played directly from the workstation or off hard drives; 2) a mixing board, the electronic switching station with sliders, faders, equalization controls, and other functions (often

Sound Recordist as Movie Hero

To honor the little-appreciated sound effects craft (and in homage to Michelangelo Antonioini's *Blow-Up* and Coppola's *The Conversation*), film director Brian De Palma made the 1981 movie, *Blow Out,* starring John Travolta. In the film, a soundman played by Travolta is recording atomosphere and effects for a movie when he inadvertently records evidence proving a car "accident" was in fact, murder.

automated) that is operated by the re-recording mixer; 3) the room itself, a small theater with real theater seats to approximate the acoustics of a theatrical environment; and 4) the sound mixer's ears. While there are all sorts of devices to measure and graph sound, there are no objective criteria for what makes a good mix. What ultimately matters is how something sounds to the mixer, the director, and the producers. Like much of filmmaking, this process is an art supported by science.

Since it's nearly impossible to physically manipulate all strands of dialogue, effects, and music at the same time (and mentally overwhelming to even hear them unmixed all together), movie sound is first prepared in "premixes." That is, the sound effects are grouped together in different categories: atmospheres, munitions, footsteps, props, horses, etc., separated out for maximum flexibility in the final mix. Each group is premixed onto a six-track master, with each track sent to three speakers arrayed behind the screen, two in the walls and one in the rear (surrounds); then all the dialogue is premixed; and, finally, the music is laid in once the effects and dialogue are set. When the time comes to do the final soundtrack, the mixer works with these prepared ingredients, though the "raw" original tracks can easily be accessed if necessary from a workstation dedicated to this purpose.

The sound arrives at the premix in "split tracks." Not only are music, dialogue, and effects separated from each other, each *type* of sound effect is segregated from other sound effects—again, for maximum flexibility. For example, 64 raw gunshot tracks in *Cold Mountain*'s battle scene have been reduced to one six-track premix, while sounds of horses' hooves are on a different premix. That way the mixer can adjust the volume relationship between just those two sounds to best represent what's on the screen—horses are made quieter because they're in the background, guns are made louder since they are in the foreground. At the sound mix of *Cold Mountain* Murch, the lead sound mixer works with two other sound mixers, Michael Prestwood-Smith and Matthew Gough. When Murch is gone from the mix to edit, attend to other duties, or at preview screenings, Prestwood-Smith will do premixes, which must continue unabated if the film is to be delivered on schedule. On the mix board, Matthew Gough supplements Prestwood-Smith and Murch by handling controls that are too spread out and numerous for one mixer to manage.

For each reel, the mixers will ultimately bring together 128 tracks of sound effects, 32 tracks of music, and 24 tracks of dialogue at the appropriate volume levels in relation to each other and to the picture. But there is more to it than just how loud, or how soft: the texture must be in the proper equalization of bass and treble (EQ); the right amount and quality of reverberation must be added to match the visuals; the sound needs to be "placed" in a three-dimensional environment to make the best use of surround speakers; and—especially important to Murch—the audio transitions between scenes must match the story appropriately, and propel it emotionally.

The sound crew in Studio A at De Lane Lea. From left to right: Allan Jenkins, Simon Chase, Martin Cantwell, Tim Bricknell, Fer Bos, Anthony Minghella, Mark Levinson, Walter Murch, Michael Prestwood-Smith, Matthew Gough, and Eddy Joseph. Not pictured: Colin Ritchie.

For Murch, to both edit a movie and mix its soundtrack is second nature. He's held both these credits on 11 previous motion pictures, beginning with *The Conversation* in 1974. For *The English Patient* he took home two Oscars, one in each of those categories, the first person in film history to do so.

Each of these jobs is a huge responsibility, a full-time commitment and a thoroughgoing artistic challenge. Doing them both may seem to overreach, a kind of grandiose ambition. While it requires a high degree of self-confidence, discipline, and physical stamina—all three of which Walter Murch has in full—it's more a measure of his personality and disposition to handle picture and sound than any overblown sense of ego. Murch embodies a creative synthesis that often goes missing in filmmaking. These two seemingly disparate threads—image and sound—become more tightly bound up with each other when they emanate together from the start of the process. Says Robert Grahamjones, Murch's former assistant: "Walter begins planning for the sound mix from the first day of editing." The resulting film has a better chance of achieving a unity of purpose and affect because those elements are integrated from the beginning. Centrifugal forces that send many films flying apart are kept in check when someone with a strong vision occupies the center of gravity, be it the producer, director, or editor/mixer.

June 13, 2003, Murch's Journal

Find the five or six places in the film that have the best quality dialogue recording and run them in the theater to tune your ears before you start premixing at DLL.

If, on this mid-June day, you open the heavy soundproof door into Studio A, the main De Lane Lea mixing theater, you see what looks like a movie playing up on the screen. The theater lights are turned down. The mix board's controls and fader lights seem to brighten in the dark—all twinkly green and orange—sharp, like runway lights. What you hear is something quite peculiar: long periods of silence (the perfect silence of what audio engineers call a "dead room") interrupted by Nicole Kidman and Renée Zellweger speaking, followed by more soundlessness until the characters speak again. This is a dialogue premix. For the moment Murch and the rest of the sound crew are working mixing on-camera dialogue tracks. They will continue, dialogue only, all the way through nine separate reels that constitute this three hour and four minute version of the film. When they are happy—or run out of time—they will begin premixing the sound effects.

Beside Murch and Prestwood-Smith, at the far left-hand side of the mixing board, dialogue editor Colin Ritchie sits at a Pro Tools sound editing workstation ready to make adjustments to the dialogue tracks as problems arise. He might need to remove a click or a pop, for example, that hadn't been audible until they entered this theatrical environment. Or he might need to cut in an alternate line reading should Minghella decide he wants to convey a slightly different meaning. Behind Murch, sitting one tier up on a blue couch, is Mark Levinson, the ADR supervisor, who leans forward paying close attention. Levinson, who favors pastel, Polo brand dress shirts and drives a vintage burgundy Triumph convertible back in Berkeley where he lives, has been in London since April, working with Minghella to record, select, and edit into place newly recorded dialogue. Levinson works closely with Minghella, even helping to conceptualize and draft new lines for the actors to read.

Today, some of the material Levinson just recorded with Nicole Kidman, Jude Law, Brendan Gleeson, Ray Winstone, Natalie Portman, and Eileen Atkins is being mixed into the soundtrack for the first time. These were the first ADR sessions among the principals. But the process of adding and replacing dialogue will continue for the next six months, right up to the last minute, literally, when they mix in Nicole Kidman's final ADR lines, turn off the mixing board, shut the lights, and close the door to Studio A.

ADR, or "looping" as it's also called, takes place in a special sound-recording studio that contains video projection and sound recording capabilities. If it's dialogue that must be matched exactly—lip-synced—a video copy with scenes from the movie gets prepared ahead of time. The scene is played over and over without stopping while the actor stands before a microphone watching it play on the screen. (In the days before video, they made a film loop of the scene so it could easily be projected over and over for the actors, hence the term "looping.") Cueing tones, which the ADR editor added to the video

Mark Levinson, ADR supervisor.

LUNCH WITH A DISH OF STRING THEORY ON THE SIDE

Mark Levinson, the ADR supervisor on *Cold Mountain*, appreciates new and better techniques of doing things, just like Murch. Beyond film, the two also share an interest in theoretical physics. Levinson first had contact with Murch while the two were working on separate films at the Zaentz Film Center in Berkeley: Murch on *The Unbearable Lightness of Being* and Levinson on *Stacking*. Murch's assistants suggested he might enjoy meeting Levinson, who earlier migrated to film post production from the University of California where he earned a PhD in physics. They had lunch together, talked string theory, and subsequently worked on three movies together prior to *Cold Mountain*.

("streamer track"), precede the specific sections needing new dialogue so the actor gets a running start before speaking his or her lines. Some actors are very good at ADR and have little difficulty finding their character and manner of speaking again many months after filming is finished, even when immersed in a role for another movie.

An ADR supervisor working with Minghella is by definition deeply involved with shaping the final version of the movie. Given his collegial approach to filmmaking, that means Levinson is in close touch with Minghella's inner workings and deepest thoughts about how to improve the film as it moves toward completion. Minghella used Levinson as his ADR supervisor on *The English Patient* and *The Talented Mr. Ripley,* and puts maximum trust in him. That's good, since ADR also means working face-to-face with famous, often demanding, actors in re-recording sessions. By the time post production rolls around, actors are often on to their next films, squeezing ADR sessions into their off days or off hours. So a director and his ADR supervisor frequently travel far and wide just to get a few precious hours in the recording studio with an actor. Nowadays, ADR sessions are sometimes handled long distance via a high-speed ISDN link and video conferencing. Levinson might direct actors doing background voices—"loop groups"—in ADR sessions if Minghella can't attend because of other pressing responsibilites. Levinson needs to fully understand what Minghella wants to accomplish in terms of story, character, and performance, while also being artistically astute and technically adept at editing that material into a pre-existing soundtrack. And like the rest of the sound editing team, an ADR supervisor needs to have a good ear.

For example, during production, while still in Northern California, Levinson wrote Murch an email about the *Cold Mountain* screenplay: "One of the things that astonished me with the script was Ant's ability to totally absorb the Southern feel of dialogue (particularly Ruby's character, where Ant has given her literacy but retained the spirit of the character from the book)." Then, remembering that Murch is using Apple's Final Cut Pro software, which may have implications for the entire sound department, Levinson adds, "Is Final Cut Pro living up to its title, or proving to be a misnomer?"

It may seem that using Final Cut for picture editing should have little bearing on what Levinson does with ADR, since he works on the Pro Tools sound-editing platform (owned by Digidesign, which is part of Avid). However, Final Cut's imprint on *Cold Mountain* post production is felt in all the departments, including Levinson's. In fact, before arriving in London, Levinson anticipates advantages Final Cut might have for the tasks that lie ahead—such as quick trips to record ADR in Los Angeles, New York, Toronto, and elsewhere.

"Are you working with OS X?" Levinson wrote to Murch back in March. "Wondering if I should explore one of the new PowerBooks to construct a sort of portable system that I could bring with me to be able to spot with Ant at the 'Chapel' or his house or hotel rooms. Have you pushed the limits of your PowerBook?"

By building a portable system, that is, an Apple PowerBook with Pro Tools and Final Cut Pro installed, Levinson could be free to prepare for ADR sessions en route—and to incorporate last-minute script rewrites Minghella hands to him, or sends by email. After a recording session, Levinson can listen immediately to new takes, pick selects, and place them in his working version of the film. After a seven-hour plane ride back to London from New York, he will walk into a mix session at De Lane Lea with newly recorded dialogue from Nicole Kidman (the best takes already chosen and edited) and in a few moments transfer them into the Pro Tools workstation on the mix stage, which Murch accesses from the mixing board and mixes into the *Cold Mountain* soundtrack.

Minghella also benefits from having Final Cut Pro on his PowerBook when he is planning for ADR sessions. "I've been able to travel with the movie," he says later. "When we were doing ADR in New York and Los Angeles, I could have the cut of the film on my laptop. I could examine the film with fluency and ease, as opposed to when you have to use a videotape machine."

JUNE 14, 2003—LONDON
It's the second day of mixing at De Lane Lea. Murch is preparing the soundtrack for the private screenings of *Cold Mountain*, which are only six days away, first in London, then in New York for Miramax. Murch now knows the MetaFlow-Titan-OMF sound conversion workaround devised by

Murch mixing *Cold Mountain*.

Sean Cullen and the sound editors is performing. Sync is holding with the movie image Murch mixes to at DLL (a digital projection from videotape output from Final Cut Pro). There will be no meltdown. This is a moment to behold. From a couch at the back of Studio A, with his PowerBook hooked up to the house high-speed line, Murch dashes off an excited email to Will Stein, Bill Hudson, Brian Meaney, and Susan Marshall (FCP product marketing) at Apple:

Date: Monday, June 16, 2003, 12:43 PM
Subject: Mixing Cold Mountain!
From: Walter Murch

Dear Apple FCP:

We are two days into our six-day temp mix, and all is going splendidly. We have finished the dialogue premixes for the whole three-hour film, and all of the EDL-Titan interface between FCP and PT worked out perfectly.

Naturally, I am interested in any advantages we can gain by using the emerging AAF - XML pathways, but I wanted to let you know that our workarounds are all functioning well.

We are also in the middle of implementing changes to the conformed 35mm picture, and that is also flowing smoothly and frame-accurately.

Best wishes,
Walter M.

Getting permission from Apple for DigitalFilm Tree and Brooks Harris to customize the unfinished XML protocol is now moot. The mix will proceed without any hidden technical issues arising. There is no response from Apple.

Ramy, back in Los Angeles, receives a similar email from Murch with the good news. He responds to Murch right away:

Date: Tue, 17 Jun 2003 22:26
Subject: Re: Mixing!
From: Ramy Katrib
To: Walter Murch

Good Day Walter,

Thank you for the update. We are extremely happy and comforted about the workarounds working. As we have learned, FCP's professional trajectory has been built on a bedrock of workarounds. We will continue to hunt down AAF/OMF - XML pathways with the hope that Apple's resistance to that will lessen, or go away. I've confirmed a free pass for Brooks from one of our Apple contacts. I just spoke with him, and if all goes as planned, he'll attend the developers conference next week, on all our behalf.

all the best, ramy

While no outright conflict ever erupted between Apple, DFT, and Murch over XML, there was an undertone of tension and frustration running through their communications. Murch, Cullen, and DFT knew a better solution for their sound workflow was very close at hand. Apple is in the business of selling reliable computers and software applications that keep customers happy. The company could not put resources into providing a "special build," as they call customized software, for a single customer, no matter how prominent and potentially useful *Cold Mountain* might be as a showcase project.

Zed Saeed at DigitalFilm Tree remains philosophical about the XML tug-of-war: "Give them credit," he says about Apple. "You know why? Look at their applications. DigitalFilm Tree is a direct descendent of that spirit. A lot of people say Apple creates an image by writing huge paychecks to ad agencies and for image campaigns," Zed continues. "Yes, I'll live with that. It allows me to use my brain, my talent, my outlook, to work on movies, help cut films, and work right next to one of my heroes."

JUNE 20, 2003—LONDON

Today is the first full screening of *Cold Mountain* to be held outside either the Chapel or De Lane Lea. It's an invited audience of 60: friends and associates of Minghella's, other filmmakers, writers, and the London Mirage company staff. It will be held at the National Film Theatre. The NFT, part of the British Film Institute, is in the South Bank complex on the Thames River. For Minghella, having recently been appointed to the prestigious position of chairman of the BFI, showing a film here is like playing football on the home pitch—a good way to test the film before taking it across the Atlantic to show Miramax. One might think a hometown crowd would be the best way to make a transition onto the main stage. However, these sorts of audiences can prove to be the most troublesome for filmmakers, especially at this point. Friends and family rarely tell you the truth about how they feel. They care more about you and your feelings than they do about the work you produce. There's a niggling sense that despite the praise, you may not hear what the audience truly believes.

Afterwards, Murch first checks in with Ramy at DigitalFilm Tree.

Date:	Sat, 21 Jun 2003
Subject:	Re: Screening
From:	Walter Murch
To:	Ramy Katrib

Dear Ramy:

Our screening at the NFT with the mixed track went without a hitch.

Looked good and sounded good. Sean loaded the cut from FCP directly into the QuBit, and then we ran the mix from our Akai dubber. Everyone very happy.

And the latest round of changes have been done to the 35mm film, so the change lists worked perfectly.

So the final two hurdles—change lists and 24bit sound export to Pro Tools—have gone along smoothly. Now all we have to do is concentrate on making the film!

Congratulations to all of us, and thanks for your invaluable help.

Best wishes and have a great time in Hawaii!
Walter

PS. Here is a link for a picture of the real Cold Mountain in NC

Date:	Sat, 21 Jun 2003
Subject:	Re: Screening
From:	Ramy Katrib
To:	Walter Murch

Hello Walter,

I was just about to leave the office for the final time before boarding a plane to Maui on Sunday. This is by far the best news of the year for us. I will pass along the wonderful developments to all. I never realized that mountain we've all been climbing was so beautiful.

sunny regards,
ramy

Then Murch gets right back to work by making some trims based on what he just saw on the screen. In an email to Debbie Ross, who will be designing the main title and end credit sequences at her studio in Los Angeles, Murch reports: "Our screening went very well—good digital projection and sound, and good response. We are still learning things, of course, and I just made changes to three reels, which shortened things by a minute."

View of Cold Mountain in North Carolina.

Having a coffee at Primrose Hill Patisserie before I go to the airport to fly to NY for the Miramax screening. God bless this endeavor and may some good come out of it. I was cleaning out the house and discovered that half of the plants on the terrace have died because I didn't water them. Embarrassing oversight. How best to fix?

In New York at the SoHo Grand at 5.30. I met Albert and Ron in the lobby. Sean is on the way to the screening room—they had experienced some "tearing" in the image when they loaded it, so they did two loads (normal and progressive).

JUNE 25, 2003—NEW YORK CITY

Within an hour of arriving and checking into his hotel, Murch walks a few blocks to the brick building at 475 Greenwich Street, home to Miramax Films, Robert De Niro's Tribeca Productions, and the Tribeca Film Center. There on the fourth floor, in the screening room, a run-through of *Cold Mountain* is about to begin. Minghella, Murch, some of the crew (costume designer Ann Roth, script supervisor Dianne Dreyer), and two of the producers, Albert Berger and Ron Yerxa, are there. Sean Cullen arrived one day earlier from London so he'd have enough time to transfer the current version of the film from Beta SP videotapes (made with output from Final Cut Pro in London) to a QuBit hard drive digital playback system—a process that takes nearly four hours, since it is done in real time.

The front entrance to Miramax Films and the Tribeca Film Center in New York City.

The video projector is an overhead box with a loud fan, and being neither bright enough nor far enough back from the screen (a distance known as the "throw-length"), the image is small. Murch is also unhappy with the sound system. It isn't as good as the NFT theater in London, and lacks high-end frequency response. There is no time to tune the room per Murch's *modus operandi*—an irritant since Murch knows how good the soundtrack really sounds. But such is the fate of the sound mixer. Compared to how it sounded inside Studio A at De Lane Lea, *Cold Mountain* will sound slightly different in every theater it is shown.

But the screening goes well. Afterward Ann Roth turns to Anthony and says, "You're not old, but this may be your masterpiece." Murch says, referring to the script supervisor, "Dianne liked it but was immediately thinking of things to cut out."

JUNE 26, 2003—NEW YORK CITY

People are assembling at 1:30 for second screening at MMX. About 40 people. We tuned the room and it now sounds much better. Bless this screening and all who sail upon her. Executives and Sydney P. are here, and like the changes we made and the work we did on the sound.

June 27, 2003, Murch's Journal

Screening for MMX yesterday went well. Much enthusiasm tempered by an awareness of what the length is, and the desire to have the relationship between Ada and Inman be as intense as it can be. Technically, all went well. They felt the image looked very good—better than the resolution they are used to in Avid output screenings. A meeting in conference room afterwards. Harvey and then Bob. Bob felt there was more heat between Sara and Inman than between Inman and Ada. "But when they get together it is great."

MMX have agreed to shoot a couple of extra days—"no budget restraints, but let's preview the film on July 15th and see if there's anything else we need."

Anthony said it was always amazing to him how much of a hot problematical potato I was for HW and other MMXers.

I am still just blinking in the sunlight of having completed the MMX showing with all its bells and whistles and complications.

Now having a mojito at a Latin bar up the street from the hotel.

Is there a way to play the mix on FCP in my room, through Dolby decoders with boom? Where can we get a CP50 Dolby decoder?

I am overwhelmed at the logistical and statistical difficulty of people getting together with an "intended"—someone who is destined for them, to enhance and complete them and vice-versa. Just looking at people walking around the streets of NY. Everyone seems so vulnerable and guarded to protect their vulnerability. How did Aggie and I get so lucky? One hour left before the car comes to pick me up.

Congratulations to Sean for guiding the film through all of its wiggling in the last six weeks. There is a screening for Charles Frazier on Sunday. Time to start thinking about going to the airport. God bless the forces that have gotten us to this place.

I am sitting on Broome Street with a solid traffic jam in front of me—four lanes. Broome and Wooster. Lovely sandblasted Mission-style brick six-story opposite. People listening to the most mindless insect music on their car radios. Now the man just turned to the theme from "The Godfather."

Minghella stays on in New York while Murch returns to London to continue editing. At a screening room on Broadway Minghella shows this version of *Cold Mountain* to author Charles Frazier, Disney Chairman Michael

Eisner (Disney owns Miramax), and others. Entertainment industry protocol behooves directors to share their incomplete work with financiers, key people, and influential opinion-makers, even if the movie is a long way from being finished. Like a Renaissance artist preparing frescoes for a Florentine chapel, when Lorenzo de Medici and the Pope want to come take a look, it's not too wise to say no.

With these screenings the concomitant set of notes—written and spoken—come, too. And for a film director whose radar gets especially sensitive from working with actors, nonverbal notes sent through body language and speaking tone can mean just as much as any memo. Now is the time when filmmakers must find space to store all this new information. Albert Berger emails a four-page memo, Charles Frazier writes two pages of notes, Michael Peretzian, Minghella's agent at Creative Artists, sends a page and a half. It's not a matter of whether the response is simply good or bad; in most cases the reaction is very positive. Simply opening up to other views and opinions takes a little getting used to after working in relatively cloistered quarters for six months. Even if a comment touches on an issue you, as director or editor, have been worried about—perhaps already struggling to address—it's disconcerting to hear about it from someone else. But in one respect, this gestation period of preliminary screenings and showings is a chance once again for Murch and Minghella to adjust to the fact that a motion picture is valuable only insofar as an audience will be there to experience it.

Date:	Mon, 30 Jun 2003 08:30 EDT
Subject:	cave be gone
To:	Walter Murch
From:	Anthony Minghella

Frazier screening went very well.

Escaping here without too much blood on our noses. Back to work.

Thanks for everything you do for me, dear friend

Rushing to adr
Love
A

Now, on regrouping in London, another milestone appears right up ahead: a public test preview screening in three weeks on July 21 in New Jersey. For Murch this means just about every post-production function required for finishing *Cold Mountain* is underway—all at once. On top of trying new editorial changes and making efforts to reduce the running time, Murch is involved in, supervising, or contributing to tasks that include special visual effects, title and credit sequences, dialogue and sound effects premixes, music recording, ADR, and even marketing (supplying material for a preview trailer to be cut in New York). It's like that Vaudeville act of keeping a dozen plates spinning simultaneously on pointed wooden sticks: forget to keep one rotating fast enough and it soon comes crashing to the floor.

With Murch at the hub for all this completion activity, so too is Final Cut Pro at the crux. All new and revised material, from music to digitally touched-up shots must be incorporated into his assembly, which sits in FCP on the hard drives in the attic at the Old Chapel. All the elements arrive here in the form of QuickTime files, Apple's powerful, cross-platform format for manipulating, enhancing, and storing image and sound. QuickTime is the universal language through which the *Cold Mountain* post-production departments talk to each other.

For example, there are many film shots that need digital touch-ups—wires removed, twinkling stars added, zoom-ins performed. These visual effects shots, done at Double Negative, a Soho-based effects-design company—can run from a few seconds to a minute or more. They are created with software applications Alias' Maya, Apple's Shake, and Pixar's Renderman, then saved as QuickTime files. Dennis Lowe, the visual effects artist, or his assistant, Fay McConkey, notifies Sean Cullen and Dei Reynolds via email when the revised shots are available on the dedicated FTP site. Then Cullen transfers that shot onto the *Cold Mountain* shared area network (SAN). He notifies Murch by email that a new shot is ready for him to review.

It may seem over the top that Cullen would email Murch, who is just 30 feet away down the hall, but this way of communicating allows Murch to attend to visual affects when he can, rather than be interrupted in the middle of cutting a scene. Murch views the new shot, compares it to the original, and decides whether it's correct or needs more work. (In most cases, it's the latter. Like most other functions in post production, digital visual effects never come out right the first time.) The portability of this visual effects shot, and its immediate viewability, is only possible because of QuickTime. Double Negative, in fact, runs on PC computers, but that's immaterial, because Mac and PC platforms read QuickTime.

Compare this pathway to traditional film-based, optically created effects. Aside from the fact that computer-generated images (CGI) are faster to create, more accurate, and better refined, a digital delivery system saves time and money. Formerly, a touched-up image would have to be printed on film at the lab (24 hours to process the negative and make a workprint copy), then shipped or sent by messenger to the editing room for screening on an editing machine. Or, if it's more convenient (and can be scheduled soon enough), the film is shown at the lab in its viewing room, which might not happen until the editor is at the lab for some other reason.

Murch describes how it was done on his film, *Return to Oz,* only 20 years ago: "We were doing claymation visual effects in Portland, Oregon. We'd get a piece of film in London by special delivery. They would have another print made from the same negative so we could see the same things. I would put the film on my Steenbeck in London, and they'd put their film on their Steenbeck in Portland, and then I'd phone them up and we'd start with the footage counter at zero. I would go forward until I saw something that needed a comment, 'Okay, everything's great, but look at frame 74. Do you see how he winks there? Let's make that a little more noticeable.' And they'd be looking at the same thing. Or, if I had an idea for how to do something different, I would put

Visual effects were used to enhance details in the explosion that started the Battle of Petersburg.

a piece of tissue paper on the screen and draw the new idea on it and fax that to them, and then they'd get it instantly and put it over their screen and do a change and send it back. Even back then, I began to get a whiff of this digital thing, even though that was before email or downloadable files. But there was fax, and digital information was in that fax signal, going back and forth, which did energize the process."

Of course, viewing visual effects in Internet time, for example, gets integrated into a compressed post-production schedule. "We don't get two extra days to do something else," as Murch says.

Date: Thu, 10 Jul 2003 10:35
Subject: Fwd: jpegs on FTP site
From: Sean
To: Walter

Walter,

These shots are in your VFX project under Shots for Review, 10/7.

Begin forwarded message:

> From: Fay McConkey
> Date: Wed Jul 9, 2003 7:24:09 PM Europe/London
> To: Dei, Sean Cullen
> Subject: jpegs on FTP site

>
> Hello
>
> I have put 2 x jpegs on to your ftp site.
>
> Please could you show them to Anthony and Walter to get some feedback.
>
> 4013
> This temp frame is to decide the size and position of the cloud in the
> background of the shot; at the moment it is 50% the size of 4014.
>
> 4014
> This is the wide shot of the mushroom cloud that needs to be
> 'zoomed'. In this test frame the cloud has been scaled to 78% - the
> smallest it can be if it is still to fit the 1.66 mask. We have just
> copied and pasted in the sides of the field for now.
>
> If you could let me know what they think, it would be much appreciated.
>
> Thanks
> Fay

An email from Double Negative, the London firm that provided *Cold Mountain* with its special visual effects. Minghella and Murch are being asked to review two visual effects shots, labeled 4013 and 4014, for the great explosion in the Battle of Petersburg.

MAKING A DIGITAL INTERMEDIATE

The digital intermediate (DI) is another filmmaking breakthrough being employed in *Cold Mountain*. Earlier, during production, Minghella requested and got approval from Miramax to make final release prints using the DI process.

In the traditional method of making release prints, the lab uses the cut negative as little as possible before making a duplicate negative—the cut camera negative is far too valuable to be running through the lab repeatedly to make thousands of release prints. The chances of it breaking, tearing, or otherwise wearing out are high. Since it's not possible to make a negative from a negative, the lab first creates an interpositive from the cut camera negative, then strikes a dupe negative from the interpositive. In this method the image quality is reduced by two generations (the interpositive and the internegative).

With a DI the interpositive is eliminated. The "dupe negative" for striking release prints is not really a duplicate—it's first generation, created directly from a digital file. *Cold Mountain* will be released in widescreen CinemaScope (2.35:1 aspect ratio). It was shot "flat" in super-35mm so the expansion to CinemaScope is also accomplished digitally. Formerly that step, "anamorphic" squeezing, would be performed using an optical printer. So this is one more compromise in picture quality averted by using the DI.

A film scanner is used to get film negative digitized into data files. It works much the same way scanners digitize photographs or flat artwork. Instead of scanning negative that's been cut, however, in the DI process whole rolls of uncut negative are threaded up on the scanner and then only the needed frames are scanned, using the edit decision list (EDL) from Final Cut Pro. The machine scans across each frame 2,000 times (called 2K scanning) and creates a digital image with 2,000 horizontal lines of data. To put that measure in context, a U.S. television displays broadcast signals as 640 lines; high-definition (HD) televisions range up to 1,920 lines. If a particular shot includes especially fine details, the scan rate will be doubled to 4,000 lines (4K), to prevent any visible degradation of the image.

One of the benefits of a DI, then, is not having to cut the original negative processed by the lab. Only after the lab completes the scanning process are shots "cut" digitally in a computer to match the current EDL. Color timing can start whenever the directory of photography is available, and then the DI master can be reconformed as the film progresses toward its final version. Not having to cut the original negative also means it will remain fully intact, just as it was processed in the lab. The pristine negative will always be available to prepare even higher quality prints using technologies and formats not yet invented. A DI also means the filmmakers can use a precise, sophisticated, digitally based color correction (or grading) system not available in the analog film world. *Cold Mountain* will be the first feature film to use both Final Cut Pro and a digital intermediate. As it turned out, the Final Cut Pro EDL used to conform the DI masters worked perfectly—"cutting the negative" was error free.

Computer Film Company lab (CFC) around the corner from De Lane Lea in Soho.

Ultimately there will be 243 visual effects shots in *Cold Mountain*. Ordering, reviewing, directing, re-reviewing, and incorporating all that material through multiple rounds of approvals takes up a major chunk of time every day. To keep track of all the visual effects shots and their status, the *Cold Mountain* assistants line the hall upstairs at the Chapel with printed frame grabs, each frame coded to indicate its stage in the process.

JULY 5, 2003—LONDON

Murch and Minghella do their first test of digital color correction on *Cold Mountain* at the Computer Film Company lab (CFC) around the corner from De Lane Lea in Soho. It's exactly one year since DigitalFilm Tree spent the Independence Day holiday weekend prepping and packing Murch's Final Cut Pro system for shipment to Romania.

That first DI color correction test was of the rainy porch scene at Black Cove Farm between Inman and Ada. "It turned out very well on first pass," Murch says later. "We incorporated a film output of that test into the 35mm print used in the first preview screening to see how it held up alongside workprint from original negative. It integrated seamlessly."

In a lengthy journal entry, Murch steps back and takes a wide view of the art and technique of film editing, amazed and curious about how it unfolds over time. Perhaps the notes are triggered by his first encounter with the digital intermediate technique, or maybe it's that his 60th birthday is two days away.

July 10, 2003, Murch Journal

Film Editing—exciting that it is still in an early stage of its evolution. The underlying values of storytelling remain the same, but the techniques of image manipulation, storage, and documentation are transforming, along with the grammar of image sequence. But by how much? Juxtapose "Conversation" with "Cold Mountain" and what is different in the grammar? In some way, "Conversation" is more advanced. Jump cuts in the workshop and the Jack Tar Hotel sequences.

There is an optimal structure to the image sequence in any particular film. Just as there is an optimal molecular structure for every particular combination of atoms. "Least energy," I think they call it. If the atoms are arranged in a different pattern, even by a small amount, the properties of the resulting molecular substance are different. A diamond and a graphite pencil are both made of the same carbon atoms, but in a different arrangement. The diamond pattern is optimal, most densely packed, "least energy," which is what gives it its density and clarity. And given a particular structure, there is an optimal cut point for every shot (atom) within that structure.

It's all well and good that the first public preview of *Cold Mountain* comes up in less than ten days, that this new version is not yet locked, and four days of temp mixing still lie ahead. Walter's birthday trumps all that. He and Aggie

Walter Murch celebrates his 60th birthday at Veeraswami's, a London restaurant where, 40 years earlier, he took Aggie on their first date. On his left are director Anthony Minghella and his wife, Carolyn Choa.

spend a long weekend in Paris to celebrate. For Walter there are deep sleeps on the train ride from London and in a friend's apartment where they are staying. Taking this kind of hiatus in the middle of the race to complete *Cold Mountain* can certainly be good for the mind and body, but suddenly slowing down from such a rapid pace can induce a certain kind of melancholia.

July 12, 2003, Murch's Journal

60th birthday: Both my father and his father, both Walter Murches, died when they were sixty. May I break the tradition, Inshallah. Dad died on December 11th 1967, just under four months after his 60th birthday. For me that will be somewhere around November 6th. I remember getting the phone call from my mother—in the evening. Aggie and I were living in the little house on Cheremoya in LA, and Aggie was working night shift at Hollywood Presbyterian. I went for a walk along the streets in the hills just above the house. I remember thinking: "Well, he was old." I was 24… what did I know. Two years later, my mother died.

Was I sad? Yes. Was I devastated? No. I had grown up with him but independent of him as far as my emotions were concerned. Still, I don't know why I wasn't more wrenched. I remember in New York that Xmas retreating into some mathematics.

SATURDAY, JULY 19, 2003—LONDON

Having spent the following week making final changes to version seven and completing the temp sound mix, Murch and Cullen prepare to fly to New York for a Monday night screening in New Jersey. Minghella had to leave a day earlier to do some ADR in New York. Less than two hours after finishing the mix, they walk to Mr. Young's, Minghella's favorite screening room in London. There, along with sound supervisor Eddy Joseph and music editor Allan Jenkins, they watch the film all the way through. Murch notes, "I feel a bit 'out of body' at the moment. Shaky." The picture looks good and is perfectly in sync, except for two places where Murch had earlier "slipped sync" during the mix to make a last-minute sound adjustment and forgot to readjust. Nearly all the N-VIS-O splices are good, meaning the film does not stutter on the splices. Dei and Walter fix the few bad splices in the projection booth at Mr. Young's. Another triumph: picture editing, sound mixing, ADR, sound editing, and 35mm picture conforming all intersect successfully—and Final Cut Pro is the hub of it all.

July 19, 2003, Murch's Journal

Eddy and Alan were at the screening and proud of the work they had done. First time any of us have seen the 35mm picture projected with all the sound effects, ADR, etc. I was (mostly) dry-eyed except when I would get "work vertigo" from contemplating how high up we are on the mountain of work that has been done. Most unstuck at the campfire scene between Ada and Inman. Bless this film and all who work on it. Another Rubicon crossed.

"I marry you. I marry you. I marry you."

The Multiplex in Edgewater, New Jersey.

CHAPTER 10

Time and Endless Patience

WEDNESDAY, OCTOBER 1, 2003—EDGEWATER, NEW JERSEY

It's 9:30 p.m. and the audience in Theater 4 is watching the concluding reel of *Cold Mountain*—the final 20 minutes of the last preview. Inside the stadium-style auditorium, 300 moviegoers will soon be filling out survey cards with their likes and dislikes. About 20 others will be invited to stay afterward for a focus group.

Walter Murch sits right in the middle of the upper section of the theater. A Russian émigré sits behind him. Earlier, before the lights went down, he leaned over and asked Murch, not possibly knowing who he was, "Is this a good movie? Is this going to be a good movie?" Before Walter could answer, the man continued: "Is it like *Scary Movie*? That was a good movie!" Walter just chuckles.

New Jersey filmgoers are a vocal audience, and they watch the film's big explosion scene with awe, the Russian vocalizing their general sentiments: "Oh, yeah—wow! Look at that!"

They're also amused. When Ruby first appears at Black Cove Farm and meets Ada, she picks up the rooster that's been terrifying Ada and breaks its neck. Zellweger, playing Ruby, gets a big laugh. When she adds, "Let's go put it in the pot," there's another round of laughter. "Kill the rooster!" the Russian guy exclaims.

These are moments that must reassure director Anthony Minghella. Harvey Weinstein of Miramax, who is sitting behind Minghella, should also be encouraged.

In the middle of the screening, Weinstein leaves the theater for a few moments during the scene of Inman recuperating at Maddie's, the goatherder and healer played by Eileen Atkins. On returning to his seat Weinstein passes behind Minghella, taps him on the shoulder, and says, "It's good." You'd have to know Weinstein well to discern whether this is a genuine conviction, meaning he will not have much criticism later, or if he's posturing for the moment. Minghella and Murch will find out the next day, during a debriefing in Miramax's offices.

So far, Weinstein has been mostly supportive of Minghella. The previous preview on August 20, also here in Edgewater, received very good audience ratings. Miramax offered to extend Minghella's delivery date to November 15, giving him one extra week.

Inman about to leave Maddy (Eileen Atkins), who nursed him back to health.

This version of *Cold Mountain* is 2:37 hours long; the end credits will add another six minutes or so. On top of all the major surgery that was done previously to reduce the running time, Murch has spent the last few weeks making little nips and tucks. One week earlier, on locking the picture for this final test screening, Murch took the film's measurements, reminding himself how far below the theoretical 30 percent limit it now is—sometimes even he forgets where all the cuts come from.

September 25, 2003, Murch's Journal

Almost 50% cut out of film. Actually 48%. When did we pass 30% (at 3:33) and how were we able to cut out almost another hour below that? Cut out the Inman-Cold Mountain-Long Walk cycle. Sara's final character beat cut out. Veaseytown and other Veasey development cut out. Swimmer. What else?

Film is 2.36.55: now that we have locked all reels. It is 2.15 am. Congratulations!! Now finished conforming the tracks at 3.30 am.

Feeling good despite the eight-hour turnaround. Home at 6am and back at work at 2 pm.

Mom said I was a happy kid until I was two, and then I became suddenly serious and preoccupied. What changed?

As Murch puts it, the story question that drove the five months of editing from the day he completed the first assembly (February 16) to the first edited version for public test screening (July 16) was this: "Will the audience engage with the characters—these strange people meeting other strange people under strange circumstances?" In particular, since Inman is quite a reticent protagonist, Murch felt the need to better reveal what is going on inside Inman's head. When his journey goes, "slightly off beam," as Murch describes it, the audience needs to see through Inman's eyes to know what he is thinking.

"With *Apocalypse Now* we had the same problem only more so," Murch explained late one night in his editing room. "In that film we're with Willard (Martin Sheen) the entire time. The film is told from his point of view, yet he hardly speaks, nor does he do very much until he finally kills Kurtz (Marlon Brando). Narration was the only way in. Contrary to *Apocalypse Now*, with Inman there are ways to find out what is going on inside. He talks—though not very much—and does things. Since Ada already speaks in voiceover through her letters, it didn't feel right for another character to also speak with a narrative voice."

After getting the balance of Inman's interior and exterior selves provisionally balanced to Walter and Anthony's satisfaction, largely through pulling Inman's actions into tighter contact with each other, Murch and Minghella spent much of their edit time from July until now focusing on Ada, both as a character and in relation to Inman. "Just as Inman goes from being a golden-haired youth to a scarred, bearded veteran, Ada matures from being a porcelain doll to having her hands dipped in blood. And it is she who survives, not Inman. In that sense the film belongs to her," Murch explains. "She is *Cold Mountain*'s Ishmael, who survives 'to tell thee.'"

AUDIENCE RESPONSE

Wise filmmakers never underestimate how movie-savvy their audience can be. Having seen and heard so many movies, filmgoers bring to the theater a sophisticated movie sense they may not even be aware of. Good editors maintain a healthy respect for the moviegoer's innate smarts about film logic and grammar. Filmmakers want to strike the right balance between exposition and discovery—pulling the moviegoers more deeply into the story, while also rewarding them for their acumen. The movies they construct need to contain exact portions of hints and foreshadowing. Too much and an audience feels talked down to; too little and they get lost. The ideal is to achieve what Murch describes as "surprising self-evidence. They don't know what is going to happen next, but when it happens it feels inevitable. Like a continuous déja vu experience."

In this screening of *Cold Mountain*, even though the film is fairly complex in its intercutting, flashbacks, and time-place discontinuities, one can feel the audience engaged, leaning into the film like a long distance runner, anticipating, but not falling off balance.

MINGHELLA'S THEORY OF CINEMATIC RELATIVITY

If Walter and I are watching the film, it goes at one speed. If you, Walter, and I watch the film, it will go at another speed. If you, Sidney, Walter, and I look at the film, it goes another speed. If there are ten people, if there are a hundred people, the collective weight on the brake of our car is extraordinary. If everybody walks away and I watch it by myself, I find it goes very quickly. The point is the film changes in front of you.

At a preview there's nobody looking to love you. They're just looking at the film and it has none of the meaning that it has when friends or family or interested parties view it. It's just what it is.

During a sequence of Inman's journey back to Cold Mountain, soon after he leaves the hospital, a close-up shot fills the screen with crabs crawling in the mud. "He's going to eat them," the Russian sitting near Murch says out loud, even before Inman is established in the scene. Audiences participate like this, using clues dropped for them, whether or not a film director plans for it. Intelligent filmmakers craft this kind of relationship with an audience, and constantly evaluate their film-in-progress from the point of view of the spectator. Murch and Minghella respect this "dialogue" with their imagined audience and as a result, moviegoers benefit from a richer film experience. Murch and Minghella benefit, too. While they work, the specter of a future audience hovers in the edit room with them, challenging their decisions and raising questions, like a Socratic third party.

One major area the phantom moviegoer questioned was *Cold Mountain*'s violence. During editing Murch and Minghella shifted the tenor of the film's bloodiest scenes—what Murch dubs a process of "desanguination." At this point in the screening the audience is watching "the Sara sequence." It may be the best example in *Cold Mountain* of not only how a scene can work better without being too full of "tang," but also how story and character get transformed as they travel from book to screenplay to film.

From the beginning when Murch first read the screenplay, he took note of potential problems with this powerful scene between Inman and the young Sara (Natalie Portman). It is Inman's last stop before making it back to Cold Mountain and to Ada. Sara is widowed and alone with her sick baby. In giving Inman shelter, she looks to him for companionship and for protection from three marauding Union soldiers. It is Inman's final temptation: a world and a woman are offered that are completely familiar to him, that need him, and to which a part of him responds more immediately than to the mysterious Ada. In the screenplay, Minghella intensified the scene with more violence (Sara is about to be raped) and tragedy (Sara kills one of the Union soldiers herself, her baby dies, Sara commits suicide) than were in the original novel. By now, however, it may be too late in the film to bring in a new major character like Sara and then ask an audience to spend emotional capital on her without deducting it from somewhere else. As producer Bill Horberg commented during editing, the viewer may begin feeling "donor fatigue."

All through post production the Sara scene seemed to galvanize people; some were moved, others felt overwhelmed. In either case, it seemed to be too much weight for the movie to carry right at that point. When Murch provided the scene to Apple in March to use as part of a presentation, word came back that they found it too depressing. In May, when Sydney Pollack came to the Old Chapel to see the cut at that point, he told Walter he thought the way it was assembled implied Sara and Inman had sex. This would jeopardize the whole purpose for the scene, which was to set up the final reunion between Inman and Ada. In June, after the first screening in New York for Miramax executives, co-chairman Bob Weinstein, Harvey's brother, felt there was more heat between Sara and Inman than between Inman and Ada. In

Sara with her sick baby, Ethan.

Sara and Inman in bed.

early September when Harvey Weinstein visited the Chapel for a day, he suggested taking out the shot of Sara breastfeeding her baby as Inman introduces himself to her.

The Sara sequence didn't achieve its ultimate form until just before this final preview. The overhaul began with a relatively minor change, when Murch tried cutting Sara's explanation of her predicament, a few lines of dialogue spoken to Inman while she breastfeeds baby Ethan:

```
                    SARA

    Used to have a cow; few goats. Raiders took them.
    Made me kill our own dog on the porch. That poor
    creature watched over me. Nothing left now save a
    hog and a couple of chickens to live off till spring.
    I'll have to kill that hog and make sense of the flesh
    and divisions—which is something I never did.
```

The cut seemed to work. Not only did the lines disappear without a trace, but in retrospect they seemed slightly out of character: why would she have revealed her vulnerability and lone resource so early to a complete stranger? Murch showed it to Minghella, who liked it and said he felt the cut put more emphasis on their tender exchange of names at the end of the scene. Maybe this was the hidden problem, the "referred pain," that had triggered Weinstein's suggestion to cut out the entire scene.

Pollack and Horberg arrived on September 11, a week after Weinstein's visit, to spend three days in the editing room going through the film inch by inch. This would be their last opportunity for such detailed work before the final preview and, given the inflexibility of the schedule, their last such opportunity, period.

When the Sara scene was run, both Pollack and Horberg liked the lift of the expository dialogue. But a few minutes later—after the Union soldiers have been killed—Inman's helpful butchering of the hog now appeared gratuitous and inexplicable, almost aggressive, because Sara's explaining her need to have it butchered (and her inability to do it herself) had already been removed. The choice was clear to everyone in the room: restore her explanation or go deeper and remove the hog butchering and everything associated with it—leading inescapably to cutting out the death of the baby and Sara's suicide. Anthony suggested cutting it all out and seeing what happens.

One simple extraction had triggered a major "lift," as editors call a wholesale removal of a scene or large portion of a scene. Will this radical cut work?

This scene of Sara and Inman butchering her hog was eliminated—the "Sara lift."

September 13, 2003, Murch's Journal

Lifting Sara's suicide became inevitable when we saw that the scene on the bed worked well without the exposition, and then Inman slaughtering the hog afterwards was redundant. Unintended consequences. I didn't plan it that way, but that's how it turned out. So we cut the Sara death scene—slaughtering of the hog, the baby's death, her suicide. Brave of Anthony to contemplate it, even in the short run. We will screen next Thursday and judge in context.

For Murch, the benefits of the foreshortened Sara scene seem numerous: narrative momentum toward the film's resolution is regained; the audience is spared emotional trauma at a point in the story arc when they've earned a denouement instead; a precious three minutes of running time is saved; tang is reduced; and Inman's character is bolstered in unexpected ways. He does not need to have any more tragedies on his shoulders—he has plenty of those already. Now the audience implicitly feels his resolve has been strengthened, since he chooses to finish his journey back to Ada rather than remain with the still-living Sara.

September 14, Murch's Journal

Sara scene thoughts: Inman now leaves her of his own free will. Formerly, he had to leave because the baby died and she died, so fate took the decision out of his hands. It is actually better for his character this way. In addition to the time and structural issues.

A lift may work for itself, but what about the film fragments that remain around it? How will they sit next to each other? After Sara shoots the third soldier, the altered scene ends with a devastating closeup of Inman. He looks blankly at scudding gray clouds, which dissolve to Black Cove Farm and Ada waking to the first heavy snowfall of the year; then a short scene of Stobrod, Pangle, and Georgia leaving prints in the fresh snow as they make their way back up the mountain. When Inman next appears, he's cresting the snowy ridge above the town of Cold Mountain and sees the valley below. His expression and his body language still convey the weight he carries. He is pulled downward, but not by Sara's suicide and her baby's death, since they no longer occur. Instead Inman's heaviness is a larger social malaise: that a young widow like Sara, who wanted to eliminate all weapons from the world ("every blade, every gun"), is so beaten down and hardened that she shoots and kills the one Union soldier—a young man probably very like her dead husband—who tried to protect her baby from the cold.

Days later, while mixing the soundtrack at De Lane Lea for this last preview in Edgewater, Walter was still pondering the story implications of the Sara scene, turning them over and over like worry beads.

The three soldiers are killed and their horses are left for Sara—she can make it through the winter if she sells them. She still has the hog. So she is better off now than before Inman arrived. Just her sick baby.

The re-imagined Sara scene prevailed. And with it, a new lesson emerges for Murch about the changing relationships between book, screenplay, and film. "It was as if film reached over the screenplay and went back to the book," Walter says later. "There was something fundamental in the book that transcended the screenplay. It was difficult for Anthony because Sara's death was something he added to the story, and he loved how the hog butchering had turned out in the shooting. It was a real 'Book of Job' moment, where a good scene was sacrificed for the larger good of the film."

Beside the removal from the Sara scene, Murch and Minghella had made two other major alterations prior to the last preview. These changes occur in the sequence when Inman and Reverend Veasey are captured by the Home Guard at Junior's, and they attempt to escape. One of the principles in editing *Cold Mountain* the last few months has been, "Don't let Inman sit down." Inman's story momentum must always be toward Ada and Cold Mountain. Murch and Minghella felt that a scene of the chain gang sitting on the street back in "Veasey Town," where Inman resists Veasey's whispered suggestion of trying an escape, violated that principle. The scene had great production values and redeemed Veasey's character—he wanted to escape with the slave girl he made pregnant. But it was backwards movement geographically, and Inman's reluctance to try an escape was hard to read: he seemed to care more about his own safety than trying to get back to Ada at any cost.

The lift of Veasey Town gave a palpable momentum to the film. It juxtaposed the night scene of the chain gang leaving Junior's with the gang on the road the next day, moments before a troop of Yankee cavalry appears in the distance. The chain gang boss, a southern Home Guard bounty hunter like Teague, is desperate not to be seen by the Yankees. He forces Inman and the other prisoners to hide behind a small rise and to remain silent until the Yankees pass. As scripted, Veasey decides this is as good an opportunity as any to try an escape, and he initiates a scramble up the hill, Inman futilely resisting.

Without the town scene, Veasey's urge to escape and Inman's resistance make no sense. The alternatives were either putting the town scene back or finding some other solution.

Remarkably, like Murch finding Frederic Forrest's alternate line reading for "He'd kill us if he had the chance," in *The Conversation*, the same thing happened here. "There was a line of Inman's ," Murch says, "where he said, 'Come on' by way of resisting Veasey's escape. And I remember before shooting began I made a note on the screenplay that this was an odd thing to say under the circumstances. Anthony said, 'No, no, what it means is, 'Come *on*, don't *do* this.' In fact, in a different context, 'come on' *could* mean 'let's go, let's do it!'' And it turned out there was one take where Jude Law's emphasis was like that: wrong for the original scripted intention, but perfect as a way to initiate and lead an escape."

"So we were able to recut the scene and create the illusion that it was *Inman* who led the escape—he was so desperate to get back to Ada that he seized the first opportunity to present itself. His line reading flipped the scene's polarity 180 degrees—it became white rather than black—and it was consequently easier to understand what was going on in his head: Inman wanted to get back to Ada at any cost."

Murch says it's common in editing, and normally easy, to steer scenes five or ten degrees in either direction from their intended course. Shading intensity, favoring a character, softening a moment—that's "the bread and butter of film editing," as he calls it. "It also seems that flipping the polarity of a scene—going completely the opposite way from where things were originally intended—is something relatively easy to do in film editing. Somebody good is now bad, or somebody who was—in this case—an unwilling participant, is now the lead conspirator."

Back in Theater 4, *Cold Mountain* is concluding. Inman and Ada are reunited, spend the night together in the old Cherokee village, and, with Ruby's assent, make their plans to be together on Black Cove Farm. Then comes the inevitable confrontation, the shootout with Captain Teague and his Home Guard. Together, Inman and Ada get Teague cornered, and the audience cheers when he is killed. Inman tracks Bosie, the albino Home Guard, and shoots him. Inman seems to survive, but his eyes glaze over and he coughs up blood. Someone nearby says, "Oh, no," pretty loudly, and there is a groan from many people. The Russian expresses their collective regret: "He's not going to die?"

Since the credit roll is not done yet, the film ends on a shot that cranes up through the trees from the Easter meal at Black Cove. A Miramax representative quickly speaks into a microphone, asking audience members to please take one of the survey cards being passed out, and to fill it in before leaving the theater. Meanwhile, producers and the other film people use this opportunity to go out into the lobby to talk, compare notes, grab their Diet Cokes, and stretch their legs before the focus group begins. Walter stays seated. He makes a few notes on his laptop then uses the walkie-talkie to reach young Walter up in the projection area. "Good job, looked great. Tell Howie and Eddy and Tim for me."

The Russian is in the lobby. "I filled out a card. I liked it," he says. "It's a good story, but I hate what happened at the end."

The focus group process that is about to begin originated in the advertising business. Ten to 20 consumers are selected who represent the age, gender, race, educational levels, and other desired traits of the market for a particular product. Clients and ad agency account executives observe the proceedings from behind a one-way viewing window. The purpose is to probe for subjective responses and latent feelings that may not come out in a strict multiple-choice questionnaire. Murch calls it "a black art."

When the focus group method is applied to films-in-progress, though, the session is held immediately after a screening, and the "clients" are sitting right there in plain sight a few rows back.

Murch moves down toward the front of the theater where the others, including Anthony Minghella and Harvey Weinstein, have regrouped to listen in on the moderated discussion that follows. "If you wrote this up for a scientific journal," Murch whispers, "and said we ran the film once, then changed it profoundly and ran it again for a different group of people a month later, and got results to compare with the first, the scientists would say that's insane because there is no control. You would need to run the two versions of the film for exactly the same group, who also need to be insulated from contact with the creators. But of course we never do that." Focus group participants are picked on the fly, based on appearances, so one never knows if the deck is loaded one way or the other. Sean Cullen was buttonholed by a focus group recruiter after the July preview because he fit the demographic. Cullen was tempted, but said he was with the film.

The focus group moderator, an energetic middle-aged man, begins by asking broad questions about how the group rated the film. Twelve of 23 raise their hands on "excellent," six respond to "good." These are called "the top two boxes," and 18 of 23, or 78 percent, for the top two boxes is considered high. Of the other five people, the moderator wants to know the reason they did not say excellent. Most of them say it was predictable. The next issue is length and pacing—close to the bone for Walter. Nine say it was just right, but thirteen hold up their hands to say it was it too long. Only three agree that the pacing "was just right." Six say it was too slow, and ten indicate it was okay, "but dragged in spots."

After another ten minutes, when the discussion is nearly over, the leader asks a final question: "Would you recommend this movie to your friends?" The people from Miramax lean forward in their seats. "The key question," Murch whispers. "Nothing else really matters." For a movie to be fully successful at the box office, word of mouth is a must. When 17 of the 23 raise their hands, the onlookers appear relieved.

Says Murch: "With more than two-thirds saying yes, you have your radio-active core, the critical mass."

It's nearly 11 p.m. when the session concludes and the participants collect their cash payments in sealed envelopes. The producers and Miramax staffers gather in the lobby and on the sidewalk, quietly discussing the screening and the focus group. One of the marketing consultants breaks in with a tally of the questionnaire results: "Top two boxes: 81, our best so far; 59 definite recommend, tied with Charleston for best; female under 25, 86 top two boxes; male under 25 top two boxes, 78." Everyone seems buoyed, except Minghella, who looks glum. Perhaps he's already thinking ahead to the next morning when he and Murch have the official post mortem with the Weinsteins at Miramax.

Wednesday, October 1, 2003, Murch's Journal

Audience same reactions as previously, loved Ruby, felt that the film didn't start until she arrived. This is the Bob Weinstein comment from June, that there wasn't enough of Ada and Inman in the film. Most of these problems are endemic and will not go away no matter what we do. I am tired and trying not to be dragged down by the incommensurability between the effort it took to get here and the results. I kept wanting to say, "Yes, but we cut out two and a half hours." Fell asleep in my clothes when I got back to the hotel, reading the book on clouds. Woke up about 6am and haven't been back to sleep.

THURSDAY OCTOBER 2, 2003—NEW YORK CITY

At 3:30 p.m. Murch goes into the Broome Street Bar on West Broadway for a late lunch. Since mid-morning he'd been a few blocks away at the Miramax offices with Anthony, Sydney, Bill Horberg, Albert Berger and Ron Yerxa. He sits in the quiet back room of this old-style New York bar and restaurant, "a relief after the neighborhood's sometimes cloying precocity," as one online guide describes it.

There were 15 to 20 people attending the morning meeting at Miramax. Murch quotes Weinstein as saying, "This is the last we're going to get together like this because we're running out of time, so I want everyone to say anything that they have to say, because you won't be able to say it again. So, Albert?"

Albert Berger and Ron Yerxa spoke first. Then, according to Murch, Sydney Pollack said, "I don't feel comfortable talking about these things in this sort of format. So I'll just talk privately to Anthony."

Murch recalls Weinstein saying that the Miramax staff got together the previous night to make their set of notes: "Here are our consolidated notes." Then Colin Vaines, Miramax's London executive, read them. "And then on top of that," Murch continues, "Harvey gave his own set of notes, which were different. So I wrote them all down. It's five handwritten pages." The commentary Murch recorded represents the producers' and studio's thoughts. By contract, however, Minghella retains ultimate authority over the film—he has "final cut."

Nothing Ever Changes, or Does It?

In early September Murch came to a dialogue premixing session at De Lane Lea with a copy of *Growing Up in Hollywood* (1976), an autobiography by director, film editor, and child actor Robert Parrish. After the lunch break Walter stood on the little mezzanine behind the mix board and addressed the sound crew: "In 1948 Columbia Studio chief Harry Cohn let director Robert Rossen hire Robert Parrish to re-edit his film, *All the King's Men*, starring Broderick Crawford as Willie Stark, loosely based on Louisiana Governor Huey Long. The film was in trouble."

Murch read from the book:

> "The preview last night was a disaster," Cohn said. "The fuckin' picture is almost three hours long and it still doesn't make any sense." He turned to Rossen and pointed at me. "What makes you think this schmuck can salvage it when the best cutter in the studio has been working on it for five months?"
>
> I told Rossen I thought I saw a way to re-cut the picture. "OK, go ahead. I'm too close to it. I've been working on it for over a year. I'm taking a holiday. I'll be back in a month and we'll preview your cut in Huntington Park, a tough factory town. They'll understand it."
>
> And that's what we did. I re-cut the entire picture, re-dubbed it using music from the film library, and we previewed it in Huntington Park.
>
> The fat cats from Santa Barbara [where the earlier preview was held] must have been in touch with the working stiffs in Huntington Park, because the reception wasn't any better. In fact, it was worse… Rossen alone still believed in it, and he somehow convinced Cohn to let us carry on.
>
> We worked on the picture for six months after the Huntington Park fiasco. We had seven more disastrous previews with all kinds of audiences.

Director Rossen had a last-ditch idea for editor Parrish, Murch says, continuing from the book: "I want you to go through the whole picture. Select what you consider to be the center of each scene, put the film in the sync machine and wind down a hundred feet (one minute) before and a hundred feet after, and chop it off, regardless of what's going on. Cut through dialogue, music, anything. Then, when you're finished, we'll run the picture and see what we've got."

> I went straight back to the cutting room, followed Rossen's instructions to the letter… when I measured it at 5:00 am we had a ninety-minute picture… his brainstorm had worked. It all made sense in an exciting, slightly confusing, montagey sort of way… We took it to our final preview in Pasadena and were relieved at the audience's enthusiastic reaction… the Pasadena fat cats stood up and applauded. After the Pasadena preview we cut the negative with all the imperfections, the mismatched cuts, and the jumps in the soundtrack.

All the King's Men won the Academy Award for best picture of the year.

"So, you see," Murch said, as he closed the book, "nothing ever changes." Then he walked to the mixing board and sat down to continue the premix.

Murch paraphrases the gist of the group's thinking: "Whatever you did between the last cut and this cut, do something like that again. Whatever rabbit you pulled out of your hat that suddenly made Inman the leader of the escape from the chain gang, we liked that. Do more stuff like that. There are some specific things, but it's more like, 'This scene now seems a little slow. Do something.' But no suggestion as to what it might be. Meanwhile, people are starting to yell about how we'll never make the date unless reels are locked today, and at the latest on Monday."

Murch is supposed to begin the final mix in ten days at De Lane Lea in London. To start sound mixing, he and Minghella must lock the picture first—finalize the picture cutting so the soundtrack can be mixed in sync with the picture. The studio wants the picture locked three days from today so the digital intermediate (DI) can be prepared in time to meet the release date.

So far, the DI is a huge data file that resides on the computers at Framestore/CFC in London. And while the director of photography, John Seale, already spent three weeks making thousands of color corrections, only a handful of DI material has been output from the computer onto actual film negative. That process takes 36 hours per reel—20 days total for *Cold Mountain*. From that negative the film lab still has to make an interpositive, followed by an internegative, and from that, film prints. Then Minghella and Murch must review and approve the quality of nine reels of film print, or send them back for fixes. "It's a complex process," Murch says, putting it mildly.

The incongruity of three competing deadlines—a re-edit leading to a final lock of the picture, a final sound mix beginning in ten days, and outputting film from the digital intermediate—reminds Murch of a similar situation on another film he worked on, *The Godfather*.

"There was a crucial issue with Nino Rota's music, which Robert Evans, the head of Paramount, didn't like," Murch says, finishing his lunch. "He *really* didn't like it—felt that it dragged the film down." Murch was there with Coppola, at a crucial 1972 meeting at Evans's house.

"Evans wanted to bring in Henry Mancini to replace the score, but Francis threatened to take his name off the film if that happened. So Evans decided on a compromise: he, Evans, would recut Nino Rota's music and preview the film, then Francis would recut Evan's recut, have another preview and may the best version win. I looked at Francis, and he looked at me. We both knew that this wasn't going to happen—there was only time to mix the film once. Whoever got to go first would win. It was one of those moments when everything hung in the balance."

"Just then actress Ali McGraw comes out, Evans's wife at the time," Murch recalls. "She says, 'Bob, don't forget, we're going to Acapulco on vacation.' 'Oh, yeah, that's right,' Evans says. 'Okay, Francis, you guys do your thing first and then I'll do mine when I come back.'"

"I looked at Francis and we both knew we had won, but we also knew we had to maintain the fiction that everything was going to go the way Evans had proposed. But it was obvious to us, and to anyone who stopped to think about it, that there just wasn't time to do two versions, evaluate everything, have the debates that would inevitably happen, and then produce a final mix."

Coppola and Murch mixed the music the way they wanted it. By the time Evans and Ali McGraw came back from Mexico, it was too late. The momentum was with the version of the film that was ultimately released, and Nino Rota's music went on to become part of popular culture.

By now it's after 4 p.m., and Murch's return flight to London is scheduled to depart JFK at 9 p.m. Before leaving he'd like to talk to Minghella, who will stay one more day in New York to do more ADR. The two of them haven't yet had time to discuss last night's screening, the focus group discussion, the Miramax meeting, or their own set of notes. Murch, who doesn't own a cell phone, borrows one to call Tim Bricknell, Minghella's assistant, to see about getting together.

"I'm jolly!" Murch says to Bricknell, who is just down the street with Minghella inside the Mercer Hotel.

"Does Mr. Minghella want to talk to Mr. Murch?" Walter asks.

A pause.

"Okay, back in London, then."

"We'll pick it up Monday when he gets back," Murch says returning the cell phone. "He wants to get some distance from the collective angst that surrounds the picture right now. It's his way of reclaiming the picture."

Murch looks at his watch and decides there's time to go to the Apple store nearby on Prince Street.

Murch comes here not to test drive the G5 computers, pick up something for his Final Cut Pro system, or check his email, but to buy his son a birthday present—an iPod. Since this is Murch's first-ever visit to an Apple store, he explores it, but does so quickly, taking only a few minutes to cruise through the crowded displays of computers and other electronics, then upstairs through the bookstore area. He swiftly purchases the music player and returns to the stunning transparent glass stairway in the center of the store that connects the two floors. For the next 15 minutes he examines the staircase, its materials, and how it's put together. He pulls out a digital camera and takes several photos, moving a companion into position on the staircase to properly

The Apple Store in New York City.

capture its scale and proportions—another case of Murch admiring Apple's attention to design and function. "Maybe something like this could work for our place in Primrose Hill," he says.

Murch is making a fair swap, being here inside the Apple store. After all, the Final Cut Pro team had come to the Old Chapel in London two weeks earlier to visit him.

RETURNING THE FAVOR

Apple's Bill Hudson, Brian Meaney, and Will Stein, along with Brett Hale and Jeff Lowe were returning home through London from the IBC broadcasting technology conference in Amsterdam, Netherlands. Hudson and Meaney had contacted Murch earlier to ask if they could come to see him, and he agreed.

From:	Walter Murch
Date:	August 31, 2003
To:	Brian Meaney
Subject:	Visit in London?

Dear Brian:

Good to hear from you, and good to know you will be coming to London.

Yes, we will be here and would love to see you all. We will be doing some recutting, premixing, recording music, and doing final visual effects and color timing. Hectic, but we will certainly make room for you.

Best wishes,
Walter Murch

Late at night on September 16, the day before the Apple delegation was scheduled to arrive, Walter walked through the quiet streets near Primrose Hill, heading home from the Old Chapel. "So, we have Apple sometime tomorrow," he says. "We've worked up three or four pages of things that it would be nice to include in the next version of Final Cut. Sean was just talking to Ramy at DigitalFilm Tree, going over that list and double-checking with him whether some of those features had already been taken care of in Final Cut 4.0."

Walter then recounted the list of surprises he'd been through the last few days. He crunched together a last-minute temp sound mix for a 35mm print version of *Cold Mountain* that Miramax could show in Tokyo to potential Japanese distributors. Pollack and Horberg were in the edit room for three days, going over the cut. Murch had expected them to be there for only one day. Since Murch has not heard anything more from Apple since the end of August, he's not sure whether or not they're still planning to come. "We haven't heard a peep out of them, they haven't told us whether they're in town or not."

Before leaving the Old Chapel a few minutes earlier, Anthony told Murch about one more surprise: Weinstein is flying in from New York the day after Apple's visit so he can see the latest cut.

He's asked about the relentlessness of it all. "You have to keep your knees loose in this game," Murch said with a smile. "You never can tell what's going to happen."

His stamina is palpable, considering he's just worked from 8:30 a.m. to midnight, on this, the 451st day of editing, which began in the morning in Soho at the premix, and ended with editing back in Hampstead.

"Is it midnight?" Murch asked guilelessly. He truly didn't know what time it was.

By this point it seemed Murch was operating far outside the parameters of normal time. The feeling is akin to exiting a very absorbing movie—that sensation of having no idea what time it is, or if it's going to be day or night when you get outside.

"Being in the zone? Yeah," Murch said. "It's even more powerful when I'm mixing," Walter says as he looked up at the western sky. "Hey, there's Mars."

The guys from Apple arrived at the Old Chapel at 1 p.m. the next day, having first gone by cab to Fleet Street instead of Fleet Road. Walter welcomes them into his edit room and invites them to watch the first reel of *Cold Mountain*. After the battle scene finishes, the large monitor goes black and Murch turns up the lights.

Murch's guests were astounded by what they saw, and a little stunned from the intensity of the battle, which is understandable.

"Thank you, that's awesome," Jeff Lowe said, breaking the momentary silence.

"Thank you to *you* guys. It was fantastic," Murch responded, meaning Final Cut Pro.

"Thank you that it actually worked," Hudson says, wiping imaginary sweat off his brow in mock relief. The group shared a laugh.

"It's been all transparency, openness, and speed," Sean Cullen said. "There were no train wrecks. No down time like we had with Avid."

Murch pointed out to the Apple guys that his experience solving Final Cut Pro problems wasn't all that different from what he previously had to do with Avid when it released a buggy new version of Film Composer just before editing began on *The Talented Mr. Ripley*. "Everyone on the ground—meaning people who were actually using it—had started to try and figure out workarounds on their own. Avid maintained that there was no problem, or if there were problems it was operator error. I said to myself back in early 2002 when I was contemplating Final Cut, that if this was the situation in Rome with Avid, what was it going to be like in Bucharest with Final Cut?" Another round of appreciative, slightly nervous laughter from the Apple delegation.

"In the end, there was never anything," Murch continued. "We would have the occasional crash, but they would be what I would term 'friendly' crashes, unlike the 'smoke out of the back of the machine' crashes that we would get with the Avid on *Ripley*. And we had this redundancy of having four machines rather than two. If one of them had really gone down, you can still roll a cart on three wheels. You don't have to have four. You just have to rebalance things. But that never happened. We were able to use the four workstations the way we had designed it, me cutting on one, Sean doing file management and cutting on another, and the two others—one for digitizing material into our system, the other for burning DVDs. That all worked great, both for stability and for the security of knowing we had redundancy, which in the end, was never called upon."

"I spent more time with the machines waiting for me," Cullen said, "which is also a sea change. On the Avid, it's always the machines telling you, 'Well, you want that, I'm in the middle of making this, and it means I have to stop.' Whereas whenever I needed to do something, if I needed more DVDs, I could always repurpose one machine to get out the DVDs I needed. It was just a whole different scenario for me as a first assistant."

"It's a great world," Hudson said. "The confluence of the technology and the creative."

Apple's Final Cut Pro team visits Murch in London. Left to right: Will Stein, Brett Hale, Brian Meaney, Walter Murch, Sean Cullen, and Bill Hudson. (Not pictured: Jeff Lowe.)

"Shall we have a sandwich?" Walter asked. The discussion continues over lunch, with Cullen and Murch going over a list of suggested improvements for future versions of Final Cut Pro. Later that night, at 11 p.m., Sean and his wife, Juliette become parents for the second time, with the arrival of their daughter, Florence.

FINAL PICTURE CUTTING

Murch returns to London from the last preview in New Jersey. The final mix is scheduled to begin October 15, less than two weeks away.

Friday, October 3, 2003, Murch's Journal

Over Atlantic on way back tired but satisfied that we got the job done. Meet this morning w/ troops and go over the landscape for the next few weeks.

All the suggestions coming out of the final New Jersey preview need to be analyzed, consolidated, reviewed, and put up against the changes Minghella and Murch also still want to try. Taking the upcoming weekend off to recoup and recharge, Murch has 12 days to do all of the remaining picture editing before locking the film.

So once again, Minghella and Murch begin from the beginning, making adjustments and removals. By Tuesday two and a half minutes are gone. Substantial changes are also still getting made—Minghella adds a third letter for Ada to read, voiceover, after Inman arrives at Cold Mountain, sitting atop the snowy ridge. Murch never leaves the old Chapel before 1 a.m. all this week. But now, at least, he has a companion on his walks home: Hana, his border terrier, who arrived with Aggie from California last June. The dog often accompanies Walter to the edit room, where she watches patiently from the couch.

Harvey Weinstein may not be there in body, but he seems to have an eye on the edit room.

Thursday, October 9, 2003, Murch's Journal

Phone conversation with HW [Harvey Weinstein], talking to Anthony. HW suggests delaying the release if we can't get the balance right. Disturbing words, to say the least. Why would he say such a thing, unless there is an ulterior motive, to frighten us into some "breakthrough" action? Which is probably what it is.

Heading home at 2.15am—another warm night like the last one.

While Anthony and Walter ought to be getting closure on sequences and reels, considering the mix begins in five days. Instead, true to form, they re-examine anything that does not yet seem quite right.

FLASHES OF FILM

I have something in my head: a clip of film, someone saying, "Have you gone maaad?" with mock disbelief. Where is it from?? A film I think, and a film I worked on… It was from "Unbearable" and it was the closeup of the Soviet interrogator grilling Tereza after she had been arrested with her photographs.

—from Murch's Journal, October 6, 2003

The porch scene from *Cold Mountain*.

Friday, October 10, 2003, Murch's Journal

*Anthony thinking of working on the porch scene [between Ada and Inman]
again. We looked at the assembly. His analysis of the problem with the scene is
that Inman is a man who says few words, and then talks a lot about how words
don't describe the world of nature and feelings. Also, the way it is cut down now,
there is no (or just a little) friction between them, so their romance is "too easy"—
an old note of mine. What if we left the scene unresolved on "I don't know you"?*

One can feel that Murch is on a roller coaster now, professionally and emotionally. He is nearing completion of the picture—editing and anticipating the
sound mixing—but without any final approval from the producers. It's not
surprising then to find two radically different journal entries on the same day:

Friday, October 10, 2003, Murch's Journal

*Amazing that we are where we are, with as few problems as we have. As intense
as it is right now, it could be much worse.*

*Strong sense of suffocation. With all the competing agendas, complete the film
but don't complete it. Harvey is coming to London on Tuesday, so no doubt
we will screen the film for him here at that time. Gurgle, gurgle. We will prevail,
Inshallah.*

On Sunday, a day off, Murch gives a three-hour lecture to the Association
of Motion Picture Sound (AMPS) at De Lane Lea. He speaks about technology and movies: the first motion picture with sound made in 1894 by W. K.
L. Dickson for Thomas Edison (which Murch helped to reconstruct for the
Library of Congress), the vacuum tube theory of power and coherence, Final
Cut Pro, and hidden regions of technical breakthroughs still to be discovered.
Then, in the afternoon, perhaps suffering a bit from early "parade syndrome,"
the sensation of moving backwards after the parade passes by, Walter tries to
relax at his house in Primrose Hill. Sometimes stopping the momentum for
even one day is not such a good idea.

Sunday, October 12, 2003, Murch's Journal

*What happens if we get to 2 hours 30 minutes and Harvey comes in and wants it
to be 15 minutes shorter or will not release this year? Harvey talking about being
worried about "Anthony and Walter's health"—ominous. That is what you say
when you are getting ready to take something away from somebody. "I am doing
this for your health." It is what they said when they fired me from Return to Oz.*

Film is 2.32.21.

Things like that do happen in the film industry. Murch has a right to be para-
noid. But neither he nor Minghella will be sent packing. It's a passing moment
of anxiety.

MURCH ON CUTTING
FOR WORDS OR
THOUGHTS

Cutting tight on a line empha-
sizes the content of the line—
the words. Cutting a beat or two
later will allow the audience to
focus their attention on the eyes
of the character, to see what he
or she really thought about what
was said.

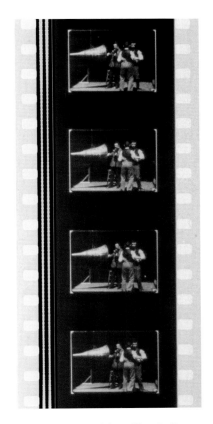

**From the Edison/Dickson film, the first
movie with sync sound, which Murch
helped to restore.**

CM is 2.29.40 (minus end credits): Under 2½ hours! Hard to believe but there it is. I restructured reel six, interposing the Christmas dance in the middle of Sara's, and dropped "Goodbye Maddy," "Goat meat in stream," "Brown leaf hill." One minute 40 secs disappeared. And the junctures are better I think. Nice cut from Ada closing the window to Inman in the rain heading for the "troll tree" with music, pre-lapping "Heathcliff" over the tree and then coming out of Heathcliff into the approach to Sara's with good music taking us there. Most remarkable is the interpose of Christmas dance during the interval at Sara's. Nice that the music creeps in as Inman is going to sleep on the corn cobs—then go to happy dancing, full flush of energy and innocence, and then out of that with thunder to Inman waking up and there is Sara asking him to come inside. So now we have cut out 2 hours 36 mins and change. In other words, we have cut The English Patient out of the assembly of Cold Mountain. Thank you for your guidance.

It's 2:30 a.m. Wednesday morning when Walter leaves the Old Chapel with Hana trotting by his side. Later that day Harvey Weinstein and Colin Vaines, Miramax's London executive, will come in for another viewing of *Cold Mountain.* Murch expects substantial conflicts.

Harvey and Colin visit. Now come and gone—3 to 7:30—went away happy, impressed with the work we had done in the last couple of weeks, tried a few ideas for cuts, loved the new reel six juxtapositions (Christmas music in the middle of Sara's), the meeting in the gorge, the Cherokee village and the shootout/death. Liked the very ending, but Anthony has some ideas there he wants to try. "Let's lock this picture," said Harvey. "Lock it by Friday." Congratulations to all. During the reel-by-reel, Hana made a beeline for Harvey, jumped up on his lap, and sat there, happily smiling. Much improved over the hangdog Hana of the last couple of days.

Murch fully recognizes what's just happened, and its implications for film editing: "Harvey signed off on the film looking at it on Final Cut Pro. One of those milestones that will go unremarked but is actually a tremendous achievement. That the image and sound presentation was more than adequate for the head of a studio to make such a fateful decision on such an expensive film."

Indeed, this same week, as if to comment on what's just occurred, Avid Technologies releases Avid Free DV, a stripped-down version of its Avid Express DV software for digital editing. *The Boston Globe*, Avid's hometown paper, reports: "Steve Jobs may have something to do with [the decision.] Today's professionals pick Avid products first. But the up-and-coming youngsters who'll be the video artists of tomorrow are buying Macintoshes and getting their first taste of video editing from an Apple product. When they're ready to upgrade, they may think Apple instead of Avid. And Apple is ready for them with Final Cut Pro, a $995 video editing product that's so good that film editor Walter Murch is using it to cut the upcoming feature film *Cold Mountain*."

Friday, October 17, 2003, Murch's Journal

2 am. Locked the film: Congratulations!! It seemed (as it always seems) anti-climactic, a kind of wobbling to a stop. But there it is. We will check screen it tomorrow morning and then release the reels to the various departments. Walking past the Chinese restaurant on England's Lane—two waiters in there having a happy loud conversation at one of the tables—2:30 am. Got a hamper of Fortnum & Mason: foodie goodies from Harvey. "Thank you so very much for all your time and endless patience. All the very best, Harvey."

Date: October 21, 2003
Subject: Lock
From: Ramy Katrib
To: Walter Murch

Dear Walter,

This is just the best. Cold Mountain locked. I think it's been around 19 months since the call from Sean. Congratulations to you for making history again, gracefully, naturally. Hats off to Anthony, to Sean, for taming the technology, and all your team.

The 'sleepless fear' throughout was that the technology would get in the way of your editing. Cheers to that damn Final Cut Pro system, withstanding your fury, refined cutting, blinking all those months.

We cannot express enough our awe for your decision to engage something new, for all your reports and encouragement, for conquering.

Best regards,
Ramy

Murch mixes sound at De Lane Lea wearing his lucky sweater. "Aggie's mother knitted it for her in 1964. A few years later I stole it. It's got a few scars on it."

CHAPTER 11

Bullets Explosions Music People

Monday, October 18, 2003, Murch's Journal

Amazing to remember in retrospect that Francis was not in the room during the mix of Conversation or Apocalypse. I played the mixes for him and he had comments, which we incorporated. Not around during the premixes of Godfather, but he was for the final.

The relationship between a film director and the sound mixer is just as intimate and complex as the one between director and film editor. After all, the mixer realizes the director's imagination of how a movie will sound. At its simplest, sound mixing means plaiting three disparate elements—music, dialogue, and sound effects—into one harmonious whole. But to achieve that requires tens of thousands, maybe millions of decisions; no one keeps track, least of all mixers, who might blanch if they ever knew. For every sound there are choices about volume, equalization (EQ, or bass/ treble), reverberation, synchronization to picture, placement within the speaker array (left, center, right, left-surround, right-surround, boom), the tonal quality of music, transitions between scenes, and more. These are subjective determinations, most of which can only be decided on a trial-and-error basis. There are no predetermined rules or formulas defining what sounds good for a particular film at a particular moment. The mixer brings together elements prepared by the sound editors and, like an orchestra leader who relies on top-notch players, succeeds only by virtue of having the best, properly prepared sound elements to work with.

Unlike filming, where the director approves the composition and angle of every shot before it's taken, much of post-production sound work happens outside the director's purview. The director may not be involved in choosing sound effects or even premixing the dialogue. Depending on the director's personality and interests, he or she will normally participate in more essential aspects of sound preparation, such as recording ADR (automated dialogue replacement) and music taping, but even that isn't a given.

For the most part, a film director is involved at arm's length in sound mixing: watching and listening until the mixer is satisfied with the work, and then giving an okay or not. It's a tedious business, and some directors don't or can't participate at such a minute level for the six to eight weeks it normally takes to do a mix from start to finish. In the scene where Inman gets shot, for example, Murch makes eight passes before he is satisfied with the equalization of Inman's cough—the proper bass/treble, the right density of sound, reverberation, and pitch. He makes 16 refinements until he is happy with the separation he creates between the sound of Ada's piano and the raindrops splattering on her window during the scene in which she sees her father die.

The mixer has to pay close attention to details, be a savvy audio engineer, operate a complex set of constantly evolving, cutting-edge controls, and work in a give-and-take style with numerous personalities—studio heads, producers, director, editor, other mixers, sound editors, and technical support. Using a professional film mixing theater can run $500 an hour or more, and that's often without counting the cost of the mixers' labor. Time and financial pressures make the sound mix a pressure cooker. A professional film sound mixer works under high stress all the time, so it's no wonder many of them have a reputation for being prickly and forbidding.

The final sound mix occurs at the end of post production, sometimes only a few weeks before the film is released in theaters. By this time, the director isn't always available to sit in at the mix. Anthony Minghella will be gone from the *Cold Mountain* mix for days at a time to attend to matters such as last-minute dialogue recording with actors in New York, or major press events, such as an interview with Jude Law and Nicole Kidman on the Barbara Walters show.

Murch made eight passes in the sound mix before being satisfied with Inman's cough.

Even when he is in London, Minghella must go off to meet with producers, write new dialogue for ADR, check film prints from the lab, and so forth. The soundtrack will not be final, however, until he approves it.

Wearing both hats, as picture editor and sound mixer, enables Murch to keep his and Minghella's confederated vision for the film intact. In the more typical filmmaking structure, where editing and mixing are handled by two different people, the editor's extra pair of eyes and ears adds another layer of complexity to an already complicated creative process. The film editor is often marginalized during the sound mix in order to maintain a workable chain of command. One sound facility manager describes "a wall" between mixer and film editor during the typical feature film sound mix.

Sunday, October 19, 2003, Murch's Journal
Heading to work at 7.20 pm. Already dark. Prep things for the temp mix on Tuesday.

Before starting the final mix on *Cold Mountain*, Murch must first complete one last temporary mix of the soundtrack so the film can be previewed at advance press screenings. Reviewers for monthly magazines and other publications with long lead times need to see the film right away to make their deadlines. It's like another dress rehearsal for Murch and the sound team— working with newly revised scenes, new ADR, and finessing their audio work one more time before the real thing. Each new mix version begins where the last one left off. The continuous temp-mixing that began back in June only improves the end result. The movie soundtrack, like sedimentary geological formations, accretes enhancements as it evolves over time.

Because he has to squeeze in a temp mix before the final mix can start, Murch turns to Final Cut Pro for a technological innovation. The sound editors are busy prepping material for the final mix, which begins on Thursday, October 23. Murch decides to do most of the preparation for the temp mix himself at the Old Chapel, in FCP. "The tracks from the previous temp mix had been imported into FCP," Murch recalls. "I recut them to match the new version, and we used my recut FCP tracks to do the last temp mix at De Lane Lea." Murch says it saved time, allowed the sound editors to do their work without being bothered, and the result sounded great. The only compromise was using 16-bit digital sound (CD quality), the highest quality Final Cut Pro 3.0 could handle, rather than 24-bit. "I can't really tell the difference," Murch admits. "It's miraculous really that we are able to do this—run FCP tracks straight into the board and get a Dolby 4-2-4, encoded/matrixed mix out of it." He had pushed Final Cut Pro past another milestone, one neither Murch, DigitalFilm Tree, nor the Apple project team could ever have anticipated.

Walter Murch mixing sound on
***Apocalypse Now* (1979).**

Today is first day of final mix. Good luck to all of us. May it go well. God willing.

Just as every scene in a movie must have a purpose if it belongs in the narrative, so the soundscape for a scene must be designed with specific intent. For example, Murch recalls wanting to use the sound of a field of crickets in one of the beginning scenes in *Apocalypse Now* when Willard is alone in his hotel room at night. "For story reasons," Murch says, "we wanted the crickets to have a hallucinatory degree of precision and focus." That led him to bring live crickets into Zoetrope's basement studio to record them individually, over and over, creating a sound-effects layer with thousands of overlapping chirps. Effective sound design rests on concrete ideas like that. And mixing together such effects, along with music and dialogue, requires the mixer to have the equivalent of a script—a blueprint of sound that instructs his choices.

Walter Murch has a map to comprehend the universe of sound, and he uses terms of light for its legend. White noise consists of every possible element of sound, just as the color white contains every color of light. Put white noise through an "audio prism" for decoding, and Murch finds the full spectrum for the language of sound. Speech, which he calls "encoded" sound, is at one end of the rainbow—violet. Language is considered to be encoded in the sense that the listener must decode it using linguistic tools to associate meaning. At the other extreme, where red exists in the light spectrum, Murch places music. He calls it "embodied sound," in the sense that it requires no code for understanding; it can be experienced directly without analysis. In between speech and music are sound effects—half language, half music. They refer to something specific, like crickets chirping or a battle explosion, that requires some thought. Neither completely uncoded like music nor coded like speech, they are yellow, midway in the rainbow of sound colors.

If sound is like color, how might audio composition compare to painting? Murch wrote about this in a 1998 article, "Dense Clarity—Clear Density": "A well-balanced painting will have an interesting and proportioned spread of colors from complementary parts of the spectrum, so the soundtrack of a film will appear balanced and interesting if it is made up of a well-proportioned spread of elements from our spectrum of 'sound-colors.'"

Like a memorable painting, be it abstract or realistic, a good soundtrack doesn't overreach. Trying to do too much with too many colors can produce an undesirable level of complexity that pleases no one. This is what Murch calls the "logjam." Avoiding excess means, among other strategies, "choosing for every moment which sounds should predominate when they can't all be included; deciding which sounds should play second fiddle," he writes. The axiom to help make these choices is Murch's "Law of Two-and-a-Half."

The mind seems capable of keeping track of one person's footsteps in a movie, for example, or even two, but not three or more. Murch had this realization early on, in 1969 when working on George Lucas's low-budget sci-fi film, *THX-1138*. In the middle of the night at the Academy of Sciences in San Francisco, Murch recorded sound effects for the movie's policemen/robots— recording himself clomping through the halls in special metal shoes he built. Later in the edit room, on syncing up the sounds to the images he realized that with two robots, their footsteps had to be in sync with the picture to be believable; but with three robots, none of the footsteps had to sync up exactly. "Our minds give up," Murch writes. "There are too many steps happening too quickly—the group of footsteps is evaluated as a single entity."

A soundtrack shouldn't contain more than two major elements and a minor third—not unlike a musical chord. Or, to put it another way, the soundtrack should simultaneously give the audience a view of both the forest and the trees: "Clarity, which comes through a feeling for the individual elements (the notes), and Density, which comes through a feeling for the whole (the chord). I found this balance point to occur most often when there were *not quite* three layers of something—my 'Law of Two-and-a-Half.'"

The physical properties of sound make such layering possible, what Murch calls "harmonic superimposure." Like musical tones, sounds can be added together while each element retains its identity. The notes C, E, and G create something new, a C-major chord, but you can also hear each of the original notes. If movie sound effects have a relationship with each other (the crickets of *Apocalypse Now*) they can be multiplied and work in harmony. Pile up too many unrelated sounds on each other (dialogue, music score, auto traffic, a car radio, horns honking, ambulance siren, jet planes, etc.), and there is too much information—white noise. The sound mixer begins with many more sound elements than he can possibly feature at any one time. Like the cinematographer who shows different options of camera angles to a film director, the sound mixer gets a plethora of elements from the sound department, each of which he arranges by priority, or eliminates, depending on his sense of the scene and its relationship to scenes before and after.

Walter Murch still walks to work, but now it's two miles in the other direction from Hampstead: south to Soho and De Lane Lea. He joins dozens of other pedestrian commuters through Regent's Park to London's central business district. Entering the park from Primrose Hill, it's a quiet, pleasant route along the Broad Walk adjacent to the London Zoo. These mornings Walter is serenaded by whistles, wails, warbles, and screeches from the nearby monkeys and exotic birds. The animals drive his dog Hana wild as she goes off leash chasing down scents and squirrels. He passes Daguerre's 1828 Diorama building, which Walter calls "a sort of early 19th Century IMAX experience." On

Sean Cullen, Hana, Walter, and Dei Reynolds meet in Walter's edit room.

leaving Regent's Park at Marylebone Road, he is swept into the clamor of a 21st Century London rush hour: buses, motor scooters, taxis, honking horns, sirens, hundreds of commuters' conversations—urban white noise, but still "a sort of morning calisthenics for the ears," he says, "and better than listening to the car radio."

Studio A at De Lane Lea is taking on a decidedly lived-in look. The *Cold Mountain* sound team has been premixing or temp-mixing the soundtrack here on and off for over four months. For two days now a pink bakery box with several chocolate croissants has been on the long table behind the mix console. Bottles of water and days-old newspapers lie around, along with empty coffee mugs, a bowl of fruit, many laptops (all PowerBooks), magazines, piled-up dishes, and assistant Tim Bricknell's mobile office: a banker's box full of files. Half a dozen green and blue Ethernet cables snake around the floor for high-speed Internet hookups. If not for the movie screen or the movie sounds, this could be the aftermath of a hacker group's all-nighter.

CAMBRIDGE TERRACE AND THE COLLISEUM REGENT'S PARK.

The London Diorama.

This was a specially constructed theater showing naturalistic illusions to the public. The first one was built in Paris in 1824 by distinguished painter Charles Bouton in partnership with Louis Jacques Mandé Daguerre, an expert in lighting and scenic effects—and later the inventor of the Daguerreotype, the first practical photographic process. Two huge pictures, 70 x 45 feet in size, were painted on translucent material. Using elaborate lighting designs and accompanied by live music to enhance the mood, the pictures took on a three-dimensional look. The amphitheatre, which held up to 360 people, swung back and forth between the two views.

A day at the final mix begins unceremoniously. The sound editors and co-mixers are at work when Walter walks in; it's like coming into a party already in progress—a very loud party. Martin Cantwell, the effects editor, sits at his ProTools station on the right-hand side of the console working on a section from the Battle of Petersburg. The crew greets Walter with cheerful good mornings between short bursts of high-decibel Civil War combat.

Before Murch takes his place at the console, he catches up on who's doing what, and where. With the finishing work moving so fast, it's critical for him to know all these details so he can plan for the tasks that lie ahead. Sound supervisor Eddy Joseph tells him that Mark Levinson just dropped off new ADR from the previous night's loop group recording session with off-camera actors' voices for the battle scene. As Joseph explains this new dialogue, sound editor Colin Ritchie puts it into the soundtrack on his ProTools workstation. Gruff male voices fill the theater: "Come on! Let's get 'em, boys!" "Them Yankees gonna die in their own holes." "We've got 'em now, boys!" "Shoot 'em!"

"Mark would have loved to have explained this to us himself," Joseph tells Murch, "and when he and Anthony are free from Harvey, of course, he will." He is referring of course to Harvey Weinstein, who has returned to London to check on the film's progress.

To commute by foot through a fountain-studded flower garden, to mix a film you enjoy working on, with people that you enjoy working with: what a blessing.

"What's the Harvey situation?" Murch inquires.

"He's arriving any minute now."

"To do what?" Murch asks in between bits of ADR.

"To destroy my edit room, I think," Joseph says facetiously.

"They're going to play Harvey the narration, the voiceover?"

"Yeah," Joseph says. "The voiceover on reel one and reel nine, but also the new letter on reel two."

"Them Yankees gonna die in their own holes!"

"I opened the door to my edit room this morning and there was Anthony," Joseph says. "He looked like a zombie."

"Really? Oh, God," Murch says.

"Damn Yankees, trapped in..."

"Hurry up! They're stuck! Shoot 'em!"

"It's not just tiredness," Joseph says. "It's that weight, isn't it?"

 Murch agrees.

"You could feel his shoulders are a little bit down," Joseph says.

"Tim said he's just getting angrier and angrier, which is not a good place to be in," Murch says.

"Not at this stage."

"Let's get 'em, boys!"

Like the process of editing the picture, finishing the sound mix consists of making a version, reviewing it, taking notes, addressing those notes in a new version, reviewing that, and so on—for as long as the schedule allows. That's the theory, anyway. In reality, on a Minghella movie, new sound elements fly in as the mix progresses (ADR from the principal actors, loop group dialogue, revised music, new closing songs, and remixes of already recorded musical score). On the picture side, opening credits, closing credits, the main title sequence, and subtitles are still in process. These new and changing visual elements may throw the soundtrack off kilter, since they could require adjustments to the soundtrack structure, such as allowing more space for Kidman's voiceover reading supplements to Ada's letters, or adjusting musical transitions. Murch and the sound crew mix at a moving target.

Unlike picture editing, where it's just Murch and Minghella (and the occasional producer), the mix is more of a team effort. With so many changes to

"Them Yankees gonna die in their own holes!"

the soundtrack still being made during the final sound mix, the sound editors from each subdepartment (dialogue, ADR, effects, Foley, music) are all there, standing by to edit the soundtrack right in the theater should that be necessary. The division between sound editing and mixing is becoming less defined. In part it's because digital sound editing technology makes instant editing possible; and automated mix boards can save settings and versions just like an audio workstation. Given that Minghella encourages collaboration (which Murch enjoys, too), sound editors are not just present, they are consulted during the mix, asked to provide notes on the mix in progress.

Each reel is just under 20 minutes long and is mixed individually whenever it becomes ready, often out of sequential order. If final audio elements are missing from a reel, or the exact running time of final visual elements is still uncertain, that reel is put off to be mixed later.

So how does Murch start? "I just kind of dive in," he says. "I'll listen to tracks in isolation and find out what works particularly well. For example, I may decide in a certain section of the battle to concentrate on people firing at each other and maybe their voices. And we won't hear much music or other effects, like footsteps."

Everyone makes a list of what still needs to be fixed as a reel plays through, pegged by timecode. An LCD counter below the screen enumerates elapsed minutes and seconds. Whoever has the first note starts the discussion. It's an audio symposium among equals; everyone's items hold equal weight and get debated only if there is disagreement, which is rare.

At this point, about halfway through discussion of reel one, Murch has a note. It concerns the section between the big explosion underneath the Confederate entrenchments and the charge of the Union Army.

"Okay, at 10:07... the horse snorts and it whinnies when it gets up. But then there's a huff-huff after that, which we could boost. Let's keep the monitor on dim here [an across-the-board level reduction to permit conversation while mixing]. At 10:42..."

Eddy Joseph jumps in. "Immediately after that, at 10:11, the first bit of the fife. I don't think you should have that."

Mike Prestwood-Smith agrees: "I don't like that, either."

"It sort of brings us out of the music," Joseph adds.

Murch agrees and goes on to the area where the Union Army makes its mad dash from screen left to screen right, Stars and Stripes flying, horses thundering, bayonets rattling, battle cries screeching.

Tuesday November 4, 2003, Murch's Journal
Finished 3 and starting 1. We ran it through and the battle sounded like a big ball of noise. Guidance and perseverance.

"In general, this is a festival of midrange sounds [600 to 2,000 cycles]," Murch says to the sound crew. "The music is right in that range; the screaming people are in there; so are the small arms, and the rifles—right in there. What is very welcome when I hear them are sounds above and below those frequencies. Like all of the cannon fire and the subharmonic stuff. So we should find out where we have an opportunity to add something down there because it anchors everything. When Oakley hits the other guy, there's a nice high metallic tinging sound. And also some ricochets and some things up around 5,000 or 6,000 cycles that will sing through. So if you know of any other effects that are like that, we can put them in."

Matt Gough hits the Play button. The projected picture (downloaded from Final Cut Pro and shown via the video track of Pro Tools for this review) jumps ahead into the peak of battle down in the pit. A chorus sings, a horse whinnies, Oakley yells as he's run through with a bayonet, explosions go off, men scream.

"We've gotten too hot on the clattery guns and stuff," Matt says.

"The firing of the guns is good," Murch says. "But it's the combination of the clatter, the screams, and the rebel yells. It's too much all on top of itself."

Later that night at 8:30 pm, walking home from De Lane Lea through the now quiet, darkened streets of central London, Walter reflects on reel one and the issue of loudness and soundtrack complexity.

"Bullets, people, explosions, music—if you're not careful everything congeals into noise that isn't particularly interesting. If you play a track loud and then some other track comes along that's louder than it, you immediately transfer your attention to the louder thing. Then a masking phenomenon takes place. A whole sound element isn't perceivable. So we have to get rid of it."

Murch describes the mixer's task as "directing the attention of the audience's ears, just as a director of photography directs its eyes." He wants to give the audience the impression that there is sound for everything, all the time. In fact, only two or three sound concepts are present at any one moment—Murch's rule of two and a half. Does it get tiring for Murch to mix a sequence like the Petersburg battle? "Because of the noise level it's exhausting work since we're immersed in it ten or twelve hours a day. The audience experiences a five-minute scene, but we're hearing it continuously for two or three days."

WEDNESDAY, NOVEMBER 5, 2003—SOHO, LONDON

At a lunch break in Studio A, Tim Bricknell, Minghella's assistant and associate producer of *Cold Mountain*, sits down on the couch next to Murch. Murch previews these newly revised opening titles and closing credits which are in QuickTime movies on Bricknell's PowerBook. Debbie Ross, the title sequence artist in Los Angeles, has been creating them using computer imagery. She finished these versions just a few hours ago, uploaded the sequences to a *Cold Mountain* FTP (file transfer protocol) server, from which Bricknell downloaded them. It's another stunning one-two punch of digital editing technology and the Internet, increasing convenience while saving time and money.

The title sequence uses visual images of sky, water, and mountains, and Walter comments about the pacing and rhythm among the three elements. "We looked at these like dailies," Murch says later. "But they are ready to be imported into the film using Final Cut because the graphic sequences are in QuickTime, and Final Cut works on QuickTime." Prior to these technological advances, Ross would have made a videotape copy of her work (or a film print, if you go back farther in time), which would have been shipped from L.A. to London (two days) for screening.

ANTHONY MINGHELLA ON BRITISH CINEMA

Rogue voices of British cinema—the independent voices, the forgotten voices, the voices from the past and from world cinema—might otherwise drown under the incessant demands of Hollywood and its irresistible machine of promotion and dissemination. I've been the beneficiary of that machine and am grateful to it, but I am also the product of an era which enjoyed a robust British Film Institute (BFI) in London and in the regions, where repertory cinema flourished and through which I learned while at university in Yorkshire, of the beautiful and complex worlds created by Fellini, Kurosawa, Ray, Visconti, Truffaut, de Sica, Lean and Bunuel. Right now the domination of the commercial cinema is unacceptable. Provocative cinema is in danger of being ignored, forgotten or suppressed. And the BFI must be its champion. The BFI's job, put simply, is to love cinema, to contextualise it, and to make its treasures available."

—Opening night address, London Film Festival, October 31, 2003

Murch quickly moves his conversation with Bricknell from visual effects to the most formidable unresolved area still facing Anthony and *Cold Mountain*: the beginning of the film. Every storyteller knows that the start and finish to a narrative are the most vital—and the hardest to get right. The success of a story is determined right up front, when an audience meets characters, locates itself in space and time, and reads stylistic clues for tone and intention. Likewise, the choices for how a story is resolved determine whether moviegoers leave the theater satisfied, feeling two-plus hours of their time was well spent.

"Pretend you are Anthony for a moment," Murch says to Bricknell, "and tell me what his thinking is on the whole reel one beginning idea."

There are three issues: Where does Kidman's voiceover reading of Ada's letter begin? Where does the initial subtitle explaining the Battle of Petersburg appear and what will it say? Which music will be used for this entire section, from the studio and producer's logos to the explosion shot?

So far, Murch hasn't had a chance to go over these questions directly with Minghella, who just returned to London that morning on the red-eye from New York where he, Bricknell, and ADR supervisor Mark Levinson went to record Kidman reading new material for the expanded voiceover letter. The answers Murch needs bear immediately upon choices he must make about how the picture might require recutting and when to mix which reel.

Bricknell has some tentative answers.

The Kidman voiceover should begin immediately after the producers' logos but before the main "Cold Mountain" title, he says. Murch asks whether there is enough time to fit it all in. Bricknell believes so, based on Levinson having tried Kidman's narration against the picture on his laptop during the flight back. The subtitle will go at the end of the initial wide shot that reveals the Southern army's encampment—what is being called "the rabbit shot," since it starts with a rabbit coming up out of a hole. But, Murch notes to Bricknell, that shot is 12 seconds too short if the subtitle is going to stay on screen long enough to be read. And since that footage was enhanced much earlier with visual effects to strengthen details in the tableau, this means going back for more visual effects, which takes time. As to the music for the opening, Bricknell reports that Minghella is still undecided: "He's trying 'Scarlet Tide' at the very beginning (a song written for the movie by Elvis Costello), he's trying 'Pretty Bird,' he's trying Ralph Stanley singing 'Tarry With Me.' He also likes the score at the very beginning, over the credits."

"Okay, Murch says, "when we're done today, I'll go back up to the Chapel and sketch that out."

In an email to producer Bill Horberg about the screenplay back in June 2002, before he had left California for Romania, Murch wrote about the way *Cold*

Mountain begins. "The beginning of the film is harder going than the material past page 35. Which is the way the book was for me—harder to get through the first hundred pages than the rest. The Battle of the Crater is the whole enchilada, and gloriously upends traditional dramatic structure. You expect a film to *end* with a big battle."

Murch likened this to *Apocalypse Now*, and how scenes with Kilgore (Robert Duvall) "front-loaded the film in a way it could never recover from. How could you top it? Nor could *Private Ryan*, for that matter. We have to watch out for this."

In addition to beginning with a big battle, there is a basic issue for the audience right at the start: Which side are we on? Who do we root for? "The first voice we hear in the film now is the voice of the Northerner," Murch says, "and then we see masked soldiers with an American flag going to blow up some other army. The natural unthinking response is the guys in blue (Union) are 'us' and those other people in grey (Confederates) are the 'enemy'—in fact it's just the opposite." Inman is the hero of the film and the people to be concerned about are the enemies of the people with the American flag. "So there's a kind of a warp at the beginning of the film," Murch continues, "when you alter people's ordinary preconceptions, which is that anyone with an American flag is on the right side and people with another kind of flag are on the wrong side."

"The beginnings of films are wildly interpreted differently by different people. Everyone is coming into the theater in a different frame of mind, attaching their own meanings to the opening images. Everyone will put it together slightly differently. It's very much like the beginning of *Touch of Evil* [which Murch re-edited in 1998]. It begins with a bomb being set, put in the trunk of a car, and then you wait three minutes and 20 seconds, and then it explodes. Here, instead of Charleton Heston and Janet Leigh, it's Jude Law and a picture of Nicole Kidman. A bomb is underneath them. Are they going to get blown up? They do, in fact."

The one-hour break from the sound mix is nearly over, but there's still enough time for Walter to take Hana out for a walk through bustling, midday Soho. "There are advantages to having me mix the film," Murch says, trying to keep Hana's retractable leash from tripping lunchtime walkers hurrying through the narrow alleys. "There is the same brain working on the sound as worked on the images. But a significant *dis*advantage is that that brain can't be cloned. I'm not available for emergencies: 'Break glass and use editor.' If I were simply the editor, I could come and go from the sound mix and be working on editorial things as the film was being mixed."

Hana gets twisted around a traffic bollard just outside Golden Square Park before Walter lets her off leash. "There's so much happening right now, and it's so end-game, that unless you keep your wits about you, it's easy to make a stupid critical mistake. We're always braced for having to stop and re-cut a whole scene. Everyone would be amazed, I think, if that didn't happen. So far, it looks like it's not happening. It's just this issue of extending the rabbit shot out by 12 seconds."

After lunch, Minghella comes to the mix studio to discuss possible answers for the three remaining issues at the beginning of the film: Kidman's voiceover, the subtitle, and the music. With Murch engaged as sound mixer, and so much uncertainty surrounding the film's opening sequence, it's understandable that Minghella wants Murch's attention as editor.

"When Walter is out of his running-the-mix-board mode, he needs to sit back here with me, and we need to play, in terms of offering up some alternatives," says Minghella. "My plan at the moment is that the movie will open with the music we've got and keep it going right up until the entry of the tunnel and the barrels. Then we lose that music, the big overture. It does something to the first five minutes that somehow generalizes it. We need to see if there is one piece of ethnic music that can go from there to the explosion. The challenge is, can we have score, silence, ethnic music, and Ada's voice without everything turning into a blob? It needs Walter to be sitting away from having to push the button so he can help me adjudicate."

There are two categories of music for *Cold Mountain*: original "score" composed solely for the film by Gabriel Yared and recorded at Abbey Road Studios in London, and "source music" from the Civil War era chosen by music producer T-Bone Burnett and recorded at his direction in Nashville with musicians such as Ralph Stanley, Alison Krauss, Stuart Duncan, Dirk Powell, and the Sacred Harp Singers. Yared and Burnett work independently of each other, but under Minghella's direction. Yared first provided musical sketches early on during production, as did Burnett. Once Murch had a first assembly and scenes became more defined, the music was elaborated.

Sometimes Murch ignores the music's original structural and emotional intentions and uses it the way he feels works best for the film. Over the course of editing for many months much of the score and source music gets shifted around, with Murch finding new places to use it, or even suggesting not to use some of it at all. Creative issues, such as whose music gets used where, can quickly get personal inside a film-in-progress. The buck in this case stops with the director. He is the person on the film whose job it is to resolve conflict and massage bruised egos. One moment this may involve two music composers; a few hours later Minghella might have to explain to an actor doing ADR why she is not rereading lines for her favorite scene—because it got cut.

Mixing reel one. Lots of Con Edison "Dig we must for a better New York" barriers up around the music at the beginning, the Ada narration, and the extension of the rabbit "Petersburg" shot. "Can I be excused, teacher?" says Anthony. "I feel sick I have to go home"—only half joking. This is where the S hits the F. Hard slog through reel one with only two hours sleep + burning blood.

THURSDAY, NOVEMBER 6, 2003—SOHO, LONDON

Everyone convenes at the mix with fresh ears. Minghella, having slept for the first time in 48 hours, explains his intentions clearly: "Whatever we do should end up with the tunnel shot [of Union soldiers laying explosives] wiping away that piece of music—the whole atmosphere of Ada—like a bit of nostalgia. And then what I'm hoping for is we have silence until we get to the caption, which is 'Petersburg, Virginia,' date, and so forth. At which point we get some so-called 'primitive music.' And what is that piece of music that carries us to the explosion and makes room for Ada's voiceover with the letter?"

"And has the right mood," Murch adds.

Ralph Stanley

Minghella likes the idea of a single singing voice to underlie tranquil scenes of Inman and the other Southern soldiers just before the explosion. He suggests "Tarry with Me," sung by Ralph Stanley, or "Pretty Bird," performed by Alison Krauss.

"Do you have an instinct, Walter?" Anthony asks.

Murch comes right to the point: "My instinct is that neither of them will work. The pucker factor is very high. I don't know if that music lets you sit back and go into this world, setting aside how it fights the dialogue, since both songs use very articulated voices. Is that the way to begin a movie like this? I know 'Pretty Bird,' and it's noble, but may be too noble. It says: This film is going to be good for you."

"Can I just see the Ralph Stanley?" Anthony asks. "Just play a little bit." Which co-mixer Michael Prestwood-Smith does. Ralph Stanley is the legendary musician who was brought to an even wider audience through the soundtrack of the Coen brothers' film, *Oh Brother, Where Art Thou?*

The initial scene of the movie begins: Union soldiers set explosives underneath unwary Confederate soldiers, and Stanley's unaccompanied voice emanates from some ancient place:

Tarry with me, O my Savior,
Tarry with me through the night;

I am lonely, Lord, without Thee,
Tarry with me through the night.

We see young Oakley push a wheelbarrow full of dead soldiers' uniforms through the trenches, stopping where Inman and Swimmer crouch, waiting. "Don't worry, son, them Yankees keep store hours," someone says to Oakley. Inman chuckles and takes a dead man's coat. The rabbit from the establishing shot emerges in the trench and a soldier chases it, shouting, "Keep your paws off my rabbit, keep your paws off my rabbit." Meanwhile the fuse is burning down below the surface, about to ignite barrels of dynamite. Ralph Stanley sings on. It's obvious by this point in the sequence that action and music are diverging, with two very different messages: bad things are coming as denoted by the darkness of Stanley's singing, but the moments on screen are peaceful and comradely.

The sequence comes to an end with the first underground explosion. With hardly any discussion, Murch and Minghella agree that the Ralph Stanley vocal isn't working here.

Minghella then asks to run the scene with no music, which they do.

Again they watch the Confederate encampment, Oakley, the wheelbarrow, Inman and Swimmer, and the rabbit chase. But it all seems to unfold at half-speed, like a pantomime. Not using any music is not going to work either. As Murch says to Minghella, "The architecture of the shots, the way it's been edited, says *music*."

Minghella realizes that none of the period, or source, music is transposable to this section. Murch agrees. "It doesn't accommodate itself to what we've got."

It is one of those "expect a miracle" moments, but none arrives at Studio A. Characteristic of the way they work, Minghella and Murch stop on a dime to probe what's going on artistically, trying to comprehend what the film is telling them while a dozen people in the mix theater wait for a cue to what they're supposed to do next. This isn't self-indulgence. Only by understanding why something doesn't work, why a filmmaker's intentions are not getting realized, does it becomes possible to figure out a good alternative.

Minghella muses that during the battle and hellish combat down in the pit, source music not only works well, it enhances and deepens those scenes. "Why is it, do you think, that the shape-note singing, 'Born to Die,' works in the battle?" he asks rhetorically.

"We've earned it," Murch responds. "We have invested in the film and in the explosion, and we've gotten to know the people. And there's this incredible thing we're looking at we've never seen before. It's the juxtaposition of that imagery with the choral voices and seeing thousands of people—souls roasting in a pit of hell. There's a resonance between souls crying out in torment and the sound of the music, and what we're looking at."

Minghella has to figure out what should be done, and do it right now. It's that literal, unglamorous part of film directing that has more to do with managing than creating. Adding to Minghella's frustration is the fact that he needs Murch to be in two, or even three places at once: with Levinson to help make selections from the previous night's loop group for the chapel-building scene; discussing music options for the pre-explosion sequence with the two music editors, Alan and Fer; and continuing the final mix by skipping over this problem area for the time being.

"You and I aren't getting the opportunity to share all the stuff that is going on in other rooms," Anthony says to Walter. Then he makes a decision: "Alan, Fer, and I would be well used just going away and having a conversation and debate about what possible music we can offer into the mix in terms of the opening. I suggest you, Walter, continue with the mix starting from Ada's conversation with Inman at the chapel."

Minghella leaves Studio A with the music editors. The mix picks up in reel one from the scene when Inman and Ada first meet and talk as the chapel is being built—Inman's flashback. Murch will mix this section knowing that additional loop group voices will be added later to build up the background atmosphere of young men alluding to the looming Southern secession.

Oakley (Lucas Black), the young Confederate soldier.

Murch continues with the mix until nearly 8 p.m. He is particularly fatigued, which is unusual, and takes a cab back to Primrose Hill. On the way home he talks about plans for the next day.

"Harvey is coming tomorrow at 9 a.m. I don't think to the mix, I think to wrangle with Anthony again." While Minghella has final cut on the film, the dance between him and the studio is complicated: a director might exercise the final cut prerogative if there's irreconcilable conflict. But the studio can always find ways to retaliate, such as decreasing what it spends to market and promote a film.

Before leaving for London, Weinstein had been phoning from New York, inquiring about what Anthony was doing, trying to figure out if the studio still has time to recommend, cajole, or argue for changes they might want. "We'll see tomorrow when Harvey shows up," Walter says.

Grading the Print

Although the primary job facing Murch is the final sound mix, there are other finishing tasks requiring his attention that are equally important and time sensitive. One is preparing the digital intermediate so it is ready to strike the thousands of release prints of the film for *Cold Mountain's* Christmas rollout. CFC, the film lab, finished scanning the camera negative into its computer system. Now the focus is on color-timing the material (called "grading" in the U.K.) using CFC's proprietary software system to give the movie the look Minghella and cinematographer John Seale intend. Color, contrast, and brightness are adjusted within each shot, and balanced shot to shot so every scene appears seamless. The film gets printed from virgin negative that itself was created from a digital file made by scanning the original camera negative. So every digital reel must be carefully examined to make sure there are no artifacts, excessive graininess, or other imperfections. Only the director can sign off and approve each reel.

Director of photography, John Seale.

Minghella was worried in October when the first answer print came out of the lab for review. The colors he saw on film weren't matching what he'd seen on the lab's computer screens. John Seale spent three weeks in September with CFC color timer Adam Glasman, making minute color adjustments in a darkened room. It's almost unheard of for a director of photography to have so much time to do color timing. But once a decision was made to use a digital intermediate, it only made sense to let Seale take full advantage of its latitude to make precise color adjustments. Normally the DP comes to the lab for color correction after the picture is locked and the negative is cut. That leaves only a small window of time, and by then a DP is often halfway around the world shooting another film. Even getting a DP to come in to do color correction the traditional way for a few days isn't guaranteed. The digital intermediate process for color correction, however, can start several months before locking picture, giving a DP more flexibility to schedule the timing. Even though grading the negative for a digital intermediate can start well before the picture gets locked, subsequent changes to the edit are easily incorporated by integrating a new edit decision list (EDL) with previously determined color settings.

"We plug in the new EDL that Sean sends us," Glasman says, "look at the data we've got, the grading decisions we've made, and make a new version. Then we can just flip through it and tweak accordingly."

Seale says his first experience with color correction on a digital intermediate is paradise. "It's so exciting. It's like being able to get inside the frame and change somebody's face, just isolate their face, change the color, pump it up a little brighter, take it down... There's a million things that you can do within the frame."

In the love scene between Ada and Inman at the end of the film, for example, Seale describes the initial images as "awful yellow-green" because of the way they were digitally scanned. In his color timing, he adds more red to give the scene a warm glow and even introduces a little flicker of yellow light: the burning campfire.

Midway through mixing on November 5, the call comes into Studio A that reel six is arriving fresh from the lab, ready for screening. Finding a stopping point, Murch walks upstairs and goes through the second floor café/lounge to De Lane Lea's small screening theater. Minghella is on his way from down the street where he's been working with Levinson selecting new ADR takes. While waiting for him to arrive, Walter engages Glasman in a conversation about the relationship between film print color and the sound mix—that nexus where Murch in particular makes his home. "I've just been looking at what we're mixing to: Final Cut Pro output being projected in video. It achieves some of its dramatic effects by alternating bright, dark, bright, dark, and that visual aggressiveness is working well with the sound. If everything in the film print comes out too muted and dark, then the chemistry between visual and sound will get spoiled."

Adam Glasman, colorist on *Cold Mountain.*

Minghella arrives with assistant Bricknell. Claire McGrane is here representing CFC, along with post-production supervisor Michael Saxton. Glasman explains that reel six, which the group is about to screen, is printed "cyan-green, two lights plus," which means the settings the lab used—the printer's lights—were too blue by an almost-imperceptible quarter of a photographic stop. These sorts of small inaccuracies are commonplace in the rush of preparing answer prints overnight. Chemicals in the "bath" through which the film travels at the lab are never absolute; neither is their temperature. These variables, along with the trial-and-error nature of film printing, often result in imperfect test prints, which is why they are also called "trial prints."

Minghella finds it disconcerting to be reviewing a reel that the lab already admits is compromised. "Why is it that they can run it through and come out two points cyan?"

"It's a hit-and-miss system," Murch says. "The mysteries of the photochemical process."

A major film director like Minghella has been through this process many times before. But with the stress of completing *Cold Mountain* and his executive producer breathing down his neck, he is too worn out to mask his feelings.

"I mean, the difficult thing is we're going to be looking at a print that's two points cyan. So it's hard to navigate the grading, because we're looking at it through a pair of sunglasses."

He gets no argument. But unless things are delayed a whole day, Minghella will have to watch the reel and make a mental adjustment as he does.

"So anyway, we'll look at it."

The lights go down and reel six begins, playing without sound since it's a test of just the film's print quality. It starts with the second part of the Christmas party where Ada, Ruby, and Sally Swanger join Stobrod, Pangle, and Georgia in festive singing and dancing. As the shots go by, Anthony and Walter comment on what they see:

"This is all positive dust, isn't it?" Anthony asks hopefully, wanting reassurance that occasional dark spots don't represent unalterable blemishes on the underlying negative.

"Yes," Glasman says.

"I'm worried about Renée's lipstick," Anthony says, thinking Zellweger may look too made up.

The reel plays on to the Sara scene, when Sara invites Inman into her bed. The scene ends with a zoom in on Inman's face that was produced using a digital visual effect Murch requested. It's designed to match, compositionally and emotionally, the incoming shot—a similar extreme close-up of Ada's face at the Christmas party. There is concern that the visual effect shows too much grain, a consequence of enlarging a dimly lit, already grainy shot.

"We were a bit concerned about that zoom to the eye because of the grain," Glasman says.

Minghella agrees, and adds that the close-up on Jude Law may reveal the makeup effects of his beard.

"Don't you want to reconsider going back to what we had before?" Minghella asks Murch. Murch agrees.

There is concern about reverse-angle shots of Ada and Ruby listening to the music in the Christmas party. They appear dark in relation to the rest of the scene.

When they're done watching the reel, Minghella seems happy after all: "The night scenes are looking really superb. You've really done beautiful work there. This has been one oasis of pleasure." The group laughs, knowing Minghella spent most of the morning sequestered with Harvey Weinstein going over another list of change notes.

Then Minghella, Bricknell, and Saxton review the schedule for approving reels from the lab over the next few days. Minghella will fly to Los Angeles the following Wednesday for five days of promotion on *Cold Mountain*. Claire says

The Christmas Party scene with Georgia (Jack White) left and Pangle (Ethan Suplee) right.

she'll have reel eight for him to see Monday, followed by one on Tuesday and reel nine on Wednesday. Minghella says he'd like to check the sound mix that is underway against these film print reels, as opposed to only hearing the mix while watching the Final Cut Pro digital video version. Using actual film will help Minghella and Murch check sync and also give them a truer idea of how the soundtrack will play in a release print.

No one confirms this request; there probably isn't time. Minghella can sense the walls closing in. He turns to Saxton and says: "What I don't want to do, Michael, and I'm not going to do, because it doesn't make any sense, I'm not going to let go of anybody until I've let go of the film. I don't want anybody to be signed off or let go until I've signed off on the movie. And I don't care what that involves."

Saxton agrees.

"I don't want people being shut down or told to return their keys and their machines until we—Walter and I—have said this is where we want to be, even if we have to go back in and keep mixing next week. What is the final day that we need to release this mix?" he asks Saxton.

"Well, it depends. The very first screening is November 24. So we need to ship it by the 22nd. We've got—what is it?—a day and a half to print master," Saxton says, referring to the final transfer of the finished sound mix, ready for marriage to the negative.

"We have to do the print master, then check it," Murch says, "and then have a buffer in case there's some problem with the optical negative."

"We're keeping everybody on until the print master is finished?" Anthony asks.

"I would if you want to," Saxton says. "Some, not all, of the sound boys were going to finish at the end of the mix, because for the print master normally it's just…"

"But when is the end of the mix?" Minghella asks.

"Well, that's… you tell me."

"I'm being asked to be schizophrenic."

"I'll do whatever you want, Anthony. We'll keep everyone on. Keep all the options open. I've got the mix theater, I think, at least another two weeks."

"We could be flying in more… I won't bore you with it all. But there's a mismatch, a disconnect between finishing the movie and the requirements of the studio."

"We won't have the film ready if you want to carry on mixing after you come back from the States," Saxton says, referring to Minghella's upcoming promotional trip.

"It's not whether I want to," Minghella says. "Want doesn't have anything to do with anything. We're still juggling. Walter hasn't heard stuff we've done. We're working on a reel where we've got new information. If there's a problem when we put all this stuff together and we don't like the effect of it, then they don't get the movie. I can't just deliver a movie when I haven't seen it."

Thursday, November 6, 2003, Murch's Journal

Harvey is here talking to Anthony about the usual issues: Inman death shot (saying it looks like a "police blotter"); and Ada voiceover. Tim said that they were talking about Anthony shooting something new for the transition after Inman's death. What will happen? Read this in four weeks and tell me. I will be in Toronto evaluating the release print master, hopefully. Endgame decisions.

CHAPTER 12

Finding the Film You Have

Miramax is in the final stages of preparing a major marketing campaign for *Cold Mountain* and making commitments to buy TV, print, and other kinds of advertising. There's a lot at stake: the prestige of the studio, its Oscar prospects, and recouping its 100 percent capital investment in the movie. This end of moviemaking has always been one of Miramax's strengths—acquiring what had traditionally been considered hard-to-market independent, international, and dramatic films, and creatively promoting them into profits at the box office. Movies such as *The Crying Game, Il Postino, The English Patient,* and *Shakespeare in Love,* among others, were rolled out to great success, in part because the Weinsteins are great marketeers.

But *Cold Mountain* isn't a small, quirky, low-budget foreign film. It's a big picture with big needs, and marketing it will be no easy matter, even for the Weinsteins, who now get ready to spend perhaps $30 million—a figure nearly half the *Cold Mountain* production budget—on promotion and advertising. Some anxiety is brewing, as the studio must decide once and for all how it's going to pitch the film to the public. Murch hears about these rumblings from Minghella: "Apparently Bob [Weinstein] called Anthony after a screening in New York," says Murch, "and said, 'I like it, Anthony, and it's really good and everything, but just what's it about? I enjoy it, but in the end, what is it about? It's not a war film; it's not a love story. That's the problem. What is it about?'"

It's disheartening for a film director to hear those kinds of questions so late in the game. After all, Miramax read the screenplay early on, saw dailies during production, and screened every assembly of the film. The conversation reminds Murch of a story, perhaps apocryphal, about Louis Mayer of Metro-Goldwyn-Mayer, who once hired violin virtuoso Jascha Heifetz to play music for a film. But Mayer was mixed up, and thought he was actually employing pianist Vladimir Horowitz. Says Murch: "Heifetz said he didn't play the piano. But Mayer told Heifetz, 'No, I hired you to play the piano, not the violin. So play! I want you to do what I hired you to do.'"

"It's the same kind of thing," Murch continues. "'I want you to be what I want you to be. I don't want you to be what you *are*. You're a musician and your name begins with H, so why can't you be what I want you to be?'"

Fer Bos, *Cold Mountain* music editor.

All good film editors (or at least the ones who continue to work) know their boundaries. Distribution and marketing are matters beyond Murch's expertise and immediate concern. He has to finish mixing this film in one week and there is still no music for the opening sequence leading to the big explosion, and no final decision about introductory subtitles—what they will say and where they go, or even if they go at all. Questions also linger about the transition at the end of the movie from Inman's death to the coda at Black Cove Farm years later.

Murch enters De Lane Lea, led by his dog Hana, as usual. There's a lot of activity already underway in the anteroom outside Studio A. This airlock chamber between the exterior world and the sound mix theatre consists of a desk, a phone, and a small couch. Producers, directors, and sound editors come out here if they need to have a conversation in peace or take a call without interrupting the mix. For the last two days, however, this tiny space has been turned into a makeshift music-editing studio. The two music editors, Fernand ("Fer") Bos and Allan Jenkins, have set up shop here with their Macintosh laptops, extra hard drives, and rented video monitor. Wearing headphones and sitting on shipping cases, they've been trying to come up with alternate musical openings for *Cold Mountain*.

Bos is T-Bone Burnett's music editor, and Jenkins is Gabriel Yared's music editor, so they normally have separate responsibilities—source music from the period and scored music composed for the movie, respectively. The music editors' work involves attending to initial recording sessions in the studio, getting that material edited into mixable tracks, and providing it to Murch, who re-records it onto the movie soundtrack. Along the way they help to prepare rough sketches so the director can review, evaluate, and begin choosing which music should go where.

Walter stands and listens as Bos and Jenkins play new opening music they've worked on together that combines source and score. Anthony sits a few inches from the TV screen, watching and listening to a conflation of Gabriel Yared's original composition played by the London Symphony Orchestra, and Sting's "My Ain True Love"—first as instrumental, then sung by Alison Krauss. Two music editors have collaborated to create a synthesis of disparate melodies—not typical of the way movie music is edited. This spontaneous partnership arose out of necessity, and it's one that Bos and Jenkins have eagerly embraced.

Allan Jenkins, *Cold Mountain* music editor.

Inman and the Confederate soldiers are in the trenches. A violin and cello duet abstracts the theme from Sting's song.

"Need a shirt, son?"

"That's Ma Oakley's boy," Inman says.

"He can't be old enough to fight, can he?"

"Morning, son."

"Got some boots and jackets. Want one?"

"Yeah, thanks."

The string duo that has been playing underneath this scene continues in the clear.

Minghella says he's not too happy with this version's lack of development—the music doesn't follow the rising tension of the sequence. Bos stops the scene. Brows are furrowed and the tension is manifest. "What are we going to do?" asks Minghella. "This isn't working."

After a second or two Murch makes a suggestion: "What if we got a cello to start adding a rhythmic element to it, so a pulse began to appear—taking those musical ideas and energizing them."

With that, the session breaks up. Anthony has a few minutes before meeting with Harvey Weinstein, so he goes off with Allan Jenkins. At this late date, there's no time to record anything new. They must find supplementary musical elements by scavenging from Yared's music.

Murch and the others go into Studio A where the mix continues.

A while later Eddy Joseph gets a cell phone call inside Studio A from Tim Bricknell, Minghella assistant. Joseph sits bolt upright and even pales slightly. "Okay, I'll tell them," he says. When Murch finishes the bit he's working on, Joseph speaks up: "That was Tim. Harvey and Anthony are coming over."

"Here?" Martin Cantwell, one of the sound editors says, incredulously.

"Yes, they're walking over from Goldcrest."

Before anyone has time to tidy up the place, the door to Studio A swings open. Weinstein, in black pants, black T-shirt, and black suspenders, walks in, followed by Minghella and Miramax executive Colin Vaines.

"Good morning," Harvey says to the group. He and Minghella take their seats on the blue couch at the rear. Anthony suggests that Walter play reel one, beginning with the explosion. Hana leaves her customary spot under the mixing board by Walter, trots over to Harvey, and as before, jumps up on his lap.

The lights come down and the last half of reel one plays. The sound and mixing crew haven't had the luxury of sitting back and listening to their work on the battle scene for a couple of days, so this is an unexpected opportunity to simply be spectators. When it's over, Weinstein is exuberant: "Great, sounds just great. I really understand the relationship between Oakley and Inman." He speaks with a deep, growly voice, but it's friendly, with a twinge of we're-all-in-this-together camaraderie, humor, and irony. "Now help get my tuxedo ready for March!"

"For my funeral?" Anthony asks under his breath.

"No way!" Harvey says.

Eddy Joseph jumps in to ask Weinstein about the controversy that's raging about banning DVD and video screeners from being sent to Academy members during Oscar season. Weinstein had recently taken a strong public position against the ban.

"We're fighting it." Harvey says. "The studios can't say anything, the executives will be fired. But they can't fire me." He pauses. "Well, they can, but…" He trails off. "Okay, thanks, everybody. Thanks, Walter. See you soon."

And with that Weinstein stands up and departs Studio A with Vaines and Minghella.

By that afternoon Fer and Allan have a new version of the opening music for Minghella to listen to. Anthony sits down again in front of the small monitor in the anteroom. The roar from the battle being mixed inside Studio A assaults the room every time someone opens the door, so Minghella puts on headphones.

For this version Fer and Allan found a drone of bass and cello; it's from an improvisational take T-Bone Burnett recorded with the players in Nashville. The editors also made a key change in Pro Tools to better connect the score to the song. They added a snare drum and timpani to the end, and used a French horn solo from Yared's score. "I like the horn," Anthony says, taking off the headphones. "It sounds like a bugle. Very nice. It'll work."

Fer and Allan are beaming. "It's like composing," Fer says after Anthony leaves, "but you take the melody as written and compose with it."

Within the hour, Murch starts mixing in the new music. First he listens to it all the way through to get a sense of its flow, dynamics, and emotional contours. But it does not begin auspiciously. Images are up on the screen, but the powerful speakers are silent.

"Where's the sound?" Murch asks.

"I don't know," Simon says. "Martin?"

There's confusion as the mixers try to figure out why nothing is happening.

All of a sudden the voice of one of the actors breaks through:

> *"This poor boy's from Alabama."*

> *"He's a long way from home."*

Then the music begins, with a sonorous bass violin followed by a long, mournful, Irish-inspired violin and other strings. The cello and the violin play the theme from "My Ain True Love." Krauss joins in, humming the melody. There is an ominous string tremolo on the cut to the explosives being set underground. Distant horns (Minghella's "bugle") play over an expansive view of Union soldiers lying in wait, on their bellies. The solo violin ascends. More ominous string tremolo. The French horn again, more humming, and then the kettledrums speak of impending battle. The strings shift into a minor key. The snare drums roll and, just as the music builds to a near-overwhelming climax that leads into the explosion, it ends.

"Great," Murch says. "Very good."

He plays the sequence again, this time punching buttons in and out on the mix board to hear one track at a time, isolating individual instruments so he can take command, like a symphony conductor, of the elements he has to work with. The sound editors and two other mixers relocate to the couches at the back of the theatre. Like a jazz soloist, Walter has the stage to himself.

He plays the three-minute piece again and suddenly the instruments seem more concentrated and integrated; he puts reverb on Alison Krauss's humming; there's more presence to the string tremolo; the horns sound stronger; and the final crescendo shimmers throughout the theater for seconds after the music ends.

Murch makes two more passes: the high end gets sharper and cleaner, Krauss's humming becomes more ethereal and is "placed" to the left side of the theater, and the horns get bigger.

When Murch is finished, Matthew Gough, one of the sound editors and co-mixers, turns to Fer and Allen: "You guys made that from bits and pieces? It's brilliant. Absolutely brilliant. It sounds like it was structured to fit everything."

"It's a Sting/Gabriel Yared collaboration," Fer says, laughing.

"They'd love it if they knew," says Allan.

"Let's leave it for tonight," Walter says, getting up from the board.

Matthew still marvels: "Very clever knitting."

"Let's go out and celebrate," Allan says with a smile.

And so they should, since a big hole is now filled. Tomorrow, Murch will confront two remaining unknowns: the opening subtitles and the closing transition.

On the way home, Murch muses about the breakthrough with the opening music: "Sting's music—it sent out its tendrils once it was in the film. It originally had a brief little job to do, which was to accompany the montage of Inman walking. Now it's the music that underscores the beginning to the explosion, and then takes us out of the explosion into the charge. Major moments." Using a film's components in unplanned ways, transforming original intentions, happens frequently during post production.

"*The English Patient* begins with a shot from a roll of inserts or cutaways that Anthony did as an afterthought on the last day of filming—cinematographer John Seale wasn't even there," Murch says. "Certainly the cameraman who shot it, if you tapped him on the shoulder and whispered, 'You are now shooting the opening image of the film,' his hand would have begun to tremble. *Unbearable Lightness of Being* also ends with a second-unit shot—the point-of-view through the windshield on the Czech country road fading to white. That's the last image of the film, but it was originally just a utilitarian shot. It's a question of getting these animals on board Noah's Ark—the raw material out of which the film winds up expressing itself—sometimes in very surprising ways."

Discovering a film's hidden secrets means finding the film you have, rather than the film you *think* you have.

Friday, November 7, 2003, Murch's Journal

Harvey came to visit the mix and listened to the battlefield from Inman emerging to the end. Pronounced it very good. We didn't finish changes to reels one & nine. Plan for card over rabbit shot abandoned because too complex.

SATURDAY, NOVEMBER 8, 2003—LONDON

It's another full ten-hour day of sound mixing at De Lane Lea. Today, among other tasks, Murch incorporates new ADR from Nicole Kidman recorded last night over high-speed Internet lines between London and New York. At the CFC lab, Minghella reviews new trial prints made from the digital intermediate. Afterward he and his wife, Carolyn, come into Studio A. Anthony and Walter arrange to return to the Old Chapel in the early evening so they can figure out the opening subtitles and the closing transition in the last reel.

By 7:30 p.m. most of the sound crew has drifted off, one by one, having made Saturday night plans. Tonight will be the peak of Guy Fawkes Night celebrations, even though the official holiday was Wednesday the 5th. Earlier, Eddy Joseph asked the mixers what they were going to do if Murch decided to work past 6 p.m., the end of their ten-hour shift. "He'll have to run it himself," said Matthew. Which Walter now does. He is operating the mix alone. Only Fer, Allan, and sound editor Simon Chase remain, seated at the back in case they are needed. Walter works with new ADR of Ada's voiceover for the final scenes of the movie and with music that goes under the Inman death scene.

Anthony watches and listens. Carolyn is asleep with a book folded on her lap. Hana lies next to her.

It's just after 8:00 p.m. when Murch finishes what seems to be a last pass on the music. "Curfew," Anthony announces from the rear couch.

Walter stands up. "Tell whoever," he says to Simon, "I'm walking away from the board. I think I did everything I was told," meaning he saved all his work to the mix board's computer, as instructed.

Walter, Anthony, and Carolyn exit De Lane Lea and are immediately engulfed by the ruckus of Soho Saturday night. They thread their way through crowds that fill the sidewalks and cluster outside the pubs until they get to a car park near Leicester Square where Carolyn has left her Mercedes. As she drives up to Hampstead, Anthony is very excited, not about the new music for *Cold Mountain*, but about soccer. The Portsmouth Football Club, his perennially losing home team, just beat Leeds. He phones to share the euphoria with his brother, who watched the match with the rest of the Minghella family.

Murch strides upstairs and back to the realm of picture editing. The clock is ticking. They must finish tonight.

On arriving at the Old Chapel, Murch strides upstairs and back to the realm of picture editing. The clock is ticking. They must finish tonight.

Final Cut Pro includes sophisticated graphics and titling functions, so Murch can try out subtitles over various shots. Last night he and Minghella had come back here after sound mixing to work on the text. For the first subtitle they agreed on: "Near the end of the Civil War, Northern troops lay explosives under the Southern defenses." And for the establishing shot of the battlefield, "Siege of Petersburg, Virginia. July, 1864. Southern troops await attack." To finalize the subtitles, Minghella invited all the assistants to come into the edit room to give their opinions. The group spent over an hour debating various modifications and rewrites. Now it was time to lock the subtitles into place.

9:30 p.m. Walter tries placing the second text card in a moment of black while Union soldiers roll barrels of explosives. Walter provides his own sound effects as he tries this position. "Rumble, rumble," he says. But there isn't enough time to read the text before the next shot comes on. Murch moves the subtitle so it comes up over the image of the barrels. Minghella has come upstairs. He likes this. One decision made.

Murch goes to work on what he's calling "the bridge shot"—getting from a close-up of Ada and Inman, who lies dying in the snow, to Black Cove Farm several years later. Miramax executives feel a high-wide shot of the two lovers from above now looks like a crime scene photo and are considering paying to have it reshot. Originally, an upward-moving crane shot was used, but the grips couldn't stabilize the dangling camera, and the jiggling made part of the shot unusable. Now it's time to see if there are alternatives.

9:55 p.m. Murch searches the dailies for all the possible shots of Inman and Ada in the snow. There is a medium shot of Jude Law but his throat moves, so he doesn't look dead. What if Murch uses the "good part" of the crane shot, after the camera settles down, and puts a dissolve from the existing medium close-up to this wide shot? This might add a sense of transition, of time passing in the gorge before we move on into the future.

Murch makes these edits with the sound turned off. The silence in the room is interrupted sporadically by Guy Fawkes fireworks from nearby Primrose Hill.

10:17 p.m. Anthony comes in. "Do you need some sustenance?" he asks Walter.

"Nah."

"Nah?" Anthony repeats. "That's just for sissies, right? What did you have to eat today, Walter?"

"I had a croissant."

Ada and Inman near the conclusion of *Cold Mountain*.

"That's it?"

"Well, and an apple."

Dean, who provides night security at the Old Chapel, sticks his head in the door to say he's on the premises if they need anything.

"Tell me when Portsmouth goals are on," Anthony says, wanting to see TV replays of his soccer team winning.

10:37 p.m. Anthony looks at the revised death scene: "I think the intersperse between the close-up and the top shot is too short. You see it and then you're out of it."

Murch adds three to four seconds to the head of the second shot. Dean calls up for Anthony to say the soccer highlights are on.

"Sorry, guys," Minghella says, and goes downstairs to watch.

10:51 p.m. Walter tries putting several new exterior landscape shots between the final image of Inman and Ada in the snow and the shot of Ada's daughter, Grace, at Black Cove Farm years later. Producer Sydney Pollack had earlier suggested interposing some neutral shots between the death of Inman and the coda to create a sense of time passing. He had done something comparable in his film *Tootsie* to address a similar need to create space between two separate chronologies. Murch adds static shots of the farmhouse in winter, the surrounding mountains, then a final wide shot of Black Cove Farm in summer. "These visuals are like chords, musical chords," he says. "This last one, the house—we've spent a lot of time there—it asks a question, gives you time to wonder, What happened to her, to Ada?"

Murch adjusts the dialogue of Kidman's letter reading accordingly ("There are days…"), bringing it forward so it begins over the last farmhouse-in-winter shot.

11:14 p.m. Anthony is back upstairs to watch this new transition. "It's a little goosebump moment for me," he says, happily.

"A voice in the clear is like that; it takes you into the end," Murch says.

Anthony goes down the hall and asks if he can borrow Sean and Susannah, who are still working, for their reactions.

They watch the revisions. "I prefer no buildings between the gorge and the house," Sean says. Anthony admits he rarely believes anything for certain, but now he's confident about what he's seen, and good-naturedly tells Sean, "You're wrong!"

"I like it," Anthony says. "We don't want to go straight away to realities. We want to keep hearts beating."

Sporadic flashes from the Guy Fawkes fireworks appear through the window, reflecting off the building next door.

11:42 p.m. Walter plays the sequence through to the end for Anthony. "This time I thought to myself maybe the four other characters could still be there, that they're survivors," Anthony says.

"It's a reminder of seasonal change, of mortality and evolution," Murch says.

Anthony considers the shot of Grace watching Ada put a sheepskin on a new-born lamb: "Did it make you think this obviates bringing Grace forward? See what happens without Grace and begin the old way."

Murch makes the edits and runs the scene with Grace now appearing in the field and walking toward the camera before we see Ada cutting off the sheepskin.

Minghella prefers this version.

"It's got the right mix of lyricism and violence," Walter says.

"Enormous changes at the last minute," says Anthony.

"Our specialty," replies Walter.

Midnight. Sean comes in to confirm that he will make tapes of the newly revised reel one for tomorrow's sound mix.

"That's it," Anthony says. He stands up, goes to Walter, and they hug.

"It's a real lock now," Murch says.

The Guy Fawkes fireworks are spent now, as Murch and his dog Hana walk home. Murch recounts what just happened with the end transition. "This afternoon I didn't really know what we were going to do, although I remembered those landscape shots of the farm. It had snowed the night before, and [visual effects supervisor] Dennis Lowe grabbed a camera and went out and got the material that we just wound up cutting into the film. The original intention was to film shots to use for background images in visual effects to be done later." Murch and Hana crunch through the fall leaves that cover sections of sidewalk between the Old Chapel and Primrose Hill.

It's fascinating to note that the final story items that had to be addressed were beginnings and endings. "That always seems to be the way it is," Murch says, chuckling slightly. "It could have easily been a day in the completion of *English Patient* or *Ripley*."

And with that Murch says goodnight. He and Hana descend Primrose Hill Road and disappear into the darkness.

Anthony Minghella is fond of rephrasing what French critic and writer Paul Valéry wrote about a poem: "A film is never finished, only abandoned." Indeed, over the next two weeks he and Murch will tweak this, adjust that, and otherwise see the film through its final technical processes and steps of quality control. It's not very creative, but it is work that must get done carefully lest an imperfection be embedded that millions of viewers will see or hear forever. Murch describes the final steps of finishing movies as a kind of petering out: "They don't end with a bang, they sort of dribble off." There is no one defining moment; no "martini shot" (during filming, the last take of the day before drinks); no tangible finish line to cross.

The next Sunday, November 9, back at De Lane Lea, Murch uses last night's picture change lists from FCP to re-conform the mix masters on the Akai dubbers and the corresponding automation files in the Harrison mixing board. They both snap into place exactly. "A big sight of relief," says mixer Matthew Gough. "High readings on the sigh-o-meter." The next day Murch finishes the print master—the absolutely final six-track sound mix used in the lab for making release prints. Two days later, Murch checks the revised mix against the complete film print struck from the digital intermediate ("Another watershed moment, one step closer to completion," he writes in his journal). On November 13, Murch fixes Ada's vision of Inman when she looks down Esco's well, swapping a few frames to make it less obvious that Inman falls down. Then, on November 17, Murch, Minghella, Harvey Weinstein, and Colin Vaines screen the answer print against the sound print master.

Wednesday, November 19, 2003, Murch's Journal
This way of doing films, everything is called into question, and nothing is certain until the very end. Anthony's secret way of liberating the film from the limits of its own intelligence, making sure the film is smarter than the author, as Kundera said the novel must be.

But hold the phone—it's not over yet. The end credit songs need to switch positions; Elvis Costello's "Scarlet Tide" now comes first, followed by Sting's "My Ain True Love." Murch makes this change, having to do a sound edit within the print master.

By now, Studio A at De Lane Lea is no longer available for these last tweaks to the soundtrack. In a November 25 email to Tim Bricknell, Murch writes: "We are scurrying around homeless in Soho, trying to find places that will let us squeeze in and do what we need to do (remix, remaster, etc.). But we will get it done, somehow, somewhere."

In car going to Deluxe: to look at the first married print. God willing, it will be good. If there are changes to be made, let us see them clearly and act decisively with wisdom.

The print looks good, except for a half-dozen shots that still require color adjustments. These are unavoidable mistakes that occur when a release print is struck from the internegative for the first time. But there are some very good things, too, especially the night scenes and dark interiors, which please Murch.

The pace slows down. Suddenly there is nothing more to accomplish. Closure, with its own rituals, is underway.

Friday, November 28, 2003, Murch's Journal

Party for Mirage at Landsdowne Pub. Very good. Awards were given out. Dei won "most athletic biking gear." I won "most promising newcomer" award. Hana won the Thalberg Achievement award, particularly cited for bravery in sitting on Harvey's lap.

On Saturday, November 29, a screening for cast and crew is held at a commercial theater in Chelsea. Murch calls it dispiriting, because much of the film is projected out of focus, and the theater's sound system is flat and unbalanced.

RESURFACING

"Finishing a film is like coming up to the surface of the ocean from a great depth. You stand now on the deck of a boat looking at the surface and wonder 'What was all the fuss about?' You know how important oxygen was, you know how deep it was, and how complex and contingent the journey was, with tangled kelp forests and sharks. But now the ocean smiles back at you, flat and sparkling in the sunlight."

—Murch's Journal

Murch and Minghella finish the mix at De Lane Lea.

MURCH ON REACHING AN AUDIENCE

Film is a popular medium, and the audience is never far from our thoughts, the way the ocean is never far from the thoughts of a shipbuilder. But that shouldn't prevent, in fact it should even encourage, beautiful ships being built.

ANTHONY MINGHELLA ON FINISHING A FILM

I love to make movies, I just hate releasing them. One's skin is very thin. At a certain point it's hard to be judged. No one wants to be judged.

Sunday, November 30, 2003, Murch's Journal

Lazy day. Got up late and had breakfast with Aggie around 11 am. Went out to the Chapel and got the Fortnum & Mason baskets and took some photographs of the scene boards. I may look normal, but I'm not. Feeling the effects of "parade syndrome." The reactive sensation that the film, though finished, is coming apart, not as good as I thought it was, all that effort for… this? When I think about it now it seems so simple and self-evident, why did it take us so long to put it together? "Are you maaaad?" etc., etc.

The next day Walter and Aggie leave early in the morning for California. They arrive in time for the first in a round of *Cold Mountain* previews in the San Francisco Bay Area and later in Los Angeles.

Wednesday, December 3, 2003, Murch's Journal

Standing in Union Square. The center of it is all paved over now. The Union Square of "The Conversation" is gone. Here is where Harry's van was parked, in front of Macy's. But remarkably still here is the bicycling Santa on Hoogasian's flower stand, which you can see in the film when the van pulls away, leaving Harry walking in the other direction into the crowd. Then I met Aggie on that same corner, going into Neiman Marcus (used-to-be-City of Paris), what a nice surprise!

Sunday, December 7, 2003, Murch's Journal

LA Premiere: Variety screening at Egyptian. Excellent sound and picture. Very good top end and great low end, especially during the explosion. Staggering. Better than De Lane Lea.

DECEMBER 25, 2003—CITRUS HEIGHTS, CALIFORNIA

The Century Greenback 16 Theatres are just off Interstate 80, past the Holiday Inn Express and a Ford dealership full of RVs. This working-class suburb is a hundred miles from San Francisco and eons from Hollywood. At 6:45 p.m. on Christmas Day there are fewer than ten empty spaces in the huge parking lot. James, the assistant manager, says five screenings have sold out today. This augurs well for a good holiday box office.

The crowd is predominantly white and Latino, with a handful of Asian Americans and African Americans. Sweatshirts and jeans are de rigueur for both sexes. Squint and you're back at the multiplex in Edgewater, New Jersey.

There are 25 people already waiting for the 7:20 p.m. showing of *Cold Mountain*, one of 2,000 theatres nationally where the movie opens today. The people in line are older and whiter than the rest of the theater patrons, with nearly twice as many women as men.

One woman says she is here because of the good reviews and the stars. "People coming out said it was very good, but sad."

"I came because of the story line," one man says. "I enjoy war action stories." "Nicole Kidman never makes a bad movie," his wife adds.

The line has swelled. Fifty people wait to go inside.

"I saw the commercial," a woman says. "I like Nicole Kidman and Jude Law. And it looks like it's action packed!"

The previous showing ends. The double doors open and the sound of "My Ain True Love" drifts out into the hall. The people waiting in line start to move forward.

FEBRUARY 25, 2003—LOS ANGELES, CALIFORNIA

It's Oscar week. Amid the flurry of parties and prognostications, Walter Murch—nominated for Best Editing for *Cold Mountain*—will appear tonight at the Los Angeles Final Cut Pro User Group's monthly meeting. By appearing here, only a few minutes drive from DigitalFilm Tree and from The Lot where he edited *K-19: The Widowmaker*, Murch is closing the loop. The group is an eclectic mix of editors who use the application for all sorts of purposes, from features to documentaries, television, and amateur video. LAFCPUG, as it's known, was formed in June 2002, the same month Murch chose FCP for *Cold Mountain* and left for Bucharest.

Murch speaks to the Los Angeles Final Cut Pro User's Group.

LAFCPUG meetings are held at the Los Angeles Film School on Sunset Boulevard in Hollywood. Members show their own works-in-progress, trailers of finished projects, and scenes that need troubleshooting. Guest speakers from the creative and technical communities often make presentations. Topics might include: "Multi-task while playing a sequence in the FCP Timeline," "35mm Plug-ins, "and "Logic Pro 6." Representatives from Apple have used these events to preview new products—Brian Meaney recently demonstrated FCP HD 4.5 for the group.

Ramy and Zed are here, along with some 200 other Final Cut devotees. Some have edited a feature film, most aspire to. All have heard or read accounts of Murch and *Cold Mountain*. By being here and telling the *Cold Mountain* story, Murch is making a powerful statement about where he belongs and what he values.

Mike Horton, the group's president, briefly introduces Murch, ending by admitting, "I'm so nervous." Murch projects his "eye on the pole" picture on the screen behind him and describes his initial surprise at finding himself editing *Cold Mountain* in Romania. As he continues, a screensaver slide show from his laptop begins to cycle images of the moon, the planets, a star nebulae, and Earth as seen from space. Murch speaks of the original motivations for changing edit systems.

"I'm here to report to you it all worked out great!"

An image of Mars dissolves into an image of the Milky Way. "I have to say, temperamentally, I'm someone who likes to make these leaps into areas that are not fully explored." The audience makes its own leap and a collective chuckle ripples around the room. Someone who wants to make sure Murch knows the laughter is not directed at him says, "Look behind you!"

"Yeah," Murch says as he turns around to see a blue and white world that seems to rotate underneath him. "Exactly." Then after a beat, like a comedian with a professional sense of rhythm (he *is* an editor), Murch quips, "Was the timing right?" More laughter.

The first audience question: "Would you use Final Cut on your next project?"

"Yes. Yes!" Murch says, and the answer is greeted with applause.

Someone asks about his artistic influences. Murch uses the opportunity to give what he calls "a fingering tip, if this was about piano playing," and proceeds to describe his "edit-on-the-fly" technique. This is a way, he says, to turn the film over, in part, to instinct and to musicality. "To make the film smarter than you are." If you're too intellectually calculating, he says, "a rhythmic tone-deafness creeps into your work."

There are anecdotes about working with directors: Coppola is like a chef using the "spaghetti-sauce method" to make a film, he says, slowly simmering all the ingredients over time; Lucas works like Procustes, lopping off whole limbs as the character from Greek mythology did. Like Coppola, some directors avoid spending too much time in the cutting room, only wanting to see nearly finished work.

Murch tells the story about director John Huston, who wasn't that interested in the detailed process of editing. "It's like seeing my wife dressing for a party," said Huston. "All those snaps and garters. I don't want to know how it's achieved, I just want to see the final results."

Director Kathryn Bigelow, on the other hand, set up her office in the back of Murch's edit room on *K-19*, complete with her own live video monitor of the editing in progress. "She'd be on the phone, making calls, and look at the monitor and say, 'Okay, Walter, great.' And I'd have to say, 'Not yet, I'm still working!'" The audience laughs sympathetically. "I hadn't worked that way before, but I got used to it and actually enjoyed it. I learned something."

His forecast for digital editing? "The future is in the Final Cut direction," Murch says. Editing systems from here on, he predicts, will give users maximum flexibility and be engineered so third-party developers can invent elegant solutions for niche users (like editors of big feature films), while also providing high-quality images at affordable prices.

But there's a catch. "As with all digital non-linear editing, its greatest strength is also its greatest weakness," says Murch." It gives you what you say you want, but that may not be what you need." The speed and precision with which digital editing systems deliver results for the editor can also cut out artistic surprises that come by accident. "These systems don't talk to you very well," Murch warns the editors. He shows photos of his scene cards and picture boards. "These are my ways to kick back at non-linear editing."

Murch has been speaking for nearly 90 minutes. He looks at his watch: "I'm perfectly happy to go on…" he says. The audience stays put.

What about working with temporary music tracks?

"If I could change one thing in the industry it would be that: No temp tracks. A composer should be on the film from the beginning, writing music that evolves with the film, working in offices down the hall, where we're all next door to each other, and at the same time, so that the music influences the edit, the sound effects influence the music, etc. What usually happens is the composer parachutes in almost at the last minute and spray-guns music onto the film. There's no time for the music to seep into the film and change it."

A brave soul puts her hand up and asks Murch about documentaries, an orphan child when it comes to most discussions about film editing. Murch pauses for a long, almost uncomfortable moment. Maybe he has nothing useful to say about the genre.

"I haven't edited a documentary since the late '60s," he finally says. "But that's where my heart is. My approach to features is a documentary approach. I don't treat the material as if it's intended for anything. That's why I don't want to know what the director thinks about any one shot. I treat the footage as if it's a found object."

"I hate to interrupt," Horton says from the side of the stage. "But the L.A. Film School says we have to leave."

It's after 11:00 p.m. and the janitor is in the auditorium, ready to begin vacuuming.

"We have a tradition," Horton says to Murch. "We're a user group and we have a raffle at the end. Would you pick for us?"

He agrees. The audience stands and applauds. Murch acknowledges the warm response. He puts his hand up and waves. Walter starts pulling ticket stubs out of a paper bag, calling out the numbers for winners of donated goodies, such as Final Cut Pro books, CDs of stock footage, FCP graphic plug-ins, training guides, and a T-shirt.

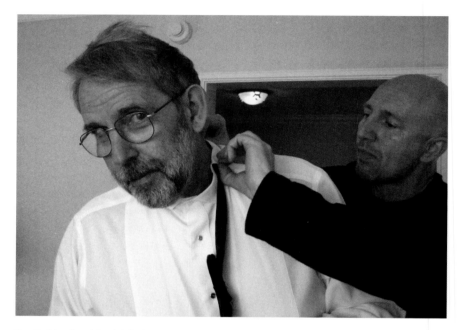

Family friend and Aggie's hair stylist, Tom Brophy, helps Walter get ready for the Oscar ceremonies.

EPILOGUE

A Jazzy Seventh Chord

In September 1965, on Walter Murch's first day of graduate film school at the University of Southern California in Los Angeles, Samuel Goldwyn was sitting at his desk at Goldwyn Studios, contemplating retirement; Jack Warner was running Warner Brothers as he had since 1918; and 92 year-old Adolf Zukor was occasionally coming in to work at Paramount, the studio he founded in 1912. But motion-picture theaters were closing all across the country, the television networks were waging their relentless war of attrition against the studios, and corporate vultures were circling: Gulf+Western, a sugar conglomerate, was poised to take over Paramount in 1966, and Kinney National—whose main interests were (ominously) parking lots and funeral homes—was sizing up Warner Brothers. Gene Peterson, the head of the USC camera department, looked around the room, smiling wanly at the hopeful faces of the 80 or so entering students. After a long, uncomfortable silence, Peterson shook his head and then finally spoke.

"Get out, now," Murch remembers him saying. "There's no work. And next year there's going to be even less. I don't know why all of you are here. Go do something sensible. You can still get your tuition back." The students reacted with uneasy laughter. Several took it to heart, though, and left the next day—quitting film school to become real estate agents, lawyers, and businessmen.

"Under those circumstances, you had to be kind of crazy to stay—which I guess we were," Murch says of himself and the other members of that 1965 class: George Lucas, John Milius, Matthew Robbins, Caleb Deschanel, John Bailey, Randal Kleiser, Hal Barwood, Robert Dalva and many others. "Jobs? Who cares about the future? We're here to make films *now!*"

Nearly 40 years later Murch and I sit in a sunny corner of his comfortable living room at Blackberry Farm. Out the front window morning sun glints off the lagoon. We're talking about filmmaking past and future, digital technology, and—now that Murch's "parade syndrome" has finally eased—what he gathered from the experience using Final Cut Pro on *Cold Mountain.*

Murch continues speaking of the mid-1960s and two terrifying undercurrents that resonate today—the Vietnam War and uncertainty about the future of cinema: "The feeling our film school generation had back then was well, shit, if the whole house is going to come crumbling down, we might as well do *something.* The old studio system paradigm was dysfunctional, but what could we do about that? The freedom of all bets being off created a vacuum into which some interesting films rushed: *The Rain People, THX-1138, The Godfather, American Graffiti, Jaws, Mean Streets, The Sugarland Express, The Black Stallion, Taxi Driver, Apocalypse Now, Star Wars.*"

The head of the USC camera department was partly right—there would be no future for cinema—at least as things had been done in Hollywood during its heyday. Unbeknownst to him and his students, American movie-making in 1965 was headed for a roller coaster ride of dips, rips, plunges, bends, and g-force changes. And that trip is still not over: not for the studios, nor for the very substance of movies themselves: film.

"Celluloid right now is at the end of its development curve, much like the four-stroke engine," Murch tells me. "We've probably wrung out of 35 millimeter film and its photo chemicals as much as we're ever going to. But digital is at the start of its development curve: no one can tell how far it will ultimately go." *Film*making may soon become a misnomer. Anthony Minghella noted this in his Foreword—as a director he glimpsed very little celluloid during the making of *Cold Mountain.* Indeed, in the last five years hundreds of shorts, documentaries, and features (from Lucas's megabudget *Attack of the Clones* to Sanchez and Myrick's microbudget *Blair Witch Project*) have been shot in digital video, edited on computers, and exhibited in film transfer, in cyber-space, or on digital projectors. Directors Wim Wenders, Steven Soderbergh, Lars von Trier, Spike Lee, Wayne Wang, Mike Figgis, Alison Anders, and Richard Linklater have all shot and released films digitally, some of them many times. Film-quality digital image recording and projection are immediately around the corner if not already parked outside the building. Does this mean the end of cinema? Doubtful.

For Murch, the cinematic experience fulfills a primal need: to sit in the dark with other people and listen to stories. "The unchanging human hunger for stories in the dark," Murch says, "has been with us since the invention of language. It bonds us together and takes us out of ourselves. For two hours we are all dreaming the same dream. But exactly what renewed form cinema takes during the 21st century will be determined by the digital forest fire now really getting into its burn."

How might those digital flames alter, reshape, and color this chimera we still call (for now) a film?

In 1982, German film director Wim Wenders shot a documentary at the Cannes Film Festival, *Chambre 666*. He invited all the film directors present to speak to camera on the future of cinema as they saw it. Werner Herzog, Rainer Werner Fassbinder, Steven Spielberg, Jean-Luc Godard, and Michelangelo Antonioni, among others, took the challenge. But only Antonioni 's statement went into the finished film unedited. I brought Wenders' book, *My Time with Antonioni,* with me to Blackberry Farm. It includes a transcript of the comments the Italian director made that day in Cannes. I read Antonioni's words to Murch:

"It's true, film is in grave danger. But we shouldn't overlook other aspects of the problem... part of the reason that the situation seems so grave to us is because we belong to an older generation. What we should do is try to adapt to the different visual technologies that are coming into being... I'm just as worried as anyone else about the future of the cinema as we know it. We're attached to it because it gave us so many ways of saying what we felt and thought we had to say. There probably always was that discrepancy between the present and the unimaginable future... High-definition video cassettes will soon bring (film) into our houses; cinemas probably won't be needed any-more... My sense is: it won't be all that hard to turn us into new people, better used to dealing with the new technologies.

"I hear what he's saying, and much of it is uncannily correct," Murch says forcefully, after I finish. "But Antonioni was 70, and at that age you can regret the passing of the familiar, then immediately second-guess that regret, and embrace the future too unconditionally. Remember, Italy was the country of..." Murch pauses, then makes a point with fine Italian pronunciation, *"Futurismo!"*

"Can we really be turned into new people by technology?" Murch asks. "The Soviet Union tried that and failed. I don't think it's true that the future is all going to be unrecognizable. There's something fundamental about storytelling. Human beings are human beings. If someone from the Stone Age walked in here we'd be chatting and laughing pretty soon, I bet. He'd tell us about something funny that happened to him on the way to the cave. Antonioni said that cinemas wouldn't be needed in the future. But I don't think so: movie-going survived the television crisis of the mid-1960s, and I think it will survive the challenges of the present. But it will change, without question—both technically and creatively. On average, DVD sales and rentals now bring in more money for a film than its theatrical exhibition. And the Internet is looming as a means of distribution."

While collective movie-going might not disappear, the processes by which those movies get made and distributed is riding a tsunami—powerful, unrelenting, and ever changing—Murch is himself right there riding its curl.

Murch likes to compare the way films get made to the way Renaissance-era frescoes were painted. Those masterpieces credited to artists such as Giotto, Piero della Francesca, and Michaelangelo were realized by teams of artists working in close collaboration. The very nature of the medium required a large group working in tight coordination under severe time pressure. The pigments were immediately embedded within wet plaster applied to the wall that morning and they changed colors as they dried. Errors were very difficult to fix and compositions had to anticipate the cracks that inevitably formed around a day's work. It took a group of artisans—journeymen, apprentices, and assistants—all led by a visionary artist, to create works that have continued to inspire over the last half-millennium.

Feature filmmaking, as we've known it, also requires a collaborative community—similarly hierarchical and likewise dependent on powerful patrons (the commercial churches of studios, distributors, investors). Filmmaking now faces the same kind of upheaval that was triggered several hundred years ago when new tools and materials meant the end of fresco painting. Oil paints, brushes, and canvas became relatively cheap and accessible, Murch says, and painting gradually turned into an individual pursuit—oil painting was easy to revise, could be done anywhere, any time, without assistants or apprentices—and sheltered from the gaze of self-interested sponsors.

We can all be painters now if we choose, and the art form has benefited from such pluralism. But there may be a price to be paid for such freedom, as Murch points out: "The presence of other people during the act of creation kept painting grounded in a way that it is obviously not today, when it's done almost exclusively in isolation." Likewise, the artist who inhabits a self-contained world of silence and imagination is vulnerable to demons and distempers—look at Van Gogh, Murch says.

Movies have only been around for 100 years but the comparison to fine art is instructive. Digital technologies are to today's filmmaker what inexpensive art supplies were to European artists four centuries ago. Economical editing systems such as Final Cut Pro, used in conjunction with other new digital filmmaking equipment and techniques, permit a filmmaker working alone to take on complex functions previously handled by dozens, even hundreds of crew members and craftspeople—shooting, editing, graphic effects, color correction, music recording, and sound mixing—and there are no apparent sacrifices in production values. (The music industry has preceded film by about a decade and a half in this regard.) Digital films can be exhibited just as widely as expensive productions made in traditional ways. For directors who prefer taking on more and more jobs themselves—and who have the energy, disposition, time, and talent to do so—methods are available for them to become one-person bands. Directors George Lucas and Robert Rodriguez come immediately to mind.

In other realms, such as documentary and corporate media, savvy clients and underwriters demand this new "crewless" approach. A very accomplished cinematographer I know recently purchased and taught himself Final Cut Pro in part because funders and clients are no longer allocating budget line items for an editor or editing facility. This may be a good thing—lower costs, more efficient workflow, singular visions being realized—but this trend discourages collaboration—not necessarily a good thing. Movies seem to magically appeal to widespread groups of people, according to Murch, because they are created by a team of diverse people, each bringing something different yet essential to the final creation. Take those creative contributions away and a pure, individually expressed conception can become odd, bizarre, and appeal only to the narrowest audience. "Is that single vision unique, communicative?" Murch wonders. "Or is it hermetic and obscure? And that's the danger of digital cinema pushed to its ultimate conclusion."

Beside empowering lone rangers, digital technology opens up another set of options for distribution and exhibition: the adaptable release print. "Why not make, say, a New England version of your film, why not a Southern version, a California version, a Bangladeshi version?" Murch asks. "Digital technology makes it quick and easy to tailor a film to a specific audience. Back in the 1930s and '40s, studios actually used to do something like this, but it was cumbersome. The distressing thing is you could spend the rest of your life on a film—it would never be finished!"

This could send film even farther down the shadowy road of test previews into a brave new world where each screening becomes an interactive focus group: "Let's give the audience exactly what *it* wants and tailor the material, geographically, locally, and temporally—meaning I, the filmmaker, don't care what I want. We'll be able to tune the film to *this* audience at 8 o'clock on Saturday the 21st of September—what it wants to see—because we can now somehow detect they're a rowdy audience and we can reconfigure the film on the fly to the rowdy version of the film. Here cinema becomes more like live theatre where actors respond to the feedback they're getting from the audience."

These kinds of scenarios take us closer to Mephistopheles' cinematic black box, as Murch calls it: a filmmaker's mythical deal with the devil. In exchange for his or her soul the filmmaker gets a black box through which the film vision inside his or her head is "thought" into existence for others to see, untouched by human hands. We're not there yet, but we're getting close. Pixar, like other animation studios, is a way station to that ultimate goal: every single pixel in every frame is put there by a conscious decision.

By now the sun is high overhead. Shadows slant at slight angles across the room since the fall equinox is not far off. Behind Murch, outside a large paned window, ripe pears hang ready for the picking.

"Some filmmakers would grab the black box and to hell with their soul! Another group would run away screaming! What the second group loves is the 'snow-flakiness' of cinema, the randomness of it, the fact that they *don't know* exactly what's going to happen next. We've always had the Hitchock types who want complete control, and the Coppola types who want to be surprised. In fact, nobody is completely one or the other. But digital technology forces the bifurcation of choices: the Snowflake or the Black Box."

The most recent iteration of "snowflake" filmmaking might just be an event Murch's son, Walter, helped organize recently in London: CinemaSports' Film-in-a-Day.

"It's a kind of art-happening done for almost no money at all. Just lots of energy and good will," Murch says.

Forty people got together, organized over the Web, and divided into eight different filmmaking teams, each group getting the same list of sketchy story elements they are obliged to include: there must be an image of falling flower petals, for instance. The participants were let loose in London with DV cameras and shot their footage in six hours. In the afternoon, using Final Cut Pro, everyone started editing their material together. At 8:30 that same night they reassembled at Mr. Young's screening room in Soho (the same place Murch and Minghella first screened a film version of *Cold Mountain*) and watched six finished short films projected digitally from DVDs they'd just burned.

"Forty people and their friends looking at 50 minutes of film, which at eight that morning not only didn't exist—these people didn't even know each other!" Murch says in wonderment. "Thanks to this technology they've come together, produced something, and they're completely jazzed by that experience, by each other, and by each other's films. Something emerges that's not contained in any of the films—it's all about people coming together to do something, be excited by the process of doing, and by its random, rapid-fire elements. There's very little control: you can't predict the weather, you can't control what you're going to find in the street when you shoot. You don't even know in advance what story you're going to tell."

Thinking about chance and fortuitous discovery—precious and invaluable to Murch—he lights up just imagining that day in London, acting out its spirit: "If *this*, then *that!* We have to have falling petals in the story? Oh, I have an idea! Yeah, let's do that! Where? I know a place in the park! These things crystallize very quickly, like a snowflake—faster than the water molecules can keep up with the crystallization—that's what makes a snowflake beautiful, unlike the ice cube, which freezes slowly and predictably. Snowflakes are endlessly fascinating because they freeze super-fast. You get beautiful randomness with an underlying pattern, the six-pointed star of the H_2O molecule, and that's a great thing."

Walter's son has since been in email contact with my own 20-year-old son, Walker, who is a college student and budding filmmaker. Walker plans to participate in an upcoming "Film-in-a-Day" event in New York where he goes to school, also sponsored by CinemaSports. He will use Final Cut Pro and at the end of the day, exchange films with Walter's London group over the Internet.

There is a midpoint, Murch says, between the Snowflake and the Black Box: an alternative direction represented by Coppola, Minghella, and other directors who savor communitarian moviemaking that favors chance and risk but relies on underlying structure. This path can be just as digitally oriented as the "Black Box"—enhanced, in fact, by systems like Final Cut Pro which made it possible for Murch's assistants to edit scenes of *Cold Mountain* on their laptops—but without aiming for total control of every aspect of the finished image, nor abandoning fine control of certain key elements of the film.

I ask Walter about Apple, and what they'd been through together on *Cold Mountain*.

"In retrospect, I'm happy that Apple wasn't holding our hand through the project," Murch says. "As frightening as it was to be in Romania and to get Will Stein's letter—'almost no chance'—it meant we had to rely on ourselves and the support team we had at DigitalFilm Tree and Aurora, along with a certain amount of luck and our gut instinct that somehow this was going to work. In hindsight, that was a good thing because if Apple had been guiding our every move, volunteering: 'Oh, give us a moment to write a subroutine for your problem,' we wouldn't have been forced to come up with our own solutions, which are almost always better, more tailored to the individual project, than the fixes someone else comes up with."

"And the public perception of what we accomplished is much better because we did it ourselves—the Little Red Hen story—which means other people can do it too, without Apple's help. Otherwise someone could say, with justification: 'Yeah, Murch's team succeeded, but only because Apple was there behind them 24/7. *I'm* not going to get that kind of support, so why should I risk it?'"

"Apple did do one crucial thing for us," Murch continues, " and that was to give us the beta version of Final Cut Pro 4 in March of '03, which allowed us to make change lists. But they were releasing it to all the other beta sites as well. Other than that, they were watching from the sidelines with a lot of good wishes and crossed fingers. The fact that we were able to get all the way through *Cold Mountain* without Apple's support solidified the achievement."

Does Murch still plan to use Final Cut on his next project? "Absolutely. I'm in negotiations, so I can't say what the film is, but Sean and I are right now discussing how best to arrange things. Hopefully, DigitalFilm Tree will be involved in some capacity. One possibility is to edit the first assembly here in the barn, like I did on *The English Patient,* and then do the rest of the post production in New York. Ultimately, it's a decision that's up to the producers. Sean and I are meeting with Brian Meaney and the FCP team down at Apple very soon. I'm looking forward to using version 4.5, which is a deep rewriting of version 3, and there have been some recent developments regarding Shared Area Networks and OS X. We have to find out about all that from Brian, and in return he gets to hear what we have been thinking."

"I love what I do!" Murch volunteers excitedly. "I just love it and always have. The old editing technology was prohibitively expensive for everyone except professionals and the most dedicated amateur filmmakers. Now the lid's off. The technology of digital video, Final Cut Pro, Final Cut Express, and I-movie—basically, it's fun. There it is! Go! That's exactly what CinemaSports is exploring—film as a way of expressing yourself—not as a means of delivering entertainment someone *else* wants to give you, but *you* doing it yourself. Feature films require a lot of work—years of dedication—and certain aspects of that won't change, at least in the short run. But there are lots of other kinds of filmmaking possibilities opening up in the wide spectrum between home movies and feature films."

"The particular open-access, non-proprietary architecture of Final Cut Pro," Murch adds, "is poised to take over larger chunks of post production, such as sound editing and color timing. There's nothing to limit its growth—to the point that someday we will be able to truly finish a film in its highest resolution right there in the edit room. Out the door into the theaters!"

Murch expects the application to begin attracting more third-party developers who will write special plug-ins to fill niche needs for the film industry. "Once that really gets going, there will be an overwhelming landslide effect. And that is all due to Apple's courageous decision to make FCP's code accessible to anyone who wants to develop a new plug-in for it."

Murch sees the long-term effect of digital films as no less earth-shattering than the invention of money. "In the middle ages you either owned land or you didn't, and that was it: you were either a duke or a serf. Money came along and emulsified everything, creating a fluid middle class. Digital is a media currency that's going to create a kind of 'middle class' that's neither filmmaker nor consumer, neither duke nor serf, but something in between—and we don't know what it is yet."

By this time it's afternoon. "My tape has run out," Murch admits.

But there's always energy for Bode and the planets.

"Want to hear some music of the spheres?" he asks.

Murch walks into the dining room and sits down at an old brown upright piano.

"This is the musical equivalent of the ratios that Bode predicts for planets. The cycles per second at which this note vibrates [he plays middle C] divided into the number of times this note vibrates [he plays B flat], is exactly the same ratio Bode predicts between the distances of Mercury and Venus."

"So these first five notes are Mercury, Venus, Earth, Mars, asteroid belt."

One at a time, like bells, five clear notes chime in succession.

"The next five planets: Jupiter, Saturn, Uranus, Neptune, and Pluto." Murch plays an arpeggio—five different notes that connect imperceptibly with the previous group.

"If you play them altogether, it's..."

Ten tones grow into one harmonic whole, filling the room. They linger until Murch lifts his foot from the sustain pedal.

"Kind of a jazzy, seventh chord variation," he says, smiling.

APPENDIX
MURCH'S EDITORIAL EQUIPMENT LIST

From Walter Murch's June 20, 2002 email to director Anthony Minghella and producers William Horberg and Ian Smith. "I have arranged the items by 'puzzle piece' and followed each item, where I could, with the approximate total retail purchase price in US dollars for all units itemized, and an explanation of the function of the item."

Piece #1—FCP stations:

4-Apple G4 2x1GHz $11980—computers

2-Radeon 7000 graphics $258—graphics card to second computer monitor

4-Final Cut Pro $3996—editing software

4-Apple Cinema Tools $3996—software to keep track of 24fps in computer

4-Aurora Igniter Studio $31996—hardware/software to digitize image converting from 30fps (beta tape) to 24fps (3/2 pulldown) and playback

4-Stealth Serial port $228—9 pin machine control to control beta deck

8-Memory 512MB $1200—1 meg extra memory for RAM in each station

4-FCP key caps $480—Final Cut Pro custom keyboards

4-RS422 cables $140—cables for machine control

6-Mitsubishi 22" CRT $5094—computer monitors. Two stations (mine and Sean's) will have two screens, and the other two stations will have one screen each.

1-Gigabit switch $1000 –to allow accelerated communication between FCP stations without going thru storage (hard drives). Important for backups.

Piece #2—Hard Drive for Media storage:

4-FibreChannel cards $6780—hardware for linking computers to data bank

1-Rorke FC 1.2TB $24000—data bank

1-Rorke FC warranty $1025—warranty

4-StudioNET VMS $3580—software for FibreChannel sharing

1-StudioNET Workgroup $1095—software for FibreChannel sharing

1-Vixel FC switch $12570—main switcher (hardware) to control media flow between four machines

6-FC SFP's $1,110—connectors for cables

2-5 meter FC cable $260—FibreChannel cable

4-50 meter FC cable $1200—FibreChannel cable

Piece #3—Outrigger equipment:

2-32" NTSC Monitors, one for me and one for Sean

2-20" NTSC Monitor—one for each of two other stations

4-16 channel audio mixers

2-Genelec reference speaker pairs 1029A $2000

2-pairs other good but not pro speakers

1-A/V cables $2,000

4 blackburst generators

4-UPS for edit stations $800 = battery backup universal power supply to maintain power in case of blackout

1-UPS Rorke stuff $649 = battery backup for the terabyte of hard drives.

2-Beta SP decks

3-VHS decks

3-8x8 Video switchers

2-Timecode/Code number burners (from to output of Beta deck to monitor-like Avid's but better)

2-Video Titlers

2-Video Maskers

2-DA88s—eight track digital recorders

3-Audio patch panels

Audio patch cables

3-CD players

Racks for Video and Sound Equipment

2-road cases for dubbers

Piece #4—35mm and Office supply equipment:

2-Laserjet Printers

1-Fax machine

1-"Avid table" (like Sean's on K-19)

1-Rolling cart for digitizing station

4-desks, chairs, and lamps

Office supplies:

2-folding tables

4-full height bookcases

Film:

3-English-style benches

Racks, splits, leader, synchronizers, bins, & other standard supplies

Power rewind

Coding machine

Film Boxes—500

(WSM is shipping over splicers, Rivas and Guillotine)

Other:

Insurance for all equipment (personal items too)

Biphase Encoder for Steenbeck (for magless dailies)

Biphase Encoder for Location Projector (for magless dailies)

Items to Purchase:

Software-Media Cleaner, After Effects, Toast

4-70GB FireWire drives for transporting media files

Blank Media:

300 Beta tapes

300 VHS tapes

100 DVDs or 600 CD-R for Media backup

500 sheets of paper for color printer

500 sheets of crack&peel labels for Daily Roll boxes

1000 labels for Beta & VHS tapes

ILLUSTRATION AND PHOTOGRAPHY

All the illustrations in this book are protected by the conventions of international copyright law and may not be reproduced without the express written permission of the respective copyright holders. We thank the many contributors for permission to use their work.

American Zoetrope Photographs courtesy of American Zoetrope, pp. 29, 29, 35, 36 top left, 39, 40, 42, 43, 52, 62 top and bottom left, 78.

Art Rogers/Point Reyes Photograph © Art Rogers/Point Reyes, p. 232.

Asheville Convention and Visitors Bureau Photograph courtesy of Asheville Convention and Visitors Bureau, p. 246.

Associated Press Photographs courtesy of Associated Press (AP), pp. 22 bottom right, 23 (Jennifer Graylock).

Berkman, Stephen Photograph by Stephen Berkman, p. 122 bottom left.

Bison Film Archives Photograph courtesy of Bison Film Archives/Marc Wannamaker, p. 49.

Blanschard, Richard Photograph by Richard Blanschard, p. 17 (Courtesy of Murch Family Collection).

Bos, Fernand Photograph courtesy of Fernand Bos, p. 310.

Brown, Michael D. Photograph by Michael D. Brown, p. 75.

Bullock, Torbin Photograph courtesy of Torbin Bullock, p. 88.

Chew, Richard Photograph courtesy of Richard Chew, p. 37 top.

Cinecitta Studios Photograph courtesy of Cinecitta Studios, p. 32.

Cruickshank, Douglas Photographs by Douglas Cruickshank, pp. 24, 33 bottom, 37 bottom.

Decordova Museum and Sculpture Park Artwork courtesy of Decordova Museum and Sculpture Park. Painting copyright Walter Murch, p. 5.

DigitalFilm Tree Photographs courtesy of DigitalFilm Tree, pp. 63 bottom left, 65, 66, 67, 68, 70, 71, 74, 77, 100, 129, 130, 131, 157, 160.

Double, Steve Cover photograph by Steve Double/RETNA.

Eismann, Katrin Photographs by Katrin Eismann, pp. 6 bottom, 258.

Framestore CFC Photographs courtesy of Framestore CFC, pp. 254, 303.

Hodes, Chuck Photographs by Chuck Hodes, p. 22 top right and left.

Hodgetts, Philip Photograph courtesy of Philip Hodgetts, p. 323.

Humboldt-University Berlin Photograph courtesy of Humboldt-University Berlin, p. 135 top right.

Ichioka, David Photograph by David Ichioka, p. 255.

James, David Photograph by David James, p. 22 bottom left.

Jenkins, Allan Photograph courtesy of Allan Jenkins, p. 311.

Joseph, Eddy Photograph courtesy of Eddy Joseph, p. 194.

Kennedy Galleries Artwork courtesy of Kennedy Galleries. Painting copyright Walter Murch, top p. 6.

Koppelman, Charles Photographs by Charles Koppelman, pp. 82, 105, 107, 176 top, 197, 243, 284.

Koppelman-Brown, Walker Photograph courtesy of Walker Koppelman-Brown, p. 58.

Lea, De Lane Photograph courtesy of De Lane Lea, p. 237.

Levinson, Mark Photographs by Mark Levinson, pp. 240, 241, 321.

Library of Congress Photograph courtesy of Library Congress, p. 279.

LucasFilms Ltd. Photograph courtesy of LucasFilms Ltd., p. 53.

Maruta, Steve Photographs by Steve Maruta, pp. 4, 10, 44, 51, 55, 86, 87, 91, 96 top left (The Saul Zaentz Company. All Rights Reserved), 98 top left, 98 top right (The Saul Zaentz Company. All Rights Reserved), 135 bottom right, 144, 176 bottom.

Meaney, Brian Illustration courtesy of Brian Meaney, p. 107.

Miramax Films Photographs Courtesy of Miramax Films, pp. 47 all, 57, 123, 127 147, 149, 170, 183, 210, 211, 212, 214, 215, 219, 227, 247, 252, 257, 260, 263, 265, 278, 286, 301, 305, 308, 317.

Mix Magazine Photograph Courtesy of *Mix* Magazine, p. 94.

Moviola Photograph courtesy of Moviola, p. 50.

Murch Family Collection Photographs courtesy of Murch Family Collection, pp. 17, 26 bottom, 32 bottom, 62 bottom left, 89, 326.

Murch, Walter Scott Photographs by Walter Scott Murch, pp. 11, 28, 55, 112, 116, 118, 119, 120, 121, 122 bottom right, 128, 134, 137, 138, 141, 142, 145, 151, 153, 158, 159, 161, 162, 163, 171, 172, 175, 178, 180, 181, 186, 202, 204 bottom left, 273, 293, 302.

Murch, Walter Slater Photographs by Walter Slater Murch, pp. 12, 14, 276.

Oliver, Barret Photograph by Oliver Barret, p. 122 bottom left.

Paramount/Kobal Picture Desk Photograph courtesy of Paramount/Kobal Picture Desk, p. 36 top right.

Piljay, Kristin Photographs by Kristin Piljay, pp. 28, 63 right, 187.

Rosenfeld, Peter Photograph by Peter Rosenfeld, p. 28 bottom left.

Shepard, Thomas H. Original drawing by Thomas H. Shepard as published in James Elmes' *Metropolitan Improvements*, London: 1827. p. 67, p. 291.

The Press Office Photograph courtesy of The Press Office, p. 299.

The Saul Zaentz Company Photographs courtesy of The Saul Zaentz Company, All Rights Reserved. p. 26 top, © 1987 The Saul Zaentz Company. P. 27, © 1987 The Saul Zaentz Company. p. 93, © 1987 The Saul Zaentz Company. p. 96 top right, © 1991 The Saul Zaentz Company. p. 97 bottom left, Maury Dann (Rip Torn) © 1975 The Saul Zaentz Company. p. 97 bottom right. R.P. McMurphy (Jack Nicholson) © 1975 The Saul Zaentz Company.

Tibor de Nagy Gallery Artwork courtesy of Tibor de Nagy Gallery. Painting copyright Walter Murch, p. 20.

Tolbert, Jeff Illustrations © Jeff Tolbert, pp. 18, 19.

Williams, Greg Photographs © Greg Williams, pp. 2, 60, 156, 189, 190, 192, 199, 201, 204 top left, 205, 207, 282, 290.

Yared, Gabriel Photograph courtesy of Gabriel Yared, p. 225.

index